Beginning Google Maps Mashups with Mapplets, KML, and GeoRSS

From Novice to Professional

Sterling Udell

Apress®

Beginning Google Maps Mashups with Mapplets, KML, and GeoRSS: From Novice to Professional

Copyright © 2009 by Sterling Udell

ISBN-13 (pbk): 978-1-4302-1620-9

ISBN-13 (electronic): 978-1-4302-1621-6

Printed and bound in the United States of America 9 8 7 6 5 4 3 2 1

Trademarked names may appear in this book. Rather than use a trademark symbol with every occurrence of a trademarked name, we use the names only in an editorial fashion and to the benefit of the trademark owner, with no intention of infringement of the trademark.

Lead Editor: Steve Anglin
Development Editor: Tom Welsh
Technical Reviewer: Victor Sumner
Editorial Board: Clay Andres, Steve Anglin, Mark Beckner, Ewan Buckingham, Tony Campbell,
    Gary Cornell, Jonathan Gennick, Michelle Lowman, Matthew Moodie, Jeffrey Pepper, Frank Pohlmann,
    Ben Renow-Clarke, Dominic Shakeshaft, Matt Wade, Tom Welsh
Project Manager: Richard Dal Porto
Copy Editor: James A. Compton
Associate Production Director: Kari Brooks-Copony
Production Editor: Kelly Gunther
Compositor: Susan Glinert Stevens
Proofreader: Kim Burton
Indexer: Ron Strauss
Artist: April Milne
Cover Designer: Kurt Krames
Manufacturing Director: Tom Debolski

Distributed to the book trade worldwide by Springer-Verlag New York, Inc., 233 Spring Street, 6th Floor, New York, NY 10013. Phone 1-800-SPRINGER, fax 201-348-4505, e-mail orders-ny@springer-sbm.com, or visit http://www.springeronline.com.

For information on translations, please contact Apress directly at 2855 Telegraph Avenue, Suite 600, Berkeley, CA 94705. Phone 510-549-5930, fax 510-549-5939, e-mail info@apress.com, or visit http://www.apress.com.

Apress and friends of ED books may be purchased in bulk for academic, corporate, or promotional use. eBook versions and licenses are also available for most titles. For more information, reference our Special Bulk Sales–eBook Licensing web page at http://www.apress.com/info/bulksales.

To Teresa, the fire of my inspiration.

Contents at a Glance

About the Author . . . . **xv**
About the Technical Reviewer . . . . **xvii**
Acknowledgments . . . . **xix**
Introduction . . . . **xxi**

PART 1 ■■■ The Geoweb and the Google Maps API

■CHAPTER 1   Introduction to the Geoweb 3
■CHAPTER 2   Getting Started with the Maps API 11
■CHAPTER 3   Consuming GeoXML in the Maps API 29
■CHAPTER 4   Building Out Your Map Page 49
■CHAPTER 5   Your Map and the Real World 79

PART 2 ■■■ Mashing Up Google Maps with Mapplets

■CHAPTER 6   Introduction to Mapplets 109
■CHAPTER 7   Creating a Mapplet 119
■CHAPTER 8   Taking Mapplets Further 137

PART 3 ■■■ Ready for the Big Leagues

■CHAPTER 9   Intermediate API Topics 173
■CHAPTER 10   Producing Geodata 221
■CHAPTER 11   Case Study: Satellite-Friendly Campground Directory 263

PART 4 ■■■ Appendixes

■APPENDIX A   Mapping Fundamentals 313

■APPENDIX B   A JavaScript Primer 325

■APPENDIX C   JavaScript Techniques for Map Developers 349

■APPENDIX D   Mapping Resources Online 365

■INDEX 373

Contents

About the Author xv
About the Technical Reviewer xvii
Acknowledgments xix
Introduction xxi

PART 1 ■■■ The Geoweb and the Google Maps API

■CHAPTER 1 **Introduction to the Geoweb** 3

The Geospatial Web 3
    The Mashup Era 4
    Machine-Readable Geodata: Part of the Semantic Web 4
    Produce All Geodata as XML 5
GeoXML 5
    KML 6
    GeoRSS 7
    Which Should You Use? 8
    Latitude and Longitude 9
Summary 10

■CHAPTER 2 **Getting Started with the Maps API** 11

An XHTML Framework 11
    The Map Container 12
    Page Style 12
Linking In the API 13
    Versions 14
    API Keys 14
Displaying the Map 16
    The JavaScript to Make It Happen 17
The Basic Maps API Objects 20
    GMap2 20
    GLatLng 21
    GMarker 21

Map Controls and Types 22

Bringing It All Together 25

Putting It to Use 26

Other Version Options 27

Summary 28

■CHAPTER 3   **Consuming GeoXML in the Maps API** 29

Using the GGeoXml Object 30

Examples of GGeoXml in Use 30

Advanced GGeoXml 34

Displaying More Than Markers 36

Polylines and Polygons 37

Ground Overlays 39

Drawbacks to Using GGeoXml 40

Inflexible Data Display 40

Closed Functionality 41

Incomplete KML Support 42

Alternatives to GeoXML 42

Putting It to Use 43

Summary 47

■CHAPTER 4   **Building Out Your Map Page** 49

Building the Basic Structure 49

Using Custom Marker Icons 53

Interacting with the User 57

"Map Blowup" Infowindows 57

Tabbed Infowindows 60

Interacting with the Rest of the Page 66

Showing an Infowindow from Outside the Map 66

Adding Optional External Content 68

Finishing Touches 72

Local Search with the GoogleBar 72

The Google Earth Map Type 73

Summary 74

■**CHAPTER 5**   **Your Map and the Real World** 79

Geocoding 80
    Coding For the Real World 83
    Geocoding Considerations 85
Driving Directions 86
Traffic 92
Street View 94
Map Advertising 100
Bringing It All Together 102
Summary 106

PART 2 ■■■ **Mashing Up Google Maps**
with Mapplets

■**CHAPTER 6**   **Introduction to Mapplets** 109

Using Mapplets 110
    Installing Mapplets 111
    Combining Mapplets 111
Developing Mapplets 112
    A Map-Centered Design 113
    A Shared Map 113
    Similarities to the Maps API 113
    Differences from the Maps API 113
    Advantages of Mapplets 116
    Drawbacks of Mapplets 117
Summary 118

■**CHAPTER 7**   **Creating a Mapplet** 119

A "Hello, World" Mapplet 119
    Gadget-Related Code 120
    Mapplet XHTML and CSS 122
    Mapplet JavaScript 123

x CONTENTS

Deploying Your Mapplet 124
  Hosting and Uploading 124
  Installing by URL 126
  Mapplet Developer Tools 127
Publishing Your Mapplet 129
  Additional Metadata 129
  Submitting Your Mapplet to the Directory 130
  Publishing a Link 130
Putting It to Use 131
  Module Preferences 132
  Sidebar Content 133
  Functionality 134
Summary 136

CHAPTER 8   Taking Mapplets Further 137

Geodata Mapplets 137
  The Placeopedia Mapplet, Revisited 137
Functionality Mapplets 143
  The Nearest Place Name Mapplet 143
  The Map Center Monitor Mapplet 154
Final Mapplet Development Notes 167
  Other Mapplets API Services 168
  Being a Good Neighbor 168
Summary 169

PART 3 ■■■ Ready for the Big Leagues

CHAPTER 9   Intermediate API Topics 173

Topic 1: Custom Marker Icons 173
  Recap of Changing Icons 174
  Pre-Made by Google 174
  Labeled Markers 175
  The Map Icon Maker 177
  Making Your Own Icons 178

Topic 2: Verified Geocoding 182
    The Basic Page 183
    Geocoding the Address 185
    Verifying the Address 186
    Saving the Coordinates 187
    Bringing It All Together................................. 188
    Additional Notes 191
Topic 3: Taking Control of GeoXml 191
Topic 4: Converting to a Mapplet 195
Topic 5: Larger Data Sets 199
    Executive Summary 199
    Loading the Data...................................... 200
    Displaying 20 Data Points 204
    Tying Up Loose Ends 208
    Mapplet Conversion Revisited: **GAsync** and
        Cross-API Development 213
    Pros and Cons of Dynamic Data Handling 219
Summary 220

■CHAPTER 10   **Producing Geodata** 221

Producing KML Manually 221
    Using Google's My Maps to Produce KML.................... 221
    Managing KML Files Yourself 225
    Validating Your KML 226
Producing Geodata with PHP and MySQL 227
    Storing Geodata in a MySQL Database 228
    Introduction to PHP: Hypertext Preprocessor................. 230
    Generating KML 232
    Generating GeoRSS 239
    Filtering by Geographic Area............................. 242
Using Geo Sitemaps 248
    Search Engine Optimization for GeoXML 248
    Creating Geo Sitemap Files 250
    Submitting Geo Sitemaps to Google........................ 254

Producing JSON Instead of XML 255
    JSON vs. GeoXML. 255
    Basic JSON Format. 256
    Producing JSON: the Nearest Place Name Server 257
    Taking JSON Further 261
Summary 261

∎CHAPTER 11 **Case Study: Satellite-Friendly Campground Directory** 263

Introducing the Satellite-Friendly Directory 263
    Background 264
    Overview of Map Architecture. 264
The Home Page 264
    The Recent Entries Map. 265
    The Click-to-Search Map. 273
Searching For Campgrounds 275
    The Main Campground Search Data Display 278
    Filtering 284
    Location Search 287
    Handling the Starting Location 289
Viewing Campground Details 291
    Displaying Both Campground and Campsite Details 296
    Adding Bells and Whistles 299
Disseminating Geodata 303
    Geo Sitemap 304
    A Satellite-Friendly Mapplet 306
Summary 310

PART 4 ∎∎∎ Appendixes

∎APPENDIX A **Mapping Fundamentals** 313

Latitude and Longitude 313
    Degrees, Minutes, and Seconds. 313
    Coordinate Precision. 316
    Calculating Distance. 318
Map Projections 319
    The Mercator Projection. 321
Summary 324

■**APPENDIX B   A JavaScript Primer** 325

Statements 325
  Semicolons 326
  Block Statements 326
  Comments... 327
Types and Objects 327
  null, the non-Value 328
  Objects.. 328
Expressions 332
  Numeric and String Operators......................... 332
  Assignment and Comparison............................ 333
  Boolean Operators 334
  Precedence 335
Control Structures 335
  The if/else Block 335
  The for Loop 336
  The while Loop....................................... 338
  The break Statement 338
  The switch Block 339
  Functions 341
Additional JavaScript Topics 343
  The Math Object...................................... 343
  The DOM 343
  Scope of Variables 346
  Function Literals and Closures 346
Summary 348

■**APPENDIX C   JavaScript Techniques for Map Developers** 349

Debugging Map Scripts 349
  Debugging Basics..................................... 349
  The GLog Object...................................... 350
  Firebug.. 351
  The Art of Debugging 357
Better Event Listeners 357
Using Multiple API Keys 360
Using the Gadgets API Cache in Mapplets 362

■APPENDIX D **Mapping Resources Online** 365

API-Related Documentation 365
    Official Google 365
    Third-Party... 366
Discussion Groups 367
    Google Maps API Group 368
    iGoogle Developer Forum................................. 368
    KML Developer Support................................... 368
    Google Earth Community 368
Map-Oriented Weblogs 368
    Google LatLon 368
    Google Geo Developers Blog 368
    Google Maps Mania 369
Related Resources 369
    GeoRSS Information 369
    XML Validators 369
    JavaScript References 370
    DOM References.. 371
    Server-Side Programming Guides 371
    Geospatial Calculations 372

■INDEX 373

About the Author

**STERLING UDELL** is a freelance web developer who has been programming with Google Maps since before the API was released. When not writing, he makes his living producing leading-edge map mashups, gadgets, and mapplets. His work has been featured at a Google Developer Day, on Google Code, and in numerous online mashup reviews.

Sterling has a degree in mathematics and computer science from Drake University, followed by graduate-level computer science study at the University of Maine. Originally from Wisconsin, Sterling lived all over the United States, including three years traveling and working full-time in an RV, before moving to his current home in the United Kingdom.

About the Technical Reviewer

VICTOR SUMNER is an Internet graphic designer and a self-taught web developer. Introduced early to video design, he has spent many late nights working in all aspects of multimedia development, leading to an honors diploma in Internet graphic design. Currently employed at We-Create Inc. as a lead architect, Victor develops and maintains `ConnectorLocal.com`, a web application, which brings local businesses, events, places, articles, and classifieds to you based on your location. He lives in Waterloo, Ontario, with his wife Alicia.

Acknowledgments

Thanks initially to Mark Lewin, for getting me started on the project in the first place. This book literally wouldn't exist with him. Similarly, I must also thank Riaan van Schoor, who "sponsored" my first professional foray into Google mapping.

Many thanks to everyone at Apress for their hard work and patience getting this, my first book, out on time, as deadlines have passed and versions changed. Especially, thanks to Tom Welsh for his unfailing support and encouragement, not to mention tolerance of my inability to get the correct plurality on my third-person pronouns.

For guiding me through pitching the book to Apress, a well-deserved thanks to Laura Olson. This may only be my first, but I'll catch you yet!

Like many, if not most, Google map programmers, I owe a debt of gratitude to Mike Williams and his unrivalled grasp of the Maps API. In particular, I'd like to thank Mike for creating the original EGeoXml object that I use (and extend) in this book.

And finally, the biggest thank you to Teresa Petrykowski, my wife and non-technical reviewer, for reading every word and sticking by me through it all, from the smirking to the hair-pulling. *Diolch yn fawr, cariad!*

Introduction

In June of 2008, while this book was being written, the Google Maps API celebrated its third birthday. In Internet terms, three is a respectable age, and the Maps API is visibly maturing. It's quite common now to find Google's excellent maps embedded in sites all over the Web; accordingly, Google Maps "expertise" is becoming more common.

With this ubiquity, however, comes a certain danger of mediocrity. The question is no longer just, "Can I put a Google map on my website?" Instead, there's now sufficient maturity in the field that the question should be, "How can I put the *best possible* Google map on my site?" There are a lot of ways to answer that question, involving considerations of good web design techniques, usability, coding best practices, and standards compliance. One of the major goals for this book is to put those kinds of answers in your hands, in ways that you can immediately use.

In fact, the last item on that list, standards compliance, is itself a big reason for writing this book. The existence of (and adherence to) geodata-publishing standards like KML and GeoRSS enables the rich world of map mashups, and by extension, the emerging geographic Web. It's a powerful and exciting movement, one that Google's mapping initiatives are supporting more and more strongly, and it's not one that's well covered in any other book.

Finally, as the API matures, I believe that the time has come to make it more accessible to nonprogrammers; that's the primary goal for this book, its real reason for being. Although some coding is unavoidable—the "P" in API stands for Programming, after all—the web-based nature of Google Maps means that it is fundamentally within the reach of anyone with some experience building web sites. But until now, all the Maps API books have been written for an audience of developers. There have been scattered tutorials and examples online, but no complete, coherent guide for beginners. So I wrote one: the book you're now holding.

Who This Book Is For

Accordingly, you don't need a programming or development background to benefit from this book. What you *do* need is a bit of grounding in web page design and construction. That's not to say that you need vast professional experience in these areas, simply that you're not completely put off by talk of XHTML and JavaScript.

Basic Web Architecture

Since all Google maps reside on web pages, you need to be comfortable with the basics of XHTML and CSS, at least enough to recognize what's going on inside a page. I'll be giving you complete code in my examples, but if you're going to integrate the concepts into your own pages, you'll need some idea of what goes where.

And because the native language of Google Maps is JavaScript, it would also be beneficial if you have seen JavaScript before, even at the level of occasional event handlers in a web page. If not, you'll find a JavaScript primer in Appendix B to help you over the rough spots.

In addition, you'll need to be familiar with the basics of web publishing, such as how to edit XHTML source files, view them in a browser, and upload them to a web server. Finally, you need to be comfortable with URLs and their structure.

Programming Experience Optional

On the other hand, I'm not saying that any programming experience you may have will be wasted, or that this isn't the book for you more seasoned developers. There's no getting away from the fact that Google Maps mashups involve *some* programming, so there's no doubt that some development background will be helpful; the more you have, the faster you'll progress.

In particular, this book will be a good fit if you have some non-web (or non-JavaScript) development experience, perhaps with another programming language or on another platform. Once you become familiar with JavaScript, you'll find that the code herein is quite elementary, and you'll be up and running in no time.

But to reiterate, programming experience is not required.

How This Book Is Structured

This book covers the use of Google's two major web mapping tools, the Maps and Mapplets APIs, with a particular focus on their use with the KML and GeoRSS dialects of geoXML. So the first two parts of the book each cover the use of one of these APIs, from fundamentals through fully functional examples. Then the third part brings it all together with more advanced, real-world code spanning both APIs.

Part 1: The Geoweb and the Google Maps API

- Chapter 1, **Introduction to the Geoweb**, lays the foundation for effective mashup development by establishing the basic concepts and data formats underlying the geographic Web.

- Chapter 2, **Getting Started with the Maps API**, is a gentle introduction to the integration of a Google map onto a web page, covering all the basics.

- Chapter 3, **Consuming GeoXML in the Maps API**, moves the basic map integration into the geoweb proper by mashing up external geodata.

- Chapter 4, **Building Out Your Map Page**, takes the map-enabled web page from Chapter 2 and adds more robust interactions with the user and the rest of the page.

- Chapter 5, **Your Map and the Real World**, covers practical topics such as geocoding, traffic displays, Street View eye-level panoramas, and map advertising.

Part 2: Mashing Up Google Maps with Mapplets

- Chapter 6, **Introduction to Mapplets**, shifts the focus to Google's *other* web-mapping API, discussing how (and why) to get your own content onto maps.google.com.

- Chapter 7, **Creating a Mapplet**, walks you through your first mapplet, with an emphasis on the differences from (and similarities to) the original Maps API.

- Chapter 8, **Taking Mapplets Further**, examines the two major types of mapplets (geodata and functionality), including plenty of tips on how to build effective mapplets yourself.

Part 3: Ready for the Big Leagues

- Chapter 9, **Intermediate API Topics**, takes your map and mapplet development to the next level with coverage of custom markers, verified geocoding, large dataset handling, and cross-API development.

- Chapter 10, **Producing Geodata**, shifts the focus from the web client to the server as it teaches you how to produce KML and GeoRSS, including database utilization and geo-search optimization.

- Chapter 11, **Case Study: Satellite-Friendly Campground Directory**, brings everything together with a guided tour of satellitefriendly.com, a real web site successfully using geodata to drive Google Maps.

Appendixes

- Appendix A, **Mapping Fundamentals**, provides an API-oriented summary of such topics as coordinate formats and map projections.

- Appendix B, **A JavaScript Primer**, covers all the basics of this powerful (but often misunderstood) programming language.

- Appendix C, **JavaScript Techniques for Map Developers**, gets you started with JavaScript debugging and then gives a few additional coding techniques that you should find useful.

- Appendix D, **Mapping Resources Online**, points you to all the best places on the Web to find Google Map-related information.

Downloading the Code

All of the code in numbered listings throughout this book can be found on the book's web site, http://sterlingudell.com/bgmm. It is also available in zip file format in the Downloads section of the Apress web site (apress.com).

Contacting the Author

If you have any comments or additional questions relating to this book, I'd love to hear from you! Full contact information can be found on sterlingudell.com, or you can e-mail me directly at sterling.udell@gmail.com.

PART 1

The Geoweb and the Google Maps API

CHAPTER 1

Introduction to the Geoweb

Everything that happens, happens somewhere! Google Maps has revolutionized how we see and use location-based information. As recently as 2005, there was no good way to put a map on your web page without paying large sums of money for solutions that still had many short-comings. Google changed all of that, first with its unprecedented draggable maps, and soon after with the release of a free API that allowed anyone to use those maps on their own websites.

It wasn't just a revolution in mapping; it was the start of a revolution in how we see information. It has led to the birth of the Geospatial Web, in which location becomes a usable aspect of almost every piece of information. It also gave birth to the idea of a *mashup*, in which every website is seen not just as a standalone entity, but as a building block for something else.

In this opening chapter, we'll explore these concepts and discover what you can do with them.

The Geospatial Web

Professional geographers commonly estimate that 80 percent of information has a geospatial component. In other words, whatever the information is, it's usually about a place. It may be a specific place, an area, or a route between places. Often this geographic aspect is implied, rather than being in the data explicitly. But it's there, more often than you may think—such as a place name referred to in a block of text or a photograph that was implicitly taken *somewhere*.

So the Geospatial Web, or *geoweb*, is an extension of the existing World Wide Web, linking it to the real world by utilizing this geospatial component of online information. It's a connection between the physical and virtual worlds.

As an example, consider a newspaper, full of articles every day about everything under the sun. Traditionally, newspaper articles have a "dateline" indicating where they're from: Washington, DC, perhaps, or New York City. This practice has continued as newspapers have moved online. The *geodata* is inherently there; each article is about a place.

For an online newspaper to participate in the geoweb, the dateline simply needs to be readable by computers, in addition to the people reading the articles. Why? Because when information is *machine-readable*, it becomes possible for other websites to *reuse* that information in new and interesting ways. For example, with the dateline reusable as geodata, you can do any of the following:

- Filter news by its relevance to a given location, such as where you live

- Plot a day's articles on a map, showing news "hotspots" at a glance

These opportunities arise precisely because the geodata is machine-readable by a search engine or by mapping software. It's the ability of these systems to work together that makes such synergies possible.

The possibilities multiply if geodata is added to *everything* in the newspaper. Not just articles, but sports results, advertisements, announcements—everything. Then you could do things like these:

- Observe trends in a sports team's performance by comparing their scores in home vs. away games, or how they perform on the road in particular geographical areas

- Plan a day's shopping by creating a route based on sales happening that day

- Combine your shopping with a trip to the movies by adding theater locations to the route, including times for the specific movies you want to see

- Avoid traffic by knowing the location of major events in the area

Add the newspaper's location into the mix and you can track the coverage of a given news story—literally, watch the news spread. It's all about reusing the geodata, often in ways that the original newspaper publisher may never have thought of.

The Mashup Era

This whole notion of reusing existing data in new ways is a relatively recent innovation on the Web. We call it a *mashup*—a new service, usually a web page, created by "mashing up" several existing services.

The classic example, often considered the first modern mashup, is HousingMaps (housingmaps.com). It's a combination of Google Maps with the realty listings from Craigslist (craigslist.org), an online classified-ads site. The property for sale and rental listings are plotted on the map—a simple idea, but one that's incredibly useful to anyone looking for a new home. It's the embodiment of the old realty maxim about "location, location, location." HousingMaps doesn't sound revolutionary now, but when it appeared in early 2005, it was the first of its kind. It's also historic for another reason: it *predated* the Google Maps API. It was created by programmer Paul Rademacher, who "hacked" Google Maps to reuse its mapping capabilities, on his own site, in conjunction with Craigslist's RSS feed. HousingMaps then attained some fame online, inspiring other Google Maps "hackers" (including myself) to try their own—all of which sufficiently impressed Google that it created the Maps API in response. Our early Google Maps "hacks", then, were the progenitors of all the geo-mashups that have come since; by sparking the creation of the first online mapping API, they made the current geoweb possible.

Machine-Readable Geodata: Part of the Semantic Web

Mashups and the geoweb are part of the much-talked-about *Semantic Web*[1], a universe of online information that's meaningful to both computers and humans. It's a web of data, not just of pages.

---

1. See the World Wide Web Consortium's Semantic Web Activity at http://www.w3.org/2001/sw/.

I have a dream for the Web [in which computers] become capable of analyzing all the data on the Web—the content, links, and transactions between people and computers. A "Semantic Web", which should make this possible, has yet to emerge, but when it does, the day-to-day mechanisms of trade, bureaucracy and our daily lives will be handled by machines talking to machines.

—Sir Tim Berners-Lee, 1999

The Semantic Web is widely perceived as where today's first- and second-generation World Wide Web is going, and by building the geoweb we're helping that process.

Produce All Geodata as XML

So the semantic geoweb is fundamentally about making the geographic component of information usable, and the key to that is *standards*. Most of the information online is not standardized; it's in freeform text on web pages. And generally, computers can't do much with that. For the information to be reusable, it needs to be in standard formats that computers can recognize and understand.

For the geoweb, that means XML. I'll cover the specifics in the next section, but for now I want to emphasize the goal that *all* geographic data should adhere to a geoXML standard. Why?

- You can use the same program code for working with your own data as you do for data from other sources. You're not reinventing the wheel each time.

- Others can reuse your data in innovative ways of their own, enabling new mashups.

- Google can index your data and include it in location-based search results.

We'll be looking at each of these concepts in more detail later in the book, but the central idea is that it's all about standards. The more standardized data is, the more useful it is.

GeoXML

So what is XML? The initials stand for eXtensible Markup Language, and as a *metalanguage*, it's a language used to create other languages. Specifically, XML is used for creating data description languages; in other words, it's a way of developing standards for data formatting, so that the information can easily be extracted programmatically.

At its most basic, XML data simply looks like this:

```
<name>value</name>
```

In a mass of information, this makes it quite easy for a computer to find a specific value given its name, because the desired data is always formatted the same way. In this book we're generally going to be avoiding the internals of XML, but you will encounter it occasionally.

Our example here is really an XML *element*; it consists of opening and closing *tags* (the <name> and </name>) enclosing the data *value*. Note its similarity to an XHTML element; XHTML is a "flavor" of XML.

XML comes in many standard flavors for different sorts of data, and each standard defines specific elements that can be used. There are two flavors we're specifically interested in for working with geodata: KML and GeoRSS.

KML

KML is a standard that was originally developed for use in Google Earth and has since come into widespread use across the geoweb. As an XML variant, the KML standard defines elements for conveying geodata concisely yet flexibly. It's currently the most widely used format for the exchange of geodata online.

ELECTRIC EYE

The "K" in KML stands for Keyhole, the company which originally developed Google Earth (before being purchased by Google). The name itself was inspired by the KH "Key Hole" series of military reconnaissance satellites, as an oblique reference to the overhead imagery that makes the software so compelling.

KML can get quite complicated, expressing an incredible richness of geospatial information, but at its most basic it looks like Listing 1-1. This is the essence of the geoweb, linking a piece of information (in this case, a description of Oregon's Crater Lake) with its geospatial location (defined by its *coordinates*—more about them in a minute), and it's what KML is all about. Figure 1-1 shows the KML from Listing 1-1 plotted at maps.google.com.

Listing 1-1. *Basic KML*

```
<?xml version="1.0" encoding="UTF-8"?>
<kml xmlns="http://earth.google.com/kml/2.2">
  <Placemark>
    <name>Crater Lake</name>
    <description>A deep blue lake in the Cascade Mountains.</description>
    <Point>
      <coordinates>-122.1089,42.9413,0</coordinates>
    </Point>
  </Placemark>
</kml>
```

■**Tip** You can display any KML or GeoRSS on the Web in the same way as Figure 1-1; simply enter its URL in the Google Maps search box and click Search Maps.

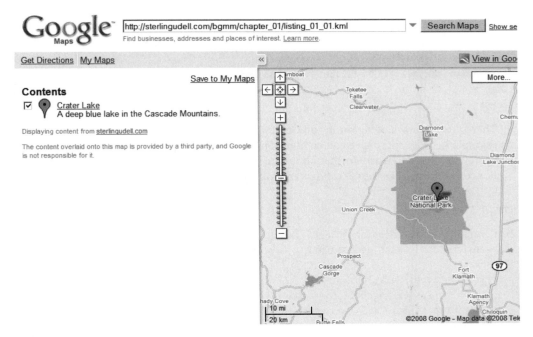

Figure 1-1. *The Crater Lake KML in action*

GeoRSS

As its name implies, GeoRSS is an extension to the widely used RSS standard, the format used for syndication of blog and news feeds across the Web. With the addition of GeoRSS elements, these same feeds can include a geospatial component. Thinking back to my newspaper example, GeoRSS is how the location would be included with each article.

Of course, RSS can be used for more than just news, as demonstrated by the multitude of blogs that use it for every topic imaginable. Generally, though, it lends itself to information that can be serialized, or that receives updates from time to time.

Despite the apparent tie to RSS, GeoRSS is equally applicable to Atom, the other major XML standard for news feeds. And in fact, Atom is my preferred format for such feeds; it's newer, slightly richer, and more standards-compliant than RSS. So my examples in this book will predominantly use Atom, rather than RSS itself, though the same principles apply.

Listing 1-2 is an example of a basic Atom feed, including a simple GeoRSS element for an entry in it. Again, this example links Crater Lake with its physical location, this time as an entry within a National Parks Tour page.

Listing 1-2. *Basic GeoRSS, in Atom*

```
<?xml version="1.0" encoding="UTF-8"?>
<feed xmlns="http://www.w3.org/2005/Atom"
      xmlns:georss="http://www.georss.org/georss">
  <title>National Park Tour</title>
  <updated>2008-05-19T19:41:10Z</updated>
```

```
<entry>
  <title>Crater Lake</title>
  <summary>A deep blue lake in the Cascade Mountains.</summary>
  <updated>2008-05-19T19:41:10Z</updated>
  <georss:point>42.9413 -122.1089</georss:point>
</entry>
</feed>
```

There are a number of variations on GeoRSS, so it won't always look exactly like this. But this example is sufficient to give you an idea of how it typically appears, and for most of this book you won't need to worry further about the internal specifics.

For completeness, Listing 1-3 shows an equivalent feed in RSS 2.0 format.

Listing 1-3. *Basic GeoRSS, in RSS 2.0*

```
<?xml version="1.0" encoding="UTF-8" ?>
<rss version="2.0" xmlns:georss="http://www.georss.org/georss">
  <channel>
    <title>National Park Tour</title>
    <link>http://sterlingudell.com/bgmm/</link>
    <description>Simple RSS feed with geodata</description>
    <item>
      <title>Crater Lake</title>
      <link>http://sterlingudell.com/bgmm/chapter_01/listing_01_03.xml</link>
      <description>A deep blue lake in the Cascade Mountains.</description>
      <georss:point>42.9413 -122.1089</georss:point>
    </item>
  </channel>
</rss>
```

If you're familiar with XML, notice that both these documents include the georss namespace in their root element.

Which Should You Use?

Both KML and GeoRSS are widely accepted standards and are good choices for publishing your geodata. Which you should use for a given project depends on the circumstances.

KML seems to enjoy wider adoption, and as such is supported by a larger number of websites and programs. So it's probably the better default choice, especially for geodata that is relatively static or that changes all at once. Here are a few examples:

- Store locations

- Weather forecasts

- Member directory entries

GeoRSS, with its roots in the news feed standards, may be a better choice for data that is logically serialized or that gets added to periodically. It's also the obvious choice when adding geodata to an existing Atom or RSS feed. Here are a few examples:

- Newspaper datelines

- Real estate listings

- Travel blogs

Both standards are equally well supported by the Google Maps API, so I'll cover both throughout this book.

Latitude and Longitude

You may have noticed that both geoXML formats use a pair of numbers to express the geospatial location. These numbers are the *latitude* and *longitude* of a place, and between them they uniquely identify any point on the Earth's surface. It's worth spending just a few minutes familiarizing yourself with what these numbers mean, using Figure 1-2 as a guide.

Latitude represents how far north a location is; positive numbers are north of the equator, negative numbers are south. If you live in the Northern Hemisphere, it's intuitive to think of them as "above" and "below" the equator.

Longitude is how far east a location is, and for historical reasons the "zero line" (analogous to the equator) is the *prime meridian*, running north-south through Greenwich, England. This is less intuitive than latitude: positive numbers are east of Greenwich (Asia, Australia, and most of Europe and Africa), while negative numbers are west (North and South America and far-western Europe and Africa).

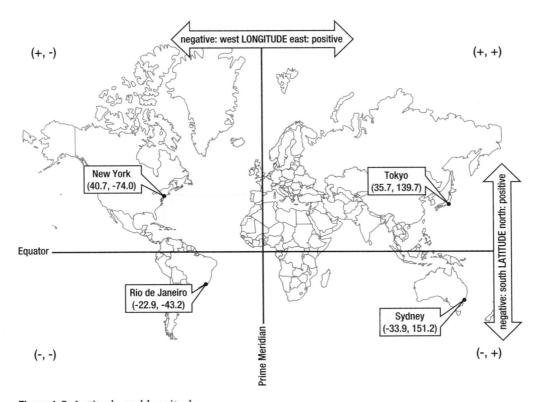

Figure 1-2. *Latitude and longitude*

WHERE DO YOU GET COORDINATES?

To make a Google map work you often need latitude and longitude coordinates. Where do you get these from? There are a number of possible sources:

- *A GPS receiver:* Hardware that is becoming widespread and inexpensive, it's often an easy way to get accurate coordinates.

- *Google Earth:* A service that displays latitude and longitude for anywhere you place your mouse cursor.

- *The Coordinate Finder mapplet:* One of several mapplets that, like Google Earth, will show you the coordinates for any point you click at maps.google.com. Install it from http://tinyurl.com/5kpcjp. (Mapplets are small map "plug-in" applications; I'll cover them thoroughly starting in Chapter 6.)

- *Geocoding:* The process of turning ordinary addresses into map coordinates, fully covered in Chapters 5 and 9.

A word of caution: Coordinates from other sources may sometimes be in a different format, leading to incorrect results on a map.

See Appendix A for more information. Latitude and longitude generally are paired together and called *coordinates*. For example, the coordinates of Crater Lake are 42.9413 north latitude and –122.1089 west longitude. In this book I'll frequently write them as simply (42.9413, –122.1089).

In GeoRSS, this is exactly how they're represented:

```
<georss:point>42.9413 -122.1089</georss:point>
```

Just to make things difficult, KML flips them around and adds a third number (for altitude, which we won't worry about):

```
<coordinates>-122.1089,42.9413,0</coordinates>
```

If you're interested, there's a more thorough discussion of map coordinates and related topics in Appendix A. It's not required reading, but it will be worthwhile if you're going to be doing much map programming.

Summary

Most of the information online relates to specific places on Earth, and the geoweb is about making that connection from cyberspace to the real world. By standardizing geospatial data on the Web, we enable anyone to "mash up" that geodata, creating endless possibilities for using those connections in new and exciting ways.

In Chapter 2, you'll lay the foundation for geo-mashups of your own by building a basic Google map that you can easily add to any web page.

CHAPTER 2

■■■

Getting Started with the Maps API

When Google Maps was introduced in February 2005, it was immediately hailed as a major advance in web mapping. By preloading the map beyond the borders of what was visible in the browser, Google was able to create an illusion that you had the entire world at your fingertips. Page refreshes to change map views became a thing of the past.

Just a few months later, Google extended this achievement by offering the same mapping system it used itself, free of charge, to anyone with minimal web programming skills. More than any other event, the release of this API fostered the creation of the geoweb and spawned a proliferation of geospatially aware sites across the Web.

Now it's your turn.

We'll start with a simple web page, and then piece by piece build a complete Google map on it, making every step clear along the way. Before the chapter's over you'll be ready to add a reasonable map to web sites of your own.

An XHTML Framework

Google Maps is fundamentally a web application; therefore, every Maps API implementation is based on a web page. Our first map example is no exception, and the basic XHTML structure for the page is shown in Listing 2-1.

Listing 2-1. *The Basic Map Page XHTML*

```
<!DOCTYPE html PUBLIC "-//W3C//DTD XHTML 1.0 Strict//EN"
                      "http://www.w3.org/TR/xhtml1/DTD/xhtml1-strict.dtd">
<html xmlns="http://www.w3.org/1999/xhtml">
  <head>
    <meta http-equiv="Content-Type" content="text/html; charset=UTF-8" />
    <title>Google Maps API Basic Example</title>
    <link type="text/css" rel="stylesheet" href="listing_02_02.css" />
  </head>
  <body>
    <div id="map"></div>
  </body>
</html>
```

As you can see, this is little more than an absolutely minimal XHTML page.

The Map Container

Your XHTML does require one very particular element, a container for the map itself. This is the `<div id="map">` line highlighted in Listing 2-1. You can use whatever `id` you want, as long as the same `id` value is used in the JavaScript we'll be writing that references it.

■**Caution** As with any XHTML `id` attribute, the map container's `id` needs to be unique on the page. It's especially important here to avoid unexpected behavior from the JavaScript.

For simplicity, my example page in Listing 2-1 contains only a map, but most of the time your Google map will be integrated with other content on a page. In any case, the `id` is how the JavaScript finds the correct XHTML container in which to build the map. Also, be aware that any other content in this map container will be erased by the Maps API.

Page Style

To make the map visible on the page, we'll also need a little bit of CSS, shown in Listing 2-2.

Listing 2-2. *The Basic Map Page Stylesheet*

```
html {
  height: 100%;
}

body {
  height: 100%;
  margin: 0;
}

#map {
  width: 100%;
  height: 100%;
}
```

Since this page contains only a map, I have included rules to make the map occupy the entire height and width of the page. If the page had other content, you'd use additional CSS as appropriate to lay the page out and place the map as desired within it.

This is a good place to say a few words about layout. Despite its distinctive appearance and high level of interactivity, there's nothing magical about a Google Map: it is built of XHTML, formatted with CSS. As such, it is part and parcel of the XHTML and CSS of your page. You position it as you would any other page element, and it can inherit style from their containing elements.

So you need to pay attention to a map page's structure and design, the same as you would for any other web page. You're likely to have trouble with a Google map on the page if your

XHTML isn't well-formed; ideally, it should pass the W3C's Markup Validation Service (http://validator.w3.org), but at the least, all your opening and closing tags need to match up. And further, if you're seeing strange behavior from a map, a good place to start troubleshooting is your page layout in CSS.

■**Caution** As frequently happens in web design, Internet Explorer presents certain challenges for laying out pages with Google Maps. In particular, IE requires additional "help" for determining the height of page elements; it doesn't automatically pick up on the size of Google Maps' dynamic XHTML. This is why the `html` and `body` tags in Listing 2-2 need `height:100%` in their CSS; without those rules IE wouldn't know how tall to render the elements.

In general, your map container always needs to have an explicit `height` supplied to it. If you have a map that works fine in other browsers but doesn't display at all in IE, this is the first thing to look for.

Linking In the API

Our page is now ready for you to add the Google Maps API itself. A single XHTML element is required to include it:

```
<script type="text/javascript"
        src="http://maps.google.com/maps?file=api&amp;v=2.124&amp;key="></script>
```

As you can see, this is a standard XHTML directive to include an external JavaScript file, served by `maps.google.com`. We'll add this element to the `head` section of the page.

WELCOME TO JAVASCRIPT 101

API stands for *Application Programming Interface*, so there is unavoidably some programming involved in its use. And specifically, JavaScript is the native language of Google Maps. So if you're completely new to JavaScript programming—or perhaps new to programming generally—you might appreciate a bit of extra help.

It's beyond the scope of this book to teach you programming or JavaScript from scratch, and if you're going to be doing much Maps API work I recommend that you take that step on your own. But for now, it'll be sufficient to just copy and paste my code examples to make your maps work. Notes like this one are here in case you'd like a bit more understanding of what the JavaScript is up to.

Right now, we have our first example of the `script` element, and it looks roughly like this:

```
<script type="text/javascript" src="script_url.js">
```

This isn't actually JavaScript; rather, it is how you attach an external JavaScript file to an XHTML page. It works much like a `<link>` tag to include CSS in the page. You supply the URL of the script file, and the browser fetches and runs it before continuing with the page load. We'll be looking at the contents of a JavaScript file in a little while.

Throughout this book, I'll be including notes like this to help bring you up to speed when key JavaScript concepts are first encountered. Also, remember that you'll find more JavaScript resources in Appendix C.

Although this `script` element as shown is sufficient to get you started, it does include a couple of options that merit a closer look before we move on.

Versions

Like most software proprietors, Google releases new versions of the Maps API periodically, usually every 1–2 weeks. The version our page uses is 2.124, determined by the `v=2.124` in the `script` element's `src` attribute.

This version number will work fine for all the examples in this book, but as the API continues to evolve, our examples will be left behind. They're stationary at `v=2.124`. The downside is obvious: we won't have access to new features that Google releases. But there is an upside, too; it does sometimes happen that new versions are incompatible with certain existing map pages, so that upgrading can break your map. We prevent this by "planting our stake" at 2.124.

■**Tip** You can always find information on current and past versions of the API in the Google Maps API wiki at `http://mapki.com`.

If you want to use a newer version of the Maps API, you do so by substituting that number for the `2.124` in the `src` URL. You then need to test your existing page functionality thoroughly, to ensure that everything still works—that nothing on your page was broken by the new version.

If everything still works, great! Go ahead and implement the new feature. If not, you basically have three options:

- Stay with the previous version and live without the new feature.

- Troubleshoot the error and find a fix, if your JavaScript skills are up to the task.

- If the problem is minor enough, ignore it and implement the new feature anyway. It's always possible that Google will fix the incompatibility on their side at some point.

None of these are ideal, but they do reflect the reality of software development.

If you'd like to learn more about Maps API versions, there's a section covering the alternatives at the end of this chapter. However, you can safely stick with `v=2.124` for the remainder of this book.

API Keys

The other URL component in the API `script` element is `key=`, and it's used for specifying your Maps API key. This is essentially your authorization to use Google Maps on your web site, and it's an important piece to understand.

When You Don't Need an API Key

You'll notice that the `key=` parameter was blank in my `script` element shown earlier, which I said was sufficient for now. That's because a key isn't required for local development work, viewing web pages through your own computer's filesystem. This means URLs that begin with `file://`, rather than the usual `http://` of pages on the Web. So a URL like this is fine without an API key:

`file:///C:/Documents+and+Settings/Sterling/My+Documents/basic_map.html`

In Windows, you can typically open an XHTML file in your default browser by simply navigating to the file in Windows Explorer and then double-clicking on it.

When You Do Need an API Key

Whenever a map page is delivered to your browser from a web server, it will need to have a valid API key. This can be a local development server, your production web server, or any public web site. The key factor is that the URL starts with `http://`.

How to Get and Use a Key

Fortunately, getting an API key is pretty easy. Simply go to `http://code.google.com/apis/maps/signup.html`, indicate your acceptance of the Terms and Conditions, and enter your web site's URL. Although Google's terms are fairly lenient, make sure your web site does comply with them.

API keys are based on the URL you supply to Google, so it's important to get this right. Here are some tips to guide you:

- Generally, it's best to enter just your site's root domain name, such as `http://mydomain.com`. Such a key will be valid for all pages within that site.

- A root domain key will also work for pages using a www prefix. (For example, a key registered for `http://mydomain.com` also works for `http://www.mydomain.com`.)

- The root key will work as well if your site is hosted at a subdomain, such as `http://webapps.mydomain.com`. (By contrast, a key you'd registered for `http://www.mydomain.com` wouldn't.)

- If your page may be served from more than one root domain, you'll need a key for each domain and additional program code to switch them dynamically. See Appendix C for a snippet of JavaScript to help you do this.

- You may also need to get a key for development servers. For example, it's fine to request a key for `http://localhost`.

- If you lose your key, don't worry: just go back and request it again. Assuming you give the same URL, Google will give you the same key, and there's no problem with this.

Once you have your key, simply paste it into the script tag that includes the API in your page, like this:

```
<script type="text/javascript"
  src="http://maps.google.com/maps?file=api&amp;v=2.124&amp;key=ABQIAAN_IKAOv">
</script>
```

Note that a real API key is much longer than I've just shown. Also, be aware that I'll omit the API key from most XHTML listings in this book, both for brevity and because my API key wouldn't work for you anyway. Don't forget to paste in a key of your own, right after key=, as needed.

Displaying the Map

All the pieces are now in place, and you're finally ready to show the map on your web page. There are two components you need to add to make this happen, and Listing 2-3 shows our XHTML with them highlighted.

Listing 2-3. *Ready to Display the Map*

```
<!DOCTYPE html PUBLIC "-//W3C//DTD XHTML 1.0 Strict//EN"
                      "http://www.w3.org/TR/xhtml1/DTD/xhtml1-strict.dtd">
<html xmlns="http://www.w3.org/1999/xhtml">
  <head>
    <meta http-equiv="Content-Type" content="text/html; charset=UTF-8" />
    <title>Google Maps API Basic Example</title>
    <link type="text/css" rel="stylesheet" href="listing_02_02.css" />
    <script type="text/javascript"
      src="http://maps.google.com/maps?file=api&amp;v=2.124&amp;key="></script>
    <script type="text/javascript" src="listing_02_04.js"></script>
  </head>
  <body onload="loadMap()" onunload="GUnload()">
    <div id="map"></div>
  </body>
</html>
```

In the head section, we have a new script element, linking in the JavaScript that puts the API to work. We'll look at that in detail in the next section. And in the body tag, we have an onload *event handler* to initialize the map when the page loads.

JAVASCRIPT 101: EVENT HANDLERS

An event handler is simply a small piece of JavaScript that the browser runs when a specific action occurs. The onload event here, for example, runs when the page has finished loading. Another common event you'll see is onclick, usually in a hyperlink or button, which runs when the user clicks on it with the mouse.

■**Note** Don't worry about GUnload; that's simply an API function to "clean up" after the map when the user leaves the page. It should be included on any page that has a map, but that's as much as you need to know about it.

The JavaScript to Make It Happen

We're now ready to look at our first real piece of JavaScript, Listing 2-4. It's mostly a single function, `loadMap`, containing the functionality to set the API in motion and display a map on the page.

Listing 2-4. *The Basic Map JavaScript*

```
var map;

function loadMap()
{
  var mapDiv = document.getElementById('map');

  if (!GBrowserIsCompatible())
  {
    mapDiv.innerHTML =
      'Sorry, your browser isn\'t compatible with Google Maps.';
  }
  else
  {
    map = new GMap2(mapDiv);
    map.setCenter(new GLatLng(39.9, -105.2), 10);
  }
};
```

JAVASCRIPT 101: VARIABLES AND FUNCTIONS

Listing 2-4 starts with a variable declaration:

```
var map;
```

In programming, *declaring a variable* simply means setting up a place for the computer to keep a piece of information. A variable is a bit like a file on your computer; the file contains information, and you use the file's name to refer to it (say, when loading it into a word processor). In this case, the map variable will hold the actual Google map object being drawn on the page, and we'll refer to it with the name "map".

Then the bulk of the JavaScript is within a function definition:

```
function loadMap()
```

A *function* is a set of actions for the computer to perform as a group; in this case, loading the map onto the page. Like a variable, a function has a name, so when you want the actions to occur you can simply use (or *call*) that name in your script. This one's named loadMap, and I chose that name because it contains the instructions needed to load the Google map onto the page. The functionality to do so is contained within the outer { and } symbols, which tell the computer where a logical unit of code begins and ends, similar to how it's done with a CSS selector.

In this example, loadMap is called by the page's onload event handler, telling the computer to load the Google map also. Event handlers are a good place to use functions, because using them keeps the amount of JavaScript embedded in your XHTML to a minimum.

Let's examine each piece of the JavaScript `loadMap` function to be clear what's going on. First, we need to get our map container from the XHTML:

```
var mapDiv = document.getElementById('map');
```

This basically gives the JavaScript a "handle" on the map container that it can work with. The text inside the parentheses and quotes needs to match the `id` of the map container `div` in the XHTML, back in Listing 2-1. As you'll recall, it's simply called `map`.

Next, it's good to make sure the user's browser is compatible with Google Maps:

```
if (!GBrowserIsCompatible())
{
  mapDiv.innerHTML =
    'Sorry, your browser isn\'t compatible with Google Maps.';
}
```

While this isn't strictly necessary to make the map work, it's definitely good practice and should always be included. Very few browsers aren't compatible, but it's much better to give those that aren't a nice message than a bunch of messy errors.

Now we're in the thick of it. The next step is to create the map object itself:

```
map = new GMap2(mapDiv);
```

I'll talk more about the `GMap2` object in a moment, but it should already be fairly clear what's going on here. We're creating a new Google map, using the `mapDiv` XHTML container.

JAVASCRIPT 101: FUNCTION PARAMETERS

Functions, introduced in the previous session of *JS101*, can also take *parameters* by including them in the parentheses after the function name. Parameters alter the way the function behaves by supplying additional information that may be different when called at different times.

Our function `loadMap` didn't need this, so it didn't have any parameters. But the API function `setCenter` is a good example, taking two parameters:

```
GMap2.setCenter(coordinates, zoom);
```

The parameters let you use the same function to place the map *viewport*, its visible geographic area, anywhere on Earth by simply changing the values of `coordinates` and `zoom`. This process of sending information into a function via its parameters is called *passing*.

Finally, we need to tell the map where on Earth we want to see. We do that with a call to the map's `setCenter` function thus:

```
map.setCenter(new GLatLng(39.9, -105.2), 10);
```

There are two parts to this, supplied as parameters:

1. The *latitude* and *longitude* where you want the map view to be centered. Here it's (39.9, -105.2), or a few miles northwest of Denver.

2. The starting *zoom level* for the map. In this case, I'm using 10, a good medium zoom.

ZOOM LEVELS

Zoom levels, illustrated here, specify how large an area the map shows.

Zoom Level 1	Zoom Level 8	Zoom Level 16

In Google Maps, zoom level 0 fits the entire Earth into 256 pixels. Each higher zoom level covers half the area but at twice the detail, so zoom level 1 would need a map 512 pixels wide to show the whole Earth. The maximum zoom varies by map type and location but is typically between 15 and 20.

That's it! With the JavaScript in place, our page now displays a map of the Colorado Front Range, as shown in Figure 2-1.

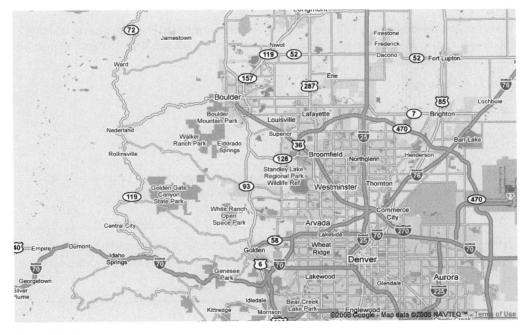

Figure 2-1. *The map appears.*

The Basic Maps API Objects

The Google Maps API makes good use of JavaScript's object orientation. All of the API functionality is encapsulated in objects, but if you haven't done object-oriented programming before, don't worry—it's not hard.

JAVASCRIPT 101: OBJECTS

JavaScript is an *object-oriented* programming language, and while this buzzword can sound intimidating, it's really a very simple concept.

For our purposes here, it's sufficient to think of JavaScript objects as self-contained bundles of related functions. For instance, everything you might want to do with a map as a whole is bundled into a GMap2 object. Actions dealing with a single marker on the map, rather than the whole map, are in the GMarker object. And so on. It's just a handy way of splitting the myriad things that the API can do into logical, manageable blocks.

Besides containing functions, objects also bundle *properties*, data that's relevant to their functionality. More examples of this will be forthcoming throughout the book, but you don't need to worry too much about it right now, so just keep it in mind as we proceed.

Let's walk through a few of the more fundamental Maps API objects. This initial description is only a taste of what's available; the API has dozens of objects for many different uses. Appendix D contains a list of resources to guide you as far as you might want to go through the Maps API.

GMap2

This is the granddaddy of them all, the core map object. Without it, you don't have a Google map on your page, so setting it up is always one of the first things you'll do. In fact, you need to both *create* the map object:

```
map = new GMap2(mapDiv);
```

and *initialize* it (as discussed earlier):

```
map.setCenter(new GLatLng(39.9, -105.2), 10);
```

before you can do anything else with the map.

Throughout the book we'll be seeing plenty of other things that can be done with GMap2, but the two basic operations just shown are enough to get you started.

■**Note**   The "2" in GMap2 signifies that we're using Version 2 of the API. It was completely overhauled from Version 1, but they coexisted for a time, hence the 2 in the name. It's simply called GMap2 regardless of which specific release of the API you're using, such as 2.124 in our case.

GLatLng

GLatLng is the Google Maps embodiment of the basic geospatial concepts *latitude* and *longitude*. It's used whenever the API needs to refer to a specific point on the globe. So it's used a *lot*.

You've already seen the GLatLng object in action as we were setting up the map in our initial block of JavaScript. Let's extract it into a variable of its own:

```
var coordinates = new GLatLng(39.9, -105.2);
map.setCenter(coordinates, 10);
```

This way, we can reuse the coordinates for something else in the next section.

GLatLng has a few other tricks up its sleeve—for instance, it can tell us how far away it is from another GLatLng—but for now, this will do.

GMarker

Here's something new to add to our little map, a marker staking out a specific point. We'll reuse the coordinates object we declared in the last section to place a marker at the center of the map, and then have a bit of fun. I've highlighted the new lines of code for you in Listing 2-5.

Listing 2-5. *Coordinates and Markers*

```
var map;

function loadMap()
{
  var mapDiv = document.getElementById('map');

  if (!GBrowserIsCompatible())
  {
    mapDiv.innerHTML =
      'Sorry, your browser isn\'t compatible with Google Maps.';
  }
  else
  {
    map = new GMap2(mapDiv);
    var coordinates = new GLatLng(39.9, -105.2);
    map.setCenter(coordinates, 10);

    var marker = new GMarker(coordinates);
    marker.bindInfoWindowHtml('<p>Hello, World!</p>');
    map.addOverlay(marker);
  }
};
```

Note what's going on in the last three lines here:

1. We create the GMarker, at the coordinates we set up earlier.

2. We give it something to say: a snippet of XHTML, within the bindInfoWindowHtml function. *Infowindow* is the Google Maps term for the "bubble" that typically pops open when a map marker is clicked.

3. We add it to the map, using the GMap2 object's own addOverlay function.

Figure 2-2 shows the results of our handiwork.

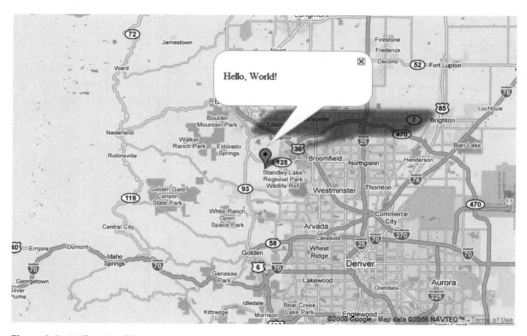

Figure 2-2. *Hello, World!*

Map Controls and Types

Our JavaScript is beginning to grow, and our map is beginning to improve. Let's round it out by adding the standard Google Maps *controls*, the onscreen tools that let a user interact with the map.

All of these controls are optional, and there may be times when you leave one or more of them out, but generally visitors to your page will be happier if they feel fully in control. And since the controls are easily added, using the GMap2 object's addControl function, there's usually little excuse not to include them on most maps.

I'll walk you through each of the basic map controls, and then we'll add them all to the JavaScript code. First up is the basic pan and zoom control (Figure 2-3), usually found at the upper left of a Google map.

```
map.addControl(new GLargeMapControl());
```

Figure 2-3. *GLargeMapControl*

Next we have the map scale (Figure 2-4), which automatically adjusts to show distance on the map.

```
map.addControl(new GScaleControl());
```

Figure 2-4. *GScaleControl*

The *overview* is the map-within-a-map at the lower right that shows a wider view of the area (Figure 2-5). It's really helpful for users to orient themselves, especially when they first jump into a map showing a small area.

```
map.addControl(new GOverviewMapControl());
```

Figure 2-5. *GOverviewMapControl*

Finally, Figure 2-6 shows the map type selection buttons.

```
map.addControl(new GMapTypeControl());
```

| Map | Satellite | Hybrid |

Figure 2-6. *GMapTypeControl*

While we're on the subject of map types, let's spruce up our map a bit by adding the Terrain map type, which isn't included on a default API map. This will also illustrate some more capabilities of the GMap2 object.

SMALL MAPS

You will probably *not* want to include all the standard map controls when your map is quite small. If a page requires a small map, less than 300 pixels or so, here are several useful techniques to make it work:

- You're probably not going to want the overview map, so leave out the `map.addControl` `(new GOverviewMapControl())` altogether.

- If your map is really small, you may also want to leave out the scale control.

- The small version of the pan and zoom control is fairly intuitive:

  ```
  map.addControl(new GSmallMapControl());
  ```

- The small map type control is less so; it's invoked by adding a parameter when creating it:

  ```
  map.addControl(new GMapTypeControl(true));
  ```

- Finally, it's a common problem for Google's copyright text to flow out of a small map, making a really ugly mess. You can prevent this with a bit of extra CSS for the map container:

  ```
  #map {
    overflow: hidden;
  }
  ```

It's done in two parts. First, we must explicitly specify a list of map types when creating the map object:

```
map = new GMap2(mapDiv,
   {mapTypes: [G_NORMAL_MAP, G_SATELLITE_MAP, G_HYBRID_MAP, G_PHYSICAL_MAP]});
```

There are many different options you can specify in the second parameter when creating GMap2, but the relevant one for now is the list of mapTypes. Note that we list the three usual types—Normal, Satellite, and Hybrid—plus the new one, Physical (what Terrain is called inside the API). This creates the GMap2 object with exactly that list of types. If we'd wanted to leave one out instead, we could have done that simply by excluding it from the list.

■**Tip** When you specify a list of map types like this, the buttons at the upper right of the map (for switching between types) will be in the same order as your types were in the JavaScript.

The second step is to start the map out with the Terrain type, and we do this by adding another parameter to setCenter, after the center coordinates and the zoom level.

```
map.setCenter(coordinates, 10, G_PHYSICAL_MAP);
```

As we move forward, you'll see that anything we might want to do with a Google map is just a variation on this process, specifying different options when calling API functions.

JAVASCRIPT 101: OPTIONAL PARAMETERS

Did you notice that `setCenter`, which we were originally calling with just two parameters, is now taking a third? This is common in JavaScript; parameters can be *optional*, meaning you can simply leave them out if you don't need to set them.

When you do leave optional parameters out of your function call, they'll usually be set internally by the function to *default values*. In our example of `setCenter`, the default value for the third parameter is the "normal" Google map type, showing roads and towns but no terrain or satellite images. This is the default value for `mapType`, and it's what you saw back in Figure 2-1.

Bringing It All Together

Our first map has come a long way in a short time, and this is a good opportunity to take stock. Combining all the extra code from the preceding sections produces the completed map shown in Figure 2-7. It's ready to publish on the Web.

Figure 2-7. *The complete map*

Listing 2-6 shows the final JavaScript for everything we've covered in this chapter, together in one place. I've highlighted the changes from Listing 2-5 for your reference.

Listing 2-6. *JavaScript for the Complete Map Page*

```
var map;

function loadMap()
{
  var mapDiv = document.getElementById('map');

  if (!GBrowserIsCompatible())
  {
    mapDiv.innerHTML =
      'Sorry, your browser isn\'t compatible with Google Maps.';
  }
  else
  {
    map = new GMap2(mapDiv,
      {mapTypes: [G_NORMAL_MAP, G_PHYSICAL_MAP, G_SATELLITE_MAP, G_HYBRID_MAP]});
    var coordinates = new GLatLng(39.9, -105.2);
    map.setCenter(coordinates, 10, G_PHYSICAL_MAP);

    var marker = new GMarker(coordinates);
    marker.bindInfoWindowHtml('<p>Hello, World!</p>');
    map.addOverlay(marker);

    map.addControl(new GScaleControl());
    map.addControl(new GOverviewMapControl());
    map.addControl(new GMapTypeControl());
    map.addControl(new GLargeMapControl());
  }
};
```

Putting It to Use

You now have everything you need to add a basic Google map to a web page of your own. I'm sure you can see how, but to make certain that you don't miss anything, here are the essential steps.

1. Lay out your page, creating and positioning a container for the map in your XHTML. Don't neglect this step.

2. Save the code from Listing 2-6 to your own site, giving it a name like *basic_map.js*.

   a. Change the latitude and longitude of the coordinates object to match the location you want your map to show.

   b. Edit the XHTML fragment in bindInfoWindowHtml to display your own message.

3. Add the two `script` elements and `body` event handlers from Listing 2-3 to your own XHTML.

   a. Register an API key for your domain and paste it into the first `script` tag.

   b. Ensure that the `src` attribute of the second `script` tag matches your JavaScript file name (such as *basic_map.js*) instead of `listing_02_04.js`.

4. Tweak other settings as needed for your own application, following the guidelines in this chapter. Don't be afraid to experiment!

Congratulations! You have your own Google map.

Other Version Options

Before we move on, and while we're on the subject of putting the map into your own page, it wouldn't hurt for you to know a bit more about Map API versions. As you'll recall from earlier in the chapter, we're using version 2.124, and that's fine up to a point. But it's not quite the full story; the Google Maps API supports four different options for version selection, controlled by what follows the `v=2` in the API `script` element. Which version you use depends mostly on how much public exposure a particular map page will receive. We've already covered one option; following are the other three.

■**Note** Version 1 of the Maps API was discontinued in 2006, and Google has yet to even mention a Version 3. So for our purposes, the major version to use is always 2.

2.s

The s stands for Stable, and that's what this version is: the latest stable release from Google. It gets moved forward now and then when Google considers a release to have been in general use long enough to have proven itself, but it always lags considerably behind the latest and greatest. For instance, at this writing 2.s is serving a release that's 16 months old.

Because of its stability, 2.s is the version that Google recommends for use on production web sites. But personally, I prefer specifying the exact version, like 2.124.

2

This is the simplest option, and it's not a bad choice during the development of your map. It will use the latest release from Google, ensuring that you have the newest enhancements. However, occasionally significant bugs do find their way into an official release, and (more rarely) a new feature will be incompatible with existing API implementations.

For these reasons, it does happen that a map which was working fine will suddenly break when Google pushes a new release. Therefore, it's not recommended that you use 2 on production web pages, only during development. And only if you're interested in keeping quite up-to-date with what Google's doing in the API.

2.x

For you thrill-seekers and adrenaline junkies, 2.x is the eXtreme version. It's essentially a preview of Google's next API release, and as such it always includes the very first look at cool new features. The disadvantage is that these prereleases often contain significant bugs and will break your map fairly frequently.

My advice is not to use 2.x until you're fairly comfortable with Maps API programming, and maybe not even then if you want to focus on your own development work rather than Google's. But definitely never, *ever* use it on a production web site.

Summary

You now have the basic framework to start building map mashups: a Google map that you can insert into any web page. It's a blank slate onto which the world's geodata can be written.

In Chapter 3 we'll begin that process, "consuming" geoXML from the Web and displaying it on our map.

CHAPTER 3

■ ■ ■

Consuming GeoXML in the Maps API

With Chapter 2 under your belt, you have the skills to add a basic Google map to any web page. Now it's time to add some geospatial data, transforming your page from a simple map into a full-fledged mashup.

True to the spirit of the geoweb, we'll do this by mapping geoXML data from various sources across the Internet. This process is known as *consuming* the geodata, which usually someone else has produced. Consuming geoXML is by far the quickest and easiest way to create a map mashup because Google makes it so simple to do; there's almost no programming involved.

Along the way, you'll learn the ins and outs of GGeoXml, the main Maps API JavaScript object that displays geodata. There are many different varieties of geodata you can map with it, but they all follow much the same pattern. We'll also look at some of the drawbacks of this approach, and then finish with an example of its use in a real-world scenario. All of the example code in this chapter builds on the base constructed in Chapter 2. You're going to add additional JavaScript to the Maps API framework you've already created. So if at any point you're unclear about what's going on in a particular listing, first make sure you understand what's happened before now.

TERMINOLOGY

Before we get started I'd like to make a bit of terminology clear, because there is room for confusion in the following two terms:

- *geoXML*: the generic term for standardized XML geodata, for our purposes KML or GeoRSS. This is the actual data tying information to its relevant latitude/longitude coordinates. Note that the "ML" is upper-case here.

- GGeoXml: a JavaScript object in the Google Maps API for mapping geodata with minimum hassle. When Google created this object in the API, they named it directly after the data it was handling; an obvious name, perhaps, but one that can cause some confusion when we're also talking about the data itself. The key distinction is that the JavaScript object's name starts with two Gs and ends with a lowercase "ml."

Using the GGeoXML **Object**

Google's own geoXML processor goes by the name GGeoXml; like most Maps API objects, its name is simply what it does preceded by a "G." It will happily process both KML and GeoRSS— the two main standards for geoXML, as discussed in Chapter 1—and its usage is exactly the same for both. Let's take a look.

Examples of GGeoXml in Use

The best way to illustrate the use of the GGeoXml object is by example, and for that we need a sample geoXML data source to work with. In the following examples, I'm using data feeds from Placeopedia, a web site dedicated to geo-locating Wikipedia entries. A *feed* is simply a source of data on the Web, usually XML of one sort or another. It's defined by a URL, just like a web page. Most data feeds change over time with updated information; hence the name—they're feeding you new data as it becomes available.

But keep in mind, one of the main reasons for using a geoXML processor in your map is that the specific data source becomes almost immaterial; your code is always going to be much the same.

Using GGeoXml with a KML Feed

My first example, in Listing 3-1, uses a KML feed of the latest Wikipedia entries to have geodata added.

Listing 3-1. *Basic GGeoXml Usage*

```
var map;
var geoXml;

function loadMap()
{
  var mapDiv = document.getElementById('map');

  if (!GBrowserIsCompatible())
  {
    mapDiv.innerHTML =
      'Sorry, your browser isn\'t compatible with Google Maps.';
  }
  else
  {
    map = new GMap2(mapDiv,
      {mapTypes: [G_NORMAL_MAP, G_SATELLITE_MAP, G_HYBRID_MAP, G_PHYSICAL_MAP]});
    var coordinates = new GLatLng(39.8, −98.5);
    map.setCenter(coordinates, 4);
```

```
map.addControl(new GLargeMapControl());
map.addControl(new GScaleControl());
map.addControl(new GOverviewMapControl());
map.addControl(new GMapTypeControl());

geoXml = new GGeoXml('http://www.placeopedia.com/cgi-bin/kml.cgi');
map.addOverlay(geoXml);
}
};
```

As you can see, most of the code is unchanged from the way we left it in Chapter 2. I've highlighted the new parts; let's go through them.

First, you need to declare the variable that will hold the GGeoXml object, much as we did for the map object initially:

```
var geoXml;
```

JAVASCRIPT 101: NAMING CONVENTIONS

You may have noticed that variables in our JavaScript are named in quite particular ways. This is no accident; code is easier to read and less error-prone if consistent standards, known as *naming conventions*, are followed.

There are two primary naming conventions widely used in JavaScript. The first is used for *types*, essentially code structures that are predefined for your use, and this convention consists of simply capitalizing the first letter of each word in the name. Good examples include LargeMapControl and GGeoXml. Because this convention causes "humps" in the middle of the name, it's often called *camel case*.

The second convention is for specific variables and functions; most of the names you'll create yourself will fall into this category. These are distinguished from type names by *not* capitalizing the first letter of the name, but still capitalizing any words that start later in the name. Examples we've seen so far include addOverlay and geoXml. Names following this convention still have "humps" in the middle, but not at the beginning, so this technique is often called *sad camel*—his head is drooping, see?

How does this make our code less error-prone? Because JavaScript is a *case-sensitive* language, it's an error to use lower-case and uppercase letters inconsistently. So in JavaScript, the names geoXml, GeoXml, and GeoXML would all be seen by the computer as referring to different things, and your code wouldn't work right if you used one when you should have used another. Consistently following the naming conventions helps avoid this error by reducing your need to remember, "Now how exactly did I capitalize that variable?"

Next, I'm starting this map out at a different location than in the previous chapter, so I need different latitude, longitude, and zoom values:

```
var coordinates = new GLatLng(39.8, -98.5);
map.setCenter(coordinates, 4);
```

The coordinates (39.8, -98.5) are in the center of the contiguous USA, and a zoom level of 4 will show those 48 states nicely on most monitors. Note that I'm also back to using the default map type, rather than G_PHYSICAL_MAP as we left things in Chapter 2.

Then comes the real heart of this section, the initialization of the `GGeoXml` object:

```
geoXml = new GGeoXml('http://www.placeopedia.com/cgi-bin/kml.cgi');
```

It's really quite simple, taking only a single parameter, the URL of the data feed we want to show on the map. As long as that URL points to data that's in an acceptable geoXML standard, the `GGeoXml` object will display it.

And finally, we need to add `geoXml` to the map:

```
map.addOverlay(geoXml);
```

If you remember, `addOverlay` is the same function we used when we added our "Hello, World" marker to the map in the previous chapter. In Google Maps terminology, an *overlay* is anything that gets placed on the map's surface, so the placement itself usually happens with `addOverlay`.

You can see typical results in Figure 3-1. I say "typical" because this is a live data feed, so reloading the page an hour or a day later will give different results, based on the latest entries at Placeopedia.

Figure 3-1. *Placeopedia, the latest Wikipedia entries with geodata*

Notice that there is some depth to the data feed; it's not just a list of coordinates. Each geodata point has associated XHTML, which `GGeoXml` displays in the infowindow for that point; this content includes a title, attribution, short description, and a link back to the Wikipedia article itself. It's this association of information—content—with geodata that truly defines the geoweb, and `GGeoXml` lets you tie into it with remarkably little effort.

■**Tip** Because GGeoXml is using Google's servers to retrieve the target XML, the page containing it must come from a real web server; that is, the page's URL in your browser needs to start with http://. It *cannot* be served from your local file system, using a URL beginning with file://. And as you'll recall from Chapter 2, this means that the page needs to use a valid Google Maps API key.

In addition, the XML file being used must be publicly available on the Internet; it can't be on your local computer or a private intranet.

THE VALUE OF GOOGLE'S CACHING

One danger inherent in all mashups is that they can be more successful than their "parents"—that is, they can get more traffic than the web sites that provide their source data. It's an indication of the power of mashup synergy, but when this happens, it's quite possible to overload the data source. Server bandwidth isn't free, and the creators of the "parent" sites probably aren't paying for more than they need. If an overload happens, not only will it break your mashup, it's also quite inconsiderate to the sites providing your data.

The GGeoXml object mitigates this danger by using a technique known as *caching*. Any geodata it uses is retrieved via Google's servers, and those servers are smart enough not to go back to the original data provider every time. Instead, they cache the data: they keep a copy of it themselves and just resend that copy when later requests for the same data arrive from mashups like yours. Only occasionally do they refresh their cache from the original source.

Not only does this avoid overloading the data source, it will also usually speed things up. Let's face it; Google has more bandwidth than whoever's providing your data, so it's probably quicker to retrieve it from Google than from the original source whenever possible.

Using GGeoXml with a GeoRSS Feed

As mentioned earlier, GGeoXml is used exactly the same way regardless of whether the data feed it's plotting is KML or GeoRSS. So to convert our example to use Placeopedia's GeoRSS feed instead, you only need to make one small change in your code:

```
geoXml = new GGeoXml('http://www.placeopedia.com/cgi-bin/rss.cgi');
```

That's it; just change the URL to point to the GeoRSS feed rather than the KML. The displayed map will be exactly the same in this case, because Placeopedia is supplying the same base geodata in both feeds, just in different formats.

■**Note** Placeopedia's GeoRSS is in W3C Geo format[1], a deprecated standard that is different internally from the GeoRSS sample given in Chapter 1. The GGeoXml object doesn't care, and at this point you don't need to, either; I only mention it in case you look "under the hood" and find something unexpected.

---

1. The deprecated W3C Geo standard can be found at http://www.w3.org/2003/01/geo.

Advanced GGeoXml

The GGeoXml object does so much for you already that there's really not a lot more to add; feed it geodata and let it go. The two areas described in the next sections cover most of the additional options. GGeoXml is still a fairly new addition to the API, however, and it's likely that more functionality will be along at some point.

Automatically Moving the Map Viewport

When data feeds change over time, the geospatial location of their contents may also change. Literally, the geodata is referring to someplace different than it was yesterday. But this means that a static map viewport, like the one I had centered on the contiguous US states earlier, is often less than ideal. You'd rather move your viewport to show whatever's currently in the feed.

Handily, GGeoXml has a function to do this. In order to use it we just need to extend our code a bit, as highlighted in Listing 3-2.

Listing 3-2. *Automatically Moving the Map Viewport*

```
var map;
var geoXml;

function loadMap()
{
  var mapDiv = document.getElementById('map');

  if (!GBrowserIsCompatible())
  {
    mapDiv.innerHTML =
      'Sorry, your browser isn\'t compatible with Google Maps.';
  }
  else
  {
    map = new GMap2(mapDiv,
      {mapTypes: [G_NORMAL_MAP, G_SATELLITE_MAP, G_HYBRID_MAP, G_PHYSICAL_MAP]});
    var coordinates = new GLatLng(39.8, -98.5);
    map.setCenter(coordinates, 4);

    map.addControl(new GLargeMapControl());
    map.addControl(new GScaleControl());
    map.addControl(new GOverviewMapControl());
    map.addControl(new GMapTypeControl());
```

```
    geoXml = new GGeoXml(
      'http://www.placeopedia.com/cgi-bin/rss.cgi?num_results=5', xmlLoaded);
    map.addOverlay(geoXml);
  }
};

function xmlLoaded()
{
  geoXml.gotoDefaultViewport(map);
};
```

All I've really done here is added a second parameter to the initialization of geoXml: the name of a callback function to be run when the geodata has been loaded into the map. And in that function is a call to geoXml.gotoDefaultViewport, which tells our GGeoXml object to move map so that the data just loaded is all nicely visible on screen.

JAVASCRIPT 101: CALLBACK FUNCTIONS

A *callback function*, like xmlLoaded here, is declared like any other JavaScript function. It's a self-contained set of actions that can be run as a group. But remember how a function has a name, just like a variable? Well, it turns out that you can pass that name as a parameter to a *second* function—just like a variable. Then the second function, GGeoXml in this case, can run the first function (xmlLoaded) at a strategic time. Literally, GGeoXml *calls back* to xmlLoaded, and then xmlLoaded does its job, moving the map viewport.

If you're interested, the reason for doing it this way is that GGeoXml is *asynchronous*—meaning that it doesn't make the rest of the code wait while it retrieves and processes the geodata. Why not? Mostly because it has to go out over the Internet to do so, and that might take a while, especially if there's a lot of data in the feed. So it lets the rest of the page continue loading and does its work in the background.

But this means that anything we want to happen *after* the data loads, such as moving the viewport, can't simply be put later in the code. If we did so, GGeoXml probably wouldn't be done loading the data yet, and wouldn't know what to do with the viewport yet either. Enter the callback function: with this mechanism, we're effectively saying "Call xmlLoaded when you're done loading data, no matter how long that takes."

Callback functions are used quite frequently in the Maps API, whenever the user experience would be improved by doing lengthy processing in the background.

I've also tweaked the Placeopedia URL to show only the last five entries, by including ?num_results=5; this is more likely to be confined to a single region of the globe than the default 50-entry data set. A typical result can be seen in Figure 3-2 (note that two of the points at Washington, DC, closely overlap).

Figure 3-2. *Map automatically sized for latest five entries*

Hide and Show

The only other GGeoXml functions that you're likely to find useful at this stage are hide and show. They do basically what you'd expect, hiding the GGeoXml overlay from view, or making it visible again if it's been hidden. Their use is equally simple:

```
geoXml.hide()
```

and

```
geoXml.show()
```

One obvious use for hide and show would be in a more complicated mashup, displaying several different sorts of geodata from different sources. It might be useful for the user to select which data they want to see at any given moment; you'd use hide and show to do so. You'll find an example of this in Chapter 4, under "Interacting with the Rest of the Page," but I wanted to introduce the GGeoXml functionality to support it here.

Displaying More Than Markers

The Placeopedia geodata in the preceding examples has all of its information tied to individual geographic points, which display as markers on the map. But the geoXML standards support a number of other sorts of geodata, and it's worth looking at a couple of them.

The usage is exactly the same each time; we simply supply the GGeoXml object with a different data feed URL. The difference is all contained in the data, and GGeoXml insulates us from having to worry about it.

Polylines and Polygons

The first example is linear geodata, describing a path along (or over) the Earth's surface rather than a single point on it. In Google Maps, such paths are called *polylines*. They're always made up of individual, straight-line segments joined together, but it's not uncommon for these segments to blend visually into an apparent curve. Polylines are supported by both KML and GeoRSS.

Figure 3-3 shows an example of polylines in action, plotting the train routes of the Chicago Transit Authority. It's placed on the map from the following geodata URL:

```
geoXml = new GGeoXml('http://mapgadgets.googlepages.com/cta.kml', xmlLoaded);
```

Figure 3-3. *Polylines showing Chicago Transit Authority routes*

Other common uses for polylines include these:

- Driving directions

- Hiking trails

- The path of a GPS-tracked object, like a weather balloon

- Line-of-sight indicators

When the start and end points of a polyline coincide, it encloses an area which we call a *polygon*. A polygon displayed on a map shows both its border (as a polyline) and, optionally, its enclosed area in color. A good example is shown in Figure 3-4, a map of population densities in Florida by county. Each county is a single polygon, tracing its border, that is then filled with a color based on its population.

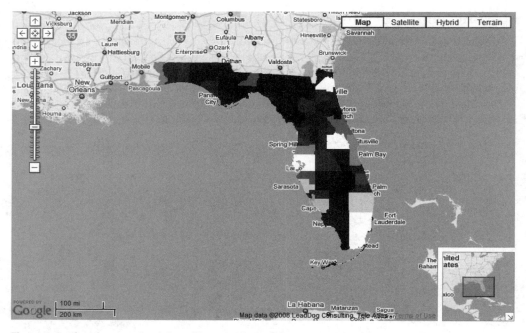

Figure 3-4. *Florida counties colored by population density*

Again, this information was added to the map by simply supplying the appropriate URL to GGeoXml:

```
geoXml = new GGeoXml(
  'http://media.juiceanalytics.com/downloads/fl_co_pd.kmz', xmlLoaded);
```

Polygons are usually used for applications such as this, showing areas of interest on the map. Common examples include these:

- Political boundaries, such as the counties in Figure 3-4

- Areas affected by some event, such as a natural disaster

- Proximity, by filling in a circle around a given point

KML AND KMZ

Most of the KML files we've been using have `.kml` in the URL, a good indication of the type of geodata within. But the Florida counties URL ends in `.kmz` instead. What's the difference?

KMZ files are simply KML that has been made smaller by compression, "abbreviating" the file's content to take up less space, so that it is quicker to download and uses less bandwidth. The specific form of compression used here is a zip file, and so the "L" in KML is replaced with a "Z" in KMZ.

Most geo software, including GGeoXml, will happily work with both KML and KMZ files interchangeably. This is pervasive enough that both are generically referred to as KML data, even if they've been zipped into a KMZ.

Ground Overlays

In addition to using polylines and polygons to create line drawings on a map, KML has the ability to superimpose a predrawn image on top of the map. Such an application is called a *ground overlay* (conceptually similar to, but not the same as, an overlay within the Maps API). It works by specifying the coordinates of all four corners of the image; GGeoXml then "glues" it in place on the map, and it will automatically remain in position as we pan or zoom.

Figure 3-5 shows an image overlay in action, with a satellite photo from NASA's LandSat orbiter placed on the map.

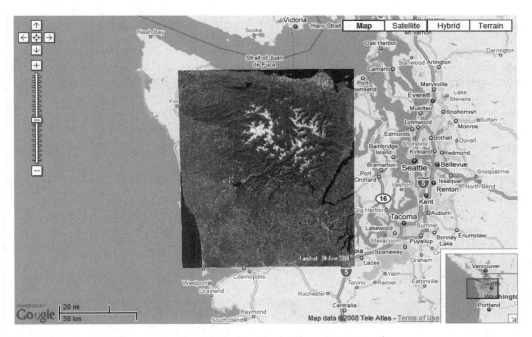

Figure 3-5. *A satellite image overlay of Washington's Olympic Peninsula*

Categories of images commonly used for ground overlays include these:

- Satellite and aerial photos, usually showing some specific detail beyond what Google's own Satellite map type does

- Special-purpose maps of a specific area, such as a park or university campus

Generally, ground overlays can be a convenient way to quickly combine existing maps—especially those scanned from paper—with Google Maps. This avoids the step of extracting all the implied geodata, such as the coordinates of individual buildings on a campus map. And for aerial or satellite photos, it's the only way to go.

Drawbacks to Using GGeoXML

The GGeoXml object is good, but of course it's not perfect, and I'd be remiss if I didn't inform you about some of its limitations. It's an excellent way to build geo-mashups quickly and easily, and by using geoXML you're advancing the geoweb as a whole, but when building real-world web applications it can be limiting.

Bear in mind that the geoweb generally, and GGeoXml specifically, are still quite new and evolving rapidly. So undoubtedly some of the disadvantages I'll mention are simply teething problems and will work themselves out as the technology matures.

Inflexible Data Display

The first limitation you're likely to encounter is that you have little control over how GGeoXml displays your geodata. Its workings are almost entirely hidden—XML goes in, and maps come out. If it does exactly what you want, that's fine, but if not, you're somewhat stuck. As a pure consumer of geodata, you'll find that aspects like icons used for markers and the colors of polylines are completely out of your control.

Which isn't to say that there's *nothing* you can do. Let's look at a couple of coping strategies for GGeoXml's autonomy.

Use CSS

You can work around some of the display limitations by the use of CSS on your map page. Specifically, the infowindow displayed by the map when a geodata marker is clicked can be styled, often extensively, by the application of well-targeted CSS. Determining what markup to target can be a bit of a challenge, but here are a couple of suggestions.

Examine the GeoXML Source

By saving a copy of a feed to your hard disk and opening it in a text editor (as you would with XHTML), you can see the XML source directly. In KML, look for the <description> tags; in GeoRSS, they're usually called <content>. In either case, this element should contain the XHTML displayed in the marker's infowindow.

View Selection Source

In Firefox, you can view the XHTML source for any page fragment by selecting it with your mouse, right-clicking on it, and choosing View Selection Source from the popup menu. This works equally well in a Google Maps infowindow, so once you have your basic geodata displaying, you can simply click on a marker, select the infowindow's content, and view its source.

Once you know the XHTML for the infowindow's content, it's often possible to devise some CSS selectors to target that content and change its presentation. A useful technique here is to keep in mind that the map is entirely within an XHTML container that we *do* have control over—in our examples so far, it's <div id="map">. You'll see an example of this CSS targeting in action toward the end of the chapter.

Control the Data Source

If you are generating the geodata yourself, as I'll discuss in Chapter 10, you have much more control over how it will display. The XML has attributes for marker image URLs, polyline weights and colors, and polygon fill colors.

You also have full control here over the XHTML content that will be displayed in infowindows, so you have the opportunity to place whatever content you like there. This approach also works well in conjunction with using the page CSS to control presentation, just as you would with any other markup.

Even if you're not producing the geodata, you may be able to contact the site that is, and discuss improvements to its presentation with them.

Closed Functionality

Just as GGeoXml keeps you from changing how your geodata displays, it also prevents you from doing very much else with the data besides displaying it. GGeoXml is fine if all you want to do is show the data on your map, but not if you want to be able to add any functionality. For instance, you may be working with a feed of hiking trails and want to show only the ones rated "strenuous." Or your web site might benefit from doing some analysis on census data by county, rather than just showing it on the map. The GGeoXml object is no help to you here.

One common additional request that mashup authors have is what's known as a *sidebar*, a list that sits alongside the map on screen and shows the data that's been mapped. Sidebars are very handy in many circumstances, providing a good place to display information that doesn't fit well onto the map, and allowing users to see the whole list at a glance without having to click on each point. It's a good complement to mapping geodata—but the GGeoXml object doesn't support it. (See "Alternatives to Google's GGeoXml Object" for third-party options if you need this capability.)

Generally, you just need to be aware of what your end goal is and what GGeoXml's limitations are.

ALTERNATIVES TO GOOGLE'S GGeoXml OBJECT

If you're a slightly more advanced JavaScript programmer, there are alternatives to Google's GGeoXml available from third-party developers. The first is called EGeoXml, and it was written by Maps API star Mike Williams as another option for processing KML data. Full information is available from his web site at http://econym.googlepages.com/egeoxml.htm, but in a nutshell, it has the following advantages over Google's object:

- Automatic sidebar generation

- Many more options for display of geodata and content

- Access to all Maps API objects created from the geodata

A second programmer, Lance Dyas, has extended EGeoXml to support GeoRSS and a greater subset of KML. His version also generates more sophisticated sidebars and includes other, more advanced features. Find out more at http://www.dyasdesigns.com/geoxml.

The JavaScript source code for both of these processors is itself available, so you can modify them yourself to suit your needs. If you're not quite ready for that, you can also contact the authors directly and suggest changes; you'll usually find that they're quite helpful and willing to extend their objects, if you ask politely. There are some disadvantages to these alternative objects, however:

- They are more complicated to use, requiring more JavaScript knowledge than Google's own object, especially to use them to full effect.

- They require that the geoXML be hosted at the same server as the map page. If you're generating your own geodata, this isn't a problem, but it definitely is an obstacle for traditional mashups.

- They support even less of the KML and GeoRSS specifications than Google's object does. Again, that's fine if you're generating your own geoXML—you can modify the XML as needed for it to work—but often, third-party geodata will display either poorly or not at all.

- They do not use the Google cache for geodata, losing the advantages to be gained there.

We'll revisit EGeoXml in Chapter 9, when your JavaScript skills are further along, but for now I recommend that you stick with GGeoXml.

Incomplete KML Support

While GGeoXml works fine for the vast majority of KML files, the KML specification is quite rich and versatile, and GGeoXml doesn't support it completely. This means that you'll occasionally find KML feeds that won't render correctly or won't appear at all on your Google map.

This is one area that's definitely improving with time; the subset of KML that GGeoXml supports now is much greater than when it was first released. By the time you read this, it may well be a nonissue, but it's good to be aware of it nonetheless.

A related problem is sheer size. There's no inherent upper bound on the size of a KML or GeoRSS feed, but GGeoXml will simply refuse to process very large datasets. As of this writing, Google gives a maximum size of 3MB for a geoXML file. However, a feed even beginning to approach this size—typically over 1MB or so—is big enough that it would usually be impractical to display it anyway. It would take too long for users on a slow connection to download, and would be completely unwieldy when drawn on the map. I'll present some solutions to this problem in Chapters 9 and 10, but it will continue to be an ongoing issue.

If you run into either of these difficulties, there's unfortunately not a lot to be done about it. If you control the feed yourself, you can change it as needed, but otherwise about all you can do is find another source for data that will work.

Alternatives to GeoXML

GeoXML is the preferred standard for disseminating geodata, but limitations like those I've just discussed mean that it's not ideal for every circumstance. If you're unable to achieve satisfactory results with KML or GeoRSS, a viable alternative is *JSON*, which stands for JavaScript Object Notation. It's essentially a shorthand method of encapsulating data directly as JavaScript, meaning that you can use it in your own code without an intermediary like the GGeoXml object.

Using JSON is fairly easy, but it does take more JavaScript than we have encountered so far. Also, there's no established standard for encoding geodata as JSON, meaning that you won't find third-party data feeds for it as you will with KML and GeoRSS. As a result, it will be left to you to do more programming work yourself, both in producing JSON and consuming it in your map. So full coverage of it won't happen until Chapters 8 and 10.

For now, just be aware that there is a viable alternative, and that we won't be permanently limited by any shortcomings of GGeoXML.

Putting It to Use

All of the preceding geoXML examples essentially exist in isolation, plotting geodata feeds by themselves on a map. That's fine, but nothing new has really been accomplished—we're just visualizing the geodata from the feed. How about doing something useful with it?

One common application for mapping on web sites is on "Contact Us" pages, showing visitors where a business is located. The following example does just that: shows an office location on a map, and includes nearby transit links to help visitors make their way there.

First, the JavaScript code. Listing 3-3 shows the .js file in its entirety; we'll go over the important bits in a moment.

Listing 3-3. *The Transit Links JavaScript*

```
var map;
var geoXml;

function loadMap()
{
  var mapDiv = document.getElementById('map');

  if (!GBrowserIsCompatible())
  {
    mapDiv.innerHTML =
      'Sorry, your browser isn\'t compatible with Google Maps.';
  }
  else
  {
    map = new GMap2(mapDiv,
      {mapTypes: [G_NORMAL_MAP, G_SATELLITE_MAP, G_HYBRID_MAP, G_PHYSICAL_MAP]});
    var coordinates = new GLatLng(49.186416, -122.842911);
    map.setCenter(coordinates, 15);

    var marker = new GMarker(coordinates);
    marker.bindInfowindowHtml('<h3>Our Office</h3>' +
      '<addr>10100 E Whalley Ring Rd<br />Vancouver, BC</addr>');
    map.addOverlay(marker); ←
    GEvent.trigger(marker, 'click');
```

```
      map.addControl(new GLargeMapControl());
      map.addControl(new GScaleControl());
      map.addControl(new GOverviewMapControl());
      map.addControl(new GMapTypeControl());

      geoXml = new GGeoXml('http://bbs.keyhole.com/ubb/download.php?Number=921371');
      map.addOverlay(geoXml);
   }
};
```

First, of course, is the map center location. My hypothetical office is at the following coordinates near Vancouver, BC, and I want the map to show good close detail, so I start it at zoom level 15:

```
var coordinates = new GLatLng(49.186416, -122.842911);
map.setCenter(coordinates, 15);
```

Next, let's have some content for the infowindow. I'll use it to show the address of my office, as an additional aid for folks trying to find us:

```
marker.bindInfowindowHtml('<h3>Our Office</h3>' +
   '<addr>10100 E Whalley Ring Rd<br />Vancouver, BC</addr>');
```

Making this content display nicely will also require a bit of CSS, because we don't want the <h3> element's customary large margins within our infowindow. Listing 3-4 shows the page CSS we already had (from Chapter 2) with the new selector added. Note that this is an example of CSS targeted at the infowindow's content, as discussed earlier.

Listing 3-4. *The Transit Links CSS*

```
html {
  height: 100%;
}

body {
  height: 100%;
  margin: 0;
}
```

```
#map {
  width: 100%;
  height: 100%;
}

#map h3 {
  margin: 0;
}
```

It would also be nice to show this address information automatically when the page opens. We can do so by taking advantage of the marker's inherent ability to open its infowindow when clicked. In the JavaScript, the following line of code simply triggers that click event, and the infowindow will follow:

```
GEvent.trigger(marker, 'click');
```

JAVASCRIPT 101: TRIGGERING EVENTS

As you'll recall from Chapter 2, an *event* refers to a specific action, usually one initiated by the user. The event here is `click`, which (not surprisingly) corresponds to a mouse click.

Events are provided by the underlying platform (like the Maps API, or JavaScript itself) as "hooks" onto which we can hang functionality, and the function we hang there—which gets called when the event occurs— is its *event handler*. The marker's click event, for example, has a handler defined by the API to open an infowindow. The API and JavaScript also let us define our own handlers, which you'll learn how to do in the next chapter.

We can also trigger an event handler manually, as is happening in this example. Doing so simply calls the event handler function, be it predefined (as here) or one we've created ourselves. It's exactly the same effect as if the user had actually clicked on the marker with their mouse—we're just not waiting for them to do so.

Finally, I'm going to include a geodata feed showing Vancouver transit information, helping my visitors reach me in an environmentally friendly manner:

```
geoXml = new GGeoXml('http://bbs.keyhole.com/ubb/download.php?Number=921371');
```

Putting it all together, Figure 3-6 shows the page as it first loads, with my office address infowindow open. Figure 3-7 then shows the same page with a sample of the additional information available when a visitor clicks on one of the transit station markers.

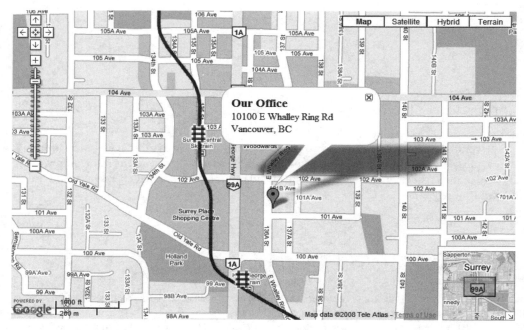

Figure 3-6. *Transit links near a business location...*

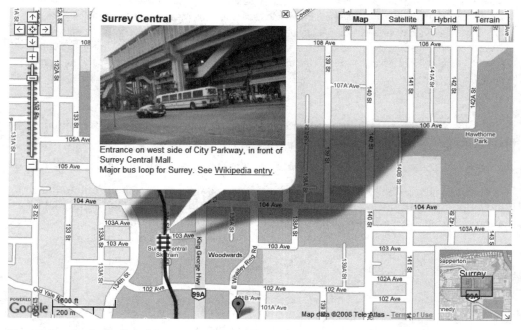

Figure 3-7. *...include clickable stop markers with extra information from the KML.*

HOW TO FIND GEOXML

Now that you're ready to add geoXML to your maps, where will it come from? I've found the following sources to be quite good:

- A Google search with `filetype:kml` will restrict the results to show only KML data. For example, if you were looking for geodata on trains, you'd type `trains filetype:kml` into the standard Google search box.

- A similar search can be run in Google Earth; here, you just enter your search query in the Fly To box. For more detailed instructions, see `http://tinyurl.com/2ck657`.

- The main Google Maps site (`maps.google.com`) is KML-aware, and you can find the data by using the Search the Map function. Look for "User-created content" in the results.

- The My Maps tab at `maps.google.com` is a great way to create geodata without needing to write code. There's a full set of graphical tools for creating geospatial content, and when you're done, the view in Google Earth link will give you the KML. This will be discussed in detail in Chapter 10.

- The Google Earth Community, at `http://bbs.keyhole.com`, is an open forum where users post KML content they've found or created. There's a bit of everything here, so the odds are that a bit of searching will turn up something useful to you.

- It's somewhat hit-and-miss, but GeoRSS content can be found at `http://del.icio.us/tag/georss`.

- Finally, Stanford University has a great tool for generating custom KML files from US Census data. Find it at `http://gecensus.stanford.edu`.

Remember, in each case we're looking for a geodata URL. If you already have a KML file open in Google Earth, do the following:

1. Right-click on the file in the Places pane and select "Share/Post..."

2. The URL will appear at the top of the Community Posting pane. Select and copy it from here.

Or, when you find a link to a file online, it's usually easiest to just right-click on it and select Copy Shortcut (in IE) or Copy Link Location (in Firefox). Either way, you'll then have the URL on your clipboard, ready to paste into your JavaScript source code.

Summary

The easiest and most standards-compliant way to create a map mashup is by consuming geoXML, and Google's GGeoXml object is the tool of choice in the Maps API. It's easy to use: just create it with the URL of a geodata feed and add it to the map. And it's powerful: it handles most geoXML from a wide variety of sources, doing all the heavy lifting of displaying it on your map while insulating you from the messy details. Although it's not without its flaws, GGeoXml is still the best game going for Maps API mashup authors, and it's getting better all the time.

In the next chapter, we'll round out our fledgling map by building interactions with both the user and the rest of the web page where it lives. We'll also look at adding some additional bells and whistles from Google, such as map advertising, local search, and an embedded 3D Google Earth view.

CHAPTER 4

■ ■ ■

Building Out Your Map Page

By now you have the basics of the Google Maps API firmly in hand. You can put a map on a web page, stake out a location with a marker, and mash up third-party geodata. You've come a long way in just a couple of chapters.

But Google Maps can do much, much more. In this chapter and the next, you'll dip your toe into the larger ocean of map functionality as we build out a couple of example map pages. We'll start with the basics you already know and demonstrate lots of ways to expand your mapping horizons; some enhancements come prepackaged from Google, while others will stretch your own JavaScript abilities. But don't worry, I'll be guiding you through every step of the way—and in all cases, you'll find plenty of examples to draw on as you begin to make your own maps come alive. Also, don't forget that Appendix B contains a JavaScript primer to help you with the basics of the language structure.

Building the Basic Structure

This chapter is focused on integrating the map into the page on which it sits, and then rounding out its functionality for a more complete user experience. The example we'll be building is a visitor guide web page for Arches National Park in Utah; the basic XHTML structure is shown in Listing 4-1.

Listing 4-1. *The Basic XHTML for the National Park Map Page*

```
<!DOCTYPE html PUBLIC "-//W3C//DTD XHTML 1.0 Strict//EN"
                      "http://www.w3.org/TR/xhtml1/DTD/xhtml1-strict.dtd">
<html xmlns="http://www.w3.org/1999/xhtml">
  <head>
    <meta http-equiv="Content-Type" content="text/html; charset=UTF-8" />
    <title>Building Out Your Map Page</title>
    <link type="text/css" rel="stylesheet" href="listing_04_02.css" />
    <script type="text/javascript"
            src="http://maps.google.com/maps?file=api&amp;v=2.124&amp;key="></script>
    <script type="text/javascript" src="listing_04_03.js"></script>
  </head>
  <body onload="loadMap()" onunload="GUnload()">
    <div id="map"></div>
    <div id="sidebar">
```

```
      <h1>Arches</h1>
      <h2>National Park Visitor Information</h2>
    </div>
  </body>
</html>
```

Notice that in addition to the now-familiar map container, we also have an area for additional content on the page, a div I've called sidebar. It's mostly empty now, but we'll add to it as we go along.

Similarly, I've extended the basic page CSS we've been using to include the sidebar div in the layout, as you can see in Listing 4-2.

Listing 4-2. *The Basic CSS, Laying Out a Sidebar Next to the Map*

```css
html {
  height: 100%;
}

body {
  height: 100%;
  margin: 0;
  font-family: sans-serif;
  font-size: 90%;
}

#map {
  width: 75%;
  height: 100%;
}

#sidebar {
  position: absolute;
  left: 75%;
  top: 0;
  right: 0;
  bottom: 0;
  overflow: auto;
  padding: 1em;
}

h1 {
  margin: 0;
  font-size: 220%;
}
h2 {
  margin: 0;
  font-size: 125%;
}
```

You can see that I've gone with a basic two-column layout, quite simple but sufficient for this example. Your pages will probably have much more complicated layout, but the principle is the same: get the structure in place first before you start on the map.

I've also added a bit of presentational style for the headings in the sidebar. We'll be expanding this as we add content along the way.

Now we're ready for the basic map JavaScript, shown in Listing 4-3. This is no different from the map code you've seen in previous chapters; it will serve as the foundation.

Listing 4-3. *JavaScript for the Basic Map*

```
// Declare variables for later use
var map;

function loadMap()
{
  // loadMap: initialize the API and load the map onto the page

  // Get the map container div
  var mapDiv = document.getElementById('map');

  // Confirm browser compatibility with the Maps API
  if (!GBrowserIsCompatible())
  {
    mapDiv.innerHTML =
      'Sorry, your browser isn\'t compatible with Google Maps.';
  }
  else
  {
    // Initialize the core map object
    map = new GMap2(mapDiv,
      {mapTypes: [G_NORMAL_MAP, G_SATELLITE_MAP, G_HYBRID_MAP, G_PHYSICAL_MAP]});

    // Set the starting map viewport, based on center coordinates and zoom level
    var coordinates = new GLatLng(38.661, -109.534);
    map.setCenter(coordinates, 11, G_PHYSICAL_MAP);

    // Add the standard map controls
    map.addControl(new GLargeMapControl());
    map.addControl(new GScaleControl());
    map.addControl(new GOverviewMapControl());
    map.addControl(new GMapTypeControl());
  }
};
```

Nothing much new here, just the basic map code plus comments (see the accompanying sidebar if you're not familiar with this feature), with center coordinates and zoom level appropriate for encompassing Arches and its nearby town, Moab. Since the terrain is one of the main attractions of the area, I've also chosen to start the map out in the Terrain type (G_PHYSICAL_MAP).

JAVASCRIPT 101: COMMENTS

As our JavaScript is getting more complicated, I'm introducing *comments* in the code to help you find your way around. You're probably familiar with comments in CSS and XHTML already: bits of text that are meant as notes for you (rather than the computer), surrounded by special characters so that the computer ignores them.

In JavaScript, there are two ways to put comments in your code. The first can be seen in Listing 4-3; anything on a line after two forward slashes // will be ignored by the computer.

```
// This is a JavaScript comment
```

The second format uses the same syntax as CSS comments:

```
/* This is also a JavaScript comment */
```

Generally, I use the first format when my comment is on only one or two lines of code, just because it's easier. I use the second option if I have a comment that will be spanning multiple lines, because you only need one set of /* and */ per comment block, rather than one per line (as with //).

And so we have our basic national park map page, ready to build upon, as seen in Figure 4-1.

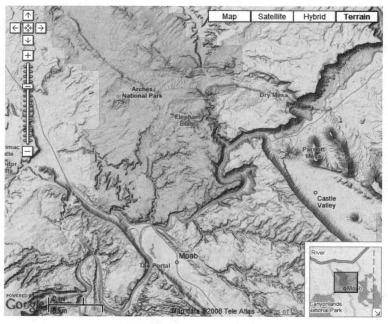

Figure 4-1. *Basic national park map page*

Using Custom Marker Icons

The first thing to do with our park map is to mark out some points of interest. Up until now, all the markers we've created have used the default Maps API marker icon, the familiar reddish-balloon-with-a-dot. For our map, we'd like to do something a bit different, so we're going to start off with a *white* marker instead.

■**Note** It's an unfortunate fact that changing marker icons in the Maps API is quite complicated. I'm easing into it for now by just changing the color; you'll find a much more complete discussion of marker icons in Chapter 9.

First, you're going to need a variable to hold the new marker:

```
var whiteIcon;
```

Then you need to initialize it:

```
whiteIcon = new GIcon(G_DEFAULT_ICON);
```

Not surprisingly, it's a GIcon object, and to avoid the complication I mentioned, Google allows you to start your new icon off with a copy of an existing one. So that's what I'm doing here: specifying G_DEFAULT_ICON, the Maps API standard, as the source icon.

Then, all you need to do is change anything that's *not* standard about it. In this case, it's just the image that we're going to use, supplied here as a relative URL:

```
whiteIcon.image = '../markers/white.png';
```

I've already created the actual icon image file, white.png, and placed it in the markers directory. As explained in the Introduction, these files are available online at http://sterlingudell.com/bgmm/markers, or in ZIP format from http://apress.com.

Now that you have your new icon, you're ready to use it with a map marker. Let's place one at the park entrance and visitor center, a natural starting place for any visitor. Here's the JavaScript code to do so; it should look quite familiar to you:

```
var entranceMarker;
coordinates = new GLatLng(38.6168, -109.61986);
entranceMarker = new GMarker(coordinates, {icon: whiteIcon});
map.addOverlay(entranceMarker);
```

In fact, the only completely new aspect is that I've specified whiteIcon as the icon for this marker to use.

MARKERS AND ICONS

In the Maps API, a *marker* is a JavaScript object that indicates a specific point on the map. The marker has latitude and longitude coordinates that identify its location, and it can respond to actions—such as opening an infowindow when clicked.

An *icon* is also an object, but it is only the small picture that you see on the map. The icon isn't the actual object staking out that location—that's the marker. While an icon has an image and a few other attributes, such as a shadow, it doesn't itself respond to actions. The icon is simply where we *encapsulate* all the various aspects that go into a marker's appearance—then we can just assign the icon to the marker, keeping everything neatly contained.

Now that you know how, let's create a couple of markers for other points of interest in the park, specifically hiking trailheads. To distinguish these from the visitor center, we'll use a different color icon, black. Listing 4-4 shows the new JavaScript with all the marker code in place.

Listing 4-4. *JavaScript with Custom Map Markers*

```
// Declare variables for later use
var map;
var whiteIcon, blackIcon;
var entranceMarker, delicateArchMarker, windowsMarker;

function loadMap()
{
  // loadMap: initialize the API and load the map onto the page

  // Get the map container div
  var mapDiv = document.getElementById('map');

  // Confirm browser compatibility with the Maps API
  if (!GBrowserIsCompatible())
  {
    mapDiv.innerHTML =
      'Sorry, your browser isn\'t compatible with Google Maps.';
  }
  else
  {
    // Initialize the core map object
    map = new GMap2(mapDiv,
      {mapTypes: [G_NORMAL_MAP, G_SATELLITE_MAP, G_HYBRID_MAP, G_PHYSICAL_MAP]});

    // Set the starting map viewport, based on center coordinates and zoom level
    var coordinates = new GLatLng(38.661, -109.534);
    map.setCenter(coordinates, 11, G_PHYSICAL_MAP);
```

```
    // Add the standard map controls
    map.addControl(new GLargeMapControl());
    map.addControl(new GScaleControl());
    map.addControl(new GOverviewMapControl());
    map.addControl(new GMapTypeControl());

    // Initialize a new icon, based on the GMaps default but in white
    whiteIcon = new GIcon(G_DEFAULT_ICON);
    whiteIcon.image = '../markers/white.png';

    // Add a marker to the map for the park entrance, using the white icon
    coordinates = new GLatLng(38.6168, -109.61986);
    entranceMarker = new GMarker(coordinates, {icon: whiteIcon});
    map.addOverlay(entranceMarker);

    // Another new icon, also based on the GMaps default but this time in black
    blackIcon = new GIcon(G_DEFAULT_ICON);
    blackIcon.image = '../markers/black.png';

    // Add two markers to the map for hiking trails, using the black icon

    coordinates = new GLatLng(38.73561, -109.52073);
    delicateArchMarker = new GMarker(coordinates, {icon: blackIcon});
    map.addOverlay(delicateArchMarker);

    coordinates = new GLatLng(38.68725, -109.53712);
    windowsMarker = new GMarker(coordinates, {icon: blackIcon});
    map.addOverlay(windowsMarker);
  }
};
```

There's really only one thing in here that I want to call your attention to. I've added two trailhead markers to the map, but since they are both using the black icon, you only need to initialize blackIcon once. You can then use it for both markers.

JAVASCRIPT 101: STRINGS

Any text embedded within a block of JavaScript, like the icon URLs in Listing 4-4, must be enclosed in either single quotes (') or double quotes ("). It doesn't matter which you use, but you do need to be consistent, and personally I find it more convenient to use single quotes. It's an indication to the computer that the text in question is not actually code; it's for use outside of JavaScript, for display to the user or interaction with another system (like XHTML or the Maps API). So, such things as event names and element IDs are always enclosed in quotes.

Such text has always been called a *string* in programming, short for a string of characters, distinguishing it from other sorts of data (like numbers). In a language like JavaScript, you don't usually need to concern yourself with the individual characters, but it's still called a string nonetheless.

I'm also going to make use of the sidebar area to display our points of interest. This is a simple matter of adding some content to the sidebar div, and a bit of CSS to present it nicely, as shown in Listings 4-5 and 4-6, respectively.

Listing 4-5. *The Sidebar Content*

```
<div id="sidebar">
  <h1>Arches</h1>
  <h2>National Park Visitor Info</h2>
  <p>
    <img width="20" height="34" alt="White" src="../markers/white.png" />
    Visitor Center
  </p>
  <h3>Hiking Trails</h3>
  <ul>
    <li>
      <img width="20" height="34" alt="Black" src="../markers/black.png" />
      Delicate Arch
    </li>
    <li>
      <img width="20" height="34" alt="Black" src="../markers/black.png" />
      The Windows
    </li>
  </ul>
</div>
```

One minor point of note here; the img elements in the sidebar are sourced from the same image files as the GIcon objects in the JavaScript.

Listing 4-6. *The Sidebar Stylesheet*

```
#sidebar img {
  vertical-align: middle;
  border: none;
}

ul, li {
  list-style: none;
  padding: 0;
  margin-top: 0;
}
li {
  margin-top: 2px;
}
```

The current state of our efforts, the map page with custom icons marking points of interest, is shown in Figure 4-2.

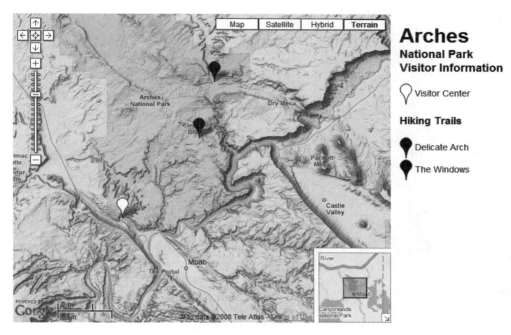

Figure 4-2. *National park map page with points of interest*

Interacting with the User

You've added points of interest to the map, but so far they're just static markers. In Chapter 2 you saw the basic Maps API infowindow in action; now, let's take that further with a couple of more advanced uses for this standard feature.

"Map Blowup" Infowindows

Arches National Park can get quite busy in the summer, with long lines to get in, so our visitor might want a quick and easy view of the road layout at the park entrance. The Maps API provides a nice function on the Marker object for doing so, `showMapBlowup`. Figure 4-3 shows what it looks like on the map.

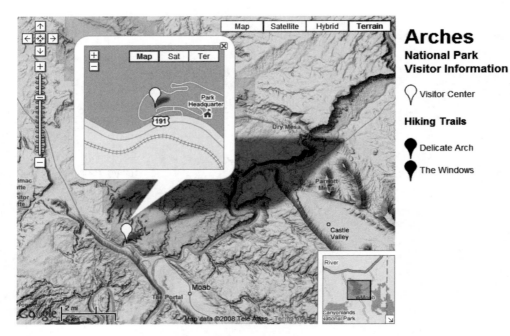

Figure 4-3. *Close-up map, or "blowup," in an infowindow*

Listing 4-7 shows it in place in our JavaScript.

Listing 4-7. *The showMapBlowup Object Added to the Page*

```
// Declare variables for later use
var map;
var whiteIcon, blackIcon;
var entranceMarker, delicateArchMarker, windowsMarker;

function loadMap()
{
  // loadMap: initialize the API and load the map onto the page

  // Get the map container div
  var mapDiv = document.getElementById('map');

  // Confirm browser compatibility with the Maps API
  if (!GBrowserIsCompatible())
  {
    mapDiv.innerHTML =
      'Sorry, your browser isn\'t compatible with Google Maps.';
  }
```

```
  else
  {
    // Initialize the core map object
    map = new GMap2(mapDiv,
      {mapTypes: [G_NORMAL_MAP, G_SATELLITE_MAP, G_HYBRID_MAP, G_PHYSICAL_MAP]});

    // Set the starting map viewport, based on center coordinates and zoom level
    var coordinates = new GLatLng(38.661, -109.534);
    map.setCenter(coordinates, 11, G_PHYSICAL_MAP);

    // Add the standard map controls
    map.addControl(new GLargeMapControl());
    map.addControl(new GScaleControl());
    map.addControl(new GOverviewMapControl());
    map.addControl(new GMapTypeControl());

    // Initialize a new icon, based on the GMaps default but in white
    whiteIcon = new GIcon(G_DEFAULT_ICON);
    whiteIcon.image = '../markers/white.png';

    // Add a marker to the map for the park entrance, using the white icon
    coordinates = new GLatLng(38.6168, -109.61986);
    entranceMarker = new GMarker(coordinates, {icon: whiteIcon});
    map.addOverlay(entranceMarker);
    GEvent.addListener(entranceMarker, 'click', entranceClick);

    // Another new icon, also based on the GMaps default but this time in black
    blackIcon = new GIcon(G_DEFAULT_ICON);
    blackIcon.image = '../markers/black.png';

    // Add two markers to the map for hiking trails, using the black icon

    coordinates = new GLatLng(38.73561, -109.52073);
    delicateArchMarker = new GMarker(coordinates, {icon: blackIcon});
    map.addOverlay(delicateArchMarker);

    coordinates = new GLatLng(38.68725, -109.53712);
    windowsMarker = new GMarker(coordinates, {icon: blackIcon});
    map.addOverlay(windowsMarker);
  }
};

function entranceClick()
{
  // entranceClick: Open a map detail infowindow showing the park entrance area
  entranceMarker.showMapBlowup({mapType: G_NORMAL_MAP, zoomLevel: 14});
};
```

As you can see, there's not a lot to adding a blowup. I've declared a function, `entranceClick`, and within it I just call the `showMapBlowup` function for `entranceMarker`. I am also telling it the map type (`G_NORMAL_MAP`) and zoom level (14) for my blowup map; these simply fine-tune the close-up map's appearance.

And to make it work, I've added a click event *listener* to `entranceMarker`, so that the blowup map appears in response to the user's mouse click.

JAVASCRIPT 101: EVENT LISTENERS

In Chapter 3's JS101, I introduced the concept of *events*, user actions like mouse clicks, and *event handlers*, JavaScript functions to be called when a particular action occurs. Linking the two together are *event listeners*—connecting each handler to its corresponding event.

In the Maps API, we create an event listener with the `GEvent.addListener` function, and its parameters are simply

1. the object we want to attach the event to

2. the name of the event

3. the handler function to use

In this case, we're attaching the `entranceClick` function we declared to show the map blowup window in response to a click on the `entranceMarker`:

```
GEvent.addListener(entranceMarker, 'click', entranceClick);
```

Most Maps API objects, from `Map2` on down, have a list of events that you can attach listeners to: actions like `moveend` (when the map view changes), `infowindowopen` (when the infowindow appears), and `mouseover` (when the user moves their mouse pointer on top of a marker). They are all attached with the same technique as you see here, using `GEvent.addListener`. You'll find a complete list in the Maps API documentation, referenced in Appendix D.

In XHTML, we need to use different techniques to attach event listeners. There's a simple one covered later in this chapter, and a more sophisticated approach in Appendix C.

Tabbed Infowindows

The Maps API's standard infowindow is a fine way to attach content to a marker, but it isn't very big. If you have more information than will comfortably fit, one option is to place it in multiple tabs. Figure 4-4 shows a tabbed infowindow in action.

If you recall, in the last two chapters we created our infowindows by embedding their content in the JavaScript. That worked fine, and it was a good way to introduce you to infowindows, but there is a better way.

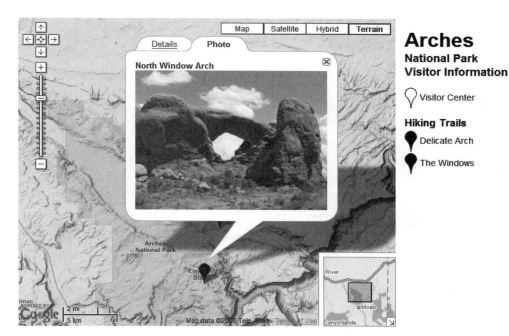

Figure 4-4. *A tabbed infowindow splits content onto multiple tabs.*

Infowindow content is page content like any other, and as such it really belongs in your XHTML. Listing 4-8 shows the content for our two tabbed infowindows, containing details and photos for both hiking trails.

Listing 4-8. *The Tabbed Infowindow Content XHTML*

```
<div id="infowindow_content">
  <div id="delicate_tab_details" class="details_tab">
    <h3>Delicate Arch trail</h3>
    <dl>
      <dt>Distance</dt><dd>3 miles (4.8 km) round trip</dd>
      <dt>Time</dt><dd>2 to 3 hours</dd>
      <dt>Difficulty</dt><dd>Moderate</dd>
    </dl>
    <p>
      One of the classic hikes of any national park, this scramble across
      exposed slickrock leads to an open sandstone bowl with stunning views of
      the freestanding Delicate Arch and the La Sal Mountains beyond.
      Especially fabulous at sunset!
    </p>
    <p>
      Carry at least 1 quart of water per person. Good balance is a plus as
      much of the hike is on sloping sandstone.
    </p>
  </div>
```

```
<div id="delicate_tab_photo" class="details_tab">
  <h3>Delicate Arch at Sunset</h3>
  <img width="300" height="225" alt="Delicate Arch" src="delicate_arch.jpg" />
</div>

<div id="windows_tab_details" class="details_tab">
  <h3>The Windows trail</h3>
  <dl>
    <dt>Distance</dt><dd>1 mile (1.6 km) round trip</dd>
    <dt>Time</dt><dd>&frac12; to 1 hour</dd>
    <dt>Difficulty</dt><dd>Easy</dd>
  </dl>
  <p>
    A fairly short, level walk that takes in several major arches, also
    providing good views across the singular landscape of the park. The same
    parking area gives access to the short trail to Double Arch.
  </p>
  <p>
    Suitable for all abilities. Initial section is wheelchair-accessible.
  </p>
</div>
<div id="windows_tab_photo" class="details_tab">
  <h3>North Window Arch</h3>
  <img width="300" height="225" alt="North Window" src="window_arch.jpg" />
</div>
</div>
```

These two divs need to be added to our page XHTML, but as you'll see in a moment, their contents will be hidden until moved into the infowindows. As such, it doesn't really matter *where* in the page source they are; I chose to place them at the end of the body, after the page's visible content (you can see them by flipping forward to Listing 4-13). Also, note the id attributes on all the various container divs. These are crucial—they are what will enable us to move the content into the infowindows.

Before we get to that, though, Listing 4-9 shows the CSS to accompany this content. It's mostly just style for the content when it appears in the infowindow, but take note of the first selector. It's targeted at the div containing our entire set of infowindow content, and the rule display: none keeps that content from showing *until* it gets into the infowindow. Before then it's just ordinary XHTML on our page, and it would otherwise be visible on screen.

Listing 4-9. *CSS for the Tabbed Infowindow Content*

```
#infowindow_content {
  display: none;
}
.details_tab {
  font-size: 80%;
}
```

```
h3 {
  margin: 0;
}
dt {
  width: 5em;
  float: left;
  clear: left;
  font-weight: bold;
  line-height: 1em;
}
dd {
  line-height: 1em;
}
```

How does it get from there into the infowindows? With a bit of JavaScript, of course. The bulk of the work is done in the following lines:

```
var tabs = [new GInfoWindowTab('Details',
                               document.getElementById('delicate_tab_details')),
            new GInfoWindowTab('Photo',
                               document.getElementById('delicate_tab_photo'))];
```

There's a lot going on here, so let's break it down:

1. Get the content from the XHTML, using `document.getElementById`. Do this for each tab:

   ```
   document.getElementById('delicate_tab_details')
   ```

2. Create a new `GInfoWindowTab` object, with the title of the tab and the content (from step 1) as parameters. Again, one object per tab:

   ```
   new GInfoWindowTab('Details', document.getElementById('delicate_tab_details'))
   ```

3. Declare a variable, `tabs`, and initialize it with the two `GInfoWindowTab` objects.

JAVASCRIPT 101: GETELEMENTBYID

The `document` object is built into JavaScript, and basically corresponds to the associated XHTML page's `<body>` element. Essentially, what its `getElementById` function does is to give your JavaScript code a "handle" on any element in your XHTML; you simply pass in that element's `id` attribute. In the example here, we're using it twice, for the `delicate_tab_details` and `delicate_tab_photo` elements.

Because JavaScript is always attached to a web page, and usually needs to interact with the elements of that page, `getElementById` is a function that you'll run across, and use, a *lot*. We actually have seen it before, starting with Listing 2-4, though I didn't mention it at the time. You had enough to worry about. But every time we've created a map, from then to now, it's been `getElementById` that has given us access to the map container `div`.

You've now created your infowindow tabs and loaded them with content. All that's left is to attach them to the marker, and that's done with this line:

```
delicateArchMarker.bindInfoWindowTabs(tabs, {maxWidth: 300});
```

The syntax of `bindInfoWindowTabs` here is similar to `bindInfoWindowHtml`, as seen in Chapters 2 and 3. It's much cleaner, though; all the heavy lifting was done earlier in setting up the `GInfoWindowTab` objects. The only option you're setting is a maximum width for the infowindow. Like floated content in XHTML, an infowindow has no inherent width, so if we want a particular size it's up to us to supply it.

For completeness, Listing 4-10 shows both calls to `bindInfoWindowTabs` and their associated code in place in the JavaScript.

Listing 4-10. *bindInfoWindowTabs in situ*

```
// Declare variables for later use
var map;
var whiteIcon, blackIcon;
var entranceMarker, delicateArchMarker, windowsMarker;

function loadMap()
{
  // loadMap: initialize the API and load the map onto the page

  // Get the map container div
  var mapDiv = document.getElementById('map');

  // Confirm browser compatibility with the Maps API
  if (!GBrowserIsCompatible())
  {
    mapDiv.innerHTML =
      'Sorry, your browser isn\'t compatible with Google Maps.';
  }
  else
  {
    // Initialize the core map object
    map = new GMap2(mapDiv,
      {mapTypes: [G_NORMAL_MAP, G_SATELLITE_MAP, G_HYBRID_MAP, G_PHYSICAL_MAP]});

    // Set the starting map viewport, based on center coordinates and zoom level
    var coordinates = new GLatLng(38.661, -109.534);
    map.setCenter(coordinates, 11, G_PHYSICAL_MAP);

    // Add the standard map controls
    map.addControl(new GLargeMapControl());
    map.addControl(new GScaleControl());
    map.addControl(new GOverviewMapControl());
    map.addControl(new GMapTypeControl());
```

```
    // Initialize a new icon, based on the GMaps default but in white
    whiteIcon = new GIcon(G_DEFAULT_ICON);
    whiteIcon.image = '../markers/white.png';

    // Add a marker to the map for the park entrance, using the white icon
    coordinates = new GLatLng(38.6168, -109.61986);
    entranceMarker = new GMarker(coordinates, {icon: whiteIcon});
    map.addOverlay(entranceMarker);
    GEvent.addListener(entranceMarker, 'click', entranceClick);

    // Another new icon, also based on the GMaps default but this time in black
    blackIcon = new GIcon(G_DEFAULT_ICON);
    blackIcon.image = '../markers/black.png';

    // Create two infowindow tabs for Delicate Arch using content from the XHTML
    var tabs = [new GInfoWindowTab('Details',
                            document.getElementById('delicate_tab_details')),
            new GInfoWindowTab('Photo',
                            document.getElementById('delicate_tab_photo'))];

    // Add a map marker for the Delicate Arch trail using the tabs and black icon
    coordinates = new GLatLng(38.73561, -109.52073);
    delicateArchMarker = new GMarker(coordinates, {icon: blackIcon});
    delicateArchMarker.bindInfoWindowTabs(tabs, {maxWidth: 300});
    map.addOverlay(delicateArchMarker);

    // Two more infowindow tabs, for the Windows trail...
    tabs = [new GInfoWindowTab('Details',
                            document.getElementById('windows_tab_details')),
            new GInfoWindowTab('Photo',
                            document.getElementById('windows_tab_photo'))];

    // ...and a map marker for the Windows trail as well, again using the black icon
    coordinates = new GLatLng(38.68725, -109.53712);
    windowsMarker = new GMarker(coordinates, {icon: blackIcon});
    windowsMarker.bindInfoWindowTabs(tabs, {maxWidth: 300});
    map.addOverlay(windowsMarker);
  }
};

function entranceClick()
{
  // entranceClick: Open a map detail infowindow showing the park entrance area
  entranceMarker.showMapBlowup({mapType: G_NORMAL_MAP, zoomLevel: 14});
};
```

The technique is a powerful one, and by separating content from presentation, it's true to the ideals of the Semantic Web. I recommend using this function—and its sibling, bindInfoWindow—whenever the content is bundled with your page like this (instead of being delivered via geoXML).

JAVASCRIPT 101: REUSING VARIABLES

In Listing 4-10, notice how the second time we load up the `tabs` variable, it doesn't have the keyword `var` in front of it? That's because `var` is only used to *declare* a variable, the first time it occurs in the code. It can be declared in isolation, like we do with `map`, or it can be declared and initialized in the same statement, as with `coordinates`. But after it has been declared, you just go ahead and use it. With `tabs`, I declare it the first time I use it, and then later reassign it to the second set of tab content (for the Windows trail).

Interacting with the Rest of the Page

We have some nice functionality on the map now, but it's still fairly isolated; our map is still basically sitting on its own within the page. In this section we'll look at a couple of ways to integrate it, making code both inside and outside the map work seamlessly together.

Showing an Infowindow from Outside the Map

As you'll recall, our sidebar contains a list of the points of interest marked on the map. Such content is handy to the page visitor because it enables her to see our points of interest at a glance. If she's interested in the Delicate Arch trail, for example, but doesn't know where in the park it is, the sidebar list lets her go straight there without having to hunt around the map for it.

However, this only works if there's a real linkage between the sidebar and the map, so that's our next task. As shown in Figure 4-5, you're going to make the sidebar list entries into links that will open their respective infowindows when clicked, enabling the user to find them directly.

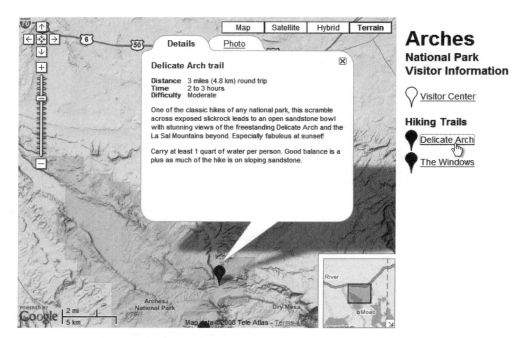

Figure 4-5. *Opening an infowindow by clicking on a link*

Because the JavaScript functionality attaching infowindows to markers is already complete, all you need to do is to link it to click events in our XHTML. I've made this change in Listing 4-11, wrapping each sidebar entry in an <a> element so that the browser will show them as links and the user will know they're clickable.

Listing 4-11. *Sidebar Links*

```
<div id="sidebar">
  <h1>Arches</h1>
  <h2>National Park Visitor Information</h2>
  <p>
    <img width="20" height="34" alt="White" src="../markers/white.png" />
    <a href="#" onclick="GEvent.trigger(entranceMarker, 'click'); return false">
      Visitor Center
    </a>
  </p>
  <h3>Hiking Trails</h3>
  <ul>
    <li>
      <img width="20" height="34" alt="Black" src="../markers/black.png" />
      <a href="#"
     onclick="GEvent.trigger(delicateArchMarker, 'click'); return false">
        Delicate Arch
      </a>
    </li>
    <li>
      <img width="20" height="34" alt="Black" src="../markers/black.png" />
      <a href="#"
        onclick="GEvent.trigger(windowsMarker, 'click'); return false">
        The Windows
      </a>
    </li>
  </ul>
</div>
```

There's a new concept here, the introduction of JavaScript within the XHTML itself, in the onclick attribute of each <a> element. This is another example of an *event listener*; onclick attaches JavaScript to the click event of the link. It's the same concept introduced earlier in the chapter, where we used GEvent.addListener to attach a handler to an event in the Maps API.

Within each event handler, there are two things going on:

1. GEvent.trigger calls the *existing* click event handler for the appropriate marker. This makes a click on the sidebar link perform exactly the same action as a click on the marker. Right now it opens the infowindow, but if you were to change the marker click behavior in the future, coding it this way means that the sidebar click would follow along with that change.

2. The return false statement prevents the default browser action for the event from
    occurring. For <a> elements, the default browser action is to follow the link, opening the
    URL specified in the href attribute. We don't want that to happen—we want the marker
    to open its infowindow instead—so we include return false to prevent it from following
    the link. Just be aware that return false is always required whenever you're *overriding*
    the default behavior for an event.

■Tip Notice the href="#" attribute in the <a> elements in Listing 4-11. What's that about?

If we didn't have an href attribute at all, most browsers wouldn't show the <a> as a clickable link. However,
since we don't really want it to link anywhere, # is a good choice: it's an internal link on the same page, but
without a real destination. So if (for some reason) our JavaScript return false failed and the browser did
try to follow the link, # means that it actually won't go anywhere.

Adding Optional External Content

As you learned in Chapter 3, an easy way to add content and value to a map is by mashing up
some geoXML with it. Let's do that now, enhancing the user experience of the Arches page by
showing nearby campgrounds on the map.

   We start with some JavaScript that should look very familiar to you after Chapter 3, simply
adding a KML geodata source to the map.

```
geoXml = new GGeoXml('http://www.satellitefriendly.com/services/popular_network.kml');
map.addOverlay(geoXml);
```

   The next step is something new. Not every visitor is interested in camping, so we're going
to give them the option of showing the campgrounds or not. To do so, you'll need some more
XHTML for the sidebar:

```
<h3>
  <input type="checkbox" id="show_campgrounds" checked="checked"
         onclick="toggleCampgrounds()" />
  Nearby Camping
</h3>
```

   That's fairly straightforward, but let's just hit the high points of what we have here:

- An h3 element, semantically indicating that it's a new section of content in the sidebar

- An input element of type checkbox; this is what the user will actually interact with to turn
  the campground overlay on and off

- An id attribute, so that we can get a handle on the checkbox from the JavaScript

- An event listener to trigger the onclick action

- A bit of JavaScript, toggleCampgrounds(), for the event handler itself

---

■**Note** Since we're not *overriding* the default checkbox behavior—I do want it to change visually between checked and unchecked—our onclick event listener for the checkbox doesn't need return false, like the events for the <a> elements did earlier.

The last item, of course, brings us back around to the main JavaScript, where you need just a bit more code to tie it all together and make it work:

```
function toggleCampgrounds()
{
  if (document.getElementById('show_campgrounds').checked)
    geoXml.show();
  else
    geoXml.hide();
};
```

It's a new event handler function, as referenced in the XHTML onchange event above. Within it, you'll see another example of document.getElementById; the code uses this to determine whether the checkbox is checked or not.

- If it is, that means the user wants to see the campgrounds, so we call the show function of the geoXml object.

- If not, they don't want to be bothered with the campgrounds, so we instead call geoXml.hide.

That's it! The result can be seen in Figure 4-6. As usual with the GGeoXml object, you get a lot of bang for your buck here, a good effect without much code.

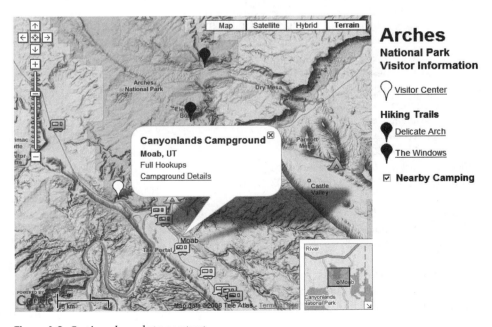

Figure 4-6. *Optional geodata content*

To make sure you're clear where everything goes, Listing 4-12 shows the complete JavaScript up to this point, with the new campground code highlighted.

Listing 4-12. *JavaScript with Optional Geodata*

```
// Declare variables for later use
var map;
var whiteIcon, blackIcon;
var entranceMarker, delicateArchMarker, windowsMarker;
var geoXml;

function loadMap()
{
  // loadMap: initialize the API and load the map onto the page

  // Get the map container div
  var mapDiv = document.getElementById('map');

  // Confirm browser compatibility with the Maps API
  if (!GBrowserIsCompatible())
  {
    mapDiv.innerHTML =
      'Sorry, your browser isn\'t compatible with Google Maps.';
  }
  else
  {
    // Initialize the core map object
    map = new GMap2(mapDiv,
      {mapTypes: [G_NORMAL_MAP, G_SATELLITE_MAP, G_HYBRID_MAP, G_PHYSICAL_MAP]});

    // Set the starting map viewport, based on center coordinates and zoom level
    var coordinates = new GLatLng(38.661, -109.534);
    map.setCenter(coordinates, 11, G_PHYSICAL_MAP);

    // Add the standard map controls
    map.addControl(new GLargeMapControl());
    map.addControl(new GScaleControl());
    map.addControl(new GOverviewMapControl());
    map.addControl(new GMapTypeControl());

    // Initialize a new icon, based on the GMaps default but in white
    whiteIcon = new GIcon(G_DEFAULT_ICON);
    whiteIcon.image = '../markers/white.png';

    // Add a marker to the map for the park entrance, using the white icon
    coordinates = new GLatLng(38.6168, -109.61986);
    entranceMarker = new GMarker(coordinates, {icon: whiteIcon});
```

```
        map.addOverlay(entranceMarker);
        GEvent.addListener(entranceMarker, 'click', entranceClick);

        // Another new icon, also based on the GMaps default but this time in black
        blackIcon = new GIcon(G_DEFAULT_ICON);
        blackIcon.image = '../markers/black.png';

        // Create two infowindow tabs for Delicate Arch using content from the XHTML
        var tabs = [new GInfoWindowTab('Details',
                                    document.getElementById('delicate_tab_details')),
                    new GInfoWindowTab('Photo',
                                    document.getElementById('delicate_tab_photo'))];

        // Add a map marker for the Delicate Arch trail using the tabs and black icon
        coordinates = new GLatLng(38.73561, -109.52073);
        delicateArchMarker = new GMarker(coordinates, {icon: blackIcon});
        delicateArchMarker.bindInfoWindowTabs(tabs, {maxWidth: 300});
        map.addOverlay(delicateArchMarker);

        // Two more infowindow tabs, for the Windows trail...
        tabs = [new GInfoWindowTab('Details',
                                    document.getElementById('windows_tab_details')),
                new GInfoWindowTab('Photo',
                                    document.getElementById('windows_tab_photo'))];

        // ...and a map marker for the Windows trail as well, again using the black icon
        coordinates = new GLatLng(38.68725, -109.53712);
        windowsMarker = new GMarker(coordinates, {icon: blackIcon});
        windowsMarker.bindInfoWindowTabs(tabs, {maxWidth: 300});
        map.addOverlay(windowsMarker);

        // Create a geodata overlay for nearby campgrounds and add it to the map
        geoXml = new GGeoXml(
                    'http://www.satellitefriendly.com/services/popular_network.kml');
        map.addOverlay(geoXml);
    }
};

function entranceClick()
{
    // entranceClick: Open a map detail infowindow showing the park entrance area
    entranceMarker.showMapBlowup({mapType: G_NORMAL_MAP, zoomLevel: 14});
};

function toggleCampgrounds()
{
    // toggleCampgrounds: Turn the campground geodata overlay on or off
```

```
if (document.getElementById('show_campgrounds').checked)
  geoXml.show();
else
  geoXml.hide();
};
```

Finishing Touches

We've covered a lot of new JavaScript in this chapter, and I think you've earned a break. So to round out our map, we'll add a couple of other "prepackaged" items from Google. Like the Maps API generally, these let you leverage the power of Google on your own page with relatively little effort.

Local Search with the GoogleBar

If you're going to harness the power of Google, what better way than by adding search capability? In the Maps API, the easiest way to do that is with the GoogleBar local search control. A single line of JavaScript is all it takes:

```
map.enableGoogleBar();
```

Doing this replaces the "Powered By Google" logo with the *GoogleBar*, a little search control. If the user types in a search query, the GoogleBar shows results within the mapped area, including details about each. It's a great, easy way to add content to your map that directly interests the user, as in Figure 4-7.

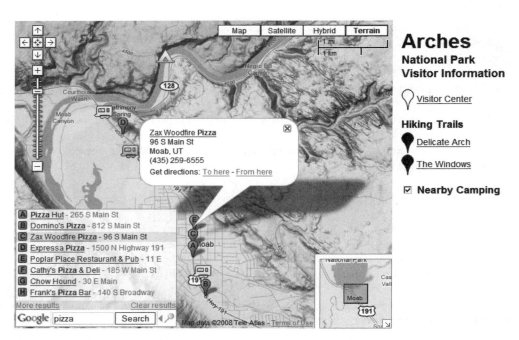

Figure 4-7. *Adding the GoogleBar allows the user to display local search results.*

The only drawback is that the GoogleBar overlaps the default location of the scale control—a curious oversight for Google, but one that's easy enough to fix. In the JavaScript that adds the GScaleControl to the map, you can specify an alternate location for it, like so:

```
map.addControl(new GScaleControl(),
               new GControlPosition(G_ANCHOR_TOP_RIGHT, new GSize(6, 31)));
```

The addition of the GControlPosition object as a second parameter moves the GScaleControl up underneath the GMapTypeControl. Without going into great detail, by running the revised JavaScript you can probably see generally how this works: the new location is 6 pixels in and 31 pixels down from the top-right corner of the map.

The Google Earth Map Type

We're going to finish up by adding the Google Earth browser plug-in. It'll enable our page visitor to see Arches and all our additional content in the full three-dimensional splendor of Google Earth.

Best of all, it's also extremely easy to add; it's been implemented by Google as just another map type. So all we need is to include it in our initialization of the Map2 object:

```
map = new GMap2(mapDiv, {mapTypes: [G_NORMAL_MAP, G_SATELLITE_MAP,
  G_HYBRID_MAP, G_PHYSICAL_MAP, G_SATELLITE_3D_MAP]});
```

This adds an additional map-type button to the upper right of the map, and when the user clicks it, Google Earth appears in place of the usual flat map (see Figure 4-8).

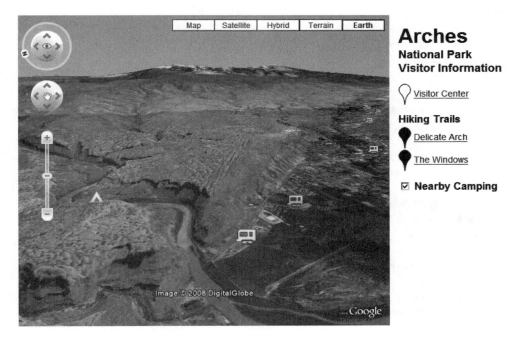

Figure 4-8. *Google Earth in the browser*

Again, there are a couple of caveats. First, the Earth map type requires a browser plug-in; it will download automatically the first time it's needed, or you can install it manually from `http://tinyurl.com/5bbo9e`. And as of this writing, that plug-in is only available for Mozilla (Firefox) and Internet Explorer on Windows, though Google is promising Mac and Linux support before this book is scheduled to go to press.

Second, because it's so new, the Earth map type still has a few issues. Its support for map functionality is incomplete, meaning that code like our "Nearby Camping" checkbox doesn't work when the Earth map type is active. Notice that there's no GoogleBar either. It even has a few bugs; for example, it's not compatible with the overview map. However, Google is clearly moving toward a greater integration of Maps and Earth, so I expect all of these issues to be sorted out in due time.

Summary

We've covered a lot of ground in this chapter, extending our basic map to one that's quite full-featured and well integrated with the rest of the page. You've learned how to change marker colors and infowindow types, as well as how to use event handlers to enhance the visitor experience, and you've seen another example of using geoXML in a real-world map. You've also seen how the GoogleBar and the Earth plug-in can enhance your map with very little effort.

By way of a summary, it's worth looking at Listings 4-13 and 4-14, containing the final XHTML and JavaScript for everything we've done in this chapter. There's nothing new here, only that it's all in one place.

Listing 4-13. *The Full XHTML for the Arches National Park Page*

```
<!DOCTYPE html PUBLIC "-//W3C//DTD XHTML 1.0 Strict//EN"
                      "http://www.w3.org/TR/xhtml1/DTD/xhtml1-strict.dtd">
<html xmlns="http://www.w3.org/1999/xhtml">
  <head>
    <meta http-equiv="Content-Type" content="text/html; charset=UTF-8" />
    <title>Building Out Your Map Page</title>
    <link type="text/css" rel="stylesheet" href="listing_04_09.css" />
    <script type="text/javascript"
            src="http://maps.google.com/maps?file=api&amp;v=2.124&amp;key="></script>
    <script type="text/javascript" src="listing_04_14.js"></script>
  </head>
  <body onload="loadMap()" onunload="GUnload()">
    <div id="map"></div>
    <div id="sidebar">
      <h1>Arches</h1>
      <h2>National Park Visitor Information</h2>
      <p>
        <img width="20" height="34" alt="White" src="../markers/white.png" />
        <a href="#" onclick="GEvent.trigger(entranceMarker, 'click'); return false">
          Visitor Center
        </a>
      </p>
```

```
    <h3>Hiking Trails</h3>
    <ul>
      <li>
        <img width="20" height="34" alt="Black" src="../markers/black.png" />
        <a href="#"
          onclick="GEvent.trigger(delicateArchMarker, 'click'); return false">
          Delicate Arch
        </a>
      </li>
      <li>
        <img width="20" height="34" alt="Black" src="../markers/black.png" />
        <a href="#"
          onclick="GEvent.trigger(windowsMarker, 'click'); return false">
          The Windows
        </a>
      </li>
    </ul>
    <h3>
      <input type="checkbox" id="show_campgrounds" checked="checked"
             onclick="toggleCampgrounds()" />
      Nearby Camping
    </h3>
</div>

<div id="infowindow_content">
  <div id="delicate_tab_details" class="details_tab">
    <h3>Delicate Arch trail</h3>
    <dl>
      <dt>Distance</dt><dd>3 miles (4.8 km) round trip</dd>
      <dt>Time</dt><dd>2 to 3 hours</dd>
      <dt>Difficulty</dt><dd>Moderate</dd>
    </dl>
    <p>
      One of the classic hikes of any national park, this scramble across
      exposed slickrock leads to an open sandstone bowl with stunning views of
      the freestanding Delicate Arch and the La Sal Mountains beyond.
      Especially fabulous at sunset!
    </p>
    <p>
      Carry at least 1 quart of water per person. Good balance is a plus as
      much of the hike is on sloping sandstone.
    </p>
  </div>
  <div id="delicate_tab_photo" class="details_tab">
    <h3>Delicate Arch at Sunset</h3>
    <img width="300" height="225" alt="Delicate Arch" src="delicate_arch.jpg" />
  </div>
```

```
        <div id="windows_tab_details" class="details_tab">
          <h3>The Windows trail</h3>
          <dl>
            <dt>Distance</dt><dd>1 mile (1.6 km) round trip</dd>
            <dt>Time</dt><dd>&frac12; to 1 hour</dd>
            <dt>Difficulty</dt><dd>Easy</dd>
          </dl>
          <p>
            A fairly short, level walk that takes in several major arches, also
            providing good views across the singular landscape of the park. The same
            parking area gives access to the short trail to Double Arch.
          </p>
          <p>
            Suitable for all abilities. Initial section is wheelchair-accessible.
          </p>
        </div>
        <div id="windows_tab_photo" class="details_tab">
          <h3>North Window Arch</h3>
          <img width="300" height="225" alt="North Window" src="window_arch.jpg" />
        </div>
      </div>
    </body>
  </html>
```

Listing 4-14. *The Complete JavaScript to Make the Arches Page Work*

```javascript
// Declare variables for later use
var map;
var whiteIcon, blackIcon;
var entranceMarker, delicateArchMarker, windowsMarker;
var geoXml;

function loadMap()
{
  // loadMap: initialize the API and load the map onto the page

  // Get the map container div
  var mapDiv = document.getElementById('map');

  // Confirm browser compatibility with the Maps API
  if (!GBrowserIsCompatible())
  {
    mapDiv.innerHTML =
      'Sorry, your browser isn\'t compatible with Google Maps.';
  }
```

```
else
{
  // Initialize the core map object, including the Google Earth maptype
  map = new GMap2(mapDiv, {mapTypes: [G_NORMAL_MAP, G_SATELLITE_MAP,
    G_HYBRID_MAP, G_PHYSICAL_MAP, G_SATELLITE_3D_MAP]});
  var coordinates = new GLatLng(38.661, -109.534);
  map.setCenter(coordinates, 11, G_PHYSICAL_MAP);

  // Add the standard map controls, moving the scale control to the upper-right
  map.addControl(new GLargeMapControl());
  map.addControl(new GScaleControl(),
                  new GControlPosition(G_ANCHOR_TOP_RIGHT, new GSize(6, 31)));
  map.addControl(new GOverviewMapControl());
  map.addControl(new GMapTypeControl());

  // Also add a local search control to the map
  map.enableGoogleBar();

  // Initialize a new icon, based on the GMaps default but in white
  whiteIcon = new GIcon(G_DEFAULT_ICON);
  whiteIcon.image = '../markers/white.png';

  // Add a marker to the map for the park entrance, using the white icon
  coordinates = new GLatLng(38.6168, -109.61986);
  entranceMarker = new GMarker(coordinates, {icon: whiteIcon});
  map.addOverlay(entranceMarker);
  GEvent.addListener(entranceMarker, 'click', entranceClick);

  // Another new icon, also based on the GMaps default but this time in black
  blackIcon = new GIcon(G_DEFAULT_ICON);
  blackIcon.image = '../markers/black.png';

  // Create two infowindow tabs for Delicate Arch using content from the XHTML
  var tabs = [new GInfoWindowTab('Details',
                                  document.getElementById('delicate_tab_details')),
              new GInfoWindowTab('Photo',
                                  document.getElementById('delicate_tab_photo'))];

  // Add a map marker for the Delicate Arch trail using the tabs and black icon
  coordinates = new GLatLng(38.73561, -109.52073);
  delicateArchMarker = new GMarker(coordinates, {icon: blackIcon});
  delicateArchMarker.bindInfoWindowTabs(tabs, {maxWidth: 300});
  map.addOverlay(delicateArchMarker);
```

```
    // Two more infowindow tabs, for the Windows trail...
    tabs = [new GInfoWindowTab('Details',
                              document.getElementById('windows_tab_details')),
           new GInfoWindowTab('Photo',
                              document.getElementById('windows_tab_photo'))];

    // ...and a map marker for the Windows trail as well, again using the black icon
    coordinates = new GLatLng(38.68725, -109.53712);
    windowsMarker = new GMarker(coordinates, {icon: blackIcon});
    windowsMarker.bindInfoWindowTabs(tabs, {maxWidth: 300});
    map.addOverlay(windowsMarker);

    // Create a geodata overlay for nearby campgrounds and add it to the map
    geoXml = new GGeoXml(
                'http://www.satellitefriendly.com/services/popular_network.kml');
    map.addOverlay(geoXml);
  }
};

function entranceClick()
{
  // entranceClick: Open a map detail infowindow showing the park entrance area
  entranceMarker.showMapBlowup({mapType: G_NORMAL_MAP, zoomLevel: 14});
};

function toggleCampgrounds()
{
  // toggleCampgrounds: Turn the campground geodata overlay on or off
  if (document.getElementById('show_campgrounds').checked)
    geoXml.show();
  else
    geoXml.hide();
};
```

It's an indication of how far you've come with the Maps API that you should now be able to look at the hundred lines of JavaScript in Listing 4-14 and be fairly comfortable with what every one of those lines is doing.

In the next chapter, we'll build out a different example in a different direction, with an emphasis on connecting your map to the real world. In the process, I'll cover traffic, driving directions, Street View, and the semi-mystical process of geocoding. You'll also learn how to monetize your mapping efforts with map advertising.

CHAPTER 5

■■■

Your Map and the Real World

In many ways, the geoweb is all about connecting the virtual, online world with the real, physical world by means of mapping. In this chapter, we'll look at various techniques for making the "last mile" of that connection. We'll examine the issues surrounding the conversion of generic place information to latitude and longitude coordinates, and then we'll tour some of the ways your map can connect with real-world, often real-time data, including traffic, driving directions, and street-level photographs. Finally, we'll connect the map with that most real of topics—money—by adding advertising to the map itself.

We'll do this by following a pattern similar to what we have done before, building out an example map to illustrate the various techniques. As in Chapter 4, there is a good quantity of JavaScript here, so there will be plenty of concrete examples for you to draw from when building your own maps. And again, I'll do my best to introduce the new concepts plainly, to walk you through them at a manageable pace.

The example we'll build in this chapter is a route finder web page for San Francisco, and the basic XHTML can be found in Listing 5-1.

Listing 5-1. *The Starting XHTML for the Route Finder Page*

```
<!DOCTYPE html PUBLIC "-//W3C//DTD XHTML 1.0 Strict//EN"
                     "http://www.w3.org/TR/xhtml1/DTD/xhtml1-strict.dtd">
<html xmlns="http://www.w3.org/1999/xhtml">
  <head>
    <meta http-equiv="Content-Type" content="text/html; charset=UTF-8" />
    <title>Your Map and the Real World</title>
    <link type="text/css" rel="stylesheet" href="../chapter_04/listing_04_02.css" />
    <script type="text/javascript"
            src="http://maps.google.com/maps?file=api&amp;v=2.124&amp;key="></script>
    <script type="text/javascript" src="listing_05_02.js"></script>
  </head>
  <body onload="loadMap()" onunload="GUnload()">
    <div id="map"></div>
    <div id="sidebar">
      <h2>Route Finder</h2>
      <p>
```

```
        Start Address
        <button onclick="geocode()">Find</button>
        <input type="text" id="start" />
      </p>
    </div>
  </body>
</html>
```

You've seen most of this code several times before; in fact, we're actually reusing the CSS from Listing 4-2. The new content is in the sidebar, where we now have a text input for the user to enter a starting address for their route. When they do so and click the Find button, a JavaScript event handler named geocode takes over. But what does geocode do?

Geocoding

Geocoding is the process of turning ordinary street addresses into latitude/longitude coordinates, and it's one of the most important tools for a map developer. Most people don't know the latitude and longitude of their home, but they do know their address. Similarly, databases that you may work with are far more likely to contain addresses than coordinates. But in either case, the coordinates are what you need for showing the information on a map. So having a geocoder at your disposal is going to be crucial; not surprisingly, Google provides one in the Maps API.

The basic use of the Maps API geocoder can be seen in Listing 5-2, where the geocode function has been added to our usual map JavaScript.

Listing 5-2. *JavaScript with Geocoder Interface*

```
// Declare variables for later use
var map;
var geocoder;
var startMarker;

function loadMap()
{
  // loadMap: initialize the API and load the map onto the page

  // Get the map container div
  var mapDiv = document.getElementById('map');

  // Confirm browser compatibility with the Maps API
  if (!GBrowserIsCompatible())
  {
    mapDiv.innerHTML =
      'Sorry, your browser isn\'t compatible with Google Maps.';
  }
```

```
  else
  {
    // Initialize the core map object
    map = new GMap2(mapDiv,
      {mapTypes: [G_NORMAL_MAP, G_SATELLITE_MAP, G_HYBRID_MAP, G_PHYSICAL_MAP]});

    // Set the starting map viewport, based on center coordinates and zoom level
    var coordinates = new GLatLng(37.75, -122.44);
    map.setCenter(coordinates, 12);

    // Add the standard map controls
    map.addControl(new GLargeMapControl());
    map.addControl(new GScaleControl());
    map.addControl(new GOverviewMapControl());
    map.addControl(new GMapTypeControl());

    // Initialize the geocoder object
    geocoder = new GClientGeocoder();
  }
};

function geocode()
{
  // geocode: Call the Google geocoder with the address supplied by the user
  var address = document.getElementById('start').value;
  geocoder.getLatLng(address, afterGeocode);
};

function afterGeocode(coordinates)
{
  // afterGeocode: Callback function for the geocoder, showing the coords on the map
  startMarker = new GMarker(coordinates);
  map.addOverlay(startMarker);
};
```

There are several parts to this, so let's go over them one at a time.

First, we always need to declare the variables we're going to be working with. In this case, it's the geocoder itself, plus a marker to show the geocoded address on the map:

```
var geocoder;
var startMarker;
```

Next, we initialize the geocoder object into the variable we declared for it. This is quite straightforward also:

```
geocoder = new GClientGeocoder();
geocoder.setViewport(map.getBounds());
```

The first line just creates GClientGeocoder (*client* because it's based in the web browser). The second line tells it to emphasize results from the current map *viewport*, the geographic area currently visible on screen. If someone just enters a street address, we want the geocoder to give preference to matching addresses here in San Francisco, rather than in some other city.

Next up is the event handler referenced by the XHTML in Listing 5-1, simply named geocode. All it does is extract the user-entered address from the XHTML (using our familiar getElementById function) and send it off to the Google geocoder:

```
var address = document.getElementById('start').value;
geocoder.getLatLng(address, afterGeocode);
```

The only thing you might not expect, then, is afterGeocode, the second parameter to geocoder.getLatLng. This is a *callback function* (as introduced in Chapter 3) that the geocoder will pass control to after it has finished its work. If you recall, callbacks are used when a process needs to go online to do its job, and it shouldn't surprise you that geocoding is in this category.

So the final block of code in Listing 5-2, naturally, is the callback function itself, afterGeocode. It receives the coordinates for the address back from Google and just places a marker there:

```
startMarker = new GMarker(coordinates);
map.addOverlay(startMarker);
```

You should recognize the basic code to place a map marker from the examples in the last three chapters, and it's no different here. The coordinates are coming from the geocoder, but the marker doesn't care.

The results can be seen in Figure 5-1. The user has entered an address, and a marker showing its location has been placed on the map.

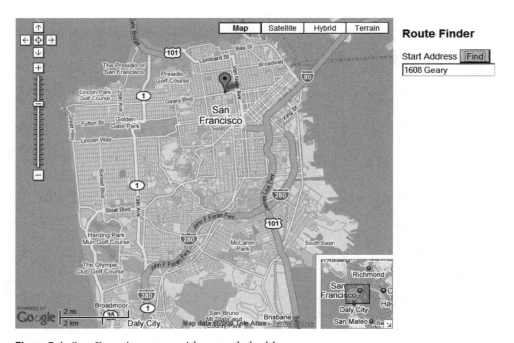

Figure 5-1. *San Francisco map with geocoded address*

■**Tip** For various licensing reasons, the geocoder supplied in the Maps API is *not* the same as that used on maps.google.com. So you can't reliably test your geocoding by comparing it with results from the main Google Maps web site; they won't always match up.

Coding For the Real World

Listing 5-2 showed the most basic use of the Maps API geocoder. In keeping with the subject of this chapter, there are a few real-world considerations that should be added to the code. This is sometimes known as *defensive coding*—programming that acknowledges that things don't always happen as we might first expect—and the changes are shown in Listing 5-3: a rewriting of the afterGeocode function from Listing 5-2.

Listing 5-3. *Defensive Coding in the Geocoder Callback Function*

```
function afterGeocode(coordinates)
{
  // afterGeocode: Callback function for the geocoder, showing the coords on the map
  if (coordinates == null)
    alert('Address not found. Please try again.');
  else if (!map.getBounds().contains(coordinates))
    alert('Address not found in map area. Please try again.');
  else
  {
    // Address was found
    if (startMarker == null)
    {
      // This is the first time we've geocoded an address, so create the marker
      startMarker = new GMarker(coordinates);
      map.addOverlay(startMarker);
    }
    else
    {
      // The marker already exists; just move it to the new coordinates
      startMarker.setPoint(coordinates);
    }
  }
};
```

JAVASCRIPT 101: NULL

In Listing 5-3, I'm checking a couple of variables to see if they're null. What's that about?

In JavaScript, null is a keyword indicating that a variable has no value assigned to it. It's not a value itself, like 'green' or 27; rather, it's a concept indicating the lack of any value. You could think of it as the programming equivalent of a vacuum—there's just nothing there.

So, if a variable is null, that means that it's been declared but has not been assigned a value. In Listing 5-2, I'm using this in two different but related circumstances:

- For coordinates, a null value is Google's way of telling us that the address couldn't be found by the geocoder.

- For startMarker, null indicates that we haven't created the marker yet, only declared it (with the var keyword at the top of Listing 5-2). So we go ahead and create it.

In both cases, null indicates that the variable in question is empty, and we can take appropriate action based on that.

First, I'm checking to see if the Google geocoder was able to find the address that the user entered. If it couldn't, the coordinates passed to the callback will be null, and we'll have no place to put a map marker. So instead, I use alert to tell the user about the problem:

```
if (coordinates == null)
  alert('Address not found. Please try again.');
```

The alert function opens a small message dialog containing the given string, and it's a simple way to display an important message to the user, as you can see in Figure 5-2.

Figure 5-2. *An alert dialog*

■**Caution** Don't overuse alert. Because the user has to click OK to dismiss the message before they can do anything else, alert can quickly become annoying to your site visitors. Only use it when you genuinely need to get their attention; consider using a DHTML message (see Chapter 10) instead.

Second, if Google found the address, I also check to confirm that it was within the map area. This covers cases where the user enters an address that the geocoder found, but in a distant location, such as in another state.

```
else if (!map.getBounds().contains(coordinates))
  alert('Address not found in map area. Please try again.');
```

Note the test here: map.getBounds returns the boundaries of the map viewport, which you can then immediately query to see if it contains the coordinates.

If the address was found in the map area by the geocoder, afterGeocode moves into the process of placing a map marker at the correct coordinates, and here we have another fork in the code: what if this isn't the first address that the user has looked up? If we naively proceed as in Listing 5-2 and just create a new marker each time, the map could soon become littered with them. So instead, we check to see if the marker has already been created:

```
if (startMarker == null)
```

In other words, a null marker tells us to proceed as before by creating a marker. Otherwise, the best course is to move the existing startMarker to the new coordinates:

```
else
  startMarker.setPoint(coordinates);
```

As your JavaScript skill advances, I'll be introducing you to more of these real-world coding situations.

Geocoding Considerations

Now that you've seen geocoding in action, you probably have some idea of how useful it can be in mapping endeavors. But before we move on, I just need to brief you on a few caveats about geocoding in general and the Google geocoder in particular.

The first is that geocoding is far from an exact science. There are many, many variations in address formats, and it's just not possible for a geocoder to decipher one hundred percent of them. Also, the data from which geocoders work is somewhat general; although the people at Google probably have a reasonable idea of the coordinates of your street, they don't actually know the coordinates of your house with absolute precision. So geocoding is a computer's educated guess at best—and its wild guess at worst. Particularly with incomplete or misspelled addresses, the results can be just completely wrong. There are also some addresses that a given geocoder will be unable to find at all.

The second issue you should be aware of is that geocoding is a complicated process. It takes some time—perhaps a second or two—to geocode each address. In fact, geocoding takes so much effort that Google limits access to the geocoder; as of this writing, it's 15,000 requests per visitor per day[1]. This may seem like a generous quota, but it's actually not hard to get into a situation where you exceed it.

Also, recall that Google's geocoder is asynchronous, requiring the afterGeocode callback function shown earlier. There are hidden dangers to asynchronous code, especially for beginners. If you were using JavaScript, like that in Listings 5-1 and 5-2, to geocode a whole list of addresses—for example, from a customer database—you'd need to be careful to not send a given address to the geocoder until the previous one had finished. Otherwise, you'd have a situation where

---

1. Note that this limit is *per web site visitor*, making it quite unlikely you'll hit it with an ordinary map application. For more information, please see http://tinyurl.com/25um3w.

later requests would "cancel out" earlier ones, causing lost geocoding requests and incomplete processing of your address list.

For these and other reasons, the best practice is to not geocode more addresses than you need to.

OHIO: Only Handle It Once

The recommended approach to follow with geocoding, therefore, is to save the latitude and longitude the first time you successfully geocode a given address. There are a number of advantages to this:

- Once you know that a given address is correctly geocoded, saving its coordinates means that a change on Google's side can't cause it to go astray.

- Geocoding all your addresses ahead of time means that later tasks, such as loading of a web page, will be faster.

- It's generally a more efficient use of computing resources, for both you and Google.

This principle is sometimes known as *OHIO*, an acronym for Only Handle It Once: it's better to get your geocoding done for good the first time and leave it alone thereafter. We'll look into techniques for doing this with geocoding in Chapters 9 and 10, but for now, just be aware of the issues and don't rush headlong into geocoding lots of addresses.

Driving Directions

Now that we have geocoded a starting address, let's press on with the Route Finder page by getting driving directions to a destination. For reasons that will become clear later in the chapter, we aren't going to support directions to arbitrary addresses, just a limited list of locations that we know to be acceptable. Listing 5-4 shows that list as XHTML content to be added to the page sidebar, within a select element. It could easily contain a much more comprehensive list of destinations in San Francisco, but this is sufficient for illustrating the technique.

Listing 5-4. *select a Destination*

```
<p>
  Destination
  <select id="finish" onchange="destinationChange()">
    <option value="">Please select:</option>
    <option value="37.809, -122.4146">The Embarcadero</option>
    <option value="37.79516, -122.39379">Ferry Terminal</option>
    <option value="37.76976, -122.46765">Golden Gate Park</option>
    <option value="37.80733, -122.47411">The Presidio</option>
    <option value="37.79482, -122.40277">Transamerica Pyramid</option>
  </select>
</p>
```

As you've seen before, this select has an event listener. Changing the selected option calls the destinationChange JavaScript function, as shown in Listing 5-5.

Listing 5-5. *The destinationChange Event Handler*

```
function destinationChange()
{
  // destinationChange: Update destination marker from the drop-down list

  // Extract the new destination from the drop-down
  var finish = document.getElementById('finish');
  var value = finish.options[finish.selectedIndex].value;
  if (value != '')
  {
    // Valid destination:  create a coordinates object from it
    var coordinates = eval('new GLatLng(' + value + ')');

    if (finishMarker == null)
    {
      // This is the first time the user has selected a destination
      finishMarker = new GMarker(coordinates);
      map.addOverlay(finishMarker);
    }
    else
    {
      // The marker already exists; just move it to the new coordinates
      finishMarker.setPoint(coordinates);
    }

    // Ensure that the destination point is visible on the map
    if (!map.getBounds().contains(coordinates))
      map.panTo(coordinates);
  }
};
```

Note that this event handler is shown in isolation here for clarity, but in practice it should be added (along with var finishMarker) to our existing JavaScript (from Listings 5-2 and 5-3).

■**Tip** All listings in this book are available for download from my web site. For example, to see destinationChange in context, Listing 5-5 may be found at http://sterlingudell.com/bgmm/ chapter_05/listing_05_05.js, or in ZIP format from http://apress.com.

There are several interesting things going on at the beginning of this function, so let's go over them one by one. First, we're using our old friend getElementById to retrieve the select element itself:

```
var finish = document.getElementById('finish');
```

Now the fun starts. We want to get the selected `option` and extract its `value` attribute (containing the latitude and longitude for the destination). All `select` elements have a built-in attribute, `selectedIndex`, that tells which `option` in their list is currently selected. So we can use this, as `finish.selectedIndex`, to get at the `option` in question. And finally, the `value` attribute of that `option` returns the coordinate pair specified in the XHTML (back in Listing 5-4):

```
var value = finish.options[finish.selectedIndex].value;
```

It's a lot to do in a single line of JavaScript, so take your time and make sure you're clear on each piece.

Now we have the coordinates as a string, such as `'37.809, -122.4146'`, in our `value` variable. We're not quite done yet, though, because we need them as a `GLatLng` object to feed back into the Maps API. We create this object by using the `eval` function:

```
var coordinates = eval('new GLatLng(' + value + ')');
```

We add (or *concatenate*) the latitude/longitude `value` into the string being evaluated and get a `GLatLng` object out the other side.

JAVASCRIPT 101: EVAL

One of the most powerful features of the JavaScript language is the humble little `eval` function. Its job is to convert text into JavaScript code. For example, the following JavaScript statement:

```
var coordinates = eval('new GLatLng(37.809, -122.4146)');
```

is exactly equivalent to this:

```
var coordinates = new GLatLng(37.809, -122.4146);
```

In other words, the text inside the `eval` function is *evaluated* as if it were itself JavaScript.

Your initial reaction might well be "so what?", but this technique opens the door to all kinds of code that adapts itself to different circumstances. In Listing 5-5, for example, the values of the destination options are text, but in order to plot them on the map we need them as API objects. With `eval`, we can make that conversion.

These few lines of code are typical of extracting data from XHTML content for use in JavaScript; it's often a bit messy, but it's essential to making a dynamic web page work. Once we've finished this, in the latter half of `destinationChange` we're ready to move on and create a destination marker, much as we did with `startMarker` in Listing 5-3. And the results of all this hard work can be seen in Figure 5-3.

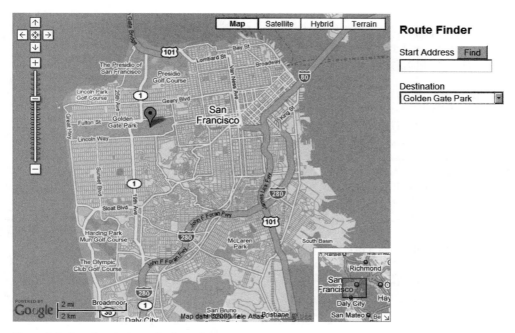

Figure 5-3. *Destination marked on the map*

So now we have both a starting point and a destination, and we're ready to get directions from one to the other. In preparation, we need to add a couple of elements to our XHTML, as highlighted in Listing 5-6.

Listing 5-6. *XHTML for Driving Directions*

```
<!DOCTYPE html PUBLIC "-//W3C//DTD XHTML 1.0 Strict//EN"
                      "http://www.w3.org/TR/xhtml1/DTD/xhtml1-strict.dtd">
<html xmlns="http://www.w3.org/1999/xhtml">
  <head>
    <meta http-equiv="Content-Type" content="text/html; charset=UTF-8" />
    <title>Your Map and the Real World</title>
    <link type="text/css" rel="stylesheet" href="../chapter_04/listing_04_02.css" />
    <script type="text/javascript
          src="http://maps.google.com/maps?file=api&amp;v=2.124&amp;key="></script>
    <script type="text/javascript" src="listing_05_07.js"></script>
  </head>
  <body onload="loadMap()" onunload="GUnload()">
    <div id="map"></div>
    <div id="sidebar">
      <h2>Route Finder</h2>
```

```
    <p>
      Start Address
      <button onclick="geocode()">Find</button>
      <input type="text" id="start" />
    </p>
    <p>
      Destination
      <select id="finish" onchange="destinationChange()">
        <option value="">Please select:</option>
        <option value="37.809, -122.4146">The Embarcadero</option>
        <option value="37.79516, -122.39379">Ferry Terminal</option>
        <option value="37.76976, -122.46765">Golden Gate Park</option>
        <option value="37.80733, -122.47411">The Presidio</option>
        <option value="37.79482, -122.40277">Transamerica Pyramid</option>
      </select>
      <button onclick="getDirections()">Directions</button>
    </p>
    <div id="directions"></div>
  </div>
  </body>
</html>
```

The button element is quite straightforward; it's really just a place for the user to click to initiate the process. The other new element, <div id="directions">, will be used by Google's driving directions object to display the results as text in the sidebar.

As with the geocoder, interacting with that object will occur in two parts: first we initialize it, and then we use it. To initialize the object, we add a couple of lines to our loadMap function:

```
var panel = document.getElementById('directions');
directions = new GDirections(map, panel);
```

Note that we're linking the directions object to both the map and the sidebar div; thus any driving directions generated will be both drawn on the map and listed in the sidebar.

The object is actually used in the getDirections event handler (attached to our new button element), as shown in Listing 5-7.

Listing 5-7. *The Driving Directions Event Handler*

```
function getDirections()
{
  // getDirections: Request driving directions from start to destination

  if ((startMarker == null) || (finishMarker == null))
    alert('Please select a starting address and destination for directions.');
  else
  {
    // Collect the start and finish points as 'lat,lon' strings
    var waypoints = [startMarker.getPoint().toUrlValue(),
                     finishMarker.getPoint().toUrlValue()];
```

```
    // Load driving directions for those points
    directions.loadFromWaypoints(waypoints);
  }
};
```

Again, what you see in Listing 5-7 is a single function in isolation, to be appended to our growing JavaScript listing. Fear not; I'll bring it all together in one place again before the end of the chapter.

We lead off here with a bit of defensive coding: if the user tries to get directions before selecting their endpoints, we remind them of this with an `alert`. Otherwise, we get on with the business of the driving directions.

The first stage is to collect the endpoints, with a multiple-step process (similar to the way we built tabbed infowindows from XHTML content in Chapter 4):

1. Get the coordinates for each marker, using its `getPoint` function:

    ```
    startMarker.getPoint()
    ```

2. Convert each point into a text string, using `toUrlValue`:

    ```
    startMarker.getPoint().toUrlValue()
    ```

3. Declare a variable, `waypoints`, and initialize it with the two strings:

    ```
    var waypoints = [startMarker.getPoint().toUrlValue(),
                        finishMarker.getPoint().toUrlValue()];
    ```

The only slightly odd thing here is that we're using `toUrlValue` to convert each coordinate pair from an object into a string, the opposite of what we did with our destination `select` earlier. Google seems to have built the `GDirections` object this way to facilitate using it with external data, but in our case it actually means an extra step.

■**Note** Directions can also be retrieved directly from addresses, rather than from coordinates as I'm doing here. While such an approach is easier in the simplest case (because you don't need to do the geocoding yourself), it becomes more complicated to handle when the geocoding inevitably goes wrong.

At any rate, we're finally ready to request the directions, and we do so as follows:

```
directions.loadFromWaypoints(waypoints);
```

It seems almost anticlimactic, because we've done all the hard work before getting to this point, but the results are well worth it, as shown in Figure 5-4.

As you can see, Google does quite a lot for you in supplying directions; details include total distance and time in the sidebar, directions and distance for each turn, and blowup maps all along the way.

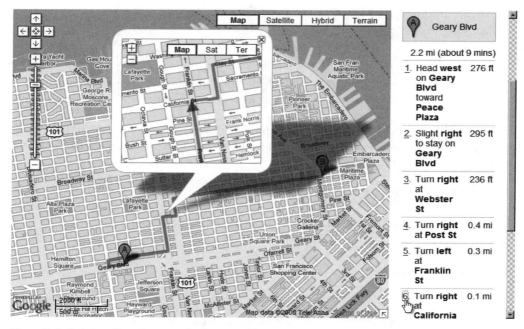

Figure 5-4. *Driving directions on the map and in the sidebar, with built-in blowup maps*

Traffic

We've had some intense JavaScript in the last couple of sections, so let's take a break and do something easy before we launch into more difficult features like Street View. As an enhancement to the driving directions, in this section we'll add a real-time traffic overlay to our map.

Again, we'll start off with a user-interface element to control the feature, highlighted in Listing 5-8.

Listing 5-8. *XHTML for the Traffic Overlay*

```
<!DOCTYPE html PUBLIC "-//W3C//DTD XHTML 1.0 Strict//EN"
                    "http://www.w3.org/TR/xhtml1/DTD/xhtml1-strict.dtd">
<html xmlns="http://www.w3.org/1999/xhtml">
  <head>
    <meta http-equiv="Content-Type" content="text/html; charset=UTF-8" />
    <title>Your Map and the Real World</title>
    <link type="text/css" rel="stylesheet" href="../chapter_04/listing_04_02.css" />
    <script type="text/javascript
          src="http://maps.google.com/maps?file=api&amp;v=2.124&amp;key="></script>
    <script type="text/javascript" src="listing_05_09.js"></script>
  </head>
  <body onload="loadMap()" onunload="GUnload()">
    <div id="map"></div>
    <div id="sidebar">
```

```
      <h2>Route Finder</h2>
      <p>
        Start Address
        <button onclick="geocode()">Find</button>
        <input type="text" id="start" />
      </p>
      <p>
        Destination
        <select id="finish" onchange="destinationChange()">
          <option value="">Please select:</option>
          <option value="37.809, -122.4146">The Embarcadero</option>
          <option value="37.79516, -122.39379">Ferry Terminal</option>
          <option value="37.76976, -122.46765">Golden Gate Park</option>
          <option value="37.80733, -122.47411">The Presidio</option>
          <option value="37.79482, -122.40277">Transamerica Pyramid</option>
        </select>
        <button onclick="getDirections()">Directions</button>
      </p>
      <p>
        <input type="checkbox" id="show_traffic" checked="checked"
               onclick="toggleTraffic()" />
        Show Traffic
      </p>
      <div id="directions"></div>
    </div>
  </body>
</html>
```

As mentioned, the traffic object is an overlay, so once it's initialized (in our loadMap function), we add it to the map as we would a GMarker or GGeoXml, with the addOverlay function:

```
traffic = new GTrafficOverlay();
map.addOverlay(traffic);
```

Similarly, the event handler to control its display looks remarkably like the toggleCampgrounds function used in Chapter 4. It's exactly the same principle: when the user has clicked the checkbox, the toggleTraffic function executes and hides or shows the overlay based on the state of the checkbox (see Listing 5-9).

Listing 5-9. *The JavaScript Function to Control the Traffic Overlay*

```
function toggleTraffic()
{
  // toggleTraffic: Turn the traffic overlay on or off
  if (document.getElementById('show_traffic').checked)
    traffic.show();
  else
    traffic.hide();
};
```

The results are visible in Figure 5-5; major highways are overlaid with thick lines in different colors based on current traffic congestion.

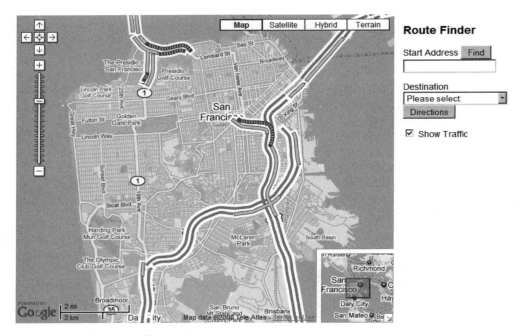

Figure 5-5. *Real-time traffic*

Street View

Google's Street View feature is a network of immersive, street-level, panoramic photos covering much of the United States and expanding in other countries. Like most Google Maps features, it's available to developers through the Maps API, so we're going to add it to our Route Finder map.

Working with panoramic photos is inherently a bit complicated, so perhaps it's not surprising that integrating Street View is not entirely simple. I've pared it back as much as I realistically can, but nonetheless, it's still the most involved piece of JavaScript we've tackled so far in this book. But it is worth it; Street View really is an impressive addition to a mapping application. We're going to use it to allow the page visitor to see any of our destinations up close and personal. It would also be a great feature for a realty web site, a travel guide, or many other types of maps.

We'll start off easily enough, adding just another button to our XHTML, as in Listing 5-10. Clicking the Street View button should open an infowindow containing the panorama for the currently selected destination. In addition, we're going to need a bit more CSS, so that's referenced here; I'll discuss it in detail in Listing 5-13, in a few pages. Note also that this is the final XHTML listing for this chapter, containing every feature we'll cover.

Listing 5-10. *XHTML with Street View Button*

```
<!DOCTYPE html PUBLIC "-//W3C//DTD XHTML 1.0 Strict//EN"
                     "http://www.w3.org/TR/xhtml1/DTD/xhtml1-strict.dtd">
<html xmlns="http://www.w3.org/1999/xhtml">
  <head>
    <meta http-equiv="Content-Type" content="text/html; charset=UTF-8" />
    <title>Your Map and the Real World</title>
    <link type="text/css" rel="stylesheet" href="listing_05_13.css" />
    <script type="text/javascript"
            src="http://maps.google.com/maps?file=api&amp;v=2.124&amp;key="></script>
    <script type="text/javascript" src="listing_05_14.js"></script>
  </head>
  <body onload="loadMap()" onunload="GUnload()">
    <div id="map"></div>
    <div id="sidebar">
      <h2>Route Finder</h2>
      <p>
        Start Address
        <button onclick="geocode()">Find</button>
        <input type="text" id="start" />
      </p>
      <p>
        Destination
        <select id="finish" onchange="destinationChange()">
          <option value="">Please select:</option>
          <option value="37.809, -122.4146">The Embarcadero</option>
          <option value="37.79516, -122.39379">Ferry Terminal</option>
          <option value="37.76976, -122.46765">Golden Gate Park</option>
          <option value="37.80733, -122.47411">The Presidio</option>
          <option value="37.79482, -122.40277">Transamerica Pyramid</option>
        </select>
        <button onclick="getDirections()">Directions</button>
        <button onclick="getView()">Street View</button>
      </p>
      <p>
        <input type="checkbox" id="show_traffic" checked="checked"
               onclick="toggleTraffic()" />
        Show Traffic
      </p>
      <div id="directions"></div>
    </div>
  </body>
</html>
```

Moving on to the JavaScript, we're going to need a variable for a Street View object, so we declare that first, at the top:

```
var streetviewClient;
```

This is the main Street View "controller" object. We'll then initialize it in the usual place, our loadMap function:

```
streetviewClient = new GStreetviewClient();
```

The pieces are now in place, so it's time to start looking at the code to make it work. The first stage can be found in Listing 5-11, the onclick event handler for the Street View button on the page.

Listing 5-11. *The getView Function*

```
function getView()
{
  // getView: Retrieve a streetview panorama for the selected destination

  if (finishMarker == null)
    alert('Please select a destination.');
  else
  {
    // Retrieve the streetview panorama for the coordinates of the marker
    var coordinates = finishMarker.getPoint();
    streetviewClient.getNearestPanorama(coordinates, afterView);
  }
};
```

We lead off here with defensive coding again, making sure that the user has selected a destination. Assuming she has, you'll need the coordinates of the destination marker, from the getPoint function that we've used before:

```
var coordinates = finishMarker.getPoint();
```

Then a fairly simple call to the getNearestPanorama function passes control to the streetviewClient object. Google's panoramic photos are all at specific points throughout the city, so this function asks for information about the one closest to our target.

```
streetviewClient.getNearestPanorama(coordinates, afterView);
```

It takes two parameters, the coordinates of our target point and the name of a callback function to be invoked after the panorama retrieval has finished. This function, afterView, can be seen in Listing 5-12. It looks daunting—the largest function we've yet written—but as usual, take it one step at a time and it should all make sense.

Listing 5-12. *The Street View Callback Function*

```
function afterView(streetviewData)
{
  // afterView: Callback function for Street View panorama retrieval

  if (streetviewData.code == G_GEO_SUCCESS)
  {
    // Create a DHTML element to contain the panorama
    var streetViewer = document.createElement('div');

    // Create the Street View panorama object
    var panorama = new GStreetviewPanorama(streetViewer);

    // Extract the precise lat/lon coordinates from the Street View data object
    var coordinates = new GLatLng(streetviewData.location.lat,
                                  streetviewData.location.lng);

    // Tell the panorama object to display view for those coordinates
    panorama.setLocationAndPOV(coordinates, streetviewData.location.pov);

    // Open an infowindow with the panorama container element
    streetViewer.className = 'streetViewer';
    finishMarker.openInfoWindow(streetViewer);
  }
};
```

We begin with defensive coding again, making sure that the panorama retrieval worked by checking its code against the predefined value G_GEO_SUCCESS. Assuming that's OK, we move into the main processing of the callback.

■**Tip** Variables in all uppercase, like G_GEO_SUCCESS here, typically signify values that are predefined for you in the API or elsewhere. This use of uppercase is not a requirement, but it is a widely used convention that makes these predefined values easier to distinguish from "ordinary" variables, and it's one that Google makes good use of in the Maps API.

If you're familiar with programming in other languages, these are the closest that JavaScript has to *constants*.

First, we need an XHTML container for the panorama. Because the viewer will go into an infowindow (which is not yet open), we need to generate this container on the fly. You do this with the `document.createElement` function; it dynamically creates an XHTML element of the supplied type (in this case, a div). We can then assign this div to a local variable, `streetViewer`, for use later in the function:

```
var streetViewer = document.createElement('div');
```

Next up is creating the Flash panorama viewer object:

```
var panorama = new GStreetviewPanorama(streetViewer);
```

Note that you pass `GStreetviewPanorama` the XHTML container where you'll want it to display; in our case, it's the `streetViewer` div created in the previous step.

Moving on, we need to get the coordinates for this panorama from the `streetviewData` object that we received in the callback. If you recall, we requested the panorama nearest to our destination point; we didn't know the precise location of that panorama. But the coordinates returned in `streetviewData` specify that location:

```
var coordinates = new GLatLng(streetviewData.location.lat,
                              streetviewData.location.lng);
```

It's a fairly simple manner of creating a new GLatLng object from the received coordinates. The next step is to initialize the panorama object from those coordinates, like so:

```
panorama.setLocationAndPOV(coordinates, streetviewData.location.pov);
```

This call also includes a second parameter for POV, or *point of view*. A panorama's point of view is essentially what direction it's looking from its base coordinates: north/south, east/west, up/down, and zoom in/out. We're just going to use the default POV for the panoramic photo from Google, contained within `location.pov` in the `streetviewData` parameter. Point of view can get quite complicated, so let's leave it at that for now; this is good enough for our purposes.

We're nearly there now; you just need to prepare the container element for display.

```
streetViewer.className = 'streetViewer';
```

The process of setting the `className` of the `streetViewer` container element is exactly the same as for adding `class="streetViewer"` in ordinary XHTML, and it allows you to target the element with CSS (as you'll see in the next listing).

Finally, all the pieces are in place, and you're ready to display an infowindow containing the panorama.

```
finishMarker.openInfoWindow(streetViewer);
```

The `openInfoWindow` function passes the supplied XHTML element—in our case, the `streetViewer` container div, with its panorama—to the standard Google Maps infowindow.

And we're done, with the fruits of our labor visible in Figure 5-6, an interactive panorama that the user can move and zoom to get a real-world view of their destination.

Figure 5-6. *Street View panorama for a destination*

As alluded to previously, there's one final aspect required, a bit of CSS to control the presentation of the panorama. Specifically, we just need to set its `height` and `width`, as highlighted in Listing 5-13. It's accomplished using the `className` of `streetViewer` that we applied in JavaScript.

Listing 5-13. *Style for the Street View Panorama*

```
html {
  height: 100%;
}

body {
  height: 100%;
  margin: 0;
  font-family: sans-serif;
  font-size: 90%;
}

#map {
  width: 75%;
  height: 100%;
}
```

```
#sidebar {
  position: absolute;
  left: 75%;
  top: 0;
  right: 0;
  bottom: 0;
  overflow: auto;
  padding: 1em;
}

h1 {
  margin: 0;
  font-size: 220%;
}
h2 {
  margin: 0;
  font-size: 125%;
}

.streetViewer {
  width: 350px;
  height: 250px;
}
```

Incidentally, Street View is why I used a `select` list for destinations, rather than geocoding addresses as we do for the starting location. Google doesn't have panoramic photos for every address, so I'm limiting the destinations to places where I know Street View exists.

Map Advertising

As a reward for getting through the Street View code, how about earning a bit of money from your map? That's exactly what the `GAdsManager` object does, placing location-sensitive Google AdSense advertisements on your map. Because they're placed geographically in an area that your page visitor is already looking at, they're likely to be relevant to that visitor, and you'll get paid with every click-through.

Because map advertising is a part of Google's AdSense program, you'll need to have an AdSense account to put ads on your own map. It's the same program used for placing standard Google ads on ordinary web pages, so if you are already doing that, you can reuse your publisher ID here. If you don't have one yet, you can sign up at `http://www.google.com/adsense`. Google will review your web site and, ideally, approve it for the AdSense program. However, be aware that not every application is approved, and it may take a few days in any case.

Assuming that you have been accepted to the AdSense program, your publisher ID ("pub-" followed by a 16-digit number, like "pub-01234567890123456") can be found in the upper-right corner of your AdSense account pages. You'll need it to place ads on your own maps.

So with your publisher ID in hand, you're ready to begin. You start by declaring a variable for the ad manager object, at the beginning of the JavaScript as usual:

```
var ads;
```

Once you've done that, showing ads on the map is as simple as initializing ads in your loadMap function.

```
ads = new GAdsManager(map, 'pub-01234567890123456', {maxAdsOnMap: 10});
ads.enable();
```

A few additional points about GAdsManager:

- I'm supplying a single option, maxAdsOnMap, meaning that my map will never show more than 10 advertisements at once.

- In addition to creating the ads object, we also have to enable it. Advertisements are disabled by default.

- Don't forget to use your own AdSense publisher ID (as a text string) in the second parameter.

The results are shown in Figure 5-7.

Figure 5-7. *Location-specific ads on the map*

It's also worth noting here that map advertising is relatively new and doesn't yet have the adoption rate enjoyed by traditional AdSense. Advertisers also come and go all the time. So don't be surprised if any given map has few ads at any given moment.

Bringing It All Together

Our Route Finder map is now complete; as a review, Listing 5-14 brings together all the code for the various components.

Listing 5-14. *The Complete Route Finder Page JavaScript*

```
// Declare variables for later use
var map;
var geocoder;
var startMarker;
var finishMarker;
var directions;
var traffic;
var streetviewClient;
var ads;

function loadMap()
{
  // loadMap: initialize the API and load the map onto the page

  // Get the map container div
  var mapDiv = document.getElementById('map');

  // Confirm browser compatibility with the Maps API
  if (!GBrowserIsCompatible())
  {
    mapDiv.innerHTML =
      'Sorry, your browser isn\'t compatible with Google Maps.';
  }
  else
  {
    // Initialize the core map object
    map = new GMap2(mapDiv,
      {mapTypes: [G_NORMAL_MAP, G_SATELLITE_MAP, G_HYBRID_MAP, G_PHYSICAL_MAP]});

    // Set the starting map viewport, based on center coordinates and zoom level
    var coordinates = new GLatLng(37.75, -122.44);
    map.setCenter(coordinates, 12);

    // Add the standard map controls
    map.addControl(new GLargeMapControl());
    map.addControl(new GScaleControl());
    map.addControl(new GOverviewMapControl());
    map.addControl(new GMapTypeControl());
```

```
    // Initialize the geocoder object and tie it to the current map view
    geocoder = new GClientGeocoder();
    geocoder.setViewport(map.getBounds());

    // Initialize the driving directions object
    var panel = document.getElementById('directions');
    directions = new GDirections(map, panel);

    // Initialize the traffic object
    traffic = new GTrafficOverlay();
    map.addOverlay(traffic);

    // Initialize the Street View controller object
    streetviewClient = new GStreetviewClient();

    // Initialize the map advertising object
    ads = new GAdsManager(map, 'pub-01234567890123456', {maxAdsOnMap: 10});
    ads.enable();
  }
};

function geocode()
{
  // geocode: Call the Google geocoder with the address supplied by the user
  var address = document.getElementById('start').value;
  geocoder.getLatLng(address, afterGeocode);
};

function afterGeocode(coordinates)
{
  // afterGeocode: Callback function for the geocoder, showing the coords on the map
  if (coordinates == null)
    alert('Address not found. Please try again.');
  else if (!map.getBounds().contains(coordinates))
    alert('Address not found in map area. Please try again.');
  else
  {
    // Address was found
    if (startMarker == null)
    {
      // This is the first time we've geocoded an address, so create the marker
      startMarker = new GMarker(coordinates);
      map.addOverlay(startMarker);
    }
```

```
        else
        {
          // The marker already exists;; just move it to the new coordinates
          startMarker.setPoint(coordinates);
        }
    }
};


function destinationChange()
{
    // destinationChange: Update destination marker from the drop-down list

    // Extract the new destination from the drop-down
    var finish = document.getElementById('finish');
    var value = finish.options[finish.selectedIndex].value;
    if (value != '')
    {
        // Valid destination:  create a coordinates object from it
        var coordinates = eval('new GLatLng(' + value + ')');

        if (finishMarker == null)
        {
            // This is the first time the user has selected a destination
            finishMarker = new GMarker(coordinates);
            map.addOverlay(finishMarker);
        }
        else
        {
            // The marker already exists; just move it to the new coordinates
            finishMarker.setPoint(coordinates);
        }

        // Ensure that the destination point is visible on the map
        if (!map.getBounds().contains(coordinates))
            map.panTo(coordinates);
    }
};


function getDirections()
{
    // getDirections: Request driving directions from start to destination

    if ((startMarker == null) || (finishMarker == null))
        alert('Please select a starting address and destination for directions.');
```

```
    else
    {
      // Collect the start and finish points as 'lat,lon' strings
      var waypoints = [startMarker.getPoint().toUrlValue(),
                       finishMarker.getPoint().toUrlValue()];

      // Load driving directions for those points
      directions.loadFromWaypoints(waypoints);
    }
};

function toggleTraffic()
{
  // toggleTraffic: Turn the traffic overlay on or off
  if (document.getElementById('show_traffic').checked)
    traffic.show();
  else
    traffic.hide();
};

function getView()
{
  // getView: Retrieve a Street View panorama for the selected destination

  if (finishMarker == null)
    alert('Please select a destination.');
  else
  {
    // Retrieve the Street View panorama for the coordinates of the marker
    var coordinates = finishMarker.getPoint();
    streetviewClient.getNearestPanorama(coordinates, afterView);
  }
};

function afterView(streetviewData)
{
  // afterView: Callback function for Street View panorama retrieval

  if (streetviewData.code == G_GEO_SUCCESS)
  {
    // Create a DHTML element to contain the panorama
    var streetViewer = document.createElement('div');

    // Create the Street View panorama object
    var panorama = new GStreetviewPanorama(streetViewer);
```

```
    // Extract the precise lat/lon coordinates from the Street View data object
    var coordinates = new GLatLng(streetviewData.location.lat,
                                  streetviewData.location.lng);

    // Tell the panorama object to display view for those coordinates
    panorama.setLocationAndPOV(coordinates, streetviewData.location.pov);

    // Open an infowindow with the panorama container element
    streetViewer.className = 'streetViewer';
    finishMarker.openInfoWindow(streetViewer);
  }
};
```

Recall that the final, complete XHTML for this chapter can be found back in Listing 5-10.

Summary

In the last two chapters we've covered a wide range of ways to improve your Maps API implementation, including plenty of practical examples that you can apply directly to your own code. You know how to geocode addresses into map coordinates—and when not to. You're also ready to create your own map mashups with all the latest bells and whistles, including these:

- Driving directions

- Traffic overlays

- Street View immersive panoramas

- Map-based advertising

So next, we're going to change gears, moving on from the core Maps API and entering the world of *mapplets*, small map "gadgets" that run on the main Google Maps web site rather than a page of your own. In the process, you'll learn how to leverage the traffic of maps.google.com to expose your mashup to a far wider audience.

PART 2

■ ■ ■

Mashing Up Google Maps with Mapplets

CHAPTER 6

■ ■ ■

Introduction to Mapplets

Part 1 of this book taught you how to use the Google Maps API, embedding a Google map in essentially any web page. Here in Part 2 we'll be working through a different but related specification, the *Mapplets API*, which instead allows us to program the main Google Maps web site itself. That's the central distinction: rather than bringing Google Maps functionality to our own site, mapplets let us bring our own content and functionality to maps.google.com.

A *mapplet*, then, is a self-contained piece of mapping functionality, ready to be "plugged in" to Google Maps. The name itself, a combination of *map* and *applet*, is a good summary of what it does: map + applet = a small mapping application. As such, building mapplets will require a bit of a shift in thinking from the Maps API programming you've done so far. You're no longer trying to integrate a map into your own, larger web site; instead, you're trying to package up what your web site has to offer in a way that's centered on the map itself.

One example of a good mapplet for many businesses could be the locations of their branches or offices. Such a mapplet would allow customers to see the branches nearest them any time they're looking at Google Maps. If the customer is planning a trip, looking at a map of their destination, this mapplet would then automatically show locations near that destination. Thus, mapplets are a way of getting your geodata onto Google's own Maps site.

In the first section of this chapter, I'll walk you through how mapplets work from a user standpoint. We'll then look at some of the key concepts involved in building your own mapplets, and we'll compare and contrast mapplets with the Maps API you're already familiar with.

MAPPLETS AS GADGETS

If you're familiar with the concept of web *gadgets* (sometimes called *widgets*)—on iGoogle, Facebook, or elsewhere—you're off to a head start with mapplets, because a good way to think of a mapplet is as a *map gadget*. Just as an iGoogle gadget is a container for embedding virtually any web content and functionality into your Google home page, so a mapplet is for embedding geospatial content and functionality into Google Maps.

In fact, Google uses its gadget architecture as the basis for mapplets, so this connection is more than abstract. If you've done any iGoogle gadget development before, you'll recognize the basic mapplet code structure in the next chapter. I'll also be pointing out useful overlaps between the Mapplets and Gadgets APIs throughout this part of the book.

Using Mapplets

Mapplets live on the My Maps page of `maps.google.com`. This is where Google Maps users customize their maps to suit themselves; they can add their own content, such as place markers, and they can install mapplets to add prepackaged content and functionality. When they do so, a list of their mapplets appears in the Created by Others section of the page, as shown in Figure 6-1.

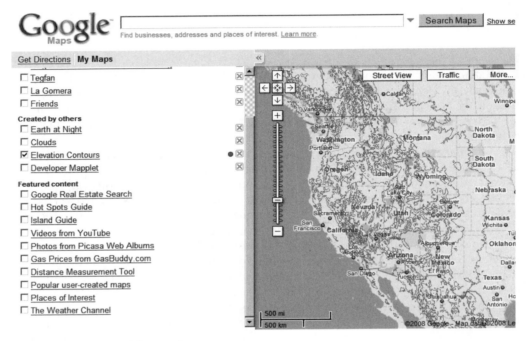

Figure 6-1. *My Maps with mapplets*

Although the user can have many different mapplets installed, they aren't necessarily all active all the time. Only active mapplets have their content shown on the map; the checkbox next to each mapplet's name in the list indicates whether or not it's active. In Figure 6-1, for example, the Elevation Contours mapplet is active, and you can see the contours it's overlaying on the map.

At any given time, one mapplet may also be *selected* by clicking its name in the list. The selected mapplet may then use the lower area of the My Maps page as a sidebar to display extra information in addition to what's on the map itself. For example, a weather mapplet might show temperature icons for different cities on the map itself, and then list the cities (with more information for each) in the sidebar, as shown in Figure 6-2. Note that Google Maps automatically displays the mapplet's name and parent URL in this area as well.

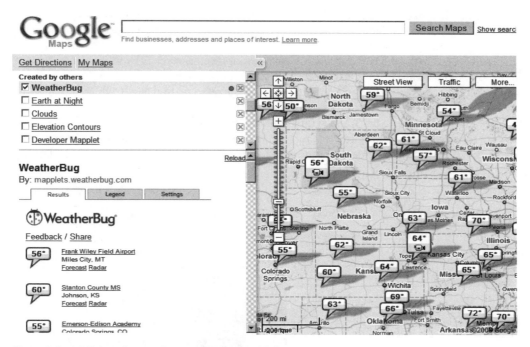

Figure 6-2. *Additional mapplet content in the sidebar*

In other words, mapplet content is divided into two areas:

- Primary content on the map itself, such as markers and overlays

- Secondary content in the sidebar, such as a list of the markers

It's also worth noting that the selected mapplet remains active after the user leaves the My Maps page. If they perform a map search, or if they leave Google Maps and return later, their selected mapplet will still be active. So a mapplet that a person finds useful may be left "on" all the time, effectively becoming a permanent addition to that person's Google Maps.

Installing Mapplets

The most common technique for installing mapplets is to use the directory that Google maintains for this purpose (although we'll see another way in the next chapter). To access it, click the Browse the Directory link at the top of the My Maps page. Doing so will take you to a searchable, categorized list of mapplets that developers have submitted to Google; from there, any mapplet can be installed by a single click on its Add It to Maps button. Newly installed mapplets are then active by default in the user's Google Maps.

Combining Mapplets

Now that you know your way around the My Maps page, let's take a look at a couple of mapplets in action. This will also help to illustrate the synergy that gives mapplets much of their potential and was a key motivator behind Google's creation of the mapplet platform.

The first half of our example is the Webcams Worldwide mapplet. It shows map markers and previews for ten public webcams nearest the map center, and it's a handy way to see real-time views of many areas.

However, most of the listed webcams are outdoors, and as a result don't have much to show after dark. So it'd be helpful to see which webcams are in daylight and which are in darkness. We can do this by installing a second mapplet, Current Day and Night, which darkens the area of the Google map corresponding to the night side of the Earth.

Then, activating both mapplets at once will instantly show which webcams are in darkness and are thus less likely to have interesting views at the moment. In the example shown in Figure 6-3, the Aleutian Islands are in the dark, while most of mainland Alaska is in daylight.

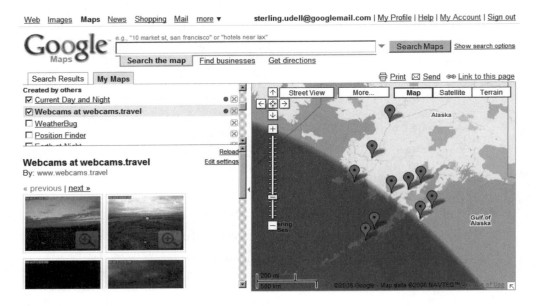

Figure 6-3. *Webcams in daylight*

This inherent cooperation between mapplets is one of their most useful features: it lets any user merge mapped content, on the fly, from disparate sources of his choosing. In doing so, ordinary users can combine geodata in ways that its creators probably never thought of, and get more out of the combination than the sum of its parts.

It's a concept that Google likes to refer to as a "mashup of mashups": each mapplet is itself a geodata mashup, and the My Maps environment gives nontechnical users the ability to mash them up further, distilling geospatial relationships that are specifically of interest to them. It's taking the geoweb another step further, empowering everyone to make the best use of it.

Developing Mapplets

Although mapplets share some common ground with the Maps API, developing them requires a somewhat different approach. First, the actual API is different, as we'll see in detail later in this chapter and the next. But at a more basic level, mapplet development requires a shift in thinking.

A Map-Centered Design

When you use the traditional Maps API to embed a map in your own web site, odds are that the map is playing a supporting role. Your web site serves a purpose that usually isn't centered on mapping; you add an API map as an enhancement.

With mapplets, conversely, a Google map is the center of attention, and your mapplet serves to enhance it. In other words, your content (as geodata) gets added to the map, rather than the map being added to your content (at your own web site).

As a result, when designing a mapplet you need to reverse your thinking, and ask, "How can my web site improve this map?" instead of "How could a map improve my web site?"

A Shared Map

The other major design consideration is that with the API you've seen until now, you have essentially had complete control over the map. However, we're now entering a realm where the map doesn't belong to you. This means that your mapplet needs to be a good neighbor, because it'll probably be sharing the map with other geodata, both from other mapplets and from Google itself.

I'll lay out some specific neighborly advice in Chapter 8, but for now, just be aware that the map is no longer your private playground. To some extent, the Mapplets API limits what you *can* do, but there is also an element of good judgment required.

Similarities to the Maps API

Although mapplets have their own, independent API, it is based on the same Maps API that this book has covered in the preceding chapters. As a result, there are more similarities between the two than there are differences.

Basic Principles

Apart from the items mentioned in the next section, all of the fundamentals of developing mapplets are unchanged from the Maps API. It's still JavaScript-based; all the same map types (Map, Terrain, Satellite, and Hybrid) are supported, and so forth. So at a basic level, most of what you have learned up until now will continue to be applicable. You should mostly find yourself in familiar territory.

JavaScript Objects

Many of the same JavaScript objects, such as GMap2, GMarker, and GLatLng, still exist. In some cases, you'll find that their behavior has changed slightly to conform to the mapplet architecture (more about that in the next section), but for the most part, they're directly comparable.

Differences from the Maps API

Of course, there are some distinctions that separate the two APIs. Let's take a look at each in turn.

Pared-Back XHTML

Because mapplets are components to be added to the Google Maps web page, they aren't complete web pages in themselves, and therefore they don't have the full XHTML structure of a web page. They do still have XHTML content, but they only include the specific elements needed: `<p>` and `<div>` tags, for example, but not `<html>`, `<head>`, nor `<body>`. You'll be seeing this in detail when we get into mapplet code in the next chapter.

Also, mapplets continue to use standard XHTML `<script>` tags for their JavaScript functionality, as well as `<style>` and `<link>` for CSS.

An Additional XML Wrapper

Replacing the missing XHTML elements is a new framework of XML, essentially containing instructions to the Google Maps page about how the mapplet should be displayed. Some of these elements simply give predictable structure to the code, helping Google Maps to integrate it, while others provide metadata similar to that found in the `<head>` section of an ordinary web page.

Again, we'll be looking at the new XML elements in detail next chapter.

XML REVISITED

We touched on XML briefly back in Chapter 1. If you remember, it's a way of developing standards for data formatting so that the information can easily be extracted programmatically. XML data simply looks like this:

```
<name>value</name>
```

XML comes in different "flavors," each of which defines a specific set of tags that makes sense for its own application. XHTML, for example, uses `<html>`, `<body>`, `<head>`, and so on. Flavors of XML that you've come across before in this book are XHTML, KML, and GeoRSS. The Mapplets API is just another flavor, defining another set of XML elements, standardizing how mapplet code is structured and enabling its integration into Google Maps.

No Need to Link In the API

Without a `<head>` section, where do you link the API into a mapplet? Answer: you don't. Because the mapplet always lives on `maps.google.com`, the "map API" is implied; it's supplied for you. There is a standard XML element that every mapplet will need to accomplish the equivalent linkage, but because it never changes, you can almost forget about it.

This also means that no API key is needed to write or use mapplets. On the downside, however, you also have no control over API versions. Theoretically, this does mean that your mapplet could break when Google releases a new version of the Mapplets API. But as a practical matter, the smaller Mapplets API—combined with the smaller form factor of mapplets themselves—means that there are fewer cutting-edge features you're likely to use. So it's very rarely an issue.

Simpler Map Object Creation

You'll recall that every map script we've written up until now required a line like the following, early in the code:

```
map = new GMap2(mapDiv, {mapTypes: [G_NORMAL_MAP, G_SATELLITE_MAP]});
```

This was necessary to initialize the core map object that controlled everything else in the API. It's still necessary in the Mapplets API, but it's less complicated in a couple of ways:

- The map container is always the same (it's the main Google Map), so it gets left out.

- There's no option to specify map types.

As a result, initializing the core mapplets object simply looks like this:

```
map = new GMap2();
```

"Good Neighbor" Enforcement

Since a mapplet is sharing the map, Google limits some of what you can do with it. This comes out in two main areas.

First, infowindow content is *sanitized*, meaning that Google disallows certain sorts of content and will remove it from infowindows you create. This is primarily a security precaution, to prevent potentially malicious code from running on the maps.google.com domain. It's not something you're likely to run into as a beginner—most basic content is allowed—but it is something to be aware of. For a complete list of allowed content tags and attributes, see http://tinyurl.com/3rabtc.

Second, there are no Mapplets API methods for disabling standard map behavior, or removing standard map controls. We haven't seen many in this book, but situations do arise where you want to reduce the functionality of API maps. For example, if your map is only showing a specific area, you might want to disable dragging the map, so that your area of interest is always in the center. The standard Maps API allows this, but mapplets do not.

It goes back to being a good neighbor—adding functionality of your own to the map without decreasing that offered by others, including Google itself.

Smaller API

Overall, the Mapplets API has significantly fewer objects and functions than the traditional Maps API. Although this sounds like a major difference, it isn't really.

First, the "good neighbor" policies described in the previous section mean that there are a number of functions that have been deliberately left out. If Google isn't going to allow you to disable dragging of the map, for example, the Mapplets API obviously doesn't need a function for it.

Second, quite a number of the Maps API objects exist solely to replicate functionality found on maps.google.com, such as traffic, driving directions, and Street View. In the Maps API, you use these objects to pick and choose which Google Maps features you want to add, but clearly there's little use for such objects in the Mapplets API. The features are all there on Google Maps already.

Third, most of the other missing functions are related to advanced map programming, such as creating new map types and controls. As a practical matter, this isn't a serious shortcoming for the majority of map developers, and applications that would use these routines are generally not well suited to being mapplets.

The upshot is that mapplets can probably do everything you need as a beginner. You might even find the more compact API less cumbersome and easier to navigate.

Asynchronous Functions

The biggest practical difference between the two APIs, and the one that *is* likely to cause you the most headaches, is that a larger proportion of mapplet functions are asynchronous. Specifically, every function that returns information from the map requires a callback.

Let's look at an example. You may recall that, in the last chapter, we occasionally needed to find out where a map marker had been placed. We did this with a simple call to the marker's getPoint function, like so:

```
coordinates = marker.getPoint();
```

To get the same information in a mapplet, we're required to use a callback function, which I'll call afterGetPoint. This introduces another step into the process:

```
function afterGetPoint(markerCoords)
{
  coordinates = markerCoords;
}
marker.getPointAsync(afterGetPoint);
```

Note that the API function, getPoint, has had Async (for "asynchronous") added to its name. It's fairly easy in this example, but in general the callback-based architecture is less convenient to use, it makes your code more complicated, and it can cause some trouble if you're not careful to follow the guidelines I'll be giving you. You'll learn more as we get into real mapplet code in the next two chapters.

If you're interested, the reason the Mapplets API does this is somewhat technical, but it boils down to an issue of security. In order to prevent mapplets from running potentially harmful code at maps.google.com, the mapplets are "sandboxed" in a separate domain. As a result, communication between a mapplet and the map needs to go through Google's servers first. Like all server functions in the API, then, the result comes in the form of a callback, rather than an immediate return value.

Advantages of Mapplets

Despite the number of differences listed in the previous section, mapplets really do have quite a lot in common with their precursor, the Maps API. And this is their biggest advantage: as a map developer, you can leverage your existing Google Map skills and create mapplets fairly easily.

In this section, we'll examine a few of the other reasons you should consider taking advantage of this and building a few mapplets.

Mapplets Complement Your Own Site

Generally, building a mapplet isn't a replacement for using the traditional API to place Google maps on your own site. If your web site has geospatial information—and, as we know from Chapter 1, most do—it's usually good to add maps to your own pages. Once you've done that, mapplets serve as a complement to those maps, opening another outlet for distributing your geodata.

One easy way to take advantage of this connection is to link to your mapplet directly from your web site. If you have a map on your site, and have built the same functionality into a mapplet, a simple link allows site visitors to install your mapplet on their My Maps with one click. Your content will then be part of their page whenever they visit Google Maps. We'll see an example of this in the next chapter.

A Potentially Huge Audience

Because they live on maps.google.com, mapplets are exposed to millions of web users every day. Even if only a tiny fraction of them install your mapplet, it still can be a very large audience for your content.

Better still, mapplets are hosted and served directly by Google, meaning that their traffic doesn't need any infrastructure investment on your part. Google also caches both the mapplet and the geodata displayed within (as discussed in Chapter 3), only returning to your own server every couple of hours to check for updates. It's a win-win situation: your content gets the traffic, but you don't need massive bandwidth.

Better Participation in the Geoweb

As another outlet for geodata, mapplets represent one more piece of the geoweb. When you build a mapplet, you're moving the geoweb one step further forward, making another bit of the world's geospatial information discoverable and usable. So not only is it good for you, by providing better dissemination of your content, it's good for the Web as a whole. With the Semantic Web still in an early stage of development, every contribution helps.

Drawbacks of Mapplets

Of course, nothing is without its downside, and mapplets are no exception. The following points summarize the main disadvantages of mapplet development, which you should be aware of as you proceed—but don't let them put you off pursuing mapplets.

Harder to Develop and Debug

Compared to the traditional Maps API, mapplets are somewhat more of a development challenge. Most of the issues stem directly from mapplet architecture; the points of divergence from the Maps API are also points of some difficulty.

To start with, the very fact that mapplets are embedded within maps.google.com makes them more difficult to work with. You can't test them from your local computer; they must be installed on My Maps to work at all. This means that all code changes during the development and debugging cycle need to be uploaded before they can be tested, and when you're trying to track down a recalcitrant bug, doing so can get a bit tedious. Also, maps.google.com has some incompatibilities with Firebug, a JavaScript debugging plug-in for Firefox and one of the most useful tools around for Maps developers (see Appendix C). So overall, the development process can be bumpier with mapplets than with the Maps API.

The second major difficulty is the asynchronous nature of many mapplet functions, as discussed earlier in this chapter. Especially for beginners, asynchronous code can be hard to get your head around, and it occasionally leads to subtle, hard-to-find bugs. Even when you get it right, it unavoidably means more code than traditional direct-return functions. You should have some familiarity with callbacks after the last few chapters, however, as we've used a good number of asynchronous functions already. Also, I'll have a few tricks for you that should help lighten your load.

Finally, the more restricted Mapplets API does occasionally present a problem when you're trying to make a mapplet from an existing map application, and your old-school API map relies upon a function or object that just doesn't exist in mapplet form. When this happens, sometimes you can work around the limitation with the tools the API gives you, but sometimes there's just not much you can do. For this reason, not every Maps application can be repackaged as a mapplet.

It's worth noting, however, that the Mapplets API is still relatively new, just over a year old as of this writing. As it matures, no doubt additional functionality will be added. So if your perfect mapplet isn't possible right now, it may well be in a few months.

Limited Adoption

In the thirteen months since their introduction, mapplets have experienced a relatively slow adoption rate, both by developers and users. The mapplet directory is still relatively sparse, with just a few thousand entries; in contrast, iGoogle gadgets (on which mapplets are based) have over 48,000 entries in their directory as of this writing. The uptake by Google Maps users has been similarly slow. A good iGoogle gadget will get tens of millions of views per month, while the equivalent mapplet will be orders of magnitude lower.

Part of the reason for this is surely that Google Maps itself gets less traffic than iGoogle. However, Google has also not promoted mapplets as strongly, neither externally nor within `maps.google.com` itself. For example, the link to add mapplets reads "Browse the directory," while the link on iGoogle to add gadgets is the shorter and friendlier "Add stuff."

It's also possible that existing Maps API developers have been put off by the more restrictive Mapplets API, or by the slightly harder development cycle. There is a bit of a chicken-and-egg problem here as well, in that usage will be low until there is a wealth of good mapplets to choose from, but developers are less inclined to spend time on a platform with relatively low usage.

With luck, the adoption rate will be another area that will continue to improve as the mapplet platform matures. Given that part of the issue lies in the hands of developers, you can contribute to the solution yourself by producing some great mapplets. And one bright point is that it's still possible to get in near the ground floor of mapplet development; if you release your mapplets soon, you'll still be ahead of the curve.

Summary

Mapplets complement the traditional Google Maps API by allowing you to build your content directly into `maps.google.com`. They're easy for users to integrate, and because they all share the same map, some excellent synergies between mapplets can appear organically.

For the Google Map developer, mapplets are a logical next step to take after learning the traditional Maps API. Although they have a distinct API of their own, there are many similarities, and experience with one will give you a head start on the other. The biggest differences lie in a more limited set of API functions and objects (mostly to do with the existing Google Maps infrastructure), and the use of callback functions to return any information from the map to the API.

In the next chapter we'll dive into mapplet coding. I'll present a simple example mapplet that we'll examine in detail, and along the way I'll bring you up to speed on the various other, ancillary topics you need to know for effective mapplet development.

CHAPTER 7

■ ■ ■

Creating a Mapplet

By now, you should have a pretty good understanding of the mapplet ecosystem: where mapplets live, what they do, and their relation to the familiar Google Maps API. By inserting your own geospatial content and functionality into `maps.google.com`, as we've seen, mapplets are an excellent way to open your geodata to millions of potential users.

So, the logical next step is to learn how to build and deploy a mapplet of your own. I'll start this chapter by presenting and analyzing a simple mapplet, giving you a guided tour of its internal structure and how it differs from code we've covered before. We'll then take a look at related mapplet programming considerations, including hosting, installing, testing, and publishing. The chapter closes with another, real-world example of a basic mapplet that can serve as a direct template for one of your own.

A "Hello, World" Mapplet

Let's jump right into our first example, which draws heavily from the "Hello, World" code of Chapter 2. Listing 7-1 shows that example converted into mapplet form. Some of the code should already look familiar to you, but I'll review it all in the next few pages.

Listing 7-1. *The "Hello, World" Mapplet*

```
<?xml version="1.0" encoding="UTF-8"?>
<Module>
  <ModulePrefs title="Creating a Mapplet">
    <Require feature="sharedmap" />
  </ModulePrefs>
  <Content type="html"><![CDATA[
    <style type="text/css">
      h1 {
        font-size: 120%;
      }
    </style>

    <h1>New York City</h1>
    <p id="hello">Hello, World!</p>
```

```
    <script type="text/javascript">
      // Initialize the map
      var map = new GMap2();
      var coordinates = new GLatLng(40.72, -73.99);
      map.setCenter(coordinates, 11);

      // Add a marker with infowindow
      var marker = new GMarker(coordinates);
      marker.bindInfoWindow(document.getElementById('hello'));
      map.addOverlay(marker);
    </script>
  ]]></Content>
</Module>
```

The base language here is XML, as discussed in the previous chapter, so all of the code is contained within XML elements. Note the first line of the mapplet:

```
<?xml version="1.0" encoding="UTF-8"?>
```

A line like this starts off every XML document and simply indicates to any computer reading it that it is indeed XML. The version is always `1.0`. The *encoding*, how the text of the document is represented internally, should usually be `UTF-8`. So as a rule, every mapplet will start with a line just like this one.

■**Caution** Although encodings other than `UTF-8` will work for English-language mapplets, XML that contains special characters from another language (such as ñ or ç) is more sensitive to encoding. To be safe, stick with `UTF-8`, unless you're working with a specific encoding for another (especially non-Western) language and you know what you're doing.

A couple of other notes about XML bear mentioning here. First, it's customary to refer to a complete unit of XML (such as Listing 7-1) as a *document*, even though it doesn't always correspond to how we traditionally use that word. In this case, the XML document specifies a mapplet, and as such you'll also see it referred to as the mapplet *specification*. I'll use both terms throughout this part of the book.

Second, you may have noticed that the tag names in this XML document are in mixed upper- and lowercase. If your only prior experience with XML is XHTML, this may look wrong to you. But every XML flavor defines its own standard for character case, and the Mapplet API specifies camel case (as described in Chapter 3). So for a mapplet, it would be wrong to use the XHTML convention of all lowercase tags.

Gadget-Related Code

As mentioned in the previous chapter, mapplets are derived from the iGoogle Gadgets API, and this shared lineage is evident in much of the basic code structure. I'll go over the basic concepts you need to know for mapplets here, and throughout this part of the book, I'll be pointing out frequent code snippets drawn from the underlying Gadgets API.

The `Module` Element

The first XML element in the document is `Module`, and the rest of the mapplet's code is always contained within its opening and closing tags. Incidentally, all well-formed XML documents have a single enclosing element like this, and it's actually called the *document element*. The `Module` element doesn't take any attributes, so it's always simply `<Module>` and `</Module>` at the beginning and end of your mapplet specification.

The name "Module" itself is a nod to the idea that each mapplet is a self-contained piece, ready to be plugged into the My Maps page, allowing the user to apply functionality in a modular way.

Module Preferences

Within `Module`, the next element in the mapplet is `ModulePrefs`. Short for "Module Preferences," `ModulePrefs` contains various *metadata* defining information *about* the mapplet, rather than the mapplet's functional code. It roughly corresponds to some of the elements found in the head section of an XHTML document, such as the `title` and `meta` tags.

Most of the metadata in `ModulePrefs` is specified as attributes. For simplicity, Listing 7-1 contains only a single attribute:

```
title="Creating a Mapplet"
```

Not surprisingly, this is the title of the mapplet, which Google Maps will display in the sidebar area whenever our mapplet is active. Unless we specify otherwise, this will also be the title shown for our mapplet in Google's directory.

We'll see some more attributes for `ModulePrefs` later in the chapter, but they'll all follow the pattern shown here, so this is sufficient as an introduction.

The Shared Map

Within the `ModulePrefs` opening and closing tags are other XML elements that serve as directives to the mapplet platform, requesting various features that our mapplet will require. In the very simple example in Listing 7-1 there is again only one of these:

```
<Require feature="sharedmap" />
```

The `sharedmap` feature is the main Google map itself, and it is actually this one line of code that marks this XML document as a mapplet specification (rather than an iGoogle gadget, which would otherwise use the same set of XML tags). As such, this line is required within the `ModulePrefs` element of every mapplet.

And again, there are other possible `features` that mapplets may `Require`. I'll cover more later in this chapter and the next, as well as in Appendix C.

The `Content` Element

After `ModulePrefs`, there's only one XML element remaining in our mapplet specification, `Content`. This is where the real mapplet functionality lives, in the form of XHTML snippets, CSS, and JavaScript, all of which I'll discuss in this section.

The `Content` element has one required attribute, `type="html"`. This is another spillover from the Gadgets API: gadgets have several possible types that behave in different ways. Only the html type is applicable to mapplets, though, so this is another piece of code that is simply required.

So as a practical matter, the main XHTML functionality of the mapplet will always be contained between the following two lines:

```
<Content type="html"><![CDATA[
```

and

```
]]></Content>
```

XML CHARACTER DATA

Notice the `<![CDATA[` and `]]>` just inside the Content element. CDATA stands for *character data*, and it's a standard XML directive that says to the computer, in effect, "Don't attempt to process what you find within as XML."

It's necessary because the mapplet content is itself XHTML, and as we know, that's actually just another "flavor" of XML. So without the CDATA directive, the functional part of the mapplet would be interpreted as part of the mapplet XML. This would be a problem, however, because the XHTML content is a different "flavor" than the mapplet specification. Google's mapplet platform doesn't actually read the Content, and in fact wouldn't know what to do with the XHTML within if it did. Instead, it passes the whole Content section off to the browser, which *does* know how to handle the XHTML, CSS, and JavaScript within. Thus, the CDATA directive prevents the mapplet platform from having to worry about the Content at all.

Put another way, CDATA is a way of wrapping one XML document within another, while maintaining a separation between the two.

Mapplet XHTML and CSS

We're now finished with the gadget-derived code; everything within the Content element is pure XHTML. Apart from the script element (which will be discussed in the next section), the content here will all be contained in the Google Maps sidebar, at the lower left of the browser window.

As such, our simple introductory mapplet doesn't have much content, just a first-level heading and a paragraph saying "Hello, World":

```
<h1>New York City</h1>
<p id="hello">Hello, World!</p>
```

I've added an id to the paragraph so that I can reuse its content from the JavaScript, but we'll get to that in a minute.

For illustration, I've also included a bit of CSS, modifying the appearance of the heading:

```
h1 {
  font-size: 120%;
}
```

You may be wondering why the CSS (and JavaScript) are internal to the code, in style and script elements, rather than linked in from external files as is the usual web design best practice. It's not a requirement of the Mapplets API—a link element will work just fine in a mapplet—but it is recommended. Here's why.

If you'll recall, in the last chapter I discussed that mapplets, because they live on maps.google.com, can potentially get a *lot* of traffic. And I also mentioned that Google hosts the actual mapplet served to site visitors, so that your host's bandwidth won't get overwhelmed if you create a popular mapplet.

However, if you link external CSS or JavaScript into your mapplet, such a linkage effectively bypasses the Google cache and goes directly to your own host. If this mapplet then becomes very popular, your host needs to support all those requests and could become overloaded. So it's generally safer to let Google handle it; they have more bandwidth than you do.

There will occasionally be times when it's impractical to avoid using external files, especially if you want to use third-party JavaScript libraries. In such a case, you may simply have to support the traffic—or use the trick for utilizing the Google cache you'll find in Appendix C. But generally, it's cleaner and simpler to just include the CSS and JavaScript internally; so that's how my examples are written.

Mapplet JavaScript

We've finally reached the code that makes the mapplet work, and it's plain JavaScript:

```
// Initialize the map
var map = new GMap2();
var coordinates = new GLatLng(40.72, -73.99);
map.setCenter(coordinates, 11);

// Add a marker with infowindow
var marker = new GMarker(coordinates);
marker.bindInfoWindow(document.getElementById('hello'));
map.addOverlay(marker);
```

If you were to compare this with the original Maps API "Hello, World" code back in Listing 2-5, you'd find that it has extremely few differences:

- Initializing the GMap2 object is easier, taking no parameters, as discussed in the preceding chapter.

- The map is centered on different coordinates and uses a different zoom level, just for a bit of variety.

- We're using bindInfoWindow for our popup content, following a lead from Chapter 4.

That's it! And with the exception of the GMap2 initialization, all of this code is *exactly as it would be in the traditional Maps API*. I've been telling you all along that mapplets are more similar to the Maps API than they are different, and here's the proof. It's actually the same JavaScript code.

■**Tip** Recall that, in the previous section, we included some CSS to style the sidebar content? With mapplets, such CSS doesn't apply to infowindows, even when we reuse the content from the sidebar (as we've done here). To style infowindow content in a mapplet, you'll generally need to use inline style attributes on the content elements themselves.

The end result can be seen in Figure 7-1: the sidebar content (including the mapplet title and URL added automatically by Google), the map marker on New York City, and the infowindow.

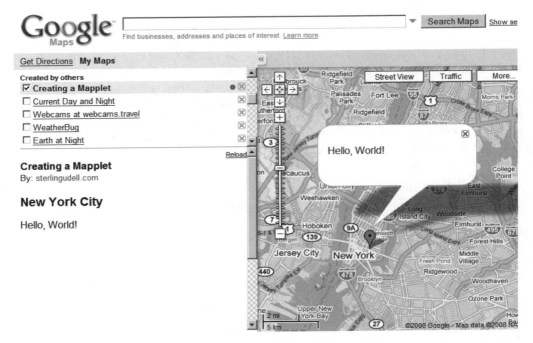

Figure 7-1. *Hello, World!*

Deploying Your Mapplet

The code for our introductory mapplet is now complete, so in this section we'll look at how to get it working on Google Maps. Because mapplets can't work in isolation, this is a more involved process than we had in the first part of the book, where we could simply place the Maps API code in a local XHTML file and look at it in our browser.

Hosting and Uploading

With mapplets, the specification (and any associated files) must be hosted on a web server where the Google Map can access it. This is true even though the mapplet code used on maps.google.com is hosted by Google itself; Google is simply caching it for you.

If you have a web server or hosting service of your own, that's usually the best place to host your mapplet. When you do so, the mapplet's XML document is no different from a web page's XHTML source; you'll edit it on your own computer and upload it as you ordinarily would. I recommend creating a separate directory or folder on your host for your mapplets, but such organization is up to you.

In any case, you'll need the URL of your mapplet's specification on your host for the next step. It'll look something like this:

```
http://www.mydomain.com/mapplets/my_mapplet.xml
```

Of course, substitute your own host's domain and mapplet path names into the URL (though it's customary for XML document file names to end with `.xml`). And as with any web development, whenever you make a change to your mapplet, you'll need to upload the latest version to your host before it will be available for use.

If you're going this route and hosting your own mapplets, you won't need to use the Google Gadget Editor, so feel free to skip the next section and rejoin the chapter at "Installing by URL."

The Google Gadget Editor

Google provides an online tool for editing and hosting iGoogle gadgets, called the Gadget Editor, and we can use the same tool for mapplets. If you don't have a web server to host your mapplets on, this is a good alternative. Even if you do have your own host, this can be a convenient place to try out new mapplet concepts, before creating an "official" version on your own server. Doing so saves the uploading step during the development cycle.

The Gadget Editor is itself a gadget, and as such, you'll need to install it before it can work. And the natural place to do so is iGoogle, the personalized Google start page. If you haven't done so yet, you'll first need to sign up for iGoogle by clicking on the iGoogle link at www.google.com. Once you're in iGoogle, you can install the Gadget Editor by browsing to http://tinyurl.com/6b8hpp and clicking Add It Now.

With the Gadget Editor installed on your iGoogle home page, you'll see that it's basically a small text editor, as shown in Figure 7-2. Generally, it supports all the common editor functions, like cut, copy, and paste. So you create your mapplet here simply by editing its XML source.

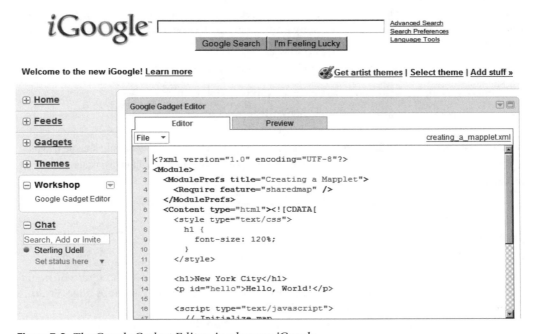

Figure 7-2. *The Google Gadget Editor, in place on iGoogle*

■Tip The Google Gadget Editor also has a preview tab, which—when editing an ordinary iGoogle gadget—is used to see your work in progress. With a mapplet, the Preview tab shows only the sidebar content, but this can be handy to preview in its own right.

When you have your mapplet ready to try, you'll need to save it. Under the File menu at the upper left of the Gadget Editor you'll find familiar options like Save and Save As; simply save your mapplet with a logical name (ending in .xml). You can also do other standard file operations like Open and Rename; you can even open a mapplet from a URL, a good way to get started with the examples from this book.

■Caution The iGoogle page will very occasionally reload itself, and when it does so, you'll lose everything not saved in the Gadget Editor. To disable its automatic reload, install the Developer gadget from http://tinyurl.com/5hkws4 onto the same iGoogle tab as the Gadget Editor. And of course, the old computer user's adage of "Save early, save often" still applies!

Then, all you need to install your mapplet on Google Maps is its URL, and this is most easily obtained from the link with your gadget's name at the upper-right corner of the editor. In Figure 7-2, for example, the link is creating_a_mapplet.xml. Simply right-click on the link and use your browser's equivalent of Copy Link Location. The result, for a file saved in the Gadget Editor, should be a URL something like this:

http://hosting.gmodules.com/ig/gadgets/file/118225708399163529220/your_mapplet.xml

This is the URL you'll need in the next section to install your mapplet.

■Note The Gadget Editor's File menu has a Publish option, which is useful for deploying iGoogle gadgets. It's of less use for Mapplets, though; the only small advantage it offers over the method just described is a bit of XML validation.

Installing by URL

Once you have your mapplet's URL, you're ready to install it into Google Maps and see it in action. So, browse to maps.google.com—you'll probably want to do this in a different browser tab from the Google Gadget Editor, if you're using that—and open the My Maps page. From there, click on the Browse the Directory link at the top of the page.

Once you're in the directory, you need to depart from the usual mapplet installation procedure. Near the top of the page, next to the Search button, you should see a link labeled Add by URL (see Figure 7-3). Clicking this will open a text entry field where you can supply the URL of your mapplet, either on your own domain, or on hosting.gmodules.com if you're using the Google Gadget Editor.

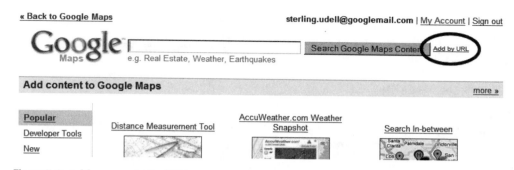

Figure 7-3. *Add a mapplet by URL*

■**Tip** If you try to add a valid mapplet URL but Google tells you it's not found, that typically means you have a problem with your XML. Try pasting your specification into the Mapplet Scratch Pad (discussed in the next section), which should give you a more informative error message.

After you've entered your URL and clicked the Add button, return to the main maps page with the Back to Google Maps link at the upper left of the directory page, and you should see your mapplet installed. Now you can try your mapplet out. Test it in different geographical areas and at different zoom levels, and in conjunction with other mapplets (as discussed in the previous chapter). And give yourself a pat on the back: your content is on the map!

CREATED BY WHOM?

As a mapplet developer, you might find it odd that your own mapplets appear on your My Maps page under Created by Others, rather than Created by Me. Just keep in mind that the vast majority of Google Maps users *aren't* developing their own mapplets, so for most people, that description is accurate.

The same explanation applies when you add one of your own mapplets, and Google gives you a security warning asking if you trust the mapplet's developer. This is normal, and you just need to click the OK button to complete the installation.

Mapplet Developer Tools

Of course, it will often happen that your mapplet doesn't work exactly as you'd like the first time out. When this occurs, you'll naturally need to return to the mapplet's source code, either on your own host or the Google Gadget Editor (as appropriate), and make changes. You won't need to repeat the installation instructions in the previous section, though, unless your mapplet's URL changes.

Also, Google has produced a couple of specialized mapplets to assist you in the development process. You can find them in the standard mapplet directory under the Developer Tools category, as shown in Figure 7-4. My advice is to install both the Mapplet Scratch Pad and the Developer mapplet; read on for a discussion of each.

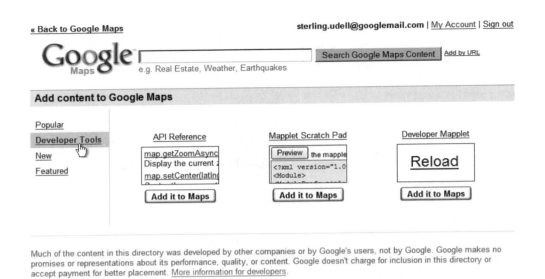

Figure 7-4. *The Developer Tools mapplets*

In case you're wondering, I don't find the other developer mapplet, API Reference, particularly useful. It's basically a long list of the functions in the Mapplets API, and in my opinion, it's unwieldy and less helpful than the official API documentation at http://code.google.com/apis/maps. You can also find additional reference resources in Appendix D of this book.

Developer Mapplet

You'll recall that Google caches your mapplet on its servers, ensuring that it's always available to Maps users without overburdening your own host. This is excellent for bandwidth conservation, but it has a downside when developing mapplets. As you're making changes to your mapplet's XML specification, adding features or hunting down bugs, your latest changes won't show up on Google Maps right away. Instead, you'll still see whatever version Google has cached on their servers, and it can be an hour or two before they refresh their cache.

The Developer Mapplet was created by Google to eliminate this problem. When active, it adds a Reload link to the upper-right corner of the sidebar area for the selected mapplet (you can actually see this link back in Figure 7-1). Clicking this link will cause Google to refresh their cache of your mapplet's XML immediately and reload it into the Maps window.

I strongly recommend that anyone working on mapplets install the Developer Mapplet tool.

Mapplet Scratch Pad

Mapplet Scratch Pad can be thought of as the Google Gadget Editor's little brother on the Maps side. At first glance, it appears similar, with an editor window for XML and a Preview button. Paste in a mapplet specification, and you can immediately see it in action on the map. Nice.

What's missing, however, are all the File operations. This means that there's no way to save your work (it'll be lost when you leave the Scratch Pad), and no way to get a URL to install your mapplet for real.

So the Mapplet Scratch Pad is of limited usefulness when you're developing a real mapplet. Nonetheless, it can be handy for early prototyping (before you copy the XML to a more permanent location), or as a fast way to debug changes to an existing mapplet. There's also hope that Google may improve the Scratch Pad with time, as the mapplet platform continues to mature.

Publishing Your Mapplet

Once you have your mapplet in satisfactory working order, you're nearly ready to share it with the world. There are a few finishing touches to be added, and then we can talk about distribution.

Additional Metadata

If you recall, toward the top of our mapplet specification is the `ModulePrefs` element, whose attributes contain metadata about the mapplet itself. So far we've only seen one, `title`, but there are a handful of others that you're recommended to complete before you release a mapplet. All of the following attributes will be included in the single ModulePrefs tag; we'll see an example in Listing 7-2 later in the chapter.

description

A short summary of what your mapplet does. For example, "Retail store locations for Acme, Inc."

author

Simply your name, as you would want it to appear on the mapplet detail page that Google automatically creates in their directory.

author_email

Your contact e-mail address, also for use in the directory. Note that there are spam considerations here; to help filter it out, Google recommends that you use a Gmail address and append a random word to your name with a plus sign, such as sterling.udell+mapplet@googlemail.com.

thumbnail

The URL of an image to display for your mapplet in the directory listing pages. The image should be 120 pixels wide and 60 pixels tall. This is essentially your mapplet's visual branding in the directory, and as such it typically makes sense to use a company logo or brand if available. But if not, a small screenshot will do.

Both this image and the next must be of type PNG, JPG, or GIF.

screenshot

Another image URL, this one is for placement on your mapplet's detail page in the directory. As its name implies, this image should be a screen capture of your mapplet in action on Google Maps, showing potential users what they'll be getting. It should be 280 pixels wide, and though it can be any height, you shouldn't make it any taller than is necessary to show what your mapplet does.

Those attributes, along with `title`, are what Google considers to be required for mapplets submitted to their directory. They're not *strictly* required—you can submit a mapplet without them—but for a good listing, you're encouraged to include as many as you can.

There are also a couple of optional attributes. Feel free to include the following in your `ModulePrefs`, or not, as you like.

directory_title

If you'd like the title for your mapplet in the directory to be different than what appears in the sidebar on Google Maps, include it here. This is most often used if the title of your mapplet is variable; what's shown in the directory must be constant.

author_location

A text string describing your physical location, such as "Key West, Florida, USA."

Submitting Your Mapplet to the Directory

With all the required metadata attributes present and correct, your creation is ready for submission to the Google mapplet directory. This is the same directory that we've been using throughout this chapter and the last, accessed from the Browse the Directory link on My Maps, and it's the single best way to publicize your new mapplet.

The submission process is quite easy: just point your browser to `http://maps.google.com/ig/submit?synd=mpl` and enter your mapplet specification's URL. Google will do some basic validation before queuing your mapplet for approval; assuming your mapplet meets their terms of service (as I'm sure it will), you can expect to see it in the main directory in one to two weeks.

Once your mapplet is submitted, you can continue to make improvements to it, and these changes will propagate to the directory automatically—there's no need to resubmit. Changes to your mapplet's functionality (in the `Content` section, mostly) will take effect within a couple of hours, subject to Google's ordinary caching procedures. Its directory is only updated every week or two, however, so changes to metadata will appear in that timeframe instead.

Publishing a Link

As well as using Google's directory, you can also publicize your mapplets yourself, on your own web pages. When you do so, it's best to supply a link that takes visitors directly to your mapplet's installation page on Google Maps, allowing users to add it quickly and easily.

The URL for such a link is as follows:

`http://maps.google.com/maps/mpl?moduleurl=[your mapplet's URL]`

Of course, you'll need to substitute your actual mapplet specification's URL for *[your mapplet's URL]*, after the `moduleurl=` parameter.

As suggested in the previous chapter, a good way to integrate such a link is by including it on a web page directly related to the mapplet's functionality. For example, if you have a Contact Us page that lists your company's locations, build that same location list into a mapplet and link to it from that page.

Putting It to Use

We've now covered the entire process of building a mapplet, from conceptualization and proto-typing through testing and deployment. To bring everything together and solidify the lesson, let's look at the specification for a real-world mapplet—and discuss some of its real-world issues.

For this example, the mapplet in question is for Placeopedia, the site dedicated to geo-locating Wikipedia entries that we first encountered back in Chapter 3. Take a look at Listing 7-2 for the complete specification XML, and we'll then go over it piece by piece.

Listing 7-2. *The Placeopedia Mapplet Specification*

```xml
<?xml version="1.0" encoding="UTF-8"?>
<Module>
  <ModulePrefs title="Placeopedia"
               description="The latest 50 Wikipedia entries with locations."
               author="Sterling Udell"
               author_email="sterling.udell+mapplet@googlemail.com"
               screenshot="http://sterlingudell.com/bgmm/chapter_07/screenshot.png"
               thumbnail="http://sterlingudell.com/bgmm/chapter_07/thumbnail.png">
    <Require feature="sharedmap" />
    <Require feature="dynamic-height"/>
  </ModulePrefs>
  <Content type="html"><![CDATA[
    <style type="text/css">
      p {
        font-size: 90%;
      }
    </style>

    <p>
      The latest 50 Wikipedia entries with locations, from
      <a href="http://www.placeopedia.com/">placeopedia.com</a>.
    </p>

    <script type="text/javascript">
      // Initialize the map
      var map = new GMap2();

      // Adjust the height of the sidebar display
      _IG_AdjustIFrameHeight();
```

```
      // Add KML feed
      var geoXml = new GGeoXml('http://www.placeopedia.com/cgi-bin/kml.cgi');
      map.addOverlay(geoXml);
    </script>
  ]]></Content>
</Module>
```

Module Preferences

As always with a mapplet, the XML opens with the `ModulePrefs` section, and here you can see that I've included all the required metadata attributes:

```
<ModulePrefs title="Placeopedia"
             description="The latest 50 Wikipedia entries with locations."
             author="Sterling Udell"
             author_email="sterling.udell+mapplet@googlemail.com"
             screenshot="http://sterlingudell.com/bgmm/chapter_07/screenshot.png"
             thumbnail="http://sterlingudell.com/bgmm/chapter_07/thumbnail.png">
```

The screenshot and thumbnail can be seen in Figures 7-5 and 7-6, containing a snapshot of the map and the Placeopedia logo, respectively.

Figure 7-5. *The Placeopedia mapplet screenshot*

Figure 7-6. *The Placeopedia thumbnail*

Next in the XML come the `Require` feature elements, and in addition to `sharedmap`, I'm also including a standard Gadget library called `dynamic-height`. It's linked in using exactly the same technique:

```
<Require feature="dynamic-height"/>
```

I recommend doing this with virtually every mapplet, and the reason is to overcome a small bug in Google's sidebar rendering. If you look back at Figure 7-1, showing our first mapplet, you'll notice a scrollbar on the lower part of the sidebar. For some reason, Google sets the mapplet sidebar content area to a height of 367 pixels, which means that (on most monitors) this superfluous scrollbar appears. The API's `dynamic-height` library allows us to overcome this bug, setting the height of the sidebar area to match our actual content height.

Don't worry if you don't fully understand that at this point, just take my word for it and include `dynamic-height` in your mapplets. There is also a line of JavaScript you'll need to make it work, but we'll get to that in a couple of pages.

■Note If you've done gadget development before, you might be familiar with the `height` metadata attribute that the Gadgets API defines. Although it sounds like a promising approach to fixing this bug, it doesn't actually work for a mapplet, necessitating the use of `dynamic-height` instead.

Sidebar Content

This conveniently brings us to the sidebar content itself, at the top of the Content element. In this particular mapplet, there's not a lot of additional content required beyond what will be plotted on the map. So, I've just included a note about what the mapplet is showing, with a link back to the Placeopedia web site:

```
<p>
  The latest 50 Wikipedia entries with locations, from
  <a href="http://www.placeopedia.com/">placeopedia.com</a>.
</p>
```

For a slightly more polished appearance, I'm also applying some light CSS to the sidebar content paragraph:

```
p {
  font-size: 90%;
}
```

■Tip One thing you generally *shouldn't* do with sidebar style is to change the font family. Doing so will visually clash with the existing Google Maps fonts and create a jarring appearance; better to simply inherit the font from the Maps page.

I recommend that, as a minimum, a mapplet's sidebar should always contain a credit and link to your site. Although Google shows the hosting domain automatically, it doesn't provide a link to it, and in some cases (like when using the Google Gadget Editor) it may not even be your domain. Not providing a link would squander the viral marketing opportunity that mapplets provide.

But usually, the sidebar is a good place to provide additional content, much as we did with the sidebar on our traditional Maps API pages in Chapters 4 and 5. Be aware, however, that the sidebar is only visible when your mapplet is selected. If the user is combining your mapplet with others into a "mashup of mashups," your mapplet may not be the one selected, and your sidebar content won't be visible. Or, the user may have left the My Maps page and returned to the Google Maps' Search Results.

Therefore, you shouldn't use this area for content that is crucial to your mapplet's function. Instead, try to use the sidebar for additional content that might helpful but isn't strictly necessary, and keep the mission-critical content on the map itself.

Functionality

And now, our feature presentation: the JavaScript that brings the mapplet to life. In this case, the core functionality is contained in the geoXML feed from Placeopedia itself, so there isn't very much coding. Let's take a look at what we do have.

As usual, we begin by initializing the map object, in the simplified Mapplets API way:

```
var map = new GMap2();
```

Next comes a line to invoke the `dynamic-height` library that we `Required` earlier:

```
_IG_AdjustIFrameHeight();
```

As its name implies, this function is adjusting the height of the sidebar area (which is actually an `iframe`). You'll need this line of code whenever you're using `dynamic-height`, but you don't want to call it until your sidebar content is finalized. In other words, if your sidebar has dynamic content placed by JavaScript, call `_IG_AdjustIFrameHeight` after that content has finished loading.

Finally, all that's left to do is to add the geoXML content to the map. The following lines do so, and you should recognize them—they're copied directly from Listing 3-1.

```
var geoXml = new GGeoXml('http://www.placeopedia.com/cgi-bin/kml.cgi');
map.addOverlay(geoXml);
```

Figure 7-7 shows this mapplet in action.

As before, geoXML (via the `GGeoXml` object) is a great, easy way to get content onto the map. However, with mapplets some care needs to be taken regarding when to use geoXML; it's not generally appropriate to bring arbitrary, external content into your own mapplet.

First, doing so would be counter to the entire mapplet philosophy; each mapplet should be a single, self-contained piece of geo-functionality, enabling the user to mix and match on their own.

For example, if you had a web site of hiking trails, it would be great to use the Maps API to map the trails on your own site. It might also make sense to add a GeoRSS feed of weather data to your own map, allowing your visitors to plan hikes based on local conditions. And, it would be perfect to repackage your trail locations as a mapplet. However, what would be less ideal would be to include the weather feed on your mapplet as well; better to let users mix in weather forecasts themselves, if they want to, using a dedicated mapplet from a weather web site.

A related consideration is that, typically, content within a mapplet should be your own. And again, this goes back to the philosophy of mapplets: they're about getting *your* content and functionality onto Google maps. When you publish a mapplet, it's your name that's attached to it, so it should really be your content within it.

This doesn't mean that other sites' content is strictly off limits, but rather that ordinary rules of respect and ownership apply. Ask permission before publishing someone else's content. And if they decline permission, abide by that.

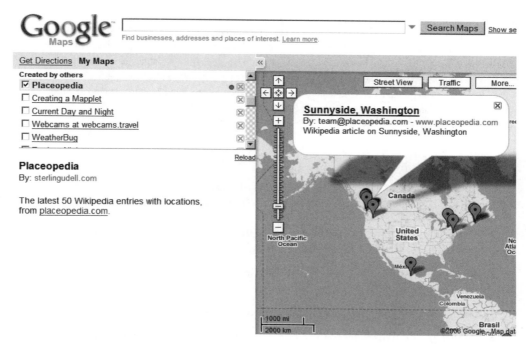

Figure 7-7. *The Placeopedia mapplet*

One exception to this rule is data that's in the public domain, such as information with a Creative Commons license, or published by U.S. government bodies. If you have an idea for a great mapplet based on data from the National Weather Service or the U.S. Geological Survey, for example, go for it!

Tip When you're publishing your own geodata to a mapplet, it's still a good idea to use geoXML. In Chapter 10 I'll cover techniques for creating your own KML and GeoRSS feeds.

QUICK AND DIRTY GEOXML MAPPLETS

In programming, *quick and dirty* refers to any technique that gets the job done with no frills. It won't be pretty, it won't be production quality, but sometimes a quick and dirty solution is exactly what's called for.

Here's a quick and dirty way to make a mapplet from any GeoXML feed. Simply type the following URL into your browser:

```
http://maps.google.com/maps/gx?output=ghapi&q=[geoXML URL]
```

For example, to do this with Placeopedia's feed, you'd substitute `http://www.placeopedia.com/cgi-bin/kml.cgi` for `[geoXML URL]` in the URL. And what you'll get back is an XML document, automatically generated by Google, for a mapplet showing that feed. Wow!

That's the *quick* part. Now for the *dirty*: the resulting mapplet has a couple of serious drawbacks compared to a hand-crafted solution like the one in Listing 7-2. First, the metadata is auto-generated, meaning that you have no control over `title`, `author`, `description`, or any other `ModulePrefs` attributes. And second, you have no control over sidebar content, either (though Google places the geoXML content there, with a technique we'll use ourselves in Chapter 9). For these reasons, you wouldn't want to publish the resulting mapplet. Nonetheless, as a fast way to create a mapplet from KML, it's tough to beat.

Summary

With the grounding you already have in the Maps API, creating mapplets is really quite easy, and this chapter has given you the tools to do it. In a nutshell, the process goes like this:

1. *Create* your mapplet by wrapping the specified XML elements around your sidebar content XHTML and map-controlling JavaScript.

2. *Save* the XML to a public web server (the Google Gadget Editor counts as public, for these purposes).

3. *Install* your mapplet on Google Maps to work the bugs out.

4. *Publish* the final mapplet to the Google directory and, usually, your own web site.

In the next chapter, you'll take your newfound mapplet skills to the next level by learning how to interact with the Google map and the user. I'll also introduce you to some other useful libraries we can borrow from the Gadgets API and give you some guidance that should help your creations integrate well into the mapplet ecosystem.

CHAPTER 8

■■■

Taking Mapplets Further

With the solid mapplet-building foundation that you now possess, you're ready to take the next step and really see what mapplets can do. In this chapter, you'll learn how the Mapplets API combines both the Google Maps and Gadgets APIs into a platform with truly unique capabilities. You'll also continue to stretch your JavaScript abilities, developing skills that will directly increase your potential everywhere in the Google Maps ecosystem.

As usual, we'll accomplish all this by examining a series of real, live mapplet examples, starting with extensions to the geoXML display introduced in the previous chapter. We'll then progress to a utility for looking up place names that will demonstrate a more generalized use of an external service; then we'll move on to a third mapplet utilizing map events and asynchronous code. The chapter finishes with notes on other Mapplets API functionality that you're now ready to tackle, and finally some last pointers on writing "neighborly" mapplet code.

In fact, the truth is that the Mapplets API isn't all *that* big, and before we're done here you'll be poised to make full use of it.

Geodata Mapplets

One of the easiest mapplets to produce, a simple wrapper for your geodata, is also one of the best. It gets your content out to the community of Google Maps users, enriching the geoweb while raising your own profile. And as you saw in the previous chapter, such a mapplet is quite easy to build. So taking the simple geodata mapplet introduced there and improving on it is a good segue into further mapplet development.

The Placeopedia Mapplet, Revisited

Listing 8-1 gets us started. It's the same Placeopedia content mapplet as you've already seen, with the significant changes from Listing 7-2 highlighted. As usual, I'll go over the changes one by one in the next few pages.

Listing 8-1. *Extending the Placeopedia Content Mapplet*

```xml
<?xml version="1.0" encoding="UTF-8"?>
<Module>
  <ModulePrefs title="Placeopedia"
               description="The latest Wikipedia entries with locations."
               author="Sterling Udell"
               author_email="sterling.udell+mapplet@googlemail.com"
            screenshot="http://sterlingudell.com/bgmm/chapter_07/screenshot.png"
            thumbnail="http://sterlingudell.com/bgmm/chapter_07/thumbnail.png">
    <Require feature="sharedmap" />
    <Require feature="dynamic-height"/>
  </ModulePrefs>
  <UserPref name="Entries"
            datatype="enum"
            default_value="25">
    <EnumValue value="10" />
    <EnumValue value="25" />
    <EnumValue value="50" />
  </UserPref>
  <Content type="html"><![CDATA[
    <style type="text/css">
      p {
        font-size: 90%;
      }
    </style>

    <p>
      The latest Wikipedia entries with locations, from
      <a href="http://www.placeopedia.com/">placeopedia.com</a>.
    </p>

    <script type="text/javascript">
      // Initialize the map
      var map = new GMap2();

      // Adjust the height of the sidebar display
      _IG_AdjustIFrameHeight();

      // Build a URL for the Placeopedia feed based on the user's preferred count
      var prefs = new _IG_Prefs();
      var entries = prefs.getString('Entries');
      var url = 'http://www.placeopedia.com/cgi-bin/rss.cgi?num_results=' + entries;
```

```
        // Retrieve and display the GeoRSS feed
        var geoXml = new GGeoXml(url);
        map.addOverlay(geoXml);
      </script>
    ]]></Content>
</Module>
```

User Preferences

The key change here is the addition of the UserPref XML element to the mapplet specification. As its name implies, this section is used for defining user preferences, allowing people who install your mapplet to change their own settings. In this case, I'm including an option for the number of Placeopedia entries to show on the map at once.

■**Note** UserPref is a standard module inherited into the Mapplets API from its Gadgets predecessor, like the dynamic-height feature introduced in the previous chapter.

A typical UserPref tag looks like this:

```
<UserPref name="Entries"
          datatype="enum"
          default_value="25">
```

Fairly self-explanatory, I hope; the attributes of the UserPref element are where you define what sort of preference-setting you want to support. Here are the attributes I'm using:

name: What this specific user preference is called, both in Google's onscreen user interface for setting it and internally in your code.

datatype: What sort of information this preference holds. In my case, enum stands for *enumerated*, meaning a specific list of options. You'll find a complete discussion of datatype in the next couple of pages.

default_value: When the user first installs the mapplet, this attribute indicates the starting value for the preference.
There are also a couple of other attributes that I'm not using here, but which you might find useful:

display_name: Related to name, this attribute if supplied will control what name Google displays to the user for this preference. In your code, you'll still use the original name value.

required: Defines whether the user is allowed to save this preference without setting a value or not. In your XML, you supply this attribute as either required="true" or required="false".

enum Values

When the datatype is enum, the UserPref element will contain the list of options available to the user, specified as EnumValue tags. For example:

```
<EnumValue value="10" />
<EnumValue value="25" />
<EnumValue value="50" />
```

In this case, I'm allowing the user the option of showing 10, 25, or 50 Placeopedia entries on the map at a time. You can supply as many EnumValue tags as you like, as appropriate for your own mapplet's needs.

The User Interface

When you include one or more UserPref elements in your specification, Google adds an Edit Settings link to your mapplet's sidebar. Clicking this link opens an automatically generated settings area where the user can make their choices; see Figure 8-1 for the Placeopedia example.

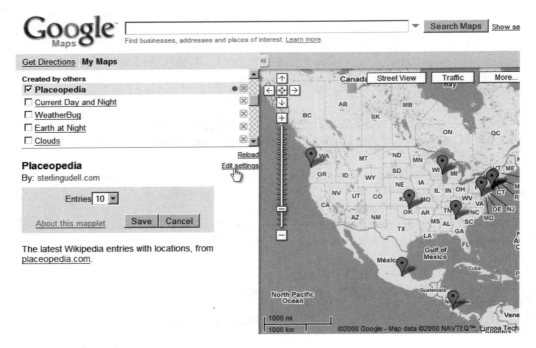

Figure 8-1. *Edit settings*

■Note You also get an About This Mapplet link in the settings area, linking back to your mapplet's directory detail page (as discussed in the previous chapter).

Other `UserPref` Data Types

As mentioned, the `datatype` attribute has other possible values besides `enum`. Here's a rundown of each and what they're used for:

`string`: The easiest data type to understand, `string` can contain any ordinary character data.

`bool`: Short for *Boolean*, `bool` contains either a "true" or "false" value, represented in the Edit Settings area with a checkbox. For example, one use for this might be to turn an optional mapplet feature on or off.

GEORGE BOOLE

Boolean data, as seen here in the `bool datatype`, is named after nineteenth-century British mathematician George Boole. Although relatively unappreciated in his own time, Boole's groundbreaking work in the study of logical expressions involving only "true" and "false" values laid the theoretical foundation for much of the modern computer era. Computers break everything down into ones and zeros (also known as *binary digits*, or *bits*), and the ways in which bits combine follow the laws worked out by Boole. So, single-bit data types are typically named in his honor.

`location`: A sort of mini-geocoder, `location` allows the user to enter a city, state, or ZIP code. Google Maps will do its best to translate it into latitude and longitude coordinates, which you can then access in your JavaScript.

`hidden`: Like a `string`, but not visible in the Edit Settings area, and therefore not changeable by the user. Your first reaction might well be, "What's the point then?" It's generally used for storing settings from your mapplet code, rather than from the user directly; you'll see `hidden` in action later in the chapter.

`list`: A set of strings that the user can edit and add to. The `list` type is more advanced in its usage, so I'm not going to cover it here. If you're interested, please see the Google Gadgets API documentation for details.

`enum`: As discussed in the previous section, a list of specific options.

Using the Preferences

So now you know the options for `UserPref`, and how the user makes her choices. What remains is to make use of it in the JavaScript code, adapting its behavior to the user's preferences. This brings us to the second set of changes in Listing 8-1, within the `script` element. Let's look at them one line at a time.

First, you need to initialize an API object for accessing the preferences. Here's how it's done:

```
var prefs = new _IG_Prefs();
```

Note that the object name begins with `_IG_`, rather than `G` as with most API objects you've run across previously. This is an indication that it's from the iGoogle Gadgets API originally, rather than the Maps API that you're more familiar with.

Next you ask the `prefs` object for the value of the preference named `Entries` and assign it to an `entries` variable of your own:

```
var entries = prefs.getString('Entries');
```

You use `getString` here because you'll want a character-string value in the next line. There are alternatives for this discussed in the next section.

So with the user's `entries` preference in hand, you can simply tack it onto the end of the appropriate Placeopedia geodata feed URL:

```
var url = 'http://www.placeopedia.com/cgi-bin/rss.cgi?num_results=' + entries;
```

This URL is a minor shift from the previous chapter, where we were using Placeopedia's KML; we need to switch to their GeoRSS to be able to limit the number of entries.

And finally, all that remains is to add the GeoRSS to the map, in the same way as we've been doing since Chapter 3:

```
var geoXml = new GGeoXml(url);
map.addOverlay(geoXml);
```

Using Other Data Types

Most of the time you'll be using `getString` to retrieve preference values, as shown in the previous section and Listing 8-1. But occasionally, you'll need to work more directly with another data type. The API provides a few alternatives to `getString` for doing so, as described in the following list.

getBool: When a `UserPref` has `datatype="bool"`, you'll usually extract the value with the `getBool` function. As an example, recall the Arches National Park example from Chapter 4, which had a user-controllable campgrounds overlay. If you were doing something similar in a mapplet, your code might look like the following (compare with the last few lines of Listing 4-12):

```
if (prefs.getBool('Campgrounds'))
  geoXml.show();
else
  geoXml.hide();
```

Since the `getBool` returns either a `true` or `false` value, we're able to use it directly in our JavaScript `if` statement.

getInt: Short for "get integer." When you need to do any sort of numerical processing with a preference value, you'll be likely to use `getInt` to get an integer out. For example, if we had a `UserPref` as in Listing 8-1 but were doing the marker processing ourselves, we'd likely use an integer in the JavaScript code to limit the results.

getArray: A more advanced data type, typically used in conjunction with `datatype="list"`. So again, it's really beyond the scope of this book to discuss in detail.

Functionality Mapplets

As discussed early in the chapter, some of the best (and easiest) mapplets are those that simply contain geodata. However, the Mapplets API is bigger than that; it actually allows you to add *functionality* to Google Maps, changing how the web site itself works. And since we've pretty well covered pure-geodata mapplets, it's time to raise your game and start building that functionality.

So in the remainder of this chapter, we'll examine two relatively simple functionality mapplets. The features they add to Google Maps aren't especially profound or exciting, but they do illustrate this next level of mapplet development's core concepts. As such, they should give you some useful tools if you want to take on the challenge and add your own workings to Google Maps.

The Nearest Place Name Mapplet

My first functionality example will look up the name of the nearest place to anywhere the user clicks on the map. Such a linkage—of map coordinates to place names—is called *geonaming*, and our mapplet will use a free web service from geonames.org to accomplish this. It's analogous to the API's own services (such as geocoding), but because it's external, bringing it on board will be a little bit more work.

■**Note** Looking up geographic information from coordinates like this is generally called *reverse geocoding*, as the opposite of the ordinary geocoding introduced in Chapter 5 (looking up coordinates from addresses).

So, I'm going to require several, mostly distinct, pieces of functionality:

1. Capture a click on the map, including its coordinates.

2. Place a marker at those coordinates.

3. Call the geoname service for those coordinates.

4. Format the results (the place name) into an infowindow for the marker from step 2.

Let's go over the code for each of those steps; then I'll bring them all together into the complete mapplet specification.

■**Caution** As a free service, geonames.org has no obligation of response time, or even availability. As always when mashing up third-party services, you use it at your own risk.

Capturing a Map Click

Map click handling starts exactly as you'd expect, with an event handler attached to a click event:

```
GEvent.addListener(map, 'click', mapClick);
```

However, the click handler itself isn't at all what you're likely to expect, because of a deceptively slight peculiarity in the Google Maps user interface. Specifically, Google has gotten its single-click and double-click events wrong. When you double-click on a Google map, you actually generate two single-click events, which isn't how it's supposed to work. A single-click event should *only* occur when it's *not* part of a double-click; that's the standard in other user interfaces.

■**Note** Google is aware of this double-click problem (see `http://tinyurl.com/6r9xjl`), but as of this writing, has issued no timetable for fixing it. If and when a fix is made, however, this workaround should continue to function.

All of this causes a problem for mapplets like ours, predominantly because Google has defined (and its users expect) a map zoom event on a double-click. Users *don't* expect a double-click on the map to place a marker. Therefore, a naive click-event implementation will lead to unexpected map behavior, quickly followed by user frustration. Not good.

So we work around the problem ourselves. My solution is based on a JavaScript feature called a *timeout*, and it's basically a way to delay a piece of code for a certain length of time before it executes. When the base click event occurs, I can use a timeout to delay the code I really want to occur (placing a marker) for a certain length of time, say half a second. This helps us because, if a *second* click occurs within that half-second, I know that the user actually intended a double-click—so I cancel the timeout, and thus my marker-placement process.

The code to implement this can be found in Listing 8-2. It's the same idea just described, only translated into JavaScript.

Listing 8-2. *The Single-Click Timeout Workaround*

```
var timeout;
var clickCoords;

function mapClick(overlay, coordinates)
{
  if (overlay != null)
    // Click wasn't on "empty" map space, so don't go any further
    return;

  if (timeout == null)
  {
    // The first click we've had recently => start a timeout for the lookup
    clickCoords = coordinates;
    timeout = setTimeout('placeMarker()', 500);
  }
  else
  {
    // Second click means it's a double-click, so cancel the lookup timeout
    clearTimeout(timeout)
```

```
      timeout = null;
   }
};
```

There are a few things to note from Listing 8-2:

- The `timeout` and `clickCoords` variables must be declared outside the `mapClick` handler function, so that their values remain from one click to the next. For more information see the section on variable scope in Appendix B.

- I use the existence of the timeout itself to establish whether this is the first or second click. If the timeout is running, then we must be in second-click territory.

- You need to save the clicked coordinates (in the `clickCoords` variable) for the `placeMarker` function that will run half a second later.

- The `setTimeout` function itself takes, as a first parameter, a *string* containing the code to be run. Its second parameter is the length of the delay, in *milliseconds* (thousandths of a second), so that 500 milliseconds = ½ second.

It's a long way around the block just to capture a map click, but unfortunately that's the way things sometimes work in the real world of programming. Hopefully, you'll find this a handy tool to have in your repertoire to avoid frustrated users when implementing click events in your mapplets.

■**Note** It's not just mapplets; the traditional Maps API suffers from this same bug in the click event. So if you need to implement a map click handler in a Maps API application, I recommend you use this same approach, for the same reasons.

Placing a Marker

After the click handler in the previous section, placing the map marker is relatively easy. See for yourself in Listing 8-3.

Listing 8-3. *Placing the Map Marker*

```
function placeMarker()
{
   if (marker == null)
   {
      // Marker doesn't exist yet, so create it now
      marker = new GMarker(clickCoords);
      map.addOverlay(marker);
   }
   else
      // Move the marker to the new coordinates
      marker.setPoint(clickCoords);
```

```
  // Prepare for the next click
  timeout = null;
};
```

It mostly follows a pattern introduced in Chapter 5 (Listing 5-3, to be precise), where you check to see if the marker exists and only create it if it doesn't. This allows you to reuse a single marker object by moving it around the map, instead of cluttering things up by repeatedly creating new ones.

There's just one other line of code worth a mention here. Right at the end of the function, I'm setting timeout back to null. This ensures that the next time a map click occurs, the handler back in Listing 8-2 will function correctly.

SAVING PRIVATE MARKERS

In the Place Name mapplet, the marker that is added to the map is temporary, meaning that after you leave Google Maps it'll be gone. What if you wanted to save a marker's location? How would you go about it?

It turns out that the easiest way is to use hidden user preferences. As I mentioned earlier in the chapter, these are useful for saving data that doesn't come explicitly from user settings—and the coordinates of a map click are a perfect example.

I'm not going to build an entire mapplet to illustrate it, but there are basically four pieces that would need to be added. First, your mapplet needs to Require one more API feature, called setprefs, to enable setting of user preferences from JavaScript:

`<Require feature="setprefs" />`

Second, you'll need the UserPref fields for the coordinates:

```
<UserPref datatype="hidden" name="latitude" />
<UserPref datatype="hidden" name="longitude" />
```

Third, you'll need to do the actual saving, which will involve adding the following lines to the placeMarker function of Listing 8-3:

```
prefs.set('latitude', clickCoords.lat());
prefs.set('longitude', clickCoords.lng());
```

The last part's the hardest. In the main mapplet code—probably right after initializing the clickIcon object—you need to place the marker at the UserPref coordinates, using getString calls much as we did earlier:

```
var prefs = new _IG_Prefs();
if (prefs.getString('latitude') != '')
{
  clickCoords = new GLatLng(parseFloat(prefs.getString('latitude')),
                       parseFloat(prefs.getString('longitude')));
  placeMarker();
}
```

That's it, in a nutshell. It's not trivial, but not especially hard either; if you have a mapplet that needs to save a map location, this should be enough to get you started.

Calling the Geoname Service

This is the easiest step of the four, and involves adding just a few lines to the `placeMarker` function you already have. Listing 8-4 highlights the new additions.

Listing 8-4. *Sending the Marker Coordinates to the Geoname Service*

```
function placeMarker()
{
  if (marker == null)
  {
    // Marker doesn't exist yet, so create it now
    marker = new GMarker(clickCoords);
    map.addOverlay(marker);
  }
  else
    // Move the marker to the new coordinates
    marker.setPoint(clickCoords);

  // Build and retrieve the placename lookup URL from the clicked coordinates
  var url = 'http://ws.geonames.org/findNearbyPlaceNameJSON?lat=' +
            clickCoords.lat() + '&lng=' + clickCoords.lng();
  _IG_FetchContent(url, afterGeoname);

  // Prepare for the next click
  timeout = null;
};
```

Building the URL should look quite familiar to you by now; we've done something like it several times, most recently in Listing 8-1. It involves adding the `lat` and `lng` from `clickCoords` to the base service URL at `geonames.org`.

So, the only really new part is the call to `_IG_FetchContent`, and it's not very hard either. It's another Gadgets API function (as evidenced by its `_IG_` prefix) that, not surprisingly, fetches the content of a given URL from the Internet. And when it's finished, it'll call back to the `afterGeoname` function, to be covered in the next section.

Formatting the Place Name

We're nearly there now. We've processed the map click, placed a marker there, and called the geoname service with the clicked coordinates. All that's left to do is handle the results, and this can be seen in Listing 8-5, the geoname callback function.

Listing 8-5. *Making an Infowindow out of the Geoname Results*

```
function afterGeoname(responseText)
{
  // Evaluate the JSON response to extract the data from it
  var responseData = json_parse(responseText);
```

```
  if (responseData.geonames.length == 0)
  {
    // No place name found; let the user know with a simple message
    var content = 'No nearby place name found.';
  }
  else
  {
    // Place name found successfully; build it into an infowindow
    var place = responseData.geonames[0];
    var miles = parseFloat(place.distance) / 1.61;
    var content = miles.toFixed(2) + ' miles from ' + place.name + ',<br />' +
                  place.adminName1 + ', ' + place.countryName;
  }

  // Attach the infowindow content to the marker, and also show it now
  marker.openInfoWindow(content);
  marker.bindInfoWindow(content);
};
```

There are quite a few things going on here, so let's break it down.

To begin with, the response from _IG_FetchContent always arrives as plain text, so your first task is to convert that response into JavaScript data that you can work with. This you'll do with the help of the json_parse function:

```
var responseData = json_parse(responseText);
```

This particular geoname service returns its results in *JSON*, or JavaScript Object Notation, and json_parse converts that to an actual JavaScript object that contains all the geoname information, ready for use.

■**Note** In Chapter 10 and Appendix B you'll learn more about JSON, its related formats, and the issues surrounding its use. For now, just notice how easy it makes importing the geoname data, and rejoice.

So let's get started using it. First up, you need to confirm that a place name was actually found (as opposed to coordinates truly in the middle of nowhere).

```
if (responseData.geonames.length == 0)
  var content = 'No nearby place name found.';
```

Fairly simple: length of zero means that no nearby place could be found, so I just put that message in the content variable for later display.

Assuming that a place name *was* found, however, you'll want more interesting content:

```
var place = responseData.geonames[0];
var miles = parseFloat(place.distance) / 1.61;
var content = miles.toFixed(2) + ' miles from ' + place.name + ',<br />' +
              place.adminName1 + ', ' + place.countryName;
```

There are three things going on here:

1. You assign a variable, `place`, to the relevant geoname result because it makes the next couple of lines easier.

2. You convert the `distance` field of `place` to miles (the native result from geonames.org is in kilometers, of which there are roughly 1.61 per mile).

3. You assemble that distance, along with the `place`'s `name`, `countryName`, and `adminName1` (state/province) into an HTML string.

So whether a place name was found or not, you now have a `content` variable that's ready to display to the user. All that remains is to do so, in the form of a standard Google Maps infowindow:

```
marker.openInfoWindow(content);
marker.bindInfoWindow(content);
```

The first line shows the infowindow to the user immediately, and the second binds the same content to the marker. This latter is necessary to ensure that the content will still be there if the user closes the infowindow and then clicks on the marker again.

parseFloat AND toFixed

Listing 8-5 introduces two new JavaScript functions that are something of a mirror image of each other, `parseFloat` and `toFixed`. If you're familiar with programming, these are *type conversion* functions. If not, they basically are used to convert variables between strings and numbers. In most programming languages, the *type* of a variable is important; you can't do math with strings, and you need to be careful how numbers print on screen.

Here's how these two work:

- `parseFloat` takes a string value, such as `'1.6852'`, and attempts to convert it to a number. In this case, we then take that number (the distance in kilometers) and do some math on it to convert it to miles.

- `toFixed` takes a number, such as `1.0467080745341614906832298136646`, and formats it as a string. The parameter to `toFixed` (2 in this case) specifies how many decimal points we want the formatted string to have. So here, the result is `'1.05'`.

In JavaScript you frequently don't need to worry too much about type conversions, but when you do, `parseFloat` and `toFixed` are helpful to have in your back pocket.

Bringing It All Together

That completes the interesting bits of the Nearest Place Name mapplet. The results are visible in Figure 8-2, and the full mapplet specification can be found in Listing 8-6.

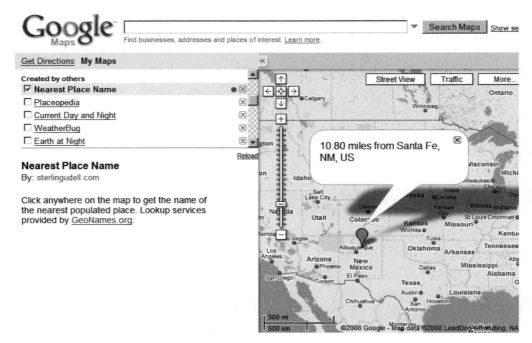

Figure 8-2. *The Nearest Place Name mapplet in action*

Listing 8-6. *The Full Specification of the Nearest Place Name Mapplet*

```
<?xml version="1.0" encoding="UTF-8"?>
<Module>
  <ModulePrefs title="Nearest Place Name"
               description="Find the name of the place nearest to a click the map."
               author="Sterling Udell"
               author_email="sterling.udell+mapplet@googlemail.com"
               screenshot="http://sterlingudell.com/bgmm/chapter_08/geoname_scr.png" ➥
               thumbnail="http://sterlingudell.com/bgmm/chapter_08/geoname_thm.png"> ➥
    <Require feature="sharedmap" />
    <Require feature="dynamic-height"/>
  </ModulePrefs>
  <Content type="html"><![CDATA[
    <style type="text/css">
      p {
        font-size: 90%;
      }
    </style>
```

```
<p>
  Click anywhere on the map to get the name of the nearest populated place.
  Lookup services provided by <a href="http://geonames.org/">GeoNames.org</a>.
</p>

<script type="text/javascript"
        src="http://sterlingudell.com/bgmm/json_parse.js"></script>
<script type="text/javascript">
  function mapClick(overlay, coordinates)
  {
    // mapClick: event handler to prepare for the placename-lookup

    if (overlay != null)
      // Click wasn't on "empty" map space, so don't go any further
      return;

    if (timeout == null)
    {
      // The first click we've had recently => start a timeout for the lookup
      clickCoords = coordinates;
      timeout = setTimeout('placeMarker()', 500);
    }
    else
    {
      // Second click means it's a double-click, so cancel the lookup timeout
      clearTimeout(timeout)
      timeout = null;
    }
  };

  function placeMarker()
  {
    // placeMarker: Only called after a true single click, so do the lookup

    if (clickCoords == null)
      // We have no clicked coordinates for some reason, so we can't proceed
      return;

    if (marker == null)
    {
      // Marker doesn't exist yet, so create it now
      marker = new GMarker(clickCoords, {icon: clickIcon});
      map.addOverlay(marker);
    }
    else
    {
```

```
      // Move the marker to the new coords and reset it to the default icon
      marker.setPoint(clickCoords);
      marker.setImage(clickIcon.image);
    }

    // Build and retrieve the placename lookup URL from the clicked coordinates
    var url = 'http://ws.geonames.org/findNearbyPlaceNameJSON?lat=' +
              clickCoords.lat() + '&lng=' + clickCoords.lng();
    _IG_FetchContent(url, afterGeoname);

    // Prepare for the next click
    timeout = null;
  };

function afterGeoname(responseText)
{
  // afterGeoname: callback when the placename lookup has completed

  // Evaluate the JSON response to extract the data from it
  var responseData = json_parse(responseText);

  if (responseData.geonames.length == 0)
  {
    // No place name found; let the user know with a simple message
    marker.setImage('http://sterlingudell.com/bgmm/markers/red.png');
    var content = 'No nearby place name found.';
  }
  else
  {
    // Place name found successfully; build it into an infowindow
    marker.setImage('http://sterlingudell.com/bgmm/markers/green.png');
    var place = responseData.geonames[0];
    var miles = parseFloat(place.distance) / 1.61;
    var content = miles.toFixed(2) + ' miles from ' + place.name + ',<br />' +
                  place.adminName1 + ', ' + place.countryName;
  }

  // Show the infowindow content, and also bind it to the marker for later use
  marker.openInfoWindow(content);
  marker.bindInfoWindow(content);
};

// END FUNCTION DECLARATIONS - BEGIN MAIN MAPPLET CODE
```

```
        // Declare variables for later use
        var timeout;
        var clickCoords;
        var marker;

        // Initialize the map
        var map = new GMap2();

        // Create the default clicked placemark icon
        var clickIcon = new GIcon(G_DEFAULT_ICON);
        clickIcon.image = 'http://sterlingudell.com/bgmm/markers/yellow.png';

        // Attach map event to handle the click behavior
        GEvent.addListener(map, 'click', mapClick);

        // Adjust the height of the sidebar display
        _IG_AdjustIFrameHeight();
    </script>
  ]]></Content>
</Module>
```

A few things have been added here, and I've highlighted those lines. First, I'm linking in the external JavaScript file json_parse.js. This contains the json_parse function introduced in Listing 8-5, which isn't part of a Google API but was written by Douglas Crockford, the creator of JSON.

Next, notice that there's some defensive coding at the beginning of both the mapClick and placeMarker functions, exiting if necessary conditions don't exist. The return statement, incidentally, just exits a function immediately.

Finally, I've included a few lines of code to change the marker color at various points in the process. When first placed on the map, and while the geoname lookup is in process, it's yellow; if the lookup fails, it turns red; or for a successful lookup, it turns green. This provides visual feedback to the user that something is happening for the few seconds that the lookup often takes.

THE ORDER OF THINGS

Possibly the most surprising aspect to the JavaScript in Listing 8-6 is the location of the callback functions from Listings 8-2 through 8-5. Here the functions come *before* the main mapplet code, where (in previous chapters) things were the other way around. Why?

It has to do with the order in which things happen in the JavaScript, and specifically, this line:

```
GEvent.addListener(map, 'click', mapClick);
```

When you add that event listener, the mapClick function needs to have already been declared, as such:

```
function mapClick(overlay, coordinates)
{
  ...
};
```

So that declaration needs to have been done before it can be referenced in the addListener call, right? Hence the placing of the function earlier in the code than the addListener. And for sake of consistency, I've grouped all the functions together at the top of the script element.

In our previous JavaScript examples, starting way back in Listing 3-2, it made more logical sense to put the main body of code first and the function declarations second. And it was OK to do this, because we didn't have anything equivalent to the addListener of Listing 8-6 in the main body of code. All such calls were themselves within other functions, and didn't get executed until after the page had loaded and all functions had been declared.

As a corollary, note that code *inside* a function declaration doesn't execute when the function is *declared*, it executes when the function is *called*. So objects, variables, etc. inside the declaration don't need to exist when the function is declared, only when it's called.

The Map Center Monitor Mapplet

My next example mapplet provides the user with a real-time display of the map's center point coordinates (Figure 8-3). The actual display is provided in the mapplet's title, and it also places a crosshair overlay at the center of the map to aid in precise positioning. Such a mapplet is one possible solution to answering the "Where am I?" question, extracting latitude/longitude coordinates out of Google Maps.

You might be wondering why I've chosen to use the mapplet's title for the coordinates display, rather than some XHTML element in the sidebar. The reason is to enhance its compatibility with other mapplets: since the title is always shown in the "Created by others" section, the coordinates will be visible *even if my mapplet isn't selected* at the moment. So if a user activates my Map Center Monitor mapplet and then activates any other mapplet, the center coordinates will still be visible, even though I no longer have control of the main sidebar area.

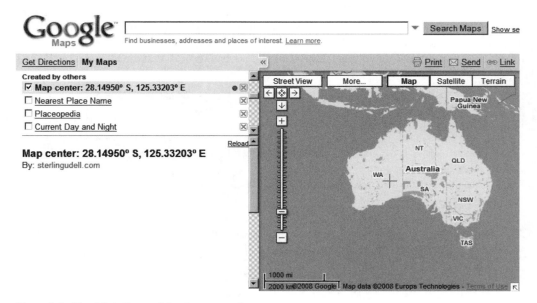

Figure 8-3. *The Map Center Monitor mapplet*

So as developers, how will we go about making this happen? As with the last example, it's best to start out with a high-level plan for what the code will need to accomplish. So here's a bird's eye view of the Map Center Monitor:

1. Set up the crosshair overlay on the map center.

2. Display the map center coordinates in the mapplet's title.

3. Whenever the map moves, display the new center coordinates.

Not surprisingly, we'll use event handlers to detect map movement, though we'll again need to work around a shortcoming of the Mapplets API.

Main Mapplet Code

First things first, though. Before you're ready to implement the events, you'll need to set things up in the main mapplet JavaScript code, as found in Listing 8-7.

Listing 8-7. *JavaScript for the Main Map Center Monitor Mapplet*

```
// Declare variables for later use
var moving = false;
var lastCenter = new GLatLng(90, 0);

// Initialize the map
var map = new GMap2();

// Create the center "crosshair" overlay
var crosshair = new GScreenOverlay(
  'http://sterlingudell.com/bgmm/markers/crosshair.png', // image URL
  new GScreenPoint(0.5, 0.5, 'fraction', 'fraction'),      // screen offset
  new GScreenPoint(11, 12, 'pixel', 'pixel'),              // overlay offset
  new GScreenSize(24, 24, 'pixel', 'pixel')                // overlay size
);
map.addOverlay(crosshair);

// Attach several events to be called when the map moves
GEvent.addListener(map, 'movestart', mapMoveStart);
GEvent.addListener(map, 'moveend',   mapMoveEnd);
GEvent.addListener(map, 'zoomend',   mapZoomEnd);

// Initialize the center display
map.getCenterAsync(afterGetCenter);

// Adjust the height of the sidebar display
_IG_AdjustIFrameHeight();
```

The first couple of sections, declaring variables and initializing the map, should look very familiar to you. We've been using minor variations on those themes all through the book.

So, let's move directly to the third section of Listing 8-7, creating the crosshair overlay—one of the main features of this mapplet, placed at the center of the map to aid users in aligning it precisely.

The mechanism you'll use to accomplish this is a new API object, GScreenOverlay. You've come across overlays of various sorts before—markers, geoXML data, and traffic, to name a few—but GScreenOverlay is fundamentally different. All the previous overlays have been geospatial, fixed to the *map surface* at specific latitude/longitude coordinates. But that's not how the crosshair should work; it needs to stay fixed to a specific *screen* location, the center of the map window, while the map surface is free to move underneath it. Hence the name, GScreenOverlay: an overlay attached to the screen instead of the map.

In order to get everything to work right, a screen overlay needs several parameters, including some new supporting objects. It's a bit complicated, but the first parameter is easy enough, the URL of the image you want to use as the overlay:

```
'http://sterlingudell.com/bgmm/markers/crosshair.png'
```

We'll look at this image in a bit more detail in a moment.

Next up is the location of the overlay on the screen, using a new GScreenPoint object:

```
new GScreenPoint(0.5, 0.5, 'fraction', 'fraction')
```

This one takes a bit of explaining. GScreenPoint can specify a location on the screen in two ways, either as absolute pixel measurements or as a fraction (both of which are measured from the bottom-left corner). This example uses the latter; I want the crosshair at the center of the screen, and one way to describe the *center* is "halfway across and halfway up." So as a *fraction* of the screen, the crosshair's position is ½, or 0.5, in both dimensions.

It may become clearer as we examine the next parameter, the offset *within* the overlay image. To make everything line up, you need the "cross" in the crosshair to be aligned with the center of the screen, meaning that you need to tell the API what the offset of that point within the image is. Here's how you do it:

```
new GScreenPoint(11, 12, 'pixel', 'pixel')
```

In other words, the alignment point is 11 pixels across and 12 pixels up from the bottom-left corner of the image. Note that the measurement unit this time is pixel rather than fraction.

Where did the 11 and 12 come from? From the crosshair image itself, as can be seen in Figure 8-4. When I created the image in a graphics program, I just counted pixels to find the correct offset.

The last parameter to GScreenOverlay is relatively simple, specifying the size of the overlay image. Again, I know from creating it that it's 24 pixels square, and the code looks like this:

```
new GScreenSize(24, 24, 'pixel', 'pixel')
```

Although this is a different object, GScreenSize rather than GScreenPoint, it works just the same. Note that GScreenSize can also take fraction as a unit; this would be used for an overlay covering a percentage of the map viewport (rather than a fixed pixel size).

Finally, you're done creating the GScreenOverlay object and are ready to add it to the map. You do this using the same AddOverlay function you're already familiar with:

```
map.addOverlay(crosshair);
```

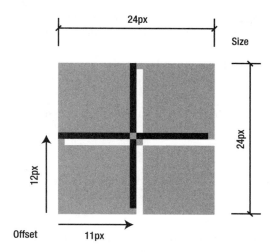

Figure 8-4. *The crosshair image, with its offset and size coordinates*

The GScreenOverlay object isn't one you're likely to use often—most geodata and functionality will be attached to the map, rather than the viewport—but there are times like this when it's indispensable.

Handling the Events

Moving on to the next section of Listing 8-7, you're ready to attach some event handlers to enable the main functionality of the mapplet, tracking the movement of the map center:

```
GEvent.addListener(map, 'movestart', mapMoveStart);
GEvent.addListener(map, 'moveend',   mapMoveEnd);
GEvent.addListener(map, 'zoomend',   mapZoomEnd);
```

You're probably wondering, why so many? Don't we just want an event for when the map moves? Well, yes, but unfortunately the GMap object doesn't have a simple move event. So, as with the click handler in the previous example, we're going to need to make the effort to build it ourselves. And as it turns out, the three events shown here will do the trick.

First up is the movestart event; as its name implies, this event triggers when the map *begins* to move for virtually any reason. Typically, movement happens in response to the user either dragging the map with her mouse or clicking on one of the arrow buttons at the upper left of the map pane. In any case, this is the signal that map movement is getting underway.

Second is movestart's counterpart, moveend. Not surprisingly, this event fires when the current bit of movement has completed; for example, when the user releases their mouse button and "drops" the map after dragging it around.

The third event, zoomend, is the analog to moveend for when the map is being zoomed in and out. Its necessity in this process is a bit more subtle: if the user double-clicks somewhere on the map, it will zoom in *on that clicked point,* changing the map center. So our Monitor needs to know about it, but unfortunately, no movestart or moveend events are fired by a double-click—and therefore, we'll again need to handle it ourselves.

Now that you're clear on when each event is triggered, we're ready to plan what you're going to do with them. Here's the plan:

movestart: Start a process that will continually update the map center display and crosshair.

moveend: Stop the process.

zoomend: Run the process once (not continually) for the new, double-clicked map center.

Implementing the Event Handlers

Once you're comfortable with this bird's-eye view of the event handlers, you'll find the JavaScript to make it happen in Listing 8-8.

Listing 8-8. *The Map Movement Event Handlers*

```
function mapMoveStart()
{
  moving = true;
  map.getCenterAsync(afterGetCenter);
};

function mapMoveEnd()
{
  moving = false;
};

function mapZoomEnd()
{
  map.getCenterAsync(afterGetCenter);
};
```

These handler implementations are actually remarkably easy. There are two keys that make this workaround work, and the Boolean variable moving is the first. As its name suggests, it's an indicator for when a map move is underway; we set it to true in mapMoveStart and false in mapMoveEnd.

All the heavy lifting is done inside the afterGetCenter callback function you see referenced here, and which I'll cover in the next section. Right now, all you need to know about afterGetCenter is that it will continually update the map center display and crosshair as long as moving is true.

FLAGS

In Listing 8-8, `moving` is a particular sort of variable we often call a *flag*. Flags are Boolean variables used to indicate the presence of some particular condition; the analogy with flags in the real world can be seen in common expressions like "I've flagged that for further review." In programming, we refer to the flag being *set* when the variable (and thus the associated condition) is `true`, and *cleared* when it's `false`.

So let's revisit our handler overview list, but at a slightly lower level:

`movestart:` Set the `moving` flag, and start the `afterGetCenter` process.

`moveend:` Clear the `moving` flag. (The `afterGetCenter` process will then stop on its own.)

`zoomend:` Run the `afterGetCenter` process once. (It will only happen once because `moving` isn't set.)

As I said, it's all work that could have been avoided if a move event had been provided in the API; such an event is common in other contexts. But without it, as with single- and double-clicks, this is the sort of solution that's required to get the mapplet functionality we want.

Using Asynchronous Mapplet Functions

Listing 8-8 also introduces our first instance of that bane of mapplet code, `Async`. As mentioned in Chapter 6, any function that returns information from the map is asynchronous and thus requires a callback. You can recognize such functions easily; they have `Async` appended to the name of the equivalent function from the traditional Maps API. So in this case, the equivalent Maps API function would be `getCenter`, and it would just return the coordinates of the map's center directly, like this:

```
coordinates = map.getCenter();
```

Conversely, in our mapplet the relevant code (as in Listing 8-8) is

```
map.getCenterAsync(afterGetCenter);
```

where `afterGetCenter` is the callback function, which will have the map center coordinates passed to it as a parameter.

■**Tip** I tend to name callback functions in a way that directly links them to their source, such as `afterGetCenter` in this case. I find this helpful in keeping the connection between source and callback straight. You may have already noticed that I usually follow a similar rule for event handlers (e.g., `moveend` and `mapMoveEnd`).

Updating the Map Center Display

There is now only one piece of JavaScript left for the Map Center Monitor, the `afterGetCenter` callback, which you can find in Listing 8-9. Don't worry; it's not as bad as it looks.

Listing 8-9. *The Callback Function to Receive the Map Center Coordinates*

```
function afterGetCenter(coordinates)
{
  if (!coordinates.equals(lastCenter))
  {
    // Map has moved since the last time we checked

    // Save the new coordinates, so we can tell next time if it's moved
    lastCenter = coordinates;

    // Reformat the map center latitude as a more readable string

    var latitude = Math.abs(coordinates.lat());
    latitude = latitude.toFixed(5);
    latitude = latitude + 'º ';

    if (coordinates.lat() > 0)
      latitude = latitude + 'N';
    else if (coordinates.lat() < 0)
      latitude = latitude + 'S';

    // Ditto for longitude

    var longitude = Math.abs(coordinates.lng());
    longitude = longitude.toFixed(5);
    longitude = longitude + 'º ';

    if (coordinates.lng() > 0)
      longitude = longitude + 'E';
    else if (coordinates.lng() < 0)
      longitude = longitude + 'W';

    var centerDisplay = 'Map center: ' + latitude + ', ' + longitude;

    // Set the mapplet's title to include the formatted center coordinates
    _IG_SetTitle(centerDisplay);
  }

  if (moving)
    // Map is still moving, so carry on updating the center display
    map.getCenterAsync(afterGetCenter);
};
```

There are primarily two aspects to this function. The first consists of updating the map center display by refreshing the coordinates in the gadget title; the second, if you recall, is continuing the process until the moving flag is cleared.

The first task is by far the largest, so it makes sense to break it down still further into its component steps, thus:

1. Confirm that the center coordinates have actually changed.

2. Format the coordinates for display.

3. Update the mapplet title with the new coordinates.

So with that in mind, let's walk through them one by one.

BREAKING IT DOWN

By now, you may be noticing a pattern, in that I approach each coding task by breaking it down into individual steps. There are several advantages to doing so:

- It allows us to get our minds around a complicated problem. Rather than trying to tackle the whole thing all at once, keep breaking it down until each step is manageable.

- It's how the computer will need to be instructed in the code. Each line of code is a single step of the process, so breaking down a large task into small steps is a logical method for writing a program.

- When you (inevitably) miss a step, it's easy to just insert it when the need for it comes up.

- It helps to identify steps that might be repeated in different parts of the process. Such steps, or groups of steps, can then be split off into functions of their own, saving you from rewriting them every time you need them. OHIO, remember—Only Handle It Once!

So keep this technique in mind as you begin to write your own mapplets, or any kind of computer program. Break every task down into smaller steps, and keep breaking it down until each step can be written as a single line of code. Nearly any programming task can be usefully approached this way.

Confirm That the Center Coordinates Have Changed

Before you begin refreshing the center-coordinates display, it makes sense to check that the coordinates have actually changed from the last time. This is a good idea because, as you'll recall, the afterGetCenter function will be called repeatedly as long as the moving flag is set. For a drag-and-drop operation, when the user is dragging the map to a new location, this means that the process continues until she "drops" the map—even if she doesn't move her mouse for a few seconds.

Like defensive coding, this is one of those steps that isn't strictly necessary but makes for a better, cleaner mapplet. The browser won't be working as hard (and so will seem less sluggish), and the user experience will be less choppy.

With this in mind, I declared a `lastCenter` variable back in Listing 8-7, the main JavaScript code:

```
var lastCenter = new GLatLng(90, 0);
```

You'll use this variable as follows: every time `afterGetCenter` runs, you'll save the map center coordinates here, so that the *next* time it runs you can compare to see if the new coordinates are different.

Tip See how I initialize `lastCenter` with a latitude of 90? This is a little trick to ensure that the first time `afterGetCenter` runs, the map center coordinates will be different from this initial `lastCenter` value. It takes advantage of the fact that 90° latitude is at the North Pole, and thus will *always* be different from the true map center coordinates. You can find more information about why this is true in Appendix A.

So here's the code for doing so, from Listing 8-8. I've distilled it down to just the lines relevant for this discussion.

```
if (!coordinates.equals(lastCenter))
{
  lastCenter = coordinates;
  ...
}
```

Reduced to its essence like this, it's fairly simple: if the new center coordinates aren't equal to the `lastCenter`, then (1) save the new center coordinates for next time around, and (2) do the rest of the center-refresh processing. Incidentally, the exclamation mark (!) in JavaScript means *not*, so applying it to the `equals` function of `coordinates` means "is not equal to."

Format the Coordinates for Display

So now you know that the coordinates have changed and that you need to refresh the map center display. The first step in doing so is to convert the raw numeric latitude and longitude (like -102.73457932456602) into readable, user-friendly strings (like '102.73458° W'). I'll talk you through the process for latitude; the code for longitude is exactly comparable.

The first step is to convert the raw number to a string, and this involves the following steps:

```
var latitude = Math.abs(coordinates.lat());
latitude = latitude.toFixed(5);
latitude = latitude + '° ';
```

You can probably see just what's going on here: I ensure that it's a positive number (*take the absolute value* in mathematical language, hence the `Math.abs` function), convert it to a string with five decimal places, and add the degree symbol. Note that it would be fine to do this all in one line of code if you're comfortable with the operations involved.

■**Note** Google keeps the latitude and longitude internally to a frightening number of decimal places, but five places is sufficient for about three feet of accuracy, good enough for this application. For more details, I again refer you to Appendix A.

So now you have a nicely formatted string. But since your first step was to convert to a positive number, you've lost the hemisphere (north or south), and need to add that back in. The following code tests whether the original latitude coordinate was positive or negative (as discussed back in Chapter 1) and modifies the latitude string accordingly:

```
if (coordinates.lat() > 0)
  latitude = latitude + 'N';
else if (coordinates.lat() < 0)
  latitude = latitude + 'S';
```

Note that a latitude of exactly zero would be on the equator, and neither N nor S.

You then repeat those steps for the longitude (substituting W for N and E for S), and combine the formatted strings into one, ready for display to the user:

```
var centerDisplay = 'Map center: ' + latitude + ', ' + longitude;
```

Update the Mapplet Title

Most of the hard work is done now; you have the formatted center coordinates ready for display to the user. A single line of code is sufficient to do so:

```
_IG_SetTitle(centerDisplay);
```

This is utilizing another iGoogle Gadgets API function, `_IG_SetTitle`, which takes a single string parameter and uses it to set the title of the mapplet displayed in the sidebar.

Continuing the Process

You're finally done with refreshing the map center display; all that's left in the `afterGetCenter` function from Listing 8-8 is to reiterate the process so long as the `moving` flag is set.

As it turns out, this is remarkably easy to do:

```
if (moving)
  map.getCenterAsync(afterGetCenter);
```

You simply test the `moving` flag, and if it's `true`, use the same asynchronous `getCenter` function as we did in the `mapMoveStart` handler back in Listing 8-7.

What will happen, of course, is that `getCenterAsync` will go off to the Google map, get its center coordinates, and pass them back to `afterGetCenter` as a callback—which will then call `getCenterAsync` again, starting the process over. As shown in Figure 8-5, this will repeat until the user "drops" the map, and the `mapMoveEnd` handler clears the `moving` flag.

It's the completion of the missing-move workaround described earlier in the chapter, literally closing the loop on our map move handler logic.

As long as moving **is set:**

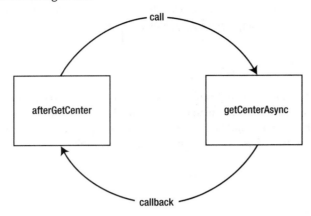

Figure 8-5. *The mapmove workaround as a callback loop*

Bringing It All Together

A lot of code has gone into this mapplet, so it's worth reviewing it all in one place. The complete mapplet specification can be found in Listing 8-10.

Listing 8-10. *The Full Map Center Monitor Mapplet Specification*

```
<?xml version="1.0" encoding="UTF-8"?>
<Module>
  <ModulePrefs title="Map Center Monitor"
               description="Continuously shows the current map center coordinates."
               author="Sterling Udell"
               author_email="sterling.udell+mapplet@googlemail.com"
               screenshot="http://sterlingudell.com/bgmm/chapter_08/center_scr.png" ➥
               thumbnail="http://sterlingudell.com/bgmm/chapter_08/center_thm.png"> ➥
    <Require feature="sharedmap" />
    <Require feature="dynamic-height"/>
    <Require feature="settitle" />
  </ModulePrefs>
  <Content type="html"><![CDATA[
    <script type="text/javascript">
      function mapMoveStart()
      {
        // mapMoveStart: event handler to initiate the recentering process
        moving = true;
        map.getCenterAsync(afterGetCenter);
      };
```

```
function mapMoveEnd()
{
  // mapMoveEnd: event handler to stop recentering when map stops moving
  moving = false;
};

function mapZoomEnd()
{
  // mapZoomEnd: also trigger the recentering code when the map is zoomed
  map.getCenterAsync(afterGetCenter);
};

function afterGetCenter(coordinates)
{
  // afterGetCenter: callback to update title with current map center coords

  if (coordinates.toUrlValue() != lastCenter.toUrlValue())
  {
    // Map has moved since the last time we checked

    // Save the new coordinates, so we can tell next time if it's moved
    lastCenter = coordinates;

    // Reformat the map center latitude as a more readable string

    var latitude = Math.abs(coordinates.lat());
    latitude = latitude.toFixed(5);
    latitude = latitude + '° ';

    if (coordinates.lat() > 0)
      latitude = latitude + 'N';
    else if (coordinates.lat() < 0)
      latitude = latitude + 'S';

    // Ditto for longitude

    var longitude = Math.abs(coordinates.lng());
    longitude = longitude.toFixed(5);

    longitude = longitude + '° ';

    if (coordinates.lng() > 0)
      longitude = longitude + 'E';
    else if (coordinates.lng() < 0)
      longitude = longitude + 'W';

    var centerDisplay = 'Map center: ' + latitude + ', ' + longitude;
```

```
                    // Set the mapplet's title to include the formatted center coordinates
                    _IG_SetTitle(centerDisplay);
                }

            if (moving)
                // Map is still moving, so carry on updating the center display
                map.getCenterAsync(afterGetCenter);
        };

        // END FUNCTION DECLARATIONS - BEGIN MAIN MAPPLET CODE

        // Declare variables for later use
        var moving = false;
        var lastCenter = new GLatLng(90, 0);

        // Initialize the map
        var map = new GMap2();

        // Create the center "crosshair" overlay
        var crosshair = new GScreenOverlay(
            'http://sterlingudell.com/bgmm/markers/crosshair.png', // image URL
            new GScreenPoint(0.5, 0.5, 'fraction', 'fraction'),     // screen offset
            new GScreenPoint(11, 12, 'pixel', 'pixel'),             // overlay offset
            new GScreenSize(24, 24, 'pixel', 'pixel')               // overlay size
        );
        map.addOverlay(crosshair);

        // Attach several events to be called when the map moves
        GEvent.addListener(map, 'movestart', mapMoveStart);
        GEvent.addListener(map, 'moveend',   mapMoveEnd);
        GEvent.addListener(map, 'zoomend',   mapZoomEnd);

        // Initialize the center display
        map.getCenterAsync(afterGetCenter);

        // Adjust the height of the sidebar display
        _IG_AdjustIFrameHeight();
    </script>
  ]]></Content>
</Module>
```

These are all the pieces we've covered before: the `ModulePrefs` XML, the event handlers and `afterGetCenter` function, and the main mapplet JavaScript code. There are just a couple of highlighted lines that I want to call your attention to.

First, there's a new `Require` element that you haven't seen before, `settitle`:

```
<Require feature="settitle" />
```

This is needed to link in the Gadgets API feature that supports the `_IG_SetTitle` function, enabling the JavaScript code to change the mapplet's title.

Second, note that near the bottom of the main JavaScript there's a single call to `afterGetCenter`:

```
map.getCenterAsync(afterGetCenter);
```

You need this call to initialize the center-coordinates display when the mapplet is first activated. Without it, the coordinates wouldn't appear in the title until the first time the map was moved.

Final Mapplet Development Notes

Although the Nearest Place Name and Map Center Monitor mapplets are the longest code listings so far in this book, they're still fairly bare-bones as functionality mapplets. You'll typically want to flesh out your own mapplets further, with additions such as these:

- Additional sidebar content, often including more information related to the functionality being presented. And as with any mapplet, it's a no-brainer to include links back to your own web site in the sidebar.

- User-interface elements in the sidebar to control aspects of your mapplet. For instance, a button to clear the Place Name marker from the map could be handy. Any options on your mapplet can also be controlled from `checkbox` or `select` elements here.

- More sophisticated infowindow content, such as greater use of styles and formatting than I've shown here. However, don't forget that the Mapplets API does limit infowindow content somewhat, as discussed in Chapter 6.

- In Appendix C, you'll find some other Gadgets API functionality that's available in mapplets.

A good example of a finished mapplet, from WeatherBug (`www.weatherbug.com`), can be found in Figure 8-6.

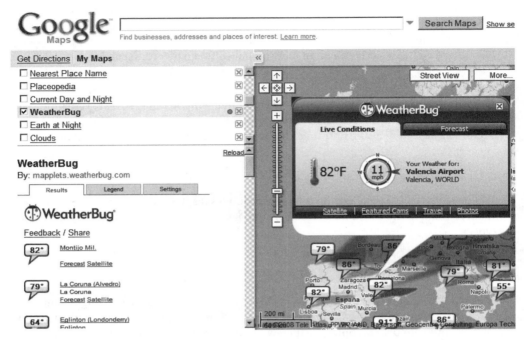

Figure 8-6. *WeatherBug's mapplet, including rich sidebar content and a well-styled infowindow*

Other Mapplets API Services

In addition to the examples I've already shown, the Mapplets API contains both the geocoding and driving-directions services that were introduced (for the Maps API) in Chapter 5. Their usage is quite similar to what you've seen before, with one slightly odd exception.

If you recall, in the Maps API the geocoder was called with a function like this:

```
getLatLng(address, callback);
```

As with most functions that have equivalents in the Mapplets API, Google has simply added Async to the name:

```
getLatLngAsync(address, callback);
```

Spot the oddity? Despite the name change, *it's the same function*—it was asynchronous (with a callback) there, and it still is here. So the good news is that you already know exactly how to use it.

Generally, there's less call for these tools in a mapplet because the Google Maps page already has them built in. However, occasions do arise where they're handy to have, so it's good to know that they're available.

Being a Good Neighbor

To close our discussion of mapplets, I'd like to leave you with a few notes on being a good resident of the maps.google.com neighborhood. In general, these are all tips that will help your mapplets work and play well with others. Such practices are more than just considerate to other mapplet developers; by following them, you can make sure that your mapplet's users will be happier as well.

The first set of suggestions is specifically to do with map markers:

- Keep custom marker icons small—no bigger than the default Google icons—so that they don't crowd other icons on the map.

- Don't place too many markers on the map, for reasons of both crowding and performance (having too many markers slows the whole map down). Try to keep your total marker count under 25 or so, with 50 as an absolute maximum.

- When creating custom icons, try to make them distinctive, so that the user can see at a glance which markers belong to which mapplet.

- Also, using custom icons allows you to convey information with the marker itself, rather than in an infowindow or sidebar entry. Examples might include using intuitive color schemes (such as the red/yellow/green in my Nearest Place Name), or icons with numbers on them to indicate quantities at different locations.

- On the other hand, don't be afraid to use the default map marker icon in a mapplet (by not specifying an `icon` when creating a `GMarker` object). By default, Google assigns different colored icons to different mapplets, helping the user to distinguish them. (However, the automatic colors don't work with the default markers that `GGeoXml` creates.)

Moving on from markers to more general topics, here are a couple of final suggestions:

- Don't move the map unnecessarily. If your geodata is confined to a specific area, a common temptation is to move the map there—but users can find this annoying. Attach the move functionality to a button instead, giving users control over it, and perhaps display a message if your data is off-screen (there's an example of this in Chapter 9).

- Be careful of interfering with standard user interactions. A good example of this is the extra effort we went to in Nearest Place Name to avoid impacting the double-click action. Naturally, users expect Google Maps to behave predictably, and if your mapplet changes those behaviors it's likely to be more irritating than useful.

Summary

We've covered a lot of ground in this chapter, with lots of code along the way. I hope you feel that your mapplet skills are beginning to blossom, and that you're ready to deploy your own geodata—and maybe even some functionality—to the Google Maps platform.

First and foremost, it's important to remember that a terrific mapplet can be terrifically easy to write. By using geoXML to integrate your geodata with Google Maps, you can both improve the geoweb and gain publicity for yourself, all without breaking a sweat. You don't need to work hard to make good mapplets.

However, if you're willing to roll up your sleeves and get your hands dirty with asynchronous JavaScript, functionality mapplets offer great potential as well. It's no accident that most of the top mapplets in Google's directory add functionality to the map. A distance-measurement or search-between tool has more universal appeal than the majority of geodata, and while it's more challenging than a simple data mapplet, it's also more bang for your development buck than a full-blown, stand-alone web application.

Whichever sort of mapplet you create, much of its strength will come from synergies with other mapplets, by participating in a "mashup of mashups." To make the most of this effort, it's also important to be considerate of your Google Maps neighbors.

So, this concludes the part of the book dedicated to mapplets. The remaining chapters are devoted to bringing your Google mapping skills together into a well-rounded whole, preparing you for real-world implementations. In the next chapter, we'll cover various intermediate JavaScript topics that should serve you well in any map integration project.

PART 3

■ ■ ■

Ready for the
Big Leagues

CHAPTER 9

■■■

Intermediate API Topics

At this point in the book, you've reached a real milestone in your development as a map programmer. You now have a solid foundation in both the Maps and Mapplets APIs, including all the building blocks required to create great geo-mashups. In this third and final section, I'm going to bring it all together and focus on real-world mapping solutions, including a number of ways to help you deploy high-quality map applications, as well as more in-depth work with geodata.

We'll get things started in this chapter with several options for custom map markers, ranging from alternatives offered by Google to building the markers yourself from scratch. We'll then revisit geocoding with a solution to help overcome its limitations, followed by a look at one of the alternatives to Google's GGeoXml object, implemented in both mapping APIs. Finally, the chapter shifts into high gear with a solution to displaying larger data sets, the toughest problem you've tackled yet.

By now, you've certainly learned to walk with Google Maps, and you're ready at least to jog. So this chapter is definitely *intermediate*, if not actually *advanced*. As such, it's intentionally pitched at a slightly higher level; while I'll still be explaining everything, I'm deliberately not going to dissect every line of code in quite the same level of detail as I have in earlier chapters. We're now approaching the point where you, the fledgling map programmer, will need to fly on your own. Think of this chapter as stretching your wings.

Also, this chapter and the next are semi-optional material. You already have the tools to build functional map mashups. I encourage you to persevere with these chapters—you'll be a better map developer for it—but they're structured in quite self-contained topics, which means you can also just dip into specific areas of interest as needed.

Topic 1: Custom Marker Icons

One of the simplest ways to give your maps a polished look is to use custom marker icons. Let's face it, G_DEFAULT_ICON is easy, but it's also used on everybody's first map, so it inevitably makes your maps look like the work of a beginner. So an excellent step in taking your maps to the next level is to replace your marker icons.

A well-designed icon can convey information, intrinsically helping your map user to find what she is looking for, rather than becoming lost in a field of identical, indistinguishable markers. Good examples include using different icons for different types of locations, intuitive use of color, or icons of varying size. Also, consider using numbered markers, either to link markers to a sidebar list or to convey a bit of data for each marker. Custom icons can enhance both form and function.

■**Note** As a counterpoint, in a mapplet there is some advantage to using the default marker icon. If you'll recall, Google assigns different colors of markers to different mapplets, helping the user to distinguish between them. If you have custom icons that convey extra information relevant to your mapplet, by all means use them. But if not, don't be afraid to stick with G_DEFAULT_ICON in mapplets.

Recap of Changing Icons

Before we get into the various sources of marker images, let's take a moment to review how you use them. As you saw in Chapter 4, the basic process looks something like this:

```
var myIcon = new GIcon(G_DEFAULT_ICON);
myIcon.image = 'http://somedomain.com/path/to/icon.png';
var options = {icon: myIcon};
var myMarker = new GMarker(coordinates, options);
```

You declare a new GIcon variable, usually basing it on G_DEFAULT_ICON when your custom image is roughly the same size and shape. You then assign its image property to the URL of your custom icon image and use it in the icon option when creating a GMarker.

You'll find some deviation from this process with more heavily customized icons discussed later, but that's the foundation—it's often just the image URL that changes.

■**Note** As I'm sure you know, it's bad practice to embed an image hosted by someone else on your web page. Exactly the same principle holds true for marker images: your map's icons should be hosted by you. So when you set the myIcon.image property, somedomain.com should be your own domain. The only exception is with icons hosted by Google; because it owns the API, you can generally use its images directly.

Also, using Google's copy of files it hosts increases the chances that your web site visitor may already have the file in her browser cache, reducing your page's load time.

Pre-Made by Google

In support of its Maps API samples, Google maintains a small library of marker icons that are simple to use in your own maps. This is the shallow end of the custom icon pool, so it's a good place to get your feet wet.

Most of the image URLs in Google's library follow a similar pattern, which looks like this:

```
http://gmaps-samples.googlecode.com/svn/trunk/markers/color/markerx.png
```

where *color* is one of blue, green, orange, pink, or red, and *x* is a number from 1 to 99. Thus, an orange icon with the number 45 in it would use the following URL:

```
http://gmaps-samples.googlecode.com/svn/trunk/markers/orange/marker45.png
```

There are two special cases that break this pattern. First, there is a blank marker in each color set, with blank in place of markerx. So a green marker with no number can be referenced this way:

```
http://gmaps-samples.googlecode.com/svn/trunk/markers/green/blank.png
```

Second, there are three blank circular markers whose URLs are substantially different:

```
http://gmaps-samples.googlecode.com/svn/trunk/markers/circular/bluecirclemarker.png
http://gmaps-samples.googlecode.com/svn/trunk/markers/circular/greencirclemarker.png
http://gmaps-samples.googlecode.com/svn/trunk/markers/circular ➥
/yellowcirclemarker.png
```

And because they're a different size and shape than G_DEFAULT_ICON, these three require a different initialization of the GIcon object. Here's the JavaScript you'll need for one of the circular icons:

```
var myIcon = new GIcon();
myIcon.image = 'http://gmaps-samples.googlecode.com/svn/trunk/' +
   'markers/circular/yellowcirclemarker.png';
myIcon.iconSize   = new GSize(31, 31);
myIcon.iconAnchor = new GPoint(15, 15);
```

I'll explain the iconSize and iconAnchor properties in a few pages, when I discuss making your own icons, but for now feel free to simply use this code.

Labeled Markers

Numbers from 1 to 99 are fine, but what if your map would benefit from some other label on the icon? Google's LabeledMarker object is for just that purpose, allowing you to place any text you'd like on a marker.

LabeledMarker isn't part of the standard Maps API—it's a separate utility library produced by Google—so to use it, you need to include it in your page. This is done with a standard XHTML script tag, like so:

```
<script type="text/javascript" src="http://gmaps-utility-library.googlecode.com ➥
/svn/trunk/labeledmarker/release/src/labeledmarker.js"></script>
```

■**Note** As with images, it's not good practice to link to JavaScript files on someone else's server directly from your code. In this case, we can again make an exception for Google, but ordinarily you'd copy the source to your own host and link to it there.

In your own map JavaScript, the first thing you need is a blank marker icon to accept the label:

```
var myIcon = new GIcon(G_DEFAULT_ICON);
myIcon.image = 'http://gmaps-samples.googlecode.com/svn/trunk/' +
   'markers/red/blank.png';
```

Note that the `circular` icons from the previous section would also be a good choice here, as they are easily large enough for two or three letters.

Next, there are a few `options` setting up what the label will contain and how it will be presented:

```
var options = {icon: myIcon,
               labelText: 'E',
               labelOffset: new GSize(-3, -32),
               labelClass: 'marker_label'};
```

I'll cover the specifics for these `options` in just a moment. For now, let's cut to the chase; integrating the `LabeledMarker` itself is simply a matter of using it instead of `GMarker`:

```
var myMarker = new LabeledMarker(coordinates, options);
```

The results can be seen in Figure 9-1.

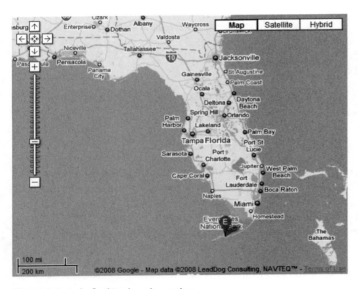

Figure 9-1. *LabeledMarker in action*

As promised, here's an explanation for the three label `options` in the example:

`labelText:` A string to superimpose on the blank marker. Obviously, this should usually be quite short to fit within the marker icon.

`labelOffset:` A `GSize` object containing the pixel distance between the marker's latitude/longitude coordinates and the upper-left corner of the label text. So in this example, the offset is 3 pixels *left* and 32 pixels *up*. The actual numbers are negative because standard web-design rules ordinarily measure position *right* and *down* (from the upper-left corner), so negative numbers reverse those directions.

labelClass: This is the clever one: a CSS class that you use to control all other aspects of the label's appearance. So to produce Figure 9-2, I also have the following CSS rule on my page:

```
div.marker_label {
  font: 12px sans-serif;
  color: white;
}
```

Notice the div.marker_label class selector, the same as you'd use for an XHTML element <div class="marker_label"> (which is exactly what LabeledMarker uses internally).

More information on LabeledMarker can be found on Google's reference page for it, at http://tinyurl.com/6kzl98.

The Map Icon Maker

Google has another handy utility, called the Map Icon Maker, for creating standard-shaped markers on the fly in any color you want. It's great on its own, but you can also use it in conjunction with LabeledMarker for full customization.

Like LabeledMarker, the Map Icon Maker is a standalone utility, which needs to be linked into your XHTML before you can use it. Here's the script tag you need:

```
<script type="text/javascript" src="http://gmaps-utility-library.googlecode.com ➡
/svn/trunk/mapiconmaker/release/src/mapiconmaker.js"></script>
```

This one's used a bit differently than the previous examples. Just as LabeledMarker was a replacement for GMarker, so MapIconMaker is a replacement for GIcon. You specify options for it and then declare a variable from it:

```
var iconOptions = {width: 48,
                   height: 48,
                   primaryColor: "#ffffff"};
var myIcon = MapIconMaker.createMarkerIcon(iconOptions);
```

The options of width, height, and primaryColor are the main ones you'll need. Rather than discussing the additional options that MapIconMaker supports, I recommend that you use Google's Icon Maker Wizard, at http://tinyurl.com/3d68xy. It's a web-based tool for setting all the options, previewing the markers, and generating the JavaScript.

With the custom icon in hand, then, you use it when you create the marker, just as you would with an ordinary GIcon:

```
var myMarker = new GMarker(coordinates, {icon: myIcon});
```

The results of this example can be seen in Figure 9-2. I'm not going to go through the additional step to combine MapIconMaker with LabeledMarker, as I have no doubt that you can accomplish that on your own. Note, however, that you can specify a width and height for MapIconMaker, potentially giving you more space in which to fit a LabeledMarker.

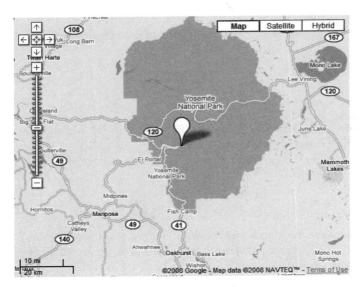

Figure 9-2. *A map marker from* `MapIconMaker`

Making Your Own Icons

The previous three sections should satisfy every conceivable need for standard-shaped Google Map icons. However, there will be times when you want an icon of a different shape, perhaps to convey specific information, or simply to make your map more distinctive. For that purpose, you'll need to create your icons.

This approach isn't for the faint of heart. To start with, you need sufficient skill with a graphics program (like Illustrator) and an eye for design to create good-looking icon images. But beyond that, for reasons of cross-browser compatibility, building a `GIcon` up from scratch is remarkably complex. In fact, full coverage of the process is beyond the scope of this book, involving various aspects of PNG and GIF formats, transparency, and image maps. So I'm only going to give you the condensed version, enough to get you started with simple icons.

ICON DESIGN CONSIDERATIONS

The design of your custom map icons is up to you, of course, but the following guidelines should help you avoid common problems:

- Keep them small, usually no more than 40 pixels or so in either dimension. If your map will have many markers, they should be correspondingly smaller to avoid overcrowding.

- At such small sizes, antialiasing becomes vital for clarity, both within the icon and at the edges (using partial transparency).

- Small icons also make it especially challenging to create designs that are easy to differentiate from each other, so keep that in mind throughout the process.

- Remember that your icon may be shown against any combination of light or dark backgrounds, so design accordingly, perhaps with a contrasting border color.

- Each icon needs to have an *anchor point* that will align with its map coordinates. If your map requires precise marker location, that anchor point should be obvious to the user, as with the "point" on G_DEFAULT_ICON.

- Combining two distinct colors per icon can be a way to make them more distinguishable; see the Map Icon Maker Wizard example in the previous section.

- Avoid over-reliance on color, however. Remember that some percentage of your audience will be color-blind.

We'll start with a simple, "flat" icon, without the three-dimensional shadow effect of G_DEFAULT_ICON. For one of my examples later in this chapter, I've created a simple, circular graphic of a star within a circle (see Figure 9-3), so let's go through the process of creating a map icon from it.

Figure 9-3. *The two-dimensional star icon (enlarged to show pixel detail)*

You begin by creating a GIcon object and setting its image property, as in the previous few sections:

```
var myIcon = new GIcon();
myIcon.image = 'http://sterlingudell.com/bgmm/markers/star.png';
```

Note that because my star icon bears very little resemblance to the default Google Maps icon, I don't base the GIcon on G_DEFAULT_ICON as I often did in my examples earlier in the chapter. This will generally be the case for two-dimensional icons.

By not basing your custom icon on the default, however, you're required to define its attributes explicitly, and that's what the next couple of lines will be about. First and foremost is the size of the icon's image:

```
myIcon.iconSize = new GSize(17, 17);
```

In this case, the star image is 17 pixels in diameter, so the two parameters (width, height) are both set to 17.

Finally, I need to set the icon's *anchor point*. This is the pixel coordinate within the image that Google will align with the marker's specified latitude and longitude when we assign the icon to it. In this case, the anchor should be in the middle of the star, halfway down and across the image—so the pixel coordinate is (8, 8). Compare that with the standard Google Map icon (in Figure 9-4); the image is 20 by 34 pixels, but the anchor point is at the middle of the bottom edge, so its coordinates are (10, 34).

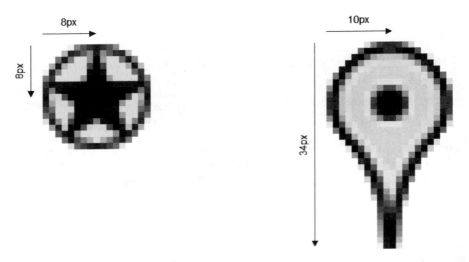

Figure 9-4. *My star icon and the standard marker icon, with their anchor point coordinates*

When you create your own icons, or find ready-made icon images from elsewhere, you'll need to locate the exact anchor point pixel coordinates in your graphics software.

■**Tip** Icons need to have an odd-numbered pixel size (like 17 for my star icon) in order to be symmetric around their anchor point.

Applying the anchor coordinates to the code, then, is simply a matter of supplying them to the iconAnchor property:

```
myIcon.iconAnchor = new GPoint(8, 8);
```

The GPoint API object is used for expressing pixel coordinates (as distinct from latitude/longitude coordinates, for which you use GLatLng).

Finally, you need an infowindow anchor. The principle here is the same as for iconAnchor—pixel coordinates within the graphic—except that this is the point on the icon where the infowindow will "attach." In my case, it's at (12, 4), or roughly the one-o'clock position on the rim of the circle:

```
myIcon.infoWindowAnchor = new GPoint(12, 4);
```

Again, you'll need to find the exact pixel coordinates using your graphics software.

And that's sufficient for a simple, flat icon like this. Bringing it all together, the full JavaScript looks like this:

```
var myIcon = new GIcon();
myIcon.image = 'http://sterlingudell.com/bgmm/markers/star.png';
myIcon.iconSize         = new GSize(17, 17);
myIcon.iconAnchor       = new GPoint(8, 8);
myIcon.infoWindowAnchor = new GPoint(12, 4);
```

To see this icon in action, please flip forward to Figure 9-9.

For a three-dimensional icon, you have the added complication of a shadow. This is a semitransparent gray outline of your icon that the API will place underneath it (and other, nearby markers) for the visual effect that your marker is standing up from the map. It is a separate graphic file from your main marker image. If you're proficient enough with your graphics software, you can make one yourself; otherwise, you can find an automated shadow generator at http://www.cycloloco.com/shadowmaker.

Once you have your shadow image, you need to tell the API about it. Not surprisingly, it's back to the GIcon object. In Listing 9-1, you can find the complete, minimal specification for a three-dimensional icon based on the graphics in Figure 9-5. I've highlighted the new shadow-related properties.

Figure 9-5. *The icon and shadow images for a three-dimensional icon (enlarged to show pixel detail)*

Listing 9-1. *JavaScript to Assign the Basic Properties for a Three-Dimensional Icon*

```
var myIcon = new GIcon(G_DEFAULT_ICON);
myIcon.image = 'http://sterlingudell.com/bgmm/markers/music.png';
myIcon.iconSize         = new GSize(25, 40);
myIcon.iconAnchor       = new GPoint(12, 40);
myIcon.infoWindowAnchor = new GPoint(12, 1);
myIcon.shadow      = 'http://sterlingudell.com/bgmm/markers/shadow.png';
myIcon.shadowSize = new GSize(41, 40);
```

The shadow property is fairly self-explanatory; it's the URL of your shadow graphic. And shadowSize is the width and height of that graphic. Note that the API will align the upper-left corners of your main icon image and its shadow, so you may need to add some top and left margin if you create your own shadow graphics.

There are many more GIcon properties that you can set, and for full cross-platform compatibility, you should. I refer you to the Google documentation (see Appendix D) for the complete list. The properties in Listing 9-1, however, are sufficient for a bare-bones three-dimensional icon, as shown in Figure 9-6.

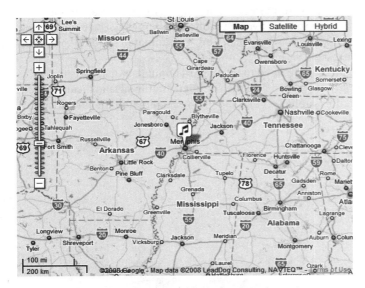

Figure 9-6. *The three-dimensional custom icon in action*

That concludes my coverage of custom map icons, though I'll continue to use them in my examples throughout the rest of the chapter.

Topic 2: Verified Geocoding

In Chapter 5 I introduced geocoding, the process of turning everyday addresses into map-compatible coordinates. And as you'll recall, I mentioned that geocoders are far from perfect; they get some addresses wrong, occasionally *very* wrong, and are unable to find other addresses at all. For this reason, it's generally unwise to rely on geocoding in an automated or unattended process. In this topic, on the other hand, we'll take a look at a process for which geocoding *is* well suited and which you can probably apply to a web project of your own at some point.

The case in point is that of a web form where a user is entering information—for example, within the context of a sign-up process. If the information on the form includes an address, then—as we know—there is implied geospatial information there. But in order to make use of it, perhaps on a member or customer map, we'll need to geocode that address, and we'd like it to be correct. So the approach will be as follows:

1. Let the user enter the address.

2. Geocode that address.

3. Display the geocoded results on the map.

4. Let the user correct the mapped location if necessary.

5. Save the verified coordinates with the user's address.

The Basic Page

Figure 9-7 shows the page we're working with: a very basic XHTML form for entry of the user's address. Of course, in a real web application this content would be contained within a larger page structure, but these are the essential elements.

Figure 9-7. *The basic location entry page*

In this example, I've used a freeform `textarea` element for the address entry; but the same technique would work fine with separate address fields—street, city, state, and so on, which some sites might need for a back-end database. In such a case, only a bit more JavaScript would be required to assemble a single address from those fields. For now, let's keep it simple.

In Listings 9-2 and 9-3 you'll find the XHTML and CSS code for the location entry form. There's only one thing I want to draw your attention to: there are two hidden `input` elements, for `latitude` and `longitude`. We'll come back to these later, but for the moment just be aware of them; they're key to this approach.

Listing 9-2. *XHTML for the Location Entry Page*

```
<!DOCTYPE html PUBLIC "-//W3C//DTD XHTML 1.0 Strict//EN"
                      "http://www.w3.org/TR/xhtml1/DTD/xhtml1-strict.dtd">
<html xmlns="http://www.w3.org/1999/xhtml">
  <head>
    <meta http-equiv="Content-Type" content="text/html; charset=UTF-8" />
    <title>Geocoding Revisted</title>
    <link type="text/css" rel="stylesheet" href="listing_09_03.css" />
    <script type="text/javascript"
          src="http://maps.google.com/maps?file=api&amp;v=2.124&amp;key="></script>
    <script type="text/javascript"
            src="http://gmaps-utility-library.googlecode.com ➥
/svn/trunk/mapiconmaker/release/src/mapiconmaker.js"></script>
    <script type="text/javascript" src="listing_09_06.js"></script>
  </head>
  <body onload="loadMap()" onunload="GUnload()">
    <div id="map"></div>
    <h1>
      Find Your Location
    </h1>
    <form method="post">
      <p>
        <label for="address">Address:</label>
        <textarea name="address" id="address"></textarea>
      </p>
      <p>
        <input type="button" value="Look Up Address"
               onclick="geocode(); return false;" />
      </p>
      <p>
        <input type="hidden" name="latitude" id="latitude" />
        <input type="hidden" name="longitude" id="longitude" />
        <input type="submit" value="Save" />
      </p>
    </form>
  </body>
</html>
```

Listing 9-3. *CSS for the Location Entry Page*

```
label {
  float: left;
  width: 5em;
}
```

```
p {
  clear: left;
}

#map {
  float: right;
  width: 400px;
  height: 400px;
  border: 1px solid;
  overflow: none;
}
```

Geocoding the Address

When the user enters his address in the `textarea` and clicks the Look Up Address button, the process gets underway. It starts the same as in Chapter 5, where you first saw geocoding: an event handler on the button calls a geocode function.

```
function geocode()
{
  var address = document.getElementById('address').value;
  geocoder.getLatLng(address, afterGeocode);
};
```

There's very little here, and certainly nothing to surprise you; the address is extracted from the XHTML and passed along to the geocoder, along with the callback function for when the process returns.

Let's take a look at that callback function, in Listing 9-4.

Listing 9-4. *The afterGeocode Callback Function*

```
function afterGeocode(coordinates)
{
  if (coordinates == null)
    alert('Address not found. Please try again.');
  else
  {
    // Address was found
    if (marker == null)
    {
      // This is the first time we've geocoded an address, so create the marker
      var iconOptions = {width: 24, height: 24, primaryColor: "#fffc1b"};
      var myIcon = MapIconMaker.createMarkerIcon(iconOptions);
      marker = new GMarker(coordinates, {icon: myIcon, draggable: true});
      map.addOverlay(marker);
```

```
    GEvent.addListener(marker, 'dragend',   markerDragEnd);
    GEvent.addListener(marker, 'dragstart', markerDragStart);
  }
  else
  {
    // The marker already exists; just move it to the new coordinates
    marker.setPoint(coordinates);
  }

  map.setCenter(coordinates, 14);

  marker.openInfoWindowHtml('Drag marker to exact location, then click Save.');
  saveCoordinates();
  }
};
```

Again, much of this should look familiar from Chapter 5:

1. Confirm that the address was found; if not, just show an `alert`.

2. If address was found, check if the marker already exists.

3. If not, create a marker at the returned coordinates. Note that it's a custom marker from `MapIconMaker`.

4. If the marker does exist, move it to the returned coordinates.

5. In either case, center the map on the marker at a reasonably high level of zoom, with `map.setCenter(coordinates, 14)`.

Verifying the Address

The new code, highlighted in Listing 9-4, is all related to the address verification process, and the approach I'm taking is based on a draggable `GMarker`. The idea is that if the geocoder got the user's address wrong, she can correct it by dragging the marker with her mouse to the right location. It's a simple and intuitive user interface; let's take a look at how it works.

The first part is that when you create the marker, you include an option of `draggable: true`. This simple flag is enough to instruct the API that the marker isn't permanently fixed but can be dragged around by the user.

Second, you need to attach a couple of event listeners to the dragging process:

```
GEvent.addListener(marker, 'dragend',   markerDragEnd);
GEvent.addListener(marker, 'dragstart', markerDragStart);
```

We'll get into what these event handlers do in a moment.

Third, you should let the user know what's going on, that she can—and should—drag the marker to confirm her address. I use the simple mechanism of an infowindow containing the instructions:

```
marker.openInfoWindowHtml('Drag marker to exact location, then click Save.');
```

Finally, save the initial returned coordinates; you never know, they just might have been right.

```
saveCoordinates();
```

I'll cover this function in detail in the next section.

So the user then drags the marker until it's stuck on top of her house in the satellite imagery. Of course, this is where the dragstart and dragend event handlers come in, as shown in Listing 9-5.

Listing 9-5. *The Marker Drag Event Handlers*

```
function markerDragStart()
{
  map.closeInfoWindow();
};

function markerDragEnd()
{
  saveCoordinates();

  var content = '<a href="#" onclick="map.zoomIn(); return false">Zoom in</a>' +
                ' if needed to place marker<br />exactly, or click Save when done.';
  marker.openInfoWindow(content);
};
```

The markerDragStart handler is quite straightforward, closing the infowindow when marker dragging commences. This covers a minor quirk in the Maps API: the marker can be dragged away from its infowindow, leaving the latter hanging awkwardly in midair. But it's simple enough to work around.

And to be honest, markerDragEnd is not much more difficult:

1. Save the new coordinates (that the marker has just been dragged to).

2. Show another instructions infowindow, with content to nudge the user along in the process.

Saving the Coordinates

All that remains is to save the new coordinates, called from both afterGeocode and markerDragEnd. The saveCoordinates function is as follows:

```
function saveCoordinates()
{
  var coordinates = marker.getPoint();
  document.getElementById('latitude').value  = coordinates.lat().toFixed(6);
  document.getElementById('longitude').value = coordinates.lng().toFixed(6);
};
```

Here's where the rubber meets the road: the function gets the current marker coordinates and then *saves them into the latitude and longitude XHTML form fields.* It's incredibly simple, but effective; with the verified coordinates in the XHTML form, they'll be passed back to the web server when the user submits the form, right alongside the address. The same server process that's already in place to handle form submissions—saving the information to a database, most likely—will now receive the latitude and longitude also.

To illustrate how this will work, Figure 9-8 shows the form, with verified address, ready for submission. I've removed the `hidden` attribute from the coordinate fields to show that their values are ready to go as well.

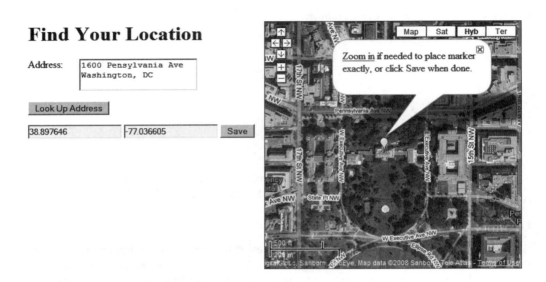

Figure 9-8. *Location form ready for submission, with latitude (38.897646) and longitude (–77.036605) shown*

Bringing It All Together

So with just a couple of additional form fields, and a really minimal amount of JavaScript, we now have a mechanism to gather accurate, verified geospatial coordinates from a user sign-up process—or anything else that involves entering an address on a web form: perhaps an order processing system, which will now have a precise destination to pass to a delivery driver. The rubber meets the road, indeed.

For completeness, the full JavaScript for this example can be found in Listing 9-6 (and for once it doesn't include any code you haven't seen before).

Listing 9-6. *JavaScript for the Geocode Verification*

```
// Declare variables for later use
var map;
var geocoder;
var marker;
```

```
function loadMap()
{
  // loadMap: initialize the API and load the map onto the page

  // Get the map container div
  var mapDiv = document.getElementById('map');

  // Confirm browser compatibility with the Maps API
  if (!GBrowserIsCompatible())
  {
    mapDiv.innerHTML =
      'Sorry, your browser isn\'t compatible with Google Maps.';
  }
  else
  {
    // Initialize the core map object
    map = new GMap2(mapDiv,
      {mapTypes: [G_NORMAL_MAP, G_SATELLITE_MAP, G_HYBRID_MAP, G_PHYSICAL_MAP]});

    // Set the starting map viewport
    var coordinates = new GLatLng(39.8, -98.5);
    map.setCenter(coordinates, 3, G_HYBRID_MAP);

    // Add the standard map controls
    map.addControl(new GSmallMapControl());
    map.addControl(new GScaleControl(),
                   new GControlPosition(G_ANCHOR_BOTTOM_LEFT, new GSize(6, 18)));
    map.addControl(new GMapTypeControl(true));

    // Initialize the geocoder object and tie it to the current map view
    geocoder = new GClientGeocoder();
  }
};

function geocode()
{
  // geocode: Call the Google geocoder with the address supplied by the user
  var address = document.getElementById('address').value;
  geocoder.getLatLng(address, afterGeocode);
};

function afterGeocode(coordinates)
{
  // afterGeocode: Callback function for the geocoder, showing the coords on the map
  if (coordinates == null)
    alert('Address not found. Please try again.');
```

```
    else
    {
      // Address was found
      if (marker == null)
      {
        // This is the first time we've geocoded an address, so create the marker
        var iconOptions = {width: 24, height: 24, primaryColor: "#fffc1b"};
        var myIcon = MapIconMaker.createMarkerIcon(iconOptions);
        marker = new GMarker(coordinates, {icon: myIcon, draggable: true});
        map.addOverlay(marker);

        GEvent.addListener(marker, 'dragend',   markerDragEnd);
        GEvent.addListener(marker, 'dragstart', markerDragStart);
      }
      else
      {
        // The marker already exists; just move it to the new coordinates
        marker.setPoint(coordinates);
      }

      map.setCenter(coordinates, 14);

      marker.openInfoWindowHtml('Drag marker to exact location, then click Save.');
      saveCoordinates();
    }
};

function markerDragStart()
{
  // markerDragStart: Close the infowindow when the marker is being dragged
  map.closeInfoWindow();
};

8function markerDragEnd()
{
  // markerDragEnd: Update the form coordinates and show more instructions

  saveCoordinates();

  var content = '<a href="#" onclick="map.zoomIn(); return false">Zoom in</a>' +
                ' if needed to place marker<br />exactly, or click Save when done.';
  marker.openInfoWindow(content);
};
```

```
function saveCoordinates()
{
  // saveCoordinates: Copy the current marker coordinates into the form fields
  var coordinates = marker.getPoint();
  document.getElementById('latitude').value  = coordinates.lat().toFixed(6);
  document.getElementById('longitude').value = coordinates.lng().toFixed(6);
};
```

Additional Notes

As usual, I've only presented the essence of the solution; although it is fully functional as it stands, a production system would probably want a few more bells and whistles. For example, code like Listing 8-2 could easily be integrated into Listing 9-6 for location selection by map click, in addition to the current geocode+drag architecture. This would support users whose addresses fail geocoding entirely, which the system as shown does not.

Also, form validation should be included, perhaps with a function such as this attached to the form element's onsubmit event:

```
function validateForm()
{
  if (document.getElementById('latitude').value == '')
  {
    alert('Please enter your address or click your location on the map.');
    return false;
  }
  else
    return true;
};
```

Such a routine could provide immediate feedback to the user, while also providing another layer of data verification.

Topic 3: Taking Control of GeoXml

Since Chapter 3, we've been making extensive use of Google's GGeoXml object to plot geodata on our map with minimal effort. As you'll recall, however, GGeoXml has certain serious drawbacks, and high on the list is a lack of control over how the geoXML data is displayed. If you don't like how the markers are shown on your map, or you want to do more with the data (like a sidebar display), GGeoXml isn't going to cooperate.

You may also recall, however, that GGeoXml isn't the only game in town. Independent developers have produced alternatives for displaying geodata quickly and easily, and they have shared their efforts with the API community. In this topic, I'll introduce you to one such alternative, an open-source object called EGeoXml, and create an enhanced display of KML data with it.

For this example, I'm displaying a KML data file of U.S. state capitals; this will be a traditional Maps API implementation, on an ordinary web page. Listing 9-7 contains the XHTML for this page; as you can see, it's pretty basic, with just a standard map `div` plus a sidebar where we'll list the markers from the KML. The only other new element is an additional `script` tag to link in the `egeoxml.js` source file; as mentioned earlier in the chapter, you always want to copy external JavaScript files to your own server and link to them there.

▓Note Download `egeoxml.js` from the code listing site for this book at `http://sterlingudell.com/bgmm/egeoxml.js`, or from the download page at `apress.com`.

Listing 9-7. *XHTML for the State Capitals Page*

```
<!DOCTYPE html PUBLIC "-//W3C//DTD XHTML 1.0 Strict//EN"
                      "http://www.w3.org/TR/xhtml1/DTD/xhtml1-strict.dtd">
<html xmlns="http://www.w3.org/1999/xhtml">
  <head>
    <meta http-equiv="Content-Type" content="text/html; charset=UTF-8" />
    <title>US State Capitals</title>
    <link type="text/css" rel="stylesheet" href="listing_09_11.css" />
    <script type="text/javascript"
            src="http://maps.google.com/maps?file=api&amp;v=2.124&amp;key="></script>
    <script type="text/javascript" src="../egeoxml.js"></script>
    <script type="text/javascript" src="listing_09_08.js"></script>
  </head>
  <body onload="loadMap()" onunload="GUnload()">
    <div id="map"></div>
    <div id="sidebar">
      <h1>US State Capitals</h1>
      <p id="list"></p>
    </div>
  </body>
</html>
```

And naturally, you'll need some JavaScript to make everything work, which can be found in Listing 9-8. Much of this listing will be very familiar to you as standard Maps API code; I've highlighted the interesting parts for further discussion.

Listing 9-8. *JavaScript for the State Capitals Page*

```
// Declare variables for later use
var map;
var geoXml;
```

```
function loadMap()
{
  // loadMap: initialize the API and load the map onto the page

  // Get the map container div
  var mapDiv = document.getElementById('map');

  // Confirm browser compatibility with the Maps API
  if (!GBrowserIsCompatible())
  {
    mapDiv.innerHTML =
      'Sorry, your browser isn\'t compatible with Google Maps.';
  }
  else
  {
    // Initialize the core map object
    map = new GMap2(mapDiv,
      {mapTypes: [G_NORMAL_MAP, G_SATELLITE_MAP, G_HYBRID_MAP, G_PHYSICAL_MAP]});

    // Set the starting map viewport
    var coordinates = new GLatLng(39.8, -98.5);
    map.setCenter(coordinates, 4);

    // Add the standard map controls
    map.addControl(new GLargeMapControl());
    map.addControl(new GScaleControl());
    map.addControl(new GOverviewMapControl());
    map.addControl(new GMapTypeControl());

    // Initialize a custom marker icon
    var starIcon = new GIcon();
    starIcon.image = '../markers/star.png';
    starIcon.iconSize        = new GSize(17, 17);
    starIcon.iconAnchor      = new GPoint(8, 8);
    starIcon.infoWindowAnchor = new GPoint(12, 4);

    // Initialize the KML processor
    var url = 'state_capitals.kml';
    var options = {sidebarid: 'list',
                   markeroptions: {icon: starIcon}};
    geoXml = new EGeoXml(map, url, options);

    // Load the KML
    geoXml.parse();
  }
};
```

First, you'll notice that I'm using a fully custom marker icon, the two-dimensional star-in-a-circle described in Topic 1 of this chapter. So the initialization of starIcon has essentially already been covered in detail. I can also now reveal that this icon was specifically designed to match the symbol often used for capitals on traditional paper maps.

Next, you're ready to proceed with initializing the EGeoXml object. This happens in the following line:

```
geoXml = new EGeoXml(map, url, options);
```

The EGeoXml object initialization takes three parameters, as follows:

1. The GMap2 object on which the data will be displayed. Here (as in all my examples) it's simply map (and it's not a string).

2. The URL of the KML file to display. In this example, I set the url variable a couple of lines earlier, using a relative URL to a file hosted in the same directory as my JavaScript source:

   ```
   var url = 'state_capitals.kml';
   ```

3. A list of options. This is where EGeoXml really shines, in all the options it provides us. Here I'm using two options, established with the following code:

   ```
   var options = {sidebarid: 'list',
                   markeroptions: {icon: starIcon}};
   ```

Let's take a look at these options in more detail.

The first option, sidebarid, is the id attribute of an XHTML element where EGeoXml will list all the KML data it processes. Refer back to Listing 9-7 and you'll see <p id="list"> in the sidebar div. So list is the element id you need here.

The second item, markeroptions, is *itself* a list of options. Specifically, these are the options that EGeoXml will use when creating GMarkers from KML Placemarks. And remember from Topic 1 that you specify custom marker icons by passing them to GMarker this way:

```
var myMarker = new GMarker(coordinates, {icon: starIcon});
```

Therefore, specifying {icon: starIcon} for EGeoXml's markeroptions will create the map markers with my custom starIcon. Any valid GMarker option (such as draggable: true, from Topic 2) can be included here.

The options list for EGeoXml can be far more extensive than I'm using here; you can include as many options as you like, and in any order. For a full list of the possible options, see the EGeoXml documentation at http://econym.googlepages.com/egeoxml.htm.

With the EGeoXml object fully initialized (in a variable named geoXml), it's a simple matter to add its KML data to the map:

```
geoXml.parse();
```

Since we specified a sidebarid option, geoXml will also list each marker there, and as a bonus these sidebar items are clickable links. You can see the results in Figure 9-9; clicking on a state in the sidebar opens the infowindow for the associated capital marker.

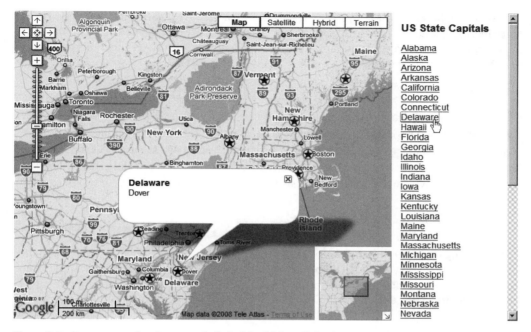

Figure 9-9. *Custom marker icons and clickable sidebar links from KML*

Of course, EGeoXml does have certain drawbacks, and it's worth reviewing them here:

- It supports only a subset of the KML specification. As a result, some KML files won't display with EGeoXml, nor will any KMZ files or GeoRSS feeds.

- The KML must be hosted on the same server as your map, because of browser security restrictions. We'll see one way around this in the next topic, however.

- Unlike Google's GGeoXml object, EGeoXml performs no caching, meaning that the KML is retrieved from your server every time the page is loaded (but again, see the next topic for more information).

Overall, though, EGeoXml is a good alternative for displaying your own KML data in a map, and I'll continue to use it throughout the chapter.

Topic 4: Converting to a Mapplet

A question that frequently arises with map developers is, "How do I convert an existing Maps API implementation to a mapplet?" In this section and the next, we'll look at some of the issues surrounding such a conversion.

The first question you should ask yourself is what aspects of your Maps application are well suited to life in a mapplet. Remember that mapplets exist in a shared environment. Will your application coexist happily with others, or does it need too much control over the underlying map?

Before embarking on a conversion, it's also worthwhile investigating its feasibility. The Mapplets API is smaller than the Maps API; not all functionality is replicated between them. So the key question is, do any of your application's core features rely on API functions or objects that don't exist on the mapplet side?

■Tip The main Google Maps site typically uses the latest released version of the Maps API internally (equivalent to `version=2` in the Maps API, from Chapter 2). As a result, many newer Maps features are available in mapplets, even if they aren't specifically documented for the Mapplets API. And in general, the Mapplets API documentation does seem to lag a good deal behind the functionality, so if there's a particular function, object, or event you want to use that's not listed in the documentation, build a small test mapplet and give it a try.

Assuming that your Maps API application is suitable, I encourage you to proceed with the transition to the Mapplets API. To help guide you, I've converted the State Capitals application (from the previous topic) to a mapplet, as shown in Figure 9-10. The specification for this mapplet can be found in Listing 9-9.

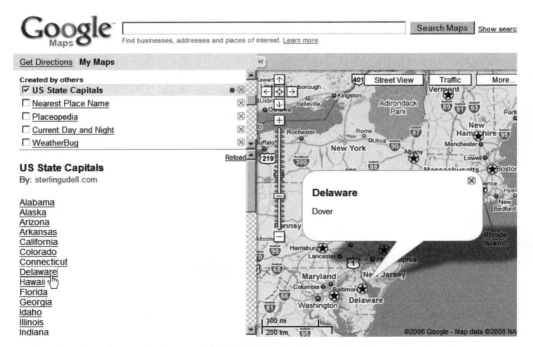

Figure 9-10. *The State Capitals mapplet, faithfully duplicating the original application*

Listing 9-9. *Specification for the State Capitals Mapplet*

```
<?xml version="1.0" encoding="UTF-8"?>
<Module>
  <ModulePrefs title="US State Capitals"
               description="The capitals (and capitols) of the 50 US states."
               author="Sterling Udell"
               author_email="sterling.udell+mapplet@googlemail.com"
            screenshot="http://sterlingudell.com/bgmm/chapter_09/state_scr.png"
            thumbnail="http://sterlingudell.com/bgmm/chapter_09/state_thm.png">
    <Require feature="sharedmap" />
    <Require feature="dynamic-height" />
  </ModulePrefs>
  <Content type="html"><![CDATA[
    <style type="text/css">
      p {
        font-size: 90%;
      }
    </style>

    <p id="list"></p>

    <script type="text/javascript"
            src="http://sterlingudell.com/bgmm/egeoxml.js"></script>
    <script type="text/javascript">
      function xmlParsed()
      {
        // xmlParsed: After KML processing, adjust the height of the sidebar display
        _IG_AdjustIFrameHeight();
      };

      // END FUNCTION DECLARATIONS - BEGIN MAIN MAPPLET CODE

      // Initialize the map
      var map = new GMap2();

      // Initialize a custom marker icon
      var starIcon = new GIcon();
      starIcon.image = 'http://sterlingudell.com/bgmm/markers/star.png';
      starIcon.iconSize        = new GSize(17, 17);
      starIcon.iconAnchor      = new GPoint(8, 8);
      starIcon.infoWindowAnchor = new GPoint(12, 4);
```

```
        // Initialize the KML processor
        var url = 'http://sterlingudell.com/bgmm/chapter_09/state_capitals.kml';
        var options = {sidebarid: 'list',
                        markeroptions: {icon: starIcon},
                        nozoom: true};
        var geoXml = new EGeoXml(map, url, options);

        // Attach an event handler for after the KML is processed
        GEvent.addListener(geoXml, 'parsed', xmlParsed);

        // Load the KML
        geoXml.parse();
      </script>
  ]]></Content>
</Module>
```

A comparison with Listing 9-8 will show that much of the core JavaScript is unchanged. I've simply removed the inapplicable aspects (predominantly GMap2 parameters, setCenter, and addControl calls) and then copied the remainder into the mapplet framework that you should be familiar with by now. The following are the high points from this conversion:

- I've moved the essential JavaScript from an external .js file into the main script element of the mapplet, as discussed in Chapter 7.

- It was impractical to move the EGeoXml source code into the mapplet, so my code is still referencing the external egeoxml.js file, using another standard script tag.

■Note The original EGeoXml object was developed for the Maps API; the beauty of open source is that I was able to modify it slightly to make it mapplet-compatible. If you want to use EGeoXml in a mapplet, you need to copy it from the URL in Listing 9-9 or the Apress download site for this book. Do *not* try to use the original code (written by Mike Williams and available from his web site) in a mapplet.

An advantage of this port is that the mapplet version is able to use a different mechanism to retrieve the KML. As a result, it's no longer limited to KML from the hosting domain (any publicly accessible URL will work), and it also uses the Google caching mechanism (to speed response time and reduce server load). Good news all around.

- All URLs are now absolute, as mapplets are served from the gmodules.com domain rather than my own server.

- In accordance with the Good Neighbor policies from Chapter 8, I'm disabling EGeoXml's default behavior that when the KML finishes loading, it automatically zooms the map to encompass all the points. I do this with an additional option, nozoom: true.

- There's an event handler, `xmlParsed`, attached to the `EGeoXml` object. It will fire when the KML parsing has completed (and therefore all data has been displayed).

- When this event fires, a call to `_IG_AdjustIFrameHeight` will resize the sidebar to accommodate its content. I also `Require` the associated `dynamic-height` module.

I'm fortunate with this application; it's simple enough that it contained no functionality incompatible with the mapplet platform. But this is potentially the biggest part of a conversion: where your application uses a Maps API function or object that is different in the Mapplets API, that code will need to be altered. You'll find more information on this in the last topic of the chapter, but beyond that, there's not a lot of specific guidance I can give you. You'll need to delve into the documentation yourself, do some testing, and perhaps ask other map developers for assistance if you get stuck. You can find links to relevant resources in Appendix D.

Topic 5: Larger Data Sets

You may recall that in previous chapters, I've recommended that you shouldn't plot more than about 50 markers on a Google map at any one time—ideally, no more than 25. It's a good guideline, and it's easy enough to comply with if your data set naturally fits within it, like the state capitals. But what about larger data sets? Especially when working with geodata from other sources, you often have no control over the quantity. What should you do when a KML file contains a thousand `Placemarks`?

Answering that question is the subject of the last topic in this chapter, and it's also the most ambitious. Although I've made it as simple as possible, the code in this topic is easily the most advanced to this point in the book, and it contains JavaScript constructs you may never have seen before. If you're up for a challenge, however, it's an extremely valuable technique to have in your map programming toolbox.

So, brave knights, if you do doubt your courage, or your strength, then come no further…

—Tim the Enchanter, *Monty Python and the Holy Grail*

Still with me? Good. At the least, I can promise you a worthy example: it's a map of all the breweries in Great Britain, 459 of them.

Executive Summary

The approach we're going to use is as follows. When the page loads, an `EGeoXml` object will load the KML, same as with the State Capitals. However, it's *not* going to create 459 map markers. Instead, it will add the data for each `Placemark` to a JavaScript *array*. Then whenever the map moves, an event handler will display markers for up to twenty data points within the map viewport. The upshot is that although we've loaded 459 data points, no more than 20 are ever shown at once. As the user pans and zooms the map, it'll be a different 20, but never more than that.

JAVASCRIPT 102: ARRAYS

Hello, and welcome to JS102. Glad you could join us!

An *array* is a special kind of variable, a numbered list, each element of which is essentially a variable in its own right. If that's not clear, just stay with me for a minute and hopefully it soon will be.

You declare an array this way:

```
var list = new Array();
```

As you can see, an array is just another object, like GMap2, GMarker, or others you're already familiar with.

Once you've declared an array, you can access individual items in the list as if they were variables themselves. Typical code looks like this:

```
list[1] = 2 + 2;
list[2] = 4;
if (list[1] == list[2])
  alert('Two plus two equals four');
```

See how it works? The square brackets [and] after the array variable's name enclose a number, called an *index*, and that determines which *element* of the array you're working with.

I'll gradually introduce you to other array operations along the way, but that should be enough to get you started. Arrays are indispensable when working with information that's essentially list-oriented, like the brewery data in this section, which consists of a number of similar items.

Loading the Data

As usual, we start with the XHTML and CSS for the page where the map will live, shown in Listings 9-10 and 9-11. You'll notice that Listing 9-10 is virtually identical to Listing 9-6, a basic map plus sidebar; only the names have been changed. They even use the same stylesheet. There is one additional JavaScript file being included, async.js, but I'll discuss that in a few pages.

Listing 9-10. *XHTML for the Basic UK Brewery Map Page*

```
<!DOCTYPE html PUBLIC "-//W3C//DTD XHTML 1.0 Strict//EN"
                      "http://www.w3.org/TR/xhtml1/DTD/xhtml1-strict.dtd">
<html xmlns="http://www.w3.org/1999/xhtml">
  <head>
    <meta http-equiv="Content-Type" content="text/html; charset=UTF-8" />
    <title>British Breweries</title>
    <link type="text/css" rel="stylesheet" href="listing_09_11.css" />
    <script type="text/javascript"
        src="http://maps.google.com/maps?file=api&amp;v=2.124&amp;key="></script>
    <script type="text/javascript" src="../egeoxml.js"></script>
    <script type="text/javascript" src="../async.js"></script>
    <script type="text/javascript" src="listing_09_15.js"></script>
  </head>
```

```
  <body onload="loadMap()" onunload="GUnload()">
    <div id="map"></div>
    <div id="sidebar">
      <h1>Breweries in Great Britain</h1>
      <ol id="list"></ol>
    </div>
  </body>
</html>
```

Listing 9-11. *CSS for the Basic UK Brewery Map Page*

```
html {
  height: 100%;
}

body {
  height: 100%;
  margin: 0;
  font-family: sans-serif;
  font-size: 90%;
}

#map {
  width: 70%;
  height: 100%;
}

#sidebar {
  position: absolute;
  left: 70%;
  top: 0;
  right: 0;
  bottom: 0;
  overflow: auto;
  padding: 1em;
}

h1 {
  margin: 0;
  font-size: 100%;
}

ul {
  padding-left: 1em;
}
li {
  padding-left: 0em;
}
```

Things begin to get interesting in the JavaScript. You can find the first part in Listing 9-12; I'll go over its important aspects before we dive into the block of code that drives the 20-marker display.

Listing 9-12. *The Basic UK Brewery Map (First Half)*

```
// Declare variables for later use
var map;
var geoXml;
var data = new Array();
var markers = new Array();

function loadMap()
{
  // loadMap: initialize the API and load the map onto the page

  // Get the map container div
  var mapDiv = document.getElementById('map');

  // Confirm browser compatibility with the Maps API
  if (!GBrowserIsCompatible())
  {
    mapDiv.innerHTML =
      'Sorry, your browser isn\'t compatible with Google Maps.';
  }
  else
  {
    // Initialize the core map object
    map = new GMap2(mapDiv,
      {mapTypes: [G_NORMAL_MAP, G_SATELLITE_MAP, G_HYBRID_MAP, G_PHYSICAL_MAP]});

    // Set the starting map viewport
    var coordinates = new GLatLng(53.6, -4.3);
    map.setCenter(coordinates, 6);

    // Add the standard map controls
    map.addControl(new GLargeMapControl());
    map.addControl(new GScaleControl());
    map.addControl(new GOverviewMapControl());
    map.addControl(new GMapTypeControl());

    // Initialize the KML processor
    var url = 'uk_breweries.kml';
    var options = {sidebarid: 'list', createmarker: createMarker, nozoom: true};
    geoXml = new EGeoXml(map, url, options);

    // Attach an event handler for after the KML is processed
    GEvent.addListener(geoXml, 'parsed', xmlParsed);
```

```
      // Load the KML
      geoXml.parse();

      // Attach an event to refresh the marker display whenever the map moves
      GEvent.addListener(map, 'moveend', mapMoveEnd);
   }
};

function addDataPoint(coordinates, name, description)
{
   // addDataPoint: save the data for a placemark found by the KML processor
   var d = data.length;
   data[d] = {coords: coordinates, title: name, details: description};
};

function xmlParsed()
{
   // xmlParsed: after KML processing, initialize the marker display
   mapMoveEnd();
};
```

The first thing to notice is the declaration of two array variables, data and markers:

```
var data = new Array();
var markers = new Array();
```

The former is the array that we'll load the KML Placemark data into, and later on we'll use the latter to manage the markers that are shown on the map.

■**Tip** Recall that when it's not in a mapplet, the KML file used with EGeoXml must be hosted on the same domain as the page that displays it. Here, that's indicated by the relative URL for uk_breweries.kml.

Second, note that I've added a further option, createmarker: addDataPoint, when initializing EGeoXml. This is a callback function that EGeoXml will use as it is processing the KML data, and by setting the createmarker option we're basically saying, "Call my addDataPoint function rather than adding a marker to the map."

Next, take a look at that addDataPoint function. When EGeoXml calls this function, it passes three parameters—coordinates, name, and description—with the data from the corresponding elements in a KML Placemark (see Listing 1-1). And EGeoXml calls this for every Placemark. In turn, we package those three pieces of information up and add them to the data array:

```
var d = data.length;
data[d] = {coords: coordinates, title: name, details: description};
```

The result is that when the EGeoXml object has finished loading the KML, the data array will contain 459 elements, each containing the coords, title, and details for a single brewery.

Then the xmlParsed function will call the mapMoveEnd event handler, and the real fun will start.

JAVASCRIPT 102: ARRAY.LENGTH

The array's `length` property returns the number of elements in the array:

```
var list = new Array();
var n = list.length;
```

After these two lines are run, n will contain the value 0, because the `list` array is newly declared and contains no elements yet. Let's look at another example:

```
var list = new Array();
list[0] = 'foo';
var n = list.length;
```

Now n == 1, because `list` contains a single element, the string 'foo' at index 0.

Yes, zero. JavaScript arrays are described as *zero-based*, meaning that the first element always has an index of 0. It can make for some confusing-looking code at times, but serious computer scientists will assure you that zero-based arrays make much more sense than one-based. And anyway, we're stuck with them.

A nice side effect of zero-based arrays is code like that found in the `addDataPoint` function of Listing 9-12:

```
var d = data.length;
data[d] = {coords: coordinates, title: name, details: description};
```

This will be called once for each data point, remember, and every time it's called, we can use the current length of the array, d, as the index of the *next* element to add to the array. So the first time, d == 0 (because the array is empty, just as in the 'foo' example); the second time, d == 1, and so on until d == 458.

Displaying 20 Data Points

After the data has finished loading, and every time the user moves the map, the `mapMoveEnd` event handler will be triggered. This is the real heart of this application: finding 20 data points within the map viewport to display. Here's how it works:

1. Get the map boundary coordinates, defining the area in which we'll display markers.

   ```
   var mapBounds = map.getBounds();
   ```

2. Remove the previous set of markers from both the map and the `markers` array. This is done by means of a JavaScript statement called a `for` loop; Appendix B contains a full explanation, but for now, just accept that it will execute a block of code repeatedly, once for every element in the array:

   ```
   for (var m = markers.length - 1; m >= 0; m--)
   {
     map.removeOverlay(markers[m]);
     markers.splice(m, 1);
   }
   ```

JAVASCRIPT 102: ARRAY.SPLICE

The `splice` function is used here to delete elements from an array. It takes two parameters, the index at which to start the deleting and the number of elements to delete. So the following code:

```
list.splice(5, 1);
```

would delete `list[5]`. Note that this doesn't leave a gap in the array; the other elements are shuffled down by one, so the old `list[6]` becomes the new `list[5]`, the old `list[7]` becomes the new `list[6]`, and so on. Of course, the array's `length` will decrease by one as well.

You can also use `splice` to add new elements in the middle of an array—even as you simultaneously delete other elements—but let's leave that for now; you have enough on your plate.

3. Look for data in the new map area. This search is done with another `for` loop, this time going through the base `data` array we set up in the last section. So for every data point we loaded with `addDataPoint`

```
for (var d = 0; d < data.length; d++)
{
```

a. Does the map viewport contain this data point?

```
if (mapBounds.contains(data[d].coords))
    {
```

b. Yes, it does. Create a new marker and add it to the array.

```
m = markers.length;
markers[m] = new GMarker(data[d].coords);
```

c. Save the associated brewery details with this marker as well.

```
markers[m].data = data[d];
```

d. Add the marker to the map.

```
map.addOverlay(markers[m]);
```

e. Also attach an event handler to show detail information when the marker is clicked. Note the creation of a `Function` on the fly, containing `m`, the index of this marker!

```
GEvent.addListener(markers[m], 'click',
    new Function('showDetail(' + m + ')'));
```

f. Create sidebar content for this data point, including a click event handler. Again, note that the event handler here has the marker array index `m` in it.

```
sidebarContent = sidebarContent +
    '<li><a href="#" onclick="showDetail(' + m + '); return false">' +
    data[d].title + '</a></li>';
```

g. Have we added 20 markers yet? If so, finish off the sidebar content and break out of the for loop.

```
if (m >= 19)
{
  sidebarContent = sidebarContent +
    '<li style="list-style: none">zoom in for more...</li>';
  break;
}
}
}
```

▪Note Why 19, when we're trying to show 20 markers? Because of the zero-based arrays, remember; when the index m is 19, we actually have 20 elements in the array.

---

4. The for loop has finished. Did we find any markers within the map viewport?

```
if (markers.length == 0)
```

a. No. Let the user know with a message in the sidebar.

```
sidebarContent = '<li style="list-style: none">' +
  'No results found in map area. ' +
  'Try zooming out or moving the map.</li>';
```

5. Almost done: all that's left to do is move the new content into the sidebar.

```
document.getElementById('list').innerHTML = sidebarContent;
```

JAVASCRIPT 102: DYNAMIC XHTML

Notice what I'm doing here with sidebarContent? I build it up as I'm placing my 20 markers on the map, adding a snippet of XHTML for each marker. Then, after the for loop finishes, I assign the whole string to the sidebar element's innerHTML property.

I expect you can see what this is doing, but it's such a valuable technique that it deserves explicit mention. The innerHTML property of a page element allows us to *change its content from within JavaScript*—whatever content that XHTML element held will be replaced by the new sidebarContent.

This technique is known as Dynamic XHTML, or *DHTML* for short. It's invaluable for applications such as this, building page content on the fly in response to user actions.

Incidentally, you first saw DHTML back in Chapter 5, with the document.createElement function. createElement and innerHTML are two alternative ways to generate DHTML, but innerHTML is usually simpler because the content of the string is ordinary XHTML, just as you'd put in your web page source.

Whew! Lots of new concepts! I don't expect that you followed every last detail, but hopefully you have the general idea. And when you've caught your breath enough for a second look, you might find a few items in there that I haven't explained but that are intriguing enough to follow up on your own. The complete mapMoveEnd function, with all the steps just described, can be found in Listing 9-14 a few pages hence. There's one more piece missing, but it's fairly easy: the event handler called by the two click events (on the markers and sidebar list items). They're calling the same handler because we want the same functionality in either case, to show the detail infowindow associated with a particular marker. And here it is:

```
function showDetail(m)
{
  markers[m].openInfoWindow(
     '<h4 style="margin: 0; font-size=120%">' + markers[m].data.title + '</h3>' +
     '<p style="margin: 0; font-size=90%">' + markers[m].data.details + '</p>');
};
```

This is where we make use of the data we attached to each marker (in step 3c). We use the function parameter m as an index into the markers array, and then we build the infowindow's XHTML content based on that data (the title and details for the individual brewery).

One final aspect was omitted from the numbered steps shown earlier, for simplicity. To make the map more usable, I'm going to assign numbered icons to each map marker and correlate them with the sidebar list (which you'll notice was an ol ordered-list element in the XHTML of Listing 9-11). Here's how:

```
var numberIcon = new GIcon(G_DEFAULT_ICON);
numberIcon.image =
   'http://gmaps-samples.googlecode.com/svn/trunk/markers/orange/marker' +
   (m + 1) + '.png';
markers[m] = new GMarker(data[d].coords, {icon: numberIcon});
```

You should recognize the basic code here from the first part of this chapter; it's one of Google's pre-made icon set, in a vaguely beer-colored orange. I use m+1 (rather than m) for the icon number because it's a zero-indexed array, but with just that small tweak the numbers will automatically correspond with the sidebar list.

And with that, we have completed the basic UK Brewery map, as you can see in Figure 9-11. Load your page in a browser and pan and zoom anywhere in Great Britain to see breweries in the area; click on a numbered marker (or a sidebar link) for more details.

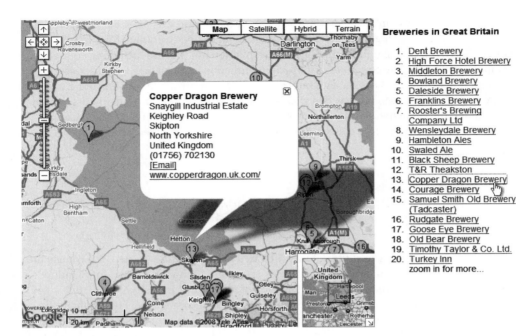

Figure 9-11. *The UK Brewery map*

Tying Up Loose Ends

It turns out that there's a slight problem with my first-pass implementation. When you open an infowindow, the API automatically pans the map so that the entire infowindow is visible. Unfortunately, this triggers our mapMoveEnd event—and this loads a new set of markers, which may or may not include the marker with the infowindow attached.

It's not actually a terribly hard problem. Listing 9-13 shows the full JavaScript, with the solution highlighted.

Listing 9-13. *JavaScript for the UK Brewery Map, with Infowindow Fix*

```
// Declare variables for later use
var map;
var geoXml;
var data = new Array();
var markers = new Array();
var clicked;
var current;

function loadMap()
{
  // loadMap: initialize the API and load the map onto the page

  // Get the map container div
  var mapDiv = document.getElementById('map');
```

```
  // Confirm browser compatibility with the Maps API
  if (!GBrowserIsCompatible())
  {
    mapDiv.innerHTML =
      'Sorry, your browser isn\'t compatible with Google Maps.';
  }
  else
  {
    // Initialize the core map object
    map = new GMap2(mapDiv,
      {mapTypes: [G_NORMAL_MAP, G_SATELLITE_MAP, G_HYBRID_MAP, G_PHYSICAL_MAP]});

    // Set the starting map viewport
    var coordinates = new GLatLng(53.6, -4.3);
    map.setCenter(coordinates, 6);

    // Add the standard map controls
    map.addControl(new GLargeMapControl());
    map.addControl(new GScaleControl());
    map.addControl(new GOverviewMapControl());
    map.addControl(new GMapTypeControl());

    // Initialize the KML processor
    var url = 'uk_breweries.kml';
    var options = {sidebarid: 'list', createmarker: addDataPoint, nozoom: true};
    geoXml = new EGeoXml(map, url, options);

    // Attach an event handler for after the KML is processed
    GEvent.addListener(geoXml, 'parsed', xmlParsed);

    // Load the KML
    geoXml.parse();

    // Attach an event to refresh the marker display whenever the map moves
    GEvent.addListener(map, 'moveend',         mapMoveEnd);
    GEvent.addListener(map, 'infowindowopen',  mapInfoWindowOpen);
    GEvent.addListener(map, 'infowindowclose', mapInfoWindowClose);
  }
};

function addDataPoint(coordinates, name, description)
{
  // addDataPoint: save the data for a placemark found by the KML processor
  var d = data.length;
  data[d] = {coords: coordinates, title: name, details: description};
};
```

```
function xmlParsed()
{
  // xmlParsed: after KML processing, initialize the marker display
  mapMoveEnd();
};

function mapMoveEnd()
{
  //  mapMoveEnd: refresh the marker display after the map has moved

  // Get the map boundary coordinates
  var mapBounds = map.getBounds();

  // Don't refresh if the currently selected marker is still in view
  if (current != null)
  {
    if (mapBounds.contains(current))
      return;
    else
      map.closeInfoWindow();
  }

  // Prepare to build new sidebar content by starting with a clean slate
  var sidebarContent = '';

  // Remove previous set of markers from the map and the array
  for (var m = markers.length - 1; m >= 0; m--)
  {
    map.removeOverlay(markers[m]);
    markers.splice(m, 1);
  }

  // Create a base icon
  var numberIcon = new GIcon(G_DEFAULT_ICON);

  // Look for data in the new map area
  for (var d = 0; d < data.length; d++)
  {
    if (mapBounds.contains(data[d].coords))
    {
      // Map does contain this data point; create a marker and add it to the map
      m = markers.length;
```

```
        numberIcon.image =
          'http://gmaps-samples.googlecode.com/svn/trunk/markers/orange/marker' +
          (m + 1) + '.png';
        markers[m] = new GMarker(data[d].coords, {icon: numberIcon});
        markers[m].data = data[d];
        map.addOverlay(markers[m]);

        // Also attach an event handler to show infowindow when marker is clicked
        GEvent.addListener(markers[m], 'click',
          new Function('showDetail(' + m + ')'));

        // Create sidebar content for this data point, including click event handler
        sidebarContent = sidebarContent +
          '<li><a href="#" onclick="showDetail(' + m + '); return false">' +
          data[d].title + '</a></li>';

        if (m >= 19)
        {
          // We've reached 20 markers, so break out of the loop
          sidebarContent = sidebarContent +
            '<li style="list-style: none">zoom in for more...</li>';
          break;
        }
      }
    }

  if (markers.length == 0)
    // No data points found in map boundaries
    sidebarContent = '<li style="list-style: none">No results found in map area. ' +
        'Try zooming out or moving the map.</li>';

  // Move the new content into the sidebar
  document.getElementById('list').innerHTML = sidebarContent;
};

function showDetail(m)
{
  // showDetail: open the infowindow for the given map marker
  current = clicked = markers[m].data.coords;
  markers[m].openInfoWindow(
    '<h4 style="margin: 0; font-size=120%">' + markers[m].data.title + '</h3>' +
    '<p style="margin: 0; font-size=90%">' + markers[m].data.details + '</p>');
};
```

```
function mapInfoWindowOpen()
{
  // mapInfoWindowOpen: set the variable that keeps track of the selected coords
  current = clicked;
};

function mapInfoWindowClose()
{
  // mapInfoWindowClose: clear the variable that keeps track of the selected coords
  current = null;
};
```

The solution is to keep track of the coordinates for the marker (if any) that currently has the infowindow open. So in the showDetail function, I set two new variables, current and clicked:

```
current = clicked = markers[m].data.coords;
```

The first of these is for the coordinates of the current marker, and the second is for the marker that's just been clicked on (the same coordinates at this point in the code).

Then in the mapMoveEnd handler, I add logic to prevent refreshing the marker display if the current coordinates are within the map viewport:

```
if (current != null)
{
  if (!mapBounds.contains(current))
    return;
  else
    map.closeInfoWindow();
}
```

Note that if the user has moved the map far enough so that current is no longer in view, I simply close the infowindow and proceed to refresh the marker display.

To finish off the fix, two more tiny event handlers set and clear current when the infowindow opens and closes:

```
function mapInfoWindowOpen()
{
  current = clicked;
};

function mapInfoWindowClose()
{
  current = null;
};
```

The clicked variable might seem a bit redundant here (as might the entire infoWindowOpen handler)—why not simply set current in showDetail? The answer is that when we call openInfoWindow in showDetail, the API actually *closes* any existing infowindow first—immediately triggering mapInfoWindowClose and clearing current. So we need to keep track of clicked separately and use it to reset current when the infowindow reopens.

Mapplet Conversion Revisited: GAsync and Cross-API Development

It shouldn't surprise you greatly that I'll want to turn such a useful map application into a mapplet as well. And this time I have even higher aspirations: I intend to drive my mapplet from *the same JavaScript code* as my traditional Maps API implementation, a *cross-API* solution.

This is easier than you might think; looking at Listing 9-13, there is only one function that doesn't exist in the Mapplets API, getBounds:

```
function mapMoveEnd()
{
  var mapBounds = map.getBounds();
...
```

If I were doing a simple mapplet conversion, I'd just rewrite that section of code to use getBoundsAsync, the asynchronous mapplet-compatible equivalent (a la Chapter 6):

```
function mapMoveEnd()
{
  map.getBoundsAsync(afterGetBounds);
};

function afterGetBounds(mapBounds)
{
...
```

However, my approach will instead use a different Mapplets API function, GAsync, which will further my cross-API goal because it's also available as an add-on for the Maps API. GAsync can be complicated to explain, but in its most basic form it's really quite simple, and it's best illustrated with an example. It allows us to rewrite the previous mapplet-compatible snippet like this:

```
function mapMoveEnd()
{
  GAsync(map, 'getBounds', afterGetBounds);
};

function afterGetBounds(mapBounds)
{
...
```

So rather than calling getBoundsAsync directly, I wrap GAsync around getBounds instead. Internally, GAsync is still calling getBoundsAsync. It works just the same—and Figure 9-12 shows the mapplet in action.

But the beauty of this approach is that when I include the async.js in my XHTML page (back in Listing 9-10), I can use the exact same GAsync code in my Maps API application.

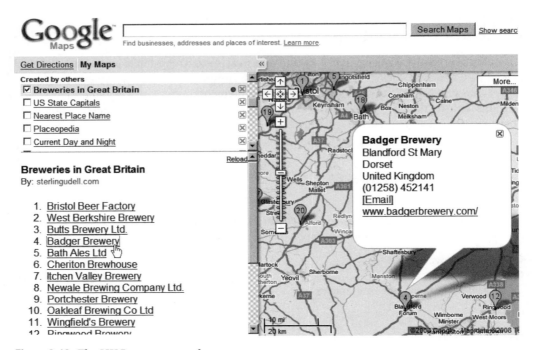

Figure 9-12. *The UK Brewery mapplet*

What does the mapplet code look like? As you'll see in Listing 9-14, it's remarkably simple, because I'm keeping the vast majority of the functionality in external JavaScript. I've highlighted the only items of note.

Listing 9-14. *Specification of the UK Brewery Mapplet*

```
<?xml version="1.0" encoding="UTF-8"?>
<Module>
  <ModulePrefs title="Breweries in Great Britain"
               directory_title="British Breweries"
               description="Map the locations of all breweries in Great Britain."
               author="Sterling Udell"
               author_email="sterling.udell+mapplet@googlemail.com"
           screenshot="http://sterlingudell.com/bgmm/chapter_09/brewery_scr.png"
           thumbnail="http://sterlingudell.com/bgmm/chapter_09/brewery_thm.png">
    <Require feature="sharedmap" />
    <Require feature="dynamic-height"/>
  </ModulePrefs>
  <Content type="html"><![CDATA[
    <style type="text/css">
      ul {
        font-size: 90%;
        padding-left: 1em;
      }
```

```
      li {
        padding-left: 0em;
      }
    </style>

    <ol id="list"></ol>

    <script type="text/javascript"
        src="http://sterlingudell.com/bgmm/egeoxml.js"></script>
    <script type="text/javascript"
        src="http://sterlingudell.com/bgmm/chapter_09/listing_09_15.js"></script>
    <script type="text/javascript">
      // Initialize the map
      map = new GMap2();

      // Initialize the KML processor
      var url = 'http://sterlingudell.com/bgmm/chapter_09/uk_breweries.kml';
      var options = {sidebarid: 'list', createmarker: addDataPoint, nozoom: true};
      geoXml = new EGeoXml(map, url, options);

      // Attach an event handler for after the KML is processed
      GEvent.addListener(geoXml, 'parsed', xmlParsed);

      // Load the KML
      geoXml.parse();

      // Attach an event to refresh the marker display whenever the map moves
      GEvent.addListener(map, 'moveend',          mapMoveEnd);
      GEvent.addListener(map, 'infowindowopen',   mapInfoWindowOpen);
      GEvent.addListener(map, 'infowindowclose', mapInfoWindowClose);
    </script>
  ]]></Content>
</Module>
```

First, I'm linking in listing_09_15.js, the same cross-API JavaScript code that the Maps API version is using (referenced in Listing 9-10). And second, I've only had to transfer a few lines of code—for loading and parsing the KML—from my loadMap function into the mapplet's main script element. The rest is still in listing_09_15.js, Listing 9-15.

■**Note** The listing_09_15.js file still contains the original loadMap function that the Maps API implementation uses. When the JavaScript is linked into the mapplet, loadMap is ignored, as the mapplet doesn't need it.

Listing 9-15. *The Final, Cross-API Version of the UK Brewery Map JavaScript*

```javascript
// Declare variables for later use
var map;
var geoXml;
var data = new Array();
var markers = new Array();
var clicked;
var current;

function loadMap()
{
  // loadMap: initialize the API and load the map onto the page

  // Get the map container div
  var mapDiv = document.getElementById('map');

  // Confirm browser compatibility with the Maps API
  if (!GBrowserIsCompatible())
  {
    mapDiv.innerHTML =
      'Sorry, your browser isn\'t compatible with Google Maps.';
  }
  else
  {
    // Initialize the core map object
    map = new GMap2(mapDiv,
      {mapTypes: [G_NORMAL_MAP, G_SATELLITE_MAP, G_HYBRID_MAP, G_PHYSICAL_MAP]});

    // Set the starting map viewport
    var coordinates = new GLatLng(53.6, -4.3);
    map.setCenter(coordinates, 6);

    // Add the standard map controls
    map.addControl(new GLargeMapControl());
    map.addControl(new GScaleControl());
    map.addControl(new GOverviewMapControl());
    map.addControl(new GMapTypeControl());

    // Initialize the KML processor
    var url = 'uk_breweries.kml';
    var options = {sidebarid: 'list', createmarker: addDataPoint, nozoom: true};
    geoXml = new EGeoXml(map, url, options);

    // Attach an event handler for after the KML is processed
    GEvent.addListener(geoXml, 'parsed', xmlParsed);
```

```
    // Load the KML
    geoXml.parse();

    // Attach an event to refresh the marker display whenever the map moves
    GEvent.addListener(map, 'moveend',         mapMoveEnd);
    GEvent.addListener(map, 'infowindowopen',  mapInfoWindowOpen);
    GEvent.addListener(map, 'infowindowclose', mapInfoWindowClose);
  }
};

function addDataPoint(coordinates, name, description)
{
  // addDataPoint: save the data for a placemark found by the KML processor
  var d = data.length;
  data[d] = {coords: coordinates, title: name, details: description};
};

function xmlParsed()
{
  // xmlParsed: after KML processing, initialize the marker display
  mapMoveEnd();
};

function mapMoveEnd()
{
  //  mapMoveEnd: get the new map boundary coordinates for use in marker display
  GAsync(map, 'getBounds', afterGetBounds);
};

function afterGetBounds(mapBounds)
{
  //  afterGetBounds: refresh the marker display

  // Don't refresh if the currently selected marker is still in view
  if (current != null)
  {
    if (mapBounds.contains(current))
      return;
    else
      map.closeInfoWindow();
  }

  // Prepare to build new sidebar content by starting with a clean slate
  var sidebarContent = '';
```

```
// Remove previous set of markers from the map and the array
for (var m = markers.length - 1; m >= 0; m--)
{
  map.removeOverlay(markers[m]);
  markers.splice(m, 1);
}

// Create a base icon
var numberIcon = new GIcon(G_DEFAULT_ICON);

// Look for data in the new map area
for (var d = 0; d < data.length; d++)
{
  if (mapBounds.contains(data[d].coords))
  {
    // Map does contain this data point; create a marker and add it to the map
    m = markers.length;
    numberIcon.image =
      'http://gmaps-samples.googlecode.com/svn/trunk/markers/orange/marker' +
      (m + 1) + '.png';
    markers[m] = new GMarker(data[d].coords, {icon: numberIcon});
    markers[m].data = data[d];
    map.addOverlay(markers[m]);

    // Also attach an event handler to show infowindow when marker is clicked
    GEvent.addListener(markers[m], 'click',
      new Function('showDetail(' + m + ')'));

    // Create sidebar content for this data point, including click event handler
    sidebarContent = sidebarContent +
      '<li><a href="#" onclick="showDetail(' + m + '); return false">' +
      data[d].title + '</a></li>';

    if (m >= 19)
    {
      // We've reached 20 markers, so break out of the loop
      sidebarContent = sidebarContent +
        '<li style="list-style: none">zoom in for more...</li>';
      break;
    }
  }
}

if (markers.length == 0)
  // No data points found in map boundaries
  sidebarContent = '<li style="list-style: none">No results found in map area. ' +
      'Try zooming out or moving the map.</li>';
```

```
  // Move the new content into the sidebar
  document.getElementById('list').innerHTML = sidebarContent;
};

function showDetail(m)
{
  // showDetail: open the infowindow for the given map marker
  current = clicked = markers[m].data.coords;
  markers[m].openInfoWindow(
    '<h4 style="margin: 0; font-size=120%">' + markers[m].data.title + '</h3>' +
    '<p style="margin: 0; font-size=90%">' + markers[m].data.details + '</p>');
};

function mapInfoWindowOpen()
{
  // mapInfoWindowOpen: set the variable that keeps track of the selected coords
  current = clicked;
};

function mapInfoWindowClose()
{
  // mapInfoWindowClose: clear the variable that keeps track of the selected coords
  current = null;
};
```

Pros and Cons of Dynamic Data Handling

This topic has shown you a useful technique for handling medium to large data sets, in both the Maps and Mapplets APIs, with what's still a relatively small amount of JavaScript. It's not the perfect solution for every geodata-mapping problem, but it should prove useful in your mapping endeavors.

How large a data set will it handle? That's more a function of the physical size of the KML data file. A drawback to any solution that attempts to handle large amounts of data purely in the browser is that by definition, all the data has to be downloaded *to* the browser. The uk_breweries.kml file is 241 kilobytes, a reasonably quick download for most users. By contrast, the global brewery data file from which it was sourced is 3.8 megabytes, too large for the average web surfer to happily download as part of an ordinary page load. So while the JavaScript will actually handle the 7,500 data points in the global KML, it's not practical to do so.

But to answer the question, this solution will generally work well up to a few thousand data points, assuming that the total file size is reasonable to download. For larger data sets, a server-based solution is usually a better choice, working in conjunction with the map page to filter the data before sending it. We'll look at these in the next couple of chapters.

Another limitation of this solution as it's written is that it always displays the *first* 20 data points it finds. For the UK brewery data, this works out well at high zoom levels, but less so when you're zoomed out; because the KML has the data points grouped by county, the first twenty are usually from only one or two counties, and they appear in clumps on the map. It would work better if data points that were more important in some way—newer data, perhaps, or highly rated on some scale—appeared earlier in the KML file. That way, the first 20 found in the viewport would also be the most important 20.

Nonetheless, a solution like this is still a vast improvement over trying to place a couple of thousand markers on the map.

Summary

This chapter has pushed your JavaScript skills as far as they'll go in this book (and possibly even a bit farther). I hope you feel it's been worth the effort; you should now be well-equipped for most mapping challenges. You've progressed beyond the beginner level and are ready to produce Google Map integrations that you can be proud of.

You've learned how to customize your marker icons in several different ways, including markers of varying sizes, colors, and with dynamic labels. You might even take a stab at creating icons from scratch.

You should also have more confidence in geocoding results after asking your users for verification. When that data comes back to you as KML, you're ready to customize the display in any way required. And finally, you now have tools at your disposal as well for handling large sets of markers and for efficiently developing applications for both the Maps and Mapplets APIs.

In short, you're finished with the pure API sections of this book. So in the next chapter, we'll explore various strategies for generating the geodata that you've been displaying up until now.

CHAPTER 10

■■■

Producing Geodata

Since Chapter 3, we've been using—or *consuming*—geodata with the Google Maps and Mapplets APIs. It's now time to try your hand at *producing* such data: taking the information assets you already have and publishing them on the geoweb. With the completion of this chapter, you'll have closed the circle. You'll be ready for the entire process of building a Google Map integration, from producing geoXML to displaying it however you want, on maps.google.com or your own web site.

We'll look first at using Google Maps itself to generate geoXML manually. This is appropriate when you have relatively little data, which doesn't change often. I'll then lead you on a whistle-stop tour of server-side programming (with examples in PHP and MySQL), giving you the basics you need to generate geodata dynamically in various circumstances. This will be the preferred technique for large, dynamic data sets, where manually building KML just isn't practical. We'll also look in on geo sitemaps, a standard for improving your geodata's visibility to search engines. Finally, I'll properly introduce JSON, an alternative data delivery format that you can use for occasions when geoXML isn't suitable.

Producing KML Manually

If you have only a fairly small amount of data, and it doesn't change very frequently, it's usually easiest to simply create KML manually for it. Although this approach is less powerful than server-side programming, it has a much shorter learning curve—and less overhead for your web host, too, as it only has to serve a static file.

An example of data well suited to this approach might be the locations of a small, local or regional restaurant chain. If there are less than a dozen or so restaurants in the chain, it won't take long to create the KML data initially. And since the chain only occasionally opens new restaurants (or relocates existing ones), the data upkeep isn't onerous. So for this section, I'll be building an example of such a restaurant chain data set.

Using Google's My Maps to Produce KML

By far the easiest way to produce map-ready geodata is directly on a map. Google has a couple of excellent tools for doing this; for our purposes, the best choice is the My Maps page at maps.google.com. My Maps has several key features that make it a good option for producing basic KML data:

- Ease of use tops the list; map markers and polylines can be created and edited quickly and efficiently with intuitive, map-based tools, right in your browser.

- Collaboration tools are included, meaning that you can invite other people to work on your map — great for team projects.

- Google hosts your KML data for you.

- If you mark your map as Public (as I'll discuss shortly), your data will automatically be indexed by Google and included in geographic searches.

- Because the KML is being generated right within Google Maps, it's guaranteed to be valid and compatible with the Maps API.

However, My Maps does have a couple of disadvantages you should be aware of:

- As a browser-based tool, it's not very convenient for working with KML files on your local computer, which is often necessary if you're using EGeoXml to display your data (as in Chapter 9). I'll discuss this situation further in a few pages.

- My Maps cannot generate GeoRSS at all. If GeoRSS is the format that makes sense for your application (see Chapter 1), there's currently little alternative to producing it from scratch.

Creating a Map

You should already be familiar with My Maps from the Mapplets API section of this book; now, however, we're going to be focusing on the "Created by me" area at the top of the My Maps page (see Figure 10-1).

On the My Maps page, click the "Create new map" link to get started, and enter a title and description for your map data file. As you can see, I've entered these details for my imaginary restaurant chain, called *Fingers Restaurants: Fork-Free Dining.* And I've selected that I want the KML to be Public; the whole idea here is that (in addition to using that data on my own maps) I'm creating geodata that's visible to everyone, as a means of publicizing my restaurants.

If you are creating geodata that's for internal use in your organization only, you'd select Unlisted here. That way, you can still access the data for your own maps, but it won't be discoverable by the general public.

With your basic map configuration set, it's time to proceed to creating the geodata itself. When you're editing your map (right after creating it, or by clicking its Edit button at any other time), Google adds buttons for the map-editing tools to the upper-left part of the map window, visible just northwest of Seattle in Figure 10-1. For my restaurant chain, I'll only be using map markers; these are created with the button that looks like the standard Google Maps marker icon (its tooltip is "Add a placemark"). Clicking the button creates a marker ready to be dropped anywhere on the map; you can then change its title, description, and icon within its editing infowindow, as shown in Figure 10-2. Click OK to save the information for each marker.

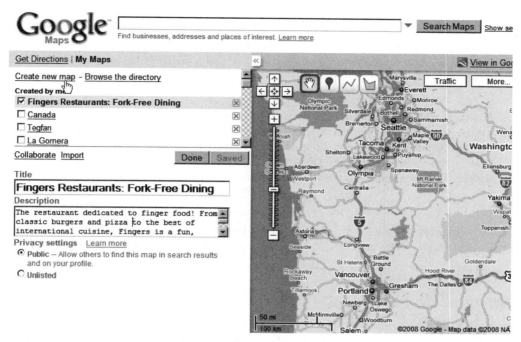

Figure 10-1. *Creating a new map for the* Fingers *restaurant chain*

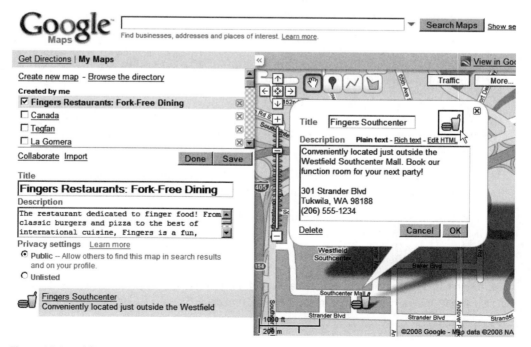

Figure 10-2. *Adding a map marker for a restaurant location*

> ■**Tip** You can change the marker for a My Maps location by clicking the icon at the upper right of the infowindow (like the "burger and drink" icon in Figure 10-2). You can even use custom icons from elsewhere on the web here—see Topic 1 in the previous chapter.

Continue adding markers for each location, using the usual Maps zoom and pan tools to place them precisely. You can also use the other two editing buttons to add polylines and polygons, if appropriate to your needs (Chapter 3 lists some typical uses for these objects).

When you're finished, click the Done button in the sidebar. Your data will be saved to Google's servers and is immediately available for use in your maps as KML.

> ■**Note** Although your geodata is immediately available, there is some delay—perhaps as much as a week or two—until Google updates its geo-search index and begins to display your content in search results.

Obtaining the KML

My Maps makes your geodata available to you as KML, ready to be used in the GGeoXml or EGeoXml objects. Here's how you obtain the KML that My Maps has created for you:

1. You need to start out in edit mode, either with a freshly created map or by clicking the map's Edit button on the Google Maps sidebar.

2. A "View in Google Earth" link should be visible above the map window. Right-click this link.

3. Select Copy Shortcut (IE) or Copy Link Location (Firefox) from the right-click menu. You now have the URL on your clipboard.

If you're using Google's own GGeoXml object, as we have through most of this book, that's all you need. Paste the URL from your clipboard into the JavaScript source code for your map page.

On the other hand, if you're using the open-source EGeoXML (a la Chapter 9), there's a bit more work to be done.

4. Paste the URL itself into the address bar of your browser, find the parameter (within the URL) that reads &output=nl, and change it to read &output=kml instead.

5. Load that URL into your browser (usually just by pressing Enter), and save the resulting KML page to your local machine.

> ■**Tip** If you're using my modified EGeoXml in a mapplet, you can skip step 5 here and simply use the URL from step 4 (with &output=nl changed to &output=kml) directly.

As you'll recall, with EGeoXml you generally need the KML to be hosted on the same server as the page it's being used in. So you'll need to upload the KML from step 5 to your web server.

Collaboration on My Maps

One of My Maps' best features is its built-in collaboration tools, which allow multiple people to contribute to a shared KML file. To enable collaboration, enter edit mode for your map and then click the Collaborate button above the title editing box. A small form will open from which you can invite colleagues to collaborate on the map with you and, afterwards, manage what permissions your collaborators have; see Figure 10-3.

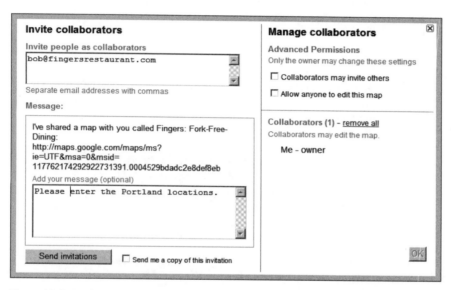

Figure 10-3. *Inviting colleagues to collaborate on a map*

Wrapping Up My Maps

Google's My Maps offers good visual tools for generating KML, so it's a good beginner's tool for producing geodata. If you're satisfied with what My Maps gives you, and you'd rather not delve into the internals of KML (or GeoRSS at all), then this is probably a good stopping point for this chapter. Otherwise, read on for a deeper look at KML and GeoRSS.

Managing KML Files Yourself

If you downloaded KML from My Maps, it will now be on your local computer, and from here you have complete flexibility with it. After downloading, a KML document is a file like any other; you'll use the same file management, editing, and uploading processes as with XHTML, CSS, or any other web page source file.

There may also be times when you need to make fine adjustments to the content of KML files after they've been downloaded. For example, you may need to tweak the appearance of infowindow content using CSS, or you may want to use a custom icon that My Maps doesn't offer (we'll discuss icons in KML later in the chapter). In such circumstances there's little alternative to editing the source code.

Editing KML or GeoRSS source directly isn't trivial, but neither is it fundamentally different from hand-coding XHTML. The basic structure of all three languages is similar; they're all forms of XML. And at its core, XML is simply text—meaning that you can probably use the same text editor for geoXML as you do for XHTML.

■**Tip** If you don't have a suitable XML editor, for Windows I recommend downloading Microsoft's free XML Notepad, from `http://tinyurl.com/qzhdt`. An alternative, more work to install but with built-in KML validation, is jEdit; Google has a guide to its use at `http://earth.google.com/outreach/tutorial_jedit.html`.

Still, I'd generally not recommend creating geoXML entirely from scratch. Often, the best route is to start by creating the initial KML in My Maps, downloading it, and making changes manually only if they couldn't be done online.

CREATING AND EDITING KML IN GOOGLE EARTH

An alternative to using a plain text editor to manipulate KML source is to use Google Earth. Essentially, Earth can function as a map-based editor for KML, with many of the same advantages as My Maps. Here's an overview:

- Under the File menu, you can Open KML files on your computer, and they'll appear in My Places.

- Right-click on any place, either in My Places or on the map itself, and select Properties to edit the title, description, and icon, much as in My Maps.

- When editing marker details, you can drag the marker itself around the map to change its location.

- Selecting Copy from the same right-click menu will put the KML for that place in your clipboard. This can be handy as a bridge between map-based and plain-text editing.

- The Add menu will allow you to create new placemarks, paths, polygons, and image overlays. The latter are supported by GGeoXml, incidentally, but can't be created from My Maps.

- When you're done, select Save As to write the KML back out to your local disk.

As a native application, Google Earth is more responsive than the browser-based My Maps and makes it easier to work with local files. There is a major disadvantage, however. Earth implements the full KML specification, and therefore it can create KML that the Google Maps API can't read, especially EGeoXml. So if you're going to use Google Earth, test all the KML features you plan to use over in the Maps API before you spend too much time creating content.

Validating Your KML

After any manual editing, I strongly recommend that you validate your XML. Generally, geodata readers (like GGeoXml) are not very forgiving of formatting errors, such as mismatched open and close tags or missing required elements. It's not like HTML, where a browser will make its best attempt to render a malformed page; GGeoXml will usually just stop at the first error it finds. So validation is more than an afterthought with geoXML, it's a crucial debugging tool.

The standard site for validating geoXML is http://feedvalidator.org. Your source file will need to be on a publicly accessible web server; then, enter its URL in the space provided and click Validate (see Figure 10-4). The service validates both KML and GeoRSS, and it will offer suggestions for greatest compatibility in addition to catching outright errors.

FEED Validator

FOR ATOM AND RSS AND KML

`http://sterlingudell.com/bgmm/chapter_10/listing_10_03.php` Validate

Congratulations!

 This is a valid KML 2.2 feed.

If you would like to create a banner that links to this page (i.e. this validation result), do the following:

1. Download the "valid KML 2.2" banner.

2. Upload the image to your own server. (This step is important. Please do not link directly to the image on this server.)

Figure 10-4. *Validating KML with feedvalidator.org*

Producing Geodata with PHP and MySQL

Creating KML manually, with My Maps or a text editor, is fine for small, static data sets. In the real world, however, we're often dealing with geodata that is neither; we may have many thousands of data points, changing on a daily basis. In such a case, there's little alternative to using database software, which in turn will require server-side programming to access.

What do I mean by *server-side programming*? It's a reference to the classic client-server model of the Internet, where a browser *client* is requesting pages (or other data) from a web *server*. Until now, this book has dealt entirely with client-side programming in JavaScript. Although there have been server interactions, our code has only been a consumer of those services—it hasn't truly been in control. And as you'll remember from the last section of Chapter 9, there comes a point where data sets become too large to process efficiently in the browser client.

With server-side programming, such limitations become largely irrelevant. Web servers can have almost unlimited disk capacity, so the efficient storage of millions of data points is not a problem. Access to this data is accomplished through program code running on the server, sending clients only the small fraction of the data that they actually need. Different programs can be running simultaneously to update the data, and because it's stored centrally, clients are assured of getting the latest possible view.

For the remainder of the chapter, we'll be looking at strategies for storing large data sets and serving them effectively to clients, using two popular open-source software packages, MySQL and PHP. Both of these are required to use any of the examples from this point forward. Many web servers have this software installed, and it's already in use behind the scenes of many web sites. If you're using the Maps API to add maps to a web site of your own, there's a good chance that your server is already running MySQL and PHP.

If you don't have any access to PHP and MySQL, but you aspire to produce geodata from a different server-side programming environment, the following examples should still be of some use to you. Many of the general principles are quite widely applicable; SQL, in particular, is fairly standardized, and the guidelines that follow shortly apply to any SQL environment.

This chapter is not meant to be a complete tutorial on using either of these packages. Rather, I want to give you a few complete code snippets and the knowledge to use them, so that you can add geodata services to any existing PHP/MySQL installation. To get the most from these sections, it would be helpful if you have some PHP and MySQL experience, or at least have a colleague with such experience that you can tap.

Storing Geodata in a MySQL Database

Software packages for storing data in a structured way are called *databases*, and one of the most widely used on web servers is MySQL. The *SQL* in MySQL stands for *Structured Query Language*, the name of the standard language used by the majority of databases for the storage and retrieval of information. A full coverage of SQL is far beyond the scope of this book; what I'll be doing instead is discussing the fundamental issues around using MySQL to effective store geodata.

Because I'm not covering MySQL from scratch, I'm not going to talk you through every aspect. So, for this section I need to assume that you either have access to some MySQL experience (as stipulated in the last section), or that your web host has a user-friendly MySQL administration interface installed. You might need to ask your web provider; one common such interface is called phpMyAdmin. But beyond that, there's not much more guidance that I can give you; too much depends on your own server's particular setup. See Appendix D for additional resources on using MySQL, especially with PHP.

Let's start by looking at a basic SQL table with geodata. In SQL, a *table* is the fundamental structure for a block of related data; it's rather like a spreadsheet, with information in rows and columns. With that in mind, take a look at Listing 10-1, which defines the columns for a MySQL table.

Listing 10-1. *The MySQL Geoname Table*

```
create table geoname (
    name        varchar(127),
    state       char(3),
    country     char(2),
    population  int(11),
    latitude    double,
    longitude   double,
```

```
    primary key (country, state, name),
    index coordinates (latitude, longitude)
)
```

This table will be used for geoname data, which as you'll recall from Chapter 8 is used to link the names of places (like cities and towns) with their map coordinates. So the first four columns, name through population, are just ordinary information about a place. It's the final two columns that really interest us, latitude and longitude; with these, as you know, we can map the places in the table on a Google Map.

A table, defined with SQL like this, is ready for filling with *rows*. Just like the rows in a spreadsheet, each row in the table will have values for these six columns; see Figure 10-5 for a sample. We can add as many rows as we like; with a table like this, we could easily store all the city and town place names on Earth. For the examples later in the chapter, I've filled my table with 73,000 rows representing virtually every populated place in North America, downloaded from the U.S. Geological Survey. So in contrast with a spreadsheet, a database table doesn't mind storing a *lot* of data.

name	state	country	population	latitude	longitude
Akiak	AK	US	289	60.9122	-161.214
Akutan	AK	US	409	54.1356	-165.773
Alakanuk	AK	US	615	62.6889	-164.615
Aleknagik	AK	US	174	59.2731	-158.618
Allakaket	AK	US	182	66.5656	-152.646
Ambler	AK	US	328	67.0861	-157.851
Anaktuvuk Pass	AK	US	311	68.1433	-151.736
Anchorage	AK	US	253649	61.2181	-149.9
Anderson	AK	US	1906	64.3442	-149.187
Angoon	AK	US	590	57.5033	-134.584
Aniak	AK	US	526	61.5783	-159.522
Atqasuk	AK	US	184	70.4694	-157.396
Barrow	AK	US	4137	71.2906	-156.789

Figure 10-5. *A few sample rows from the geoname table*

To run the examples in this part of the chapter, you'll need to create the geoname table using the SQL in Listing 10-1. If you have phpMyAdmin, this can be done from the SQL tab (see Figure 10-6); if not, I have to assume that you can manage on your own. The sample data I'm using throughout this part of the chapter can be downloaded from http://sterlingudell.com/bgmm/chapter_10/geoname_data.zip, ready to load into the MySQL table from Listing 10-1 (on the Import tab, if you're using phpMyAdmin).

There are two other specific aspects of this table that I want to draw your attention to. Even if you're not able to follow along and run my examples on a server environment of your own, they are applicable to any SQL database.

The first is the *data type* of the latitude and longitude columns, double. Short for *double-precision*, double is used for numbers that must be accurate to many decimal places. The alternatives in standard SQL (float and decimal, if you're interested) either aren't precise enough or aren't efficient ways to store such numbers. So if you're adding map coordinates to an SQL table, it's a good rule of thumb to use double.

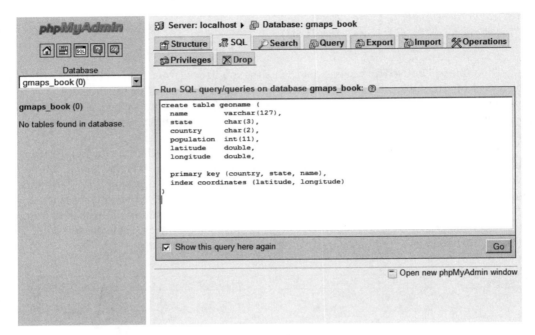

Figure 10-6. *Creating the geoname table in phpMyAdmin*

Second is the index on the geospatial columns, defined with the following line:

```
index coordinates (latitude, longitude)
```

Put simply, an *index* lets a database access specific rows quickly, much as the index in a book lets you go directly to the page containing a topic of interest. In this case, an index that I've named `coordinates` is on the `latitude` and `longitude` columns. Later in the chapter, we'll see this index in action as we access data in a specific geographic area. The database engine will use the two columns in the index to narrow down the result set; it will filter first on the latitude and then on the longitude, to arrive at the precise rows required. Structure like this is another way in which database tables differ from spreadsheets; they are more than simply data in columns and rows.

This is an extremely minimal introduction to database tables and SQL, but it is sufficient to support some realistic geodata-production scenarios. For those scenarios, though, we'll need functionality, and for that we'll use PHP.

Introduction to PHP: Hypertext Preprocessor

My choice of server-side programming language for this chapter is PHP. In a nutshell, what PHP does is run *before* any given web page is served. By executing some program code embedded in the server version of that page, it *changes the content of that page*, before the page goes out across the Internet to your browser. Hence the name: it preprocesses the HTML before it's served.

It might be easiest to see how PHP works with a simple example. Consider the following very basic PHP script.

```
<p>
<?php
  echo 'Hello, world!';
?>
</p>
```

When a browser requests this script from a PHP-enabled web server, everything between `<?php` and `?>`—the PHP open and close tags—gets executed as program code. In this case, it's just a single line:

```
echo 'Hello, world!';
```

The `echo` statement simply copies whatever comes after it to the resulting web document. So when PHP runs, the following HTML comes out the other side:

```
<p>
Hello, world!
</p>
```

And this will be served back to the requesting browser, just as if these three lines had been contained within an ordinary `.html` document.

At this point, you might well be asking, "Why bother? Why not just write the XHTML?" The answer is that PHP scripts will generally contain some *logic* to perform different actions under different circumstances. So here's a slightly longer example, with logic:

```
<p>
<?php
  if (date('H') < 12)
    echo 'Good morning, world!';
  else
    echo 'Hello, world!';
?>
</p>
```

As you can see, I've extended the PHP to examine the hour of the day, using its built-in `date` function; if the hour is less than 12, it echoes the "Good morning" message instead. Still quite trivial, but more than could be accomplished with XHTML alone.

You'll notice that PHP's syntax is quite like JavaScript in a number of ways: it has an identical `if`/`else` construct, each line ends with a semicolon, and the strings are contained in quotes (as in JavaScript, either single or double quotes will do). The similarities will continue; much of the language structure will look familiar to you.

There is, however, a basic divide between PHP and JavaScript that I want to stress at this point. JavaScript is fundamentally a *client-side* programming language; it runs in the browser, after a page has been received over the web. Conversely, PHP is *server-side*; it runs on the web host, before a page is sent. This distinction translates into basic strengths and weaknesses for each language; you'll see more of these as we go along.

Like MySQL in the previous section, PHP is open-source and very widely used on web servers worldwide. It's an extremely flexible programming language, which is what makes it suitable for this chapter; I'll be producing geoXML with it, not XHTML. But PHP doesn't care; it will produce whatever it's told to produce, and if the results get served as KML, that's fine all around.

Generating KML

For this example, I'm going to produce KML for a list of the larger cities in Pennsylvania, though (as you'll see) the technique used will generalize to any selection of our place name data. By way of planning our attack, then, Listing 10-2 shows what we want our KML to look like. It's fairly simple, there's a name element describing the document and then a Placemark for each city containing its name, population, and coordinates.

Listing 10-2. *The KML Document to Be Generated*

```
<?xml version="1.0" encoding="UTF-8"?>
<kml xmlns="http://earth.google.com/kml/2.2">
<Document>
  <name>Cities in Pennsylvania</name>
  <Placemark>
    <name>Allentown</name>
    <description><![CDATA[
      Population 105339
    ]]></description>
    <Point>
      <coordinates>-75.491,40.608,0</coordinates>
    </Point>
  </Placemark>/n
  <Placemark>
    <name>Altoona</name>
    <description><![CDATA[
      Population 52531
    ]]></description>
    <Point>
      <coordinates>-78.395,40.519,0</coordinates>
    </Point>
  </Placemark>
  ...
</Document>
</kml>
```

This KML will be produced in response to a request from a Maps API JavaScript. In previous chapters, such scripts have been loading static KML documents; the big difference now is that the KML will be produced on demand by PHP.

So on the server, we need a PHP script that will

1. Extract the Pennsylvania city data from the geoname table.

2. Format that data as the KML in Listing 10-2.

3. Return the KML to the client.

Let's go through the pieces one by one before assembling them into a complete PHP program.

Retrieving the Data

The database retrieval works by embedding a SQL statement in the PHP, as follows:

```
$query = "select *
          from geoname
          where (country = 'US')
            and (state = 'PA')
            and (population > 25000)";
```

In PHP, all variables start with the $ symbol (and you don't need var). So we're setting $query to a block of SQL that says, "select data from the geoname table where the following conditions are true: the country is USA, and the state is Pennsylvania, and the population is over 25,000." Basic SQL is quite intuitive in this way; you can almost read it as abbreviated English.

■**Tip** PHP strings, unlike those in JavaScript, don't need to be confined to a single line. So the SQL statement string in the previous listing, for example, spans five lines of code—a handy technique that you'll see me use often.

With the SQL statement (often called a *query*, hence the variable name) in hand, it's a simple matter to send it to the MySQL database:

```
$result = mysql_query($query);
```

It's one function call, mysql_query, and I'm placing the return value into another variable, $result, which we'll use in the next section.

Creating the KML

We get the KML started by creating a "header" string as follows:

```
$header = '<?xml version="1.0" encoding="UTF-8"?>
<kml xmlns="http://earth.google.com/kml/2.2">
<Document>
  <name>Cities in Pennsylvania</name>';
```

This header is all the KML (from Listing 10-2) that precedes the Placemarks. So our PHP statement places the KML header text, as a string, into the $header variable.

The Placemarks themselves will be generated from the data retrieved out of MySQL; this data is organized into rows, remember, with one row per city. So for each row, we need to create the KML for one Placemark. This is the heart of generating geodata dynamically, and here's how it's done:

```
$placemarks = $placemarks.'
<Placemark>
  <name>'.htmlentities($row['name']).'</name>
  <description><![CDATA[
    Population '.$row['population'].'
  ]]></description>
  <Point>
    <coordinates>'.$row['longitude'].','.$row['latitude'].',0</coordinates>
  </Point>
</Placemark>';
```

Essentially, this is very like the $header statement earlier; you build a $placemarks variable containing the row data for the city—compare with Listing 10-2. A few additional PHP notes are in order, however:

- $row is an array here, but unlike the arrays in Chapter 9, the index is a string (rather than a number).

- In PHP, strings like $placemarks are added together with a dot (as opposed to JavaScript, which used a plus sign +).

- The htmlentities function on the name makes sure that no special characters—like <, >, or "—find their way into the KML without being properly encoded (such as < for <). Just as in XHTML, failing to do this could invalidate the KML by unbalancing the angle brackets (for example).

But where does the $row array come from—how does each database row come to be there? By wrapping our $placemark statement in a language construct called a while loop:

```
while ($row = mysql_fetch_array($result))
{
  $placemarks .= '
<Placemark>
  ...
</Placemark>';
}
```

Like the for loop introduced in Chapter 9, the while loop repeatedly executes the code within its control. In this case, it's controlled by mysql_fetch_array, a great PHP function that extracts a database row from the query execution $result and creates a PHP array. This allows us to access the elements of $row by the column name, as seen above. And mysql_fetch_array will keep "fetching" the next $row, each time the while loop comes around, until there are no more rows to fetch—at which point it will break the loop. It's a powerful little piece of code.

When it's done, you just need to finish up the KML. The PHP to do this should look quite reasonable to you by now:

```
$footer = '
</Document>
</kml>';
```

Looking back at Listing 10-2, these closing tags for `Document` and `kml` are all that remain in the KML after the `Placemarks`.

Returning the Results

So by this point, we have all the required KML created in PHP, and all that's left is to return it to the client as a KML document. Four lines of code will do the job:

```
header('Content-type: application/vnd.google-earth.kml+xml');
echo $header;
echo $placemarks;
echo $footer;
```

The first line is a PHP function, `header`, which marks the returning document internally as KML. It's not strictly required if the client is unequivocally going to process the document as KML (as our JavaScript will), but for standards compliance it's a good idea—a bit like the `DOCTYPE` in XHTML. And the remaining lines simply `echo` our KML-holding variables from the previous section—$header, $placemarks, and $footer—to the resulting KML document.

That's it! We've created the KML for Listing 10-2 from the database rows and sent it back to the client, who neither knows nor cares that it was created on the fly. The Pennsylvania cities have been extracted from the database and will be displayed on the map, as shown in Figure 10-7.

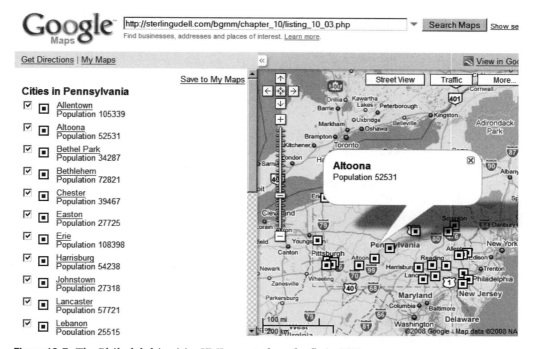

Figure 10-7. *The Philadelphia cities KML, created on the fly in PHP*

> ■**Note** This is example data; although it was sourced from real USGS place-name data, at `http://`
> `geonames.usgs.gov`, it's not production-quality, and the population numbers shown here are not to be
> relied on!

Bringing It All Together

You're now ready for the complete PHP script, producing KML by combining the steps from
the previous few sections, and Listing 10-3 lays it all out. Although this is essentially the same
code as earlier, I've filled in a few additional items for better, more complete KML.

Listing 10-3. *The PHP to Produce Dynamic KML*

```php
<?php
  // Connect to the database.
  include 'database_connect.php';

  // Execute the MySQL query to retrieve the data
  $query = "select *
              from geoname
              where (country = 'US')
                and (state = 'PA')
                and (population > 25000)";
  $result = mysql_query($query);
  if (!$result)
    die("Unable to retrieve data");

  // Prepare the KML header
  $header = '<?xml version="1.0" encoding="UTF-8"?>
<kml xmlns="http://earth.google.com/kml/2.2">
<Document>
  <name>Cities in Pennsylvania</name>
  <Style id="city_style">
    <IconStyle>
      <Icon>
        <href>http://maps.google.com/mapfiles/kml/pal4/icon56.png</href>
      </Icon>
    </IconStyle>
  </Style>';

  // Generate KML placemarks for the retrieved data
  while ($row = mysql_fetch_array($result))
  {
    $placemarks = $placemarks.'
<Placemark id="'.$row['country'].'_'.$row['state'].'_'.urlencode($row['name']).'">
  <name>'.htmlentities($row['name']).'</name>
```

```
    <description><![CDATA[
      Population '.$row['population'].'
    ]]></description>
    <styleUrl>#city_style</styleUrl>
    <Point>
      <coordinates>'.$row['longitude'].','.$row['latitude'].',0</coordinates>
    </Point>
  </Placemark>';
  }

  // Prepare the KML footer
  $footer = '
</Document>
</kml>';

  // Output the final KML
  header('Content-type: application/vnd.google-earth.kml+xml');
  echo $header;
  echo $placemarks;
  echo $footer;
?>
```

Connecting to the Database

Right at the top of the listing, notice the following line:

```
include 'database_connect.php';
```

The include statement runs an external PHP file, much like a script tag in XHTML. In this case, the external file connects PHP to the database, in preparation for the mysql_query that comes next.

There are a couple of reasons why I've not included the database connection directly in Listing 10-3. First, it's a common and good practice to make the connection in a separate file like this, so if you're trying to use my PHP on an established web site, it's likely that your site already has an equivalent to database_connect.php. But second, the database connection process varies greatly by site—meaning that my connection parameters will be no good to you.

To create your own database_connect.php, you'll need to know your database address, database name, user ID, and password (see why my script wouldn't help you?). You'll then need to fill all those parameters into a script like the following, named database_connect.php, on your server:

```
<?php
  $db = mysql_connect('database address', 'user id', 'password');
  mysql_select_db('database name');
?>
```

For compatibility with my PHP code, your database_connect.php will need to set a variable named $db from the mysql_connect function, as shown here.

Styling the Markers

Moving on, the next addition to Listing 10-3 involves *style*, and it illustrates the technique for setting marker icons within KML. It begins with a Style element in the "header" section; you'll then need the Icon and IconStyle elements shown within, and finally href, containing the URL of the marker icon to use.

KML marker icons have less flexibility than the API icons discussed in Chapter 9; they'll always be rendered by Google Maps as 32 pixels square, and without separate shadows. You can create your own icons in this size, or you can use one of the standard Google Earth icons, as I have here. For a complete list of the available Earth icons, please see http://econym.googlepages.com/geicons.htm.

Note that the Style element in the header has an id, "city_style" in this case. You can apply this style to all the Placemarks by inserting the following in each:

```
<styleUrl>#city_style</styleUrl>
```

Be careful to include a hash character (#) in front of the style id in the styleUrl. Additionally, you can define multiple Styles in the header area and use them for different Placemarks simply by using different ids.

▪**Caution** It's also valid KML to include style with each Placemark, rather than once in the header as I'm doing here, and you may see KML like this from time to time. However, doing so isn't compatible with EGeoXml, so I advise you to stick with this method.

Preparing the Geodata for Indexing

Speaking of ids, that brings me to the other addition to Listing 10-3, the id in the Placemark tag. While this isn't strictly required for KML, it is recommended, especially if you want your geodata to be indexed by Google (more on that later in the chapter). If it is included, the id needs to be unique for each Placemark. In this case, I accomplish that by stringing together the location's country code, state abbreviation, and URL-encoded city name:

```
id="'.$row['country'].'_'.$row['state'].'_'.urlencode($row['name']).'"
```

The quotation marks can get confusing with multiple strings like this; you do need to be careful that they all match up!

And with that, we have complete, valid KML (recall Figure 10-4). It's still quite minimal, though; sufficient to illustrate the PHP technique, but a pale shadow of the richness that the format can convey. I encourage you to delve into the KML specification and tutorials at http://code.google.com/apis/kml and try your hand at generating more interesting geodata.

Dynamic Data?

Before we move on, there's one last point I want to address. You might well have noticed that this example isn't truly *dynamic*—it always returns the same list of Pennsylvania cities. So what's the point of all the PHP?

First, you could completely change the KML with absolutely minimal changes to the source code; for example, you could see cities in Wisconsin instead simply by changing PA to WI. Move the population threshold up or down from 25000 just as easily. You don't need to spend hours researching cities and rebuilding KML by hand; the data's all there, just waiting for you to select.

Second, it's an easy additional step to *parameterize* the code so that the data can be controlled by the client. There's an example of this later in the chapter, but for now, just imagine the client JavaScript allowing the user to select her state of interest (perhaps with an XHTML select element, as in Listing 5-4). The URL to this PHP would then include the requested state code, which would be used to drive the SQL retrieval.

Third, the data itself could be variable. Imagine that, rather than a table of geonames, we were working with data from a chain of stores—and rather than population, we were filtering by monthly sales numbers. Then the map would always show the top-performing stores for the month, automatically updating as the underlying data was changed.

However, if you are selecting data that is intrinsically static, it *doesn't* make sense to serve it from PHP like this. It may be useful to write the PHP to generate the KML once, but if the data isn't going to change, save the resulting KML and serve that to clients instead. It'll be significantly less server load (and thus faster) than running PHP and hitting the database every time.

■Tip When you've finished a script like this to generate KML, don't forget to enter its URL at http://feedvalidator.com to ensure that all elements are in its proper place. And of course, try out its URL at Google Maps!

Generating GeoRSS

The process for generating GeoRSS via PHP is almost identical to that for KML: select the data, format the XML, and return it to the client. So you won't need me to go through every step of the process in great detail. And for simplicity, I'm using exactly the same data as in the previous example.

Listing 10-4 shows the PHP code required to produce a simple GeoRSS feed. The main difference from Listing 10-3 is that the content being generated is Atom XML rather than KML. I've highlighted a few other interesting items and will go over them following the listing.

Listing 10-4. *The PHP to Produce Dynamic GeoRSS*

```php
<?php
  // Connect to the database
  include 'database_connect.php';

  // Execute the MySQL query to retrieve the data
  $query = "select *
              from geoname
              where (country = 'US')
                and (state = 'PA')
                and (population > 25000)";
  $result = mysql_query($query);
```

```php
  if (!$result)
    die("Unable to retrieve data");

  $now = mktime();

  // Prepare the Atom header
  $header = '<?xml version="1.0" encoding="UTF-8"?>
<feed xmlns="http://www.w3.org/2005/Atom"
      xmlns:georss="http://www.georss.org/georss">
  <title>Cities in Pennsylvania</title>
  <subtitle>with population over 25,000</subtitle>
  <updated>'.date('c', $now).'</updated>
  <id>urn:978-1-4302-1620-9:chapter_10</id>
  <author>
    <name>Sterling Udell</name>
  </author>
  <link href="http://sterlingudell.com/bgmm/" rel="related" />
  <link href="http://'.$_SERVER['HTTP_HOST'].$_SERVER['SCRIPT_NAME'].'"
        rel="self" type="application/atom+xml" />';

  // Generate GeoRSS entries for the retrieved data
  while ($row = mysql_fetch_array($result))
  {
    $urlname = str_replace('_', ' ', $row['name']);
    $entries = $entries.'
  <entry>
    <title>'.htmlentities($row['name']).'</title>
    <link href="http://en.wikipedia.org/wiki/'.$urlname.',_Pennsylvania"/>
    <id>urn:978-1-4302-1620-9:'.$row['country'].$row['state'].'_'.$urlname.'</id>
    <summary>Population '.$row['population'].'</summary>
    <updated>'.date('c', $now--).'</updated>
    <georss:point>'.$row['latitude'].' '.$row['longitude'].'</georss:point>
  </entry>';
  }

  // Prepare the Atom footer
  $footer = '
</feed>';

  // Output the final Atom/GeoRSS
  header('Content-type: application/atom+xml');
  echo $header;
  echo $entries;
  echo $footer;
?>
```

First, note that I'm setting a variable called $now using PHP's mktime function, which stores the current date and time from the server. I do this because Atom requires the use of updated elements (also highlighted in Listing 10-4). In the "header" section, updated is quite easy, simply $now formatted with the use of the date function. But the individual row entries all need to have *different* updated values; I actually kludge it by decreasing the timestamp in $now by one second every time the while loops, using $now--.

KLUDGE

If you spend any time around programmers, sooner or later you'll hear the word *kludge*. It means a coding solution that isn't pretty, and isn't really the right way to do things, but gets the job done. My use of $now-- here is undeniably a kludge, and it's used only because the geoname data is not inherently well suited to GeoRSS distribution.

I'm reusing the geonames in this example purely for simplicity, to avoid burdening you with another SQL table definition and different select statement. But if you'll recall from Chapter 1, GeoRSS is better suited for data which gets added to periodically, such as blog entries. Such data would normally have a date/time stamp attached to each row, and it would have no need for my $now-- kludge.

■Note PHP's date function can format a date/time variable in many different ways, the 'c' parameter I'm using in Listing 10-4 just happens to be the format that Atom expects (ISO 8601, such as 2008-09-26T15:09:24+00:00). For a complete list of format specifiers, see http://php.net/date.

The next item of interest also occurs in the header section:

```
<link href="http://'.$_SERVER['HTTP_HOST'].$_SERVER['SCRIPT_NAME'].'"
    rel="self" type="application/atom+xml" />';
```

Again, this is direct from the Atom specification; it's a recommendation that any feed include a link back to itself, for use by reader software. I make this happen by use of $_SERVER, an array that's *predefined* by PHP with a variety of useful data. You don't need to understand exactly how this works; the beauty of it is that you can simply include this code in your own PHP, and it will always supply the URL of the current script. Handy.

Within the while loop that generates the GeoRSS entries, you have another id, similar to the KML Placemark id you saw earlier:

```
<id>urn:978-1-4302-1620-9:'.$row['country'].$row['state'].'_'.$urlname.'</id>
```

The major difference here is that Atom likes this id to be *globally unique*, that is, any other entry in any other feed with the same id should refer to *the same data*.

To avoid conflicting with anyone else's feed, I've included this book's unique ISBN in the string. You'll need to find some similarly unique identifier for your own feed entries. Often, this can be derived from your site's domain name. If that's not practical, you can generate a Universally Unique Identifier—details at http://tinyurl.com/67cz2t.

A close reading of Listing 10-4 will reveal a few other tweaks to support additional fields, but that covers the main differences for generating GeoRSS. All that's left is to send it back to the client, and for this, we have a different header parameter near the bottom of the script:

```
header('Content-type: application/atom+xml');
```

This is exactly analogous to the header call when were producing KML, except that application/atom+xml indicates that this is an Atom feed.

And the result can be seen in Figure 10-8; it's quite similar to 10-7, subject to the distinctions between the two XML formats.

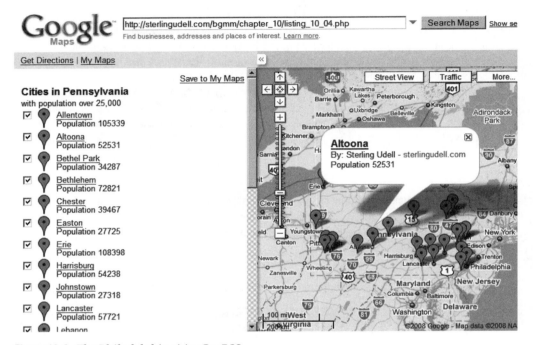

Figure 10-8. *The Philadelphia cities GeoRSS*

As with my KML example, this Atom document is quite minimal; I encourage you to enrich your own feeds with the full range of elements that the standard has to offer. For more information, the official Atom specification and documentation are available at http://atomenabled.org.

■**Tip** Again, validation is your friend. For GeoRSS, the tool to use is http://feedvalidator.org.

Filtering by Geographic Area

Returning to KML, I want to introduce you to a feature that will make excellent use of dynamic geodata, an aspect called *network links*. These can almost be thought of as "meta-KML"; rather than containing geospatial data itself, a network link *refers to another KML file* where the data can be found. What makes this bit of redirection useful is that, like a function in JavaScript or PHP, the link can include *parameters* that refine the data returned.

Let's look at an example. The specific parameterized link I'll be using in this section is based on the map viewport, and the idea is that when the map is moved, the KML link will retrieve new data—but only within the map's visible area. This way, no matter where the user moves the map or how far he zooms in and out, we can specifically show data points within that viewport.

This is a particularly powerful technique because it is another, more scalable approach to handling large data sets. You may recall that, late in Chapter 9, I introduced a method for handling a few thousand data points purely on the client—but said that for more data, a server-side solution was needed. This is it.

We begin with the network link KML, in Listing 10-5. It's remarkably simple, because it's not doing the real work. The important piece is the href element: this is the network link itself, containing the URL for a PHP script that will accept the viewport parameters and return dynamic KML for data points within it. The other new elements shown here, such as flyToView, viewRefreshMode, and viewRefreshTime, will be the same for any KML using this technique.

Listing 10-5. *The Map-Viewport Network Link KML*

```
<?xml version="1.0" encoding="UTF-8"?>
<kml xmlns="http://earth.google.com/kml/2.2">
  <Document>
    <name>Largest Cities</name>
    <description>
      The 10 largest cities in the map area (North America only)
    </description>
  </Document>
  <NetworkLink>
    <flyToView>0</flyToView>
    <Link>
      <href>http://sterlingudell.com/bgmm/chapter_10/listing_10_06.php</href>
      <viewRefreshMode>onStop</viewRefreshMode>
      <viewRefreshTime>1</viewRefreshTime>
    </Link>
  </NetworkLink>
</kml>
```

So let's jump straight into the KML-producing script, in Listing 10-6. I've highlighted the lines where it differs from Listing 10-3, our basic KML generator; you'll notice that (apart from changing the name) the new code is confined to only two sections, handling the parameters and the SQL select.

Listing 10-6. *The Viewport-Parameterized KML Generator*

```
<?php
  // Connect to the database
  include 'database_connect.php';

  // Make sure the URL parameters are numbers in the valid range
```

```php
$viewport = split(',', $_GET['BBOX']);

while ($viewport[0] > $viewport[2])
  $viewport[0] -= 360;

$north = (float) min(90,   $viewport[3]);
$north = min(90,   (float) $viewport[3]);
$south = max(-90,  (float) $viewport[1]);
$east  = min(180,  (float) $viewport[2]);
$west  = max(-180, (float) $viewport[0]);

// Execute the MySQL query to retrieve the data
$query = "select *
            from geoname
            where (latitude between $south and $north)
              and (longitude between $west and $east)
            order by population desc
            limit 10";
$result = mysql_query($query);
if (!$result)
  die("Unable to retrieve data");

// Prepare the KML header
$header = '<?xml version="1.0" encoding="UTF-8"?>
<kml xmlns="http://earth.google.com/kml/2.2">
<Document>
  <name>Largest Cities</name>
  <Style id="city_style">
    <IconStyle>
      <Icon>
        <href>http://maps.google.com/mapfiles/kml/pal4/icon56.png</href>
      </Icon>
    </IconStyle>
  </Style>';

// Generate KML placemarks for the retrieved data
while ($row = mysql_fetch_array($result))
{
  $placemarks = $placemarks.'
<Placemark id="'.$row['country'].'_'.$row['state'].'_'.urlencode($row['name']).'">
  <name>'.htmlentities($row['name']).'</name>
  <description><![CDATA[
    Population '.$row['population'].'
  ]]></description>
  <styleUrl>#city_style</styleUrl>
```

```
      <Point>
        <coordinates>'.$row['longitude'].','.$row['latitude'].',0</coordinates>
      </Point>
    </Placemark>';
    }

    // Prepare the KML footer
    $footer = '
</Document>
</kml>';

    // Output the final KML
    header('Content-type: application/vnd.google-earth.kml+xml');
    echo $header;
    echo $placemarks;
    echo $footer;
?>
```

Receiving the Viewport Parameters

When the client map moves and the new viewport is applied to the network link, it's in the form of a URL parameter named BBOX (for *bounding box*). The parameterized URL will look like this:

```
http://sterlingudell.com/bgmm/chapter_10/dynamic.kml.php?BBOX=west,south,east,north
```

where *west*, *south*, *east*, and *north* are numbers representing the latitude or longitude of the edges of the viewport.

PHP is quite used to dealing with URL parameters; it's a common aspect of server-side programming. It places them in another predefined array variable, this time named $_GET. You can then extract the individual ordinates like this:

```
$viewport = split(',', $_GET['BBOX']);
```

$_GET is a PHP array, remember, so the element of interest is indexed by the string 'BBOX'. Then the handy split function creates another array (stored in $viewport) by separating *west,south,east,north* on the commas. Result: $viewport has the four compass point ordinates as separate array elements.

I don't want to dwell too much on the next bit, because I don't want to get distracted from the business at hand and I'll cover it thoroughly in Appendix A. For now, suffice it to say that if the map viewport spans the 180-degree longitude line, *west* will be on the wrong side of *east*, and it will need to be modified:

```
while ($viewport[0] > $viewport[2])
  $viewport[0] -= 360;
```

The remaining parameter handling is some defensive coding:

```
$north = min(90,   (float) $viewport[3]);
$south = max(-90,  (float) $viewport[1]);
$east  = min(180,  (float) $viewport[2]);
$west  = max(-180, (float) $viewport[0]);
```

For each of the four values, you need to make sure it's just a number (with the `float` type-conversion, similar to JavaScript's `parseFloat`) and limit it to a realistic value (using the `max` and `min` functions). Essentially, this "cleans" the parameters to ensure that the SQL statement that's coming next will be happy with them.

■**Caution** Failing to clean parameters can pose a security risk in your PHP code, opening your server to an attack known as *SQL Injection*. In this case, the crucial part is the `float` conversion, but if your parameters include strings, please see `http://php.net/mysql_real_escape_string` for details on cleaning them. For more information on SQL injection attacks, please see `http://en.wikipedia.org/wiki/SQL_injection`.

Filtering the Data

With good viewport parameters in hand, it's time to hit the database. Again, the SQL syntax is remarkably intuitive:

```
select *
  from geoname
  where (latitude between $south and $north)
    and (longitude between $west and $east)
  order by population desc
  limit 10
```

It starts out exactly as before (in Listings 10-3 and 10-4), `selecting` rows from the `geoname` table. But instead of limiting the search to big cities in Pennsylvania, this time the `where` clause is limiting our result set to coordinates within the viewport, using of the `between` operator.

■**Note** The two `between` statements here utilize the `coordinates` index (which we set up back when we defined the geoname table) to quickly and efficiently filter the rows that will be returned from the query, rather than looking through all 73,000 place names.

There are also two entirely new lines here. The first, `order by population desc`, ensures that we get the largest cities in the first rows—sorting by `population` in `descending` order. So if the viewport encompasses the entire USA, the retrieved rows will start with New York City, Los Angeles, Chicago, and so on. And finally, `limit 10` does exactly what you might expect, ending the retrieval after the first 10 rows.

Once the data is retrieved, the rest of this script is no different from Listing 10-3, illustrating the power of dynamic geodata. The difference is all in the data; formatting it into KML and returning it to the client remain the same.

The result of the network link KML can be seen in Figures 10-9 and 10-10. For a wide range of zoom levels, the same script returns the ten largest cities (or towns) in view. Note that, although our KML has the largest cities first, Google Maps' sidebar automatically sorts them by name.

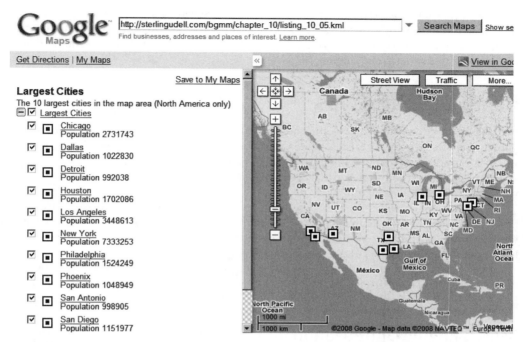

Figure 10-9. *The dynamic city KML, zoomed out to show the contiguous USA…*

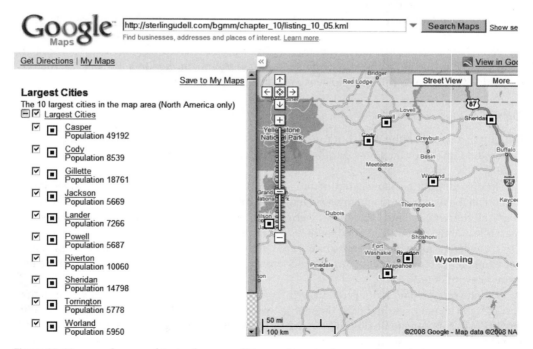

Figure 10-10. *…and zoomed in to show small towns in a single area of one state.*

The big advantage of network links, of course, is that the client-side programming is almost trivial; this KML will work fine with the JavaScript code from way back in Listing 3-1. And although EGeoXml is not natively compatible with network links, you will find an alternative method for dealing with this situation in Chapter 11.

Using Geo Sitemaps

By this point, I hope you're fairly comfortable with producing KML and GeoRSS. But for full participation in the geoweb, the rest of the world needs to be able to find that geodata. How can you make it more discoverable? In this next part of the chapter, you'll learn about geo sitemaps, special index files on your web site that help Google (and other geo-aware search engines) find your data and add it to their index.

If you haven't come across them before, *sitemaps* are standardized XML files that the major search engines use as an aid in crawling your web site. A sitemap document lists what files your site has available, how often they change, and their relative importance. For more information on sitemaps in general, the definitive source is http://sitemaps.org.

And as the name implies, *geo sitemaps* are a geospatial extension to the existing sitemap protocol. Ordinary sitemaps list conventional web documents; you turn an ordinary sitemap into a geo sitemap by including tags that indicate which of your documents contain geodata.

Search Engine Optimization for GeoXML

Before you get started creating geo sitemaps, however, you need to make certain that your geodata is ready. Effectively, this means applying *search engine optimization* (or SEO) principles to your geodata documents, ensuring that both the XML structure and its content are fully ready for indexing.

Search engine optimization is the subject of many books in its own right; in this section, I'll simply touch on a couple of specific items relevant to optimizing geodata. But overall, many general SEO principles will apply to geospatial documents as well.

Content Is King

It's a bit of a cliché on the Web, but the importance of content is no less true for geodata. The richer and more relevant your information, the better your placement will be in geo search results.

In my restaurant-chain example from Figure 10-2, for instance, note that I included information on the types of food that my restaurants specialized in, as well as key words and phrases like "function rooms" and "party." Geoweb or no, this is still web content, and if you want good search result placement, you need to include relevant text.

Conversely, my code examples have kept content to a minimum, as my main emphasis has been on the structure. For your own documents, you should make an effort to include far more relevant detail.

When your geodata is delivered in KML, such additional content will typically go into the description elements, both in the "header" section and for individual Placemarks. Essentially any XHTML content can be placed here to be indexed for geo search results. However, don't neglect descriptive names as well!

With its roots in news feeds, GeoRSS offers additional SEO opportunities in the form of more specialized XML elements. For Atom, this means tags such as author, content, summary, category, contributor, and source; in RSS, the equivalents include category, author, description, and comments. See the documentation referenced earlier in the chapter (and in Appendix D) for more details.

Finally, don't neglect links within your geoXML content. As with any web document, embedded links are important both for directing visitors to your own site and for informing search result rankings.

Optimizing GeoXML Structure

Google, at the forefront of geo search, recommends a few specific elements to include in your XML. The purpose of these elements is *attribution*; Google will use them in its results to display a "byline" for your content, encouraging interested users to visit your own site.

These tags—author, name, and link—can be found in Listing 10-4, my Atom feed example. Here they are, as they would appear in the actual feed:

```
<author>
  <name>Sterling Udell</name>
</author>
<link href="http://sterlingudell.com/bgmm/" rel="related" />
```

As you can see, name should contain your name (or your company name), and link the URL of your web site. You can see the attribution in action back in Figure 10-8, as the second line of text in the infowindow.

Since these elements are native to the Atom standard, using them in KML or RSS documents requires a slightly different format. First, the root XML element needs to include an additional *namespace* attribute, pointing to the Atom specification (where a feed reader can find a definition for the tag names). Here's how you do it:

```
<kml xmlns="http://earth.google.com/kml/2.2"
     xmlns:atom="http://www.w3.org/2005/Atom">
```

Simply replace your opening kml tag with this code. The usage in RSS is similar:

```
<rss version="2.0" xmlns:georss="http://www.georss.org/georss"
                    xmlns:atom="http://www.w3.org/2005/Atom">
```

Then, each of the actual elements needs to be prefixed with atom:, indicating the namespace that it's drawn from. So the three attribution elements will now look like this:

```
<atom:author>
  <atom:name>Sterling Udell</atom:name>
</atom:author>
<atom:link href="http://sterlingudell.com/bgmm/" rel="related" />
```

These elements should be inserted into the "header" section of your KML or RSS; in other words, add them to Listing 10-3 in the same area where they appear in Listing 10-4.

■**Note** Although RSS has an author element, it's not the same as Atom's. So it's still important that these author attribution elements carry the atom: namespace prefix in RSS.

Creating Geo Sitemap Files

With your geodata content ready for indexing, the next step is to create the geo sitemap files. Basically, a sitemap is an XML file listing the actual content documents of your web site. For a conventional sitemap, these documents are web pages; for a geo sitemap, they're geoXML documents.

■**Tip** If all your geodata is in static KML created on Google's My Maps, there's no need for a sitemap. Remember, Google automatically crawls and indexes all geodata marked as Public on My Maps.

Basic Geo Sitemaps

It's easiest to demonstrate a geo sitemap by example. Listing 10-7 contains a simple sitemap for the geoXML documents created earlier in this chapter.

Listing 10-7. *A Basic Geo Sitemap*

```
<?xml version="1.0" encoding="UTF-8"?>
<urlset xmlns="http://www.sitemaps.org/schemas/sitemap/0.9"
        xmlns:geo="http://www.google.com/geo/schemas/sitemap/1.0">
  <url>
    <loc>http://sterlingudell.com/bgmm/chapter_10/listing_10_03.php</loc>
    <geo:geo>
      <geo:format>kml</geo:format>
    </geo:geo>
  </url>
  <url>
    <loc>http://sterlingudell.com/bgmm/chapter_10/listing_10_04.php</loc>
    <geo:geo>
      <geo:format>georss</geo:format>
    </geo:geo>
  </url>
</urlset>
```

As you can see, there's not much to it; each url element contains a single loc with the URL of the geodata document. Then the geo-namespaced elements, geo:geo and geo:format, contain the format for the document in question. The allowable values for geo:format are kml, kmz (not shown here, but see Chapter 3), and georss.

As usual, it's worth noting that the document in Listing 10-7 is quite minimal; the sitemap specification includes a number of optional tags to aid in indexing your content. I encourage you to visit http://sitemaps.org/protocol.php for the definitive list, where you can determine which are appropriate for your geodata.

With your geo sitemap created, it should be uploaded to the highest directory of your web server that it applies to. For the example in Listing 10-7, this would be http://sterlingudell.com/bgmm/chapter_10/. It's now ready for submitting to Google; we'll get to that in a moment.

Dynamic Geo Sitemaps

You may have noticed that Listing 10-7 only included the basic geoXML from this chapter, not the network-linked dynamic KML. That's because some additional effort is required to sitemap these files.

The basic issue is that there is no actual URL to list in a `loc` tag for such data. The "meta-KML" of Listing 10-5 doesn't contain any geodata itself, and the linked KML generated by Listing 10-6 only does if parameterized. It's unlikely that Google arbitrarily creates such parameterized URLs simply to crawl geodata; to start with, the correct parameters to use will vary by data provider, and aren't easily guessable. So it's safest to assume that Google doesn't.

In this case, how do you get your geodata indexed by Google? Since the geo sitemap is essentially just a list of URLs, it's possible to create a sitemap containing URLs *with parameters already included*, guiding Google to crawl your dynamic KML in a way that is sure to produce results.

For a large dataset, producing such a list of parameterized URLs can be a challenge. But since the parameters are viewport-based, the approach I'll take is to overlay the geographic area covered by my data with a grid, and generate one URL for a "viewport" covering each grid cell.

Figure 10-11 gets us started. I've superimposed a grid on the continental USA; my area of coverage spans latitudes from 25 to 50 degrees, and longitudes from –130 to –60 (west longitudes are negative, remember). And I've chosen grid cells covering five degrees of latitude by ten degrees of longitude each.

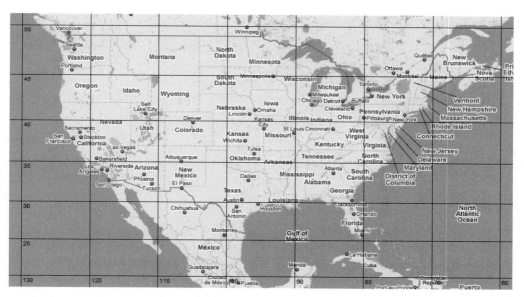

Figure 10-11. *Dividing the USA with a grid[1]*

Having done this, each geodata URL will cover one grid square. So the northwest cell will have the following URL, defining the `BBOX` for its latitude and longitude bounds:

```
http://sterlingudell.com/bgmm/chapter_10/dynamic.kml.php?BBOX=-130,45,-120,50
```

---

1. My thanks to Bill Chadwick, `http://www.bdcc.co.uk`, for the grid overlay.

Then all that remains is to generate a geo sitemap file accordingly, with one `url` element for each grid cell. Part of such a sitemap can be found in Listing 10-8.

Listing 10-8. *A Grid-Based Geo Sitemap*

```
<?xml version="1.0" encoding="UTF-8"?>
<urlset xmlns="http://www.sitemaps.org/schemas/sitemap/0.9"
        xmlns:geo="http://www.google.com/geo/schemas/sitemap/1.0">
  <url>
    <loc>
     http://sterlingudell.com/bgmm/chapter_10/listing_10_06.php?BBOX=-130,25,-120,30
    </loc>
    <geo:geo>
      <geo:format>kml</geo:format>
    </geo:geo>
  </url>
  <url>
    <loc>
     http://sterlingudell.com/bgmm/chapter_10/listing_10_06.php?BBOX=-120,25,-110,30
    </loc>
    <geo:geo>
      <geo:format>kml</geo:format>
    </geo:geo>
  </url>
  <url>
    <loc>
     http://sterlingudell.com/bgmm/chapter_10/listing_10_06.php?BBOX=-110,25,-100,30
    </loc>
    <geo:geo>
      <geo:format>kml</geo:format>
    </geo:geo>
  </url>
  ...
</urlset>
```

Now, it's certainly possible to do this manually, and for a fairly coarse grid that might be easiest. But what if your geodata is dense enough to warrant a one-degree grid? Covering the area shown in Figure 10-11 would take 1750 URLs—not a sitemap you'd want to build by hand.

Fortunately, you now have the resources of PHP to draw upon, and repetitive tasks like this are perfect for scripting. Listing 10-9 shows the PHP required to generate the sitemap for the grid in Figure 10-11.

Listing 10-9. *Generating a Grid-Based Geo Sitemap*

```
<?php
  // Boundaries for sitemap grid
  $north = 50;
  $south = 25;
```

```
    $east  = -60;
    $west  = -130;

    // Grid size, in degrees, with separate sizes for latitude and longitude
    $lat_grid = 5;
    $lon_grid = 10;

    // Prepare the sitemap XML header
    $header = '<?xml version="1.0" encoding="UTF-8"?>
<urlset xmlns="http://www.sitemaps.org/schemas/sitemap/0.9"
        xmlns:geo="http://www.google.com/geo/schemas/sitemap/1.0">';

    // Create a sitemap url element for each grid cell
    for ($lat = $south; $lat < $north; $lat += $lat_grid)
      for ($lon = $west; $lon < $east; $lon += $lon_grid)
      {
        $urls = $urls.'
  <url>
    <loc>
      http://sterlingudell.com/bgmm/chapter_10/listing_10_06.php?BBOX='.
          $lon.','.$lat.','.($lon + $lon_grid).','.($lat + $lat_grid).'
    </loc>
    <geo:geo>
      <geo:format>kml</geo:format>
    </geo:geo>
  </url>';
      }

    // Prepare the sitemap XML footer
    $footer = '
</urlset>';

    // Output the final sitemap XML
    header('Content-type: application/xml');
    echo $header;
    echo $urls;
    echo $footer;
?>
```

Since its job is to generate XML, this script follows the same basic pattern as all the previous PHP in this chapter. Here's the rundown:

1. Set up the boundaries and size of the grid: $north, $south, $east, $west, $lat_grid, and $lon_grid, all drawn directly from Figure 10-11.

2. Place the "header" XML into the $header variable; the same as we did with the geoXML earlier in the chapter (though of course the XML itself is for a sitemap here).

3. Loop through each grid cell, using two for loops, one inside the other (this configuration is called a *nested loop*):

```
for ($lat = $south; $lat < $north; $lat += $lat_grid)
    for ($lon = $west; $lon < $east; $lon += $lon_grid)
```

4. Each grid cell's URL is based on the $lat and $lon variables that we're looping on; the north and east components of the BBOX are calculated by adding the grid size:

```
<loc>
 http://sterlingudell.com/bgmm/chapter_10/listing_10_06.php?BBOX='.
        $lon.','.$lat.','.($lon + $lon_grid).','.($lat + $lat_grid).'
</loc>
```

5. After the nested loops finish, create the XML footer. Again, this is very much like what we've been doing in each PHP script.

6. echo the XML variables, creating the XML document (with the appropriate Content-type of application/xml).

When the time comes to submit this sitemap to Google (in the next section), use the URL for this PHP script, as in http://sterlingudell.com/bgmm/chapter_10/listing_10_09.php. When Google's spider fetches it, the PHP will generate the necessary sitemap on the fly (as in Listing 10-8), and Google will happily index it.

■**Tip** If your data set is large, the load of generating a full sitemap on demand can be prohibitive, causing the requesting spider to time out before the sitemap can be returned to it. In such a case, you might consider pre-generating the sitemap in advance and saving the XML to your server instead, as described for the Pennsylvania cities KML earlier in the chapter.

The PHP of Listing 10-9 is general enough that it will work for any sitemap grid; all you need to change are the boundaries and size to fit your own data's geographic area.

■**Caution** Any one sitemap can contain a maximum of 50,000 URLs. When laying out your grid parameters for Listing 10-9, ensure that you won't exceed 50,000 grid cells.

Submitting Geo Sitemaps to Google

So you now have one or more sitemaps listing search-engine-optimized geo-content. All that's left is to submit them to Google for indexing.

This is accomplished using Google's Webmaster Tools, at http://www.google.com/webmasters/tools. If you haven't used the Webmaster Tools before, you'll need to create an account and verify that you manage the web site for which you want to submit a geo sitemap. Follow the instructions on the site to do so.

Once logged into Webmaster Tools for your web site, select Sitemaps on the menu and click Add a Sitemap. You'll be prompted for the type; select Geo Sitemap, enter the URL to your sitemap document, and then click the Add Geo Sitemap button (see Figure 10-12).

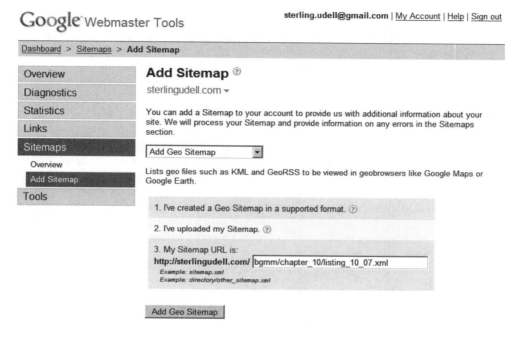

Figure 10-12. *Submitting a geo sitemap to Google*

Once Google has your sitemap, it'll be added to the crawl queue, and your content will typically be indexed within about a week. Afterwards, your geodata will begin to appear as "user-created content" in search results on Google Maps. Welcome to the geoweb!

Producing JSON Instead of XML

To finish off this chapter, we're going to step away from the path of geoXML with a detour into JSON, an alternate format for producing geodata.

JSON stands for *JavaScript Object Notation* and is pronounced like the name "Jason." As its name implies, JSON is closely tied to the JavaScript language, which naturally makes it a good fit for the JavaScript-based Google mapping APIs. In fact, it's no overstatement to say that JSON *is* JavaScript, just applied to defining data rather than executable code.

JSON vs. GeoXML

JSON's main strength is its *flexibility*: because it is JavaScript, it can encapsulate *any* JavaScript data. Contrast this with KML and GeoRSS, where the data must fit into predefined XML elements; that's fine for the data items that those formats define, but if you want anything else, you're stuck.

For example, consider the largest-city data that we've been generating geoXML for throughout this chapter. In each example, we included the population of each city in the description or summary elements, from where it would automatically display in the map infowindow and perhaps the sidebar. But what if we wanted to *do* something with those population numbers—allow the user to filter by them, perhaps, or compute some statistics from them? The geoXML wouldn't have been very helpful for this. It's possible to extract numeric data from freeform text fields, but it's a kludge, far from ideal. Therefore, geoXML wouldn't be the preferred solution for such a task.

If the data were sent using JSON, on the other hand, it would be trivial to include a population field for each city, and it would be readily available in JavaScript for anything we might want to do with it.

So why not always use JSON—why mess around with geoXML at all?

The first reason is *standards*. As you'll recall from Chapter 1, consistent data standards make the geoweb work; KML and GeoRSS are the embodiments of those standards. JSON, by contrast, has no standards; you define the fields you need as you need them, making it up as you go along. This flexibility is also its Achilles' heel; JSON data exists outside the mainline geoweb and is neither searchable nor readily reusable.

This leads us into the second reason for preferring geoXML to JSON whenever possible: the KML and GeoRSS standards allow you to use them much more easily in your Google Maps application. Just feed the data to a GGeoXml or EGeoXml object and they'll appear on your map. With JSON, you need to do it manually.

The upshot is that, on the geoweb, JSON is a supplement to geoXML—not a replacement for it.

Basic JSON Format

You probably don't realize it, but you've actually been using JSON for much of this book. Starting way back in Listing 2-6, and every time since that we've set options for a JavaScript object, those options have been in JSON.

Here's a simple example, taken from the custom marker icons in the previous chapter:

```
var iconOptions = {width: 48,
                    height: 48,
                    primaryColor: "#ffffff"};
```

Essentially, everything between (and including) the curly braces ({ and }) is JSON. We haven't dwelled on the fact, but what the code here is doing is *creating a JavaScript object on the fly* and then assigning it to the iconOptions variable. The object in question has three properties—width, height, and primaryColor—that are declared and initialized (to two numbers and a string) in one fell swoop. That's *JSON*: the format, or *N*otation, for placing data into a *J*ava*S*cript *O*bject on the fly.

■**Note** For the definitive (if somewhat technical) guide to JSON, I refer you to the web site of JavaScript guru Douglas Crockford, who invented it: http://www.json.org.

Another thing that makes JSON useful as a data interchange format is that it's plain text; essentially, it's JavaScript source code. So we can generate it from PHP as easily as we have been doing with XML, and we can just as easily send it out across the Web to the client.

Producing JSON: the Nearest Place Name Server

We first used JSON for data interchange back in Chapter 8, when we retrieved geoname data proximate to the user's clicked map coordinates in the Nearest Place Name mapplet. If you recall, the data was retrieved from the aptly named geonames.org web service and then imported into JavaScript for display in an infowindow. As an introduction to producing JSON, we're going to replicate that server ourselves, using the same geoname table defined earlier in the chapter.

As a review, recall that the geonames.org server was called with a URL like this:

```
http://ws.geonames.org/findNearbyPlaceNameJSON?lat=39&lng=-105
```

which would look up the place-name details nearest to coordinates (39, –105).

Retrieving the Nearest Place Name

Our first task, then, is to ask MySQL for the row from the geoname table that's closest to the given coordinates. The query to do so can be found in Listing 10-10.

Listing 10-10. *The Nearest Place Name Query*

```
select *,
       (6371 * acos(cos(radians($lat)) * cos(radians(latitude)) *
                   cos(radians(longitude) - radians($lng)) +
                   sin(radians($lat)) * sin(radians(latitude)))) as distance
  from geoname
  where latitude between ($lat - 1) and ($lat + 1)
    and longitude between ($lng - 1) and ($lng + 1)
  order by distance asc
  limit 1
```

Don't panic—yes, there's a bunch of math in there, involving big numbers, trigonometry, and who knows what else. But I'm actually going to gloss over that part; for now, suffice it to say that everything after select * and before from geoname is a standard formula for calculating distance on the surface of the Earth in kilometers. You can find a more complete explanation in Appendix A, if you're interested, but for now you really needn't concern yourself with it. The important part is that, for rows in the geoname table, MySQL is calculating distance from our target coordinates ($lat, $lng).

■**Tip** For more advanced MySQL users, the distance equation from Listing 10-10 is an excellent candidate for a user-defined function, which would simplify the final query.

The interesting parts of the query occur a bit later. Note the where clause:

```
where latitude between ($lat - 1) and ($lat + 1)
  and longitude between ($lng - 1) and ($lng + 1)
```

As you'll recall from Listing 10-6, the between operator is telling MySQL that we want rows whose latitude and longitude fall within the given limits. In this case, I'm constructing a "bounding box" of one degree (in all four directions) around our target point, and I'm filtering the geoname rows to those whose coordinates fall within that box.

This seems like a roundabout way to find the nearest point, doesn't it? My rationale goes back to the concept of a database *index*; if you remember, an index allows MySQL to find specific rows in a table efficiently. But unfortunately, there's no easy way to index a table on the notion of "nearest coordinates," and without an index, MySQL would have to look through all 73,000 rows to find the nearest one. The bounding box trick allows MySQL to use an index it *does* have to narrow the search down greatly, probably to no more than a couple of hundred rows, which it can then look through reasonably quickly.

■**Note** Newer versions of MySQL (and some other databases) support *geospatial extensions* that do allow explicit indexing on coordinates. But they're rather involved, both to set up and to use, and your MySQL installation might not even support them. This chapter's just a very basic introduction to SQL, remember.

So the between operators get you in the neighborhood, and the last two lines find the actual closest point, by making use of the order by and limit clauses introduced earlier in the chapter. Within the bounding box, finding the closest point is a simple matter of ordering by distance (ascending) and taking the first row, the 1 with the lowest distance:

```
order by distance asc
limit 1
```

■**Tip** If you're ever tasked with finding several nearest locations—the five stores nearest to a customer, for example—you can use the same distance calculation as in Listing 10-10 and just change the limit to 5.

Generating the JSON

The hard work's now done: the nearest place-name row is in hand, and all you need to do is format the data as JSON for return to the client. Listing 10-11 shows the way, and you'll immediately see that it has the same basic structure as every other PHP script in this chapter: get the data, format it, and return it to the client. The major difference here is that the format in question is JSON rather than XML.

Listing 10-11. *The PHP for the Nearest Place Name Server*

```php
<?php
  // Connect to the database.
  include 'database_connect.php';
```

```php
// Make sure the URL parameters are numbers in the valid range
$lat = (float) min(90, max(-90, $_GET['lat']));
$lng = (float) min(180, max(-180, $_GET['lng']));

// Execute the MySQL query to retrieve the data
$query = "select *,
                (6371 * acos(cos(radians($lat)) * cos(radians(latitude)) *
                    cos(radians(longitude) - radians($lng)) +
                    sin(radians($lat)) * sin(radians(latitude)))) as distance
            from geoname
            where latitude between ($lat - 1) and ($lat + 1)
              and longitude between ($lng - 1) and ($lng + 1)
            order by distance asc
            limit 1";
$result = mysql_query($query);
if (!$result)
  die("Unable to retrieve data");

// Prepare the JSON header
$header = '{geonames: [';

// Generate JSON for the retrieved data
if ($row = mysql_fetch_array($result))
{
  $json = '{countryCode: "'.$row['country'].'",
            countryName: "'.$row['country'].'",
            adminCode1:  "'.$row['state'].'",
            adminName1:  "'.$row['state'].'",
            name:        "'.addslashes($row['name']).'",
            lat:         '.$row['latitude'].',
            lng:         '.$row['longitude'].',
            population:  '.$row['population'].',
            distance:    '.round($row['distance'], 3).'}';
}

// Prepare the JSON footer
$footer = ']}';

// Output the final JSON
header('Content-type: text/plain');
echo $header;
echo $json;
echo $footer;
?>
```

There are a few lines highlighted in Listing 10-11 that I do want to call your attention to:

- Near the top, I'm cleaning the URL parameters by ensuring that they're numbers within the valid range for latitude and longitude.

- Since this script returns only one row, the main body isn't a while loop as you've seen before. It's replaced by a simple if statement that ensures we actually got a "nearest" row back from MySQL; it's possible that the bounding box was empty (the "middle of nowhere" case from Listing 8-5).

- Within the JSON generation itself, the field names (like countryCode, countryName, and adminCode1) were established by the geonames.org server that we're replicating. A few of these are a bit odd here, because our geoname table doesn't have state or country names, just codes. In a real-world situation, you'll probably have more realistic data.

- Finally, note that the distance is being rounded to the nearest meter. Close enough!

And we're done. The server is invoked by calling a URL like the following:

```
http://sterlingudell.com/bgmm/chapter_10/listing_10_11.php?lat=39&lng=-105
```

which will return JSON like the following—for Woodland Park, Colorado, the nearest place to (39, –105).

```
{geonames: [{countryCode: "US",
            countryName: "US",
            adminCode1:  "CO",
            adminName1:  "CO",
            name:        "Woodland Park",
            lat:         38.9939,
            lng:         -105.056,
            population:  5722,
            distance:    4.892}]}
```

JSON ARRAYS

In the JSON returned from Listing 10-11, notice the square brackets ([and])? Those tell you that what's inside is a JavaScript array. As introduced in Chapter 9, arrays are a language construct for storing lists of (usually similar) data items, and like any JavaScript data structure, they work fine in JSON.

In JSON, a basic array might look like this:

```
{myArray: ['red', 'green', 'blue']}
```

In other words, myArray is an array with three elements—all strings—and myArray[0] is 'red'.

We had no real need for arrays in our example of Listing 10-11; we had no list of data to include in the JSON. But to replicate geoname.org's data format, we had to follow their lead; some of their services can return multiple place names, so for consistency they just always put their results in an array.

Incidentally, you can declare arrays using this same syntax in ordinary JavaScript, and you'll often see it done this way—it's a lot more concise than the new Array() construct introduced in Chapter 9.

Integrating the Server

Because we built it as such, Listing 10-11 is a drop-in replacement for geoname.org's findNearbyPlaceNameJSON server. In a client like the Nearest Place Name mapplet, we need only change the server URL. So in Listing 8-6, this would be the only change:

```
var url = 'http://sterlingudell.com/bgmm/chapter_10/listing_10_11.php?lat=' +
          clickCoords.lat() + '&lng=' + clickCoords.lng();
```

Taking JSON Further

The preceding example lays out the basics of producing JSON, and the technique as shown is suitable for any small, specialized data retrieval like this. As with this mapplet, such retrievals are frequently used to provide additional details in response to user interaction.

If necessary, JSON can be used for much larger data transfers as well, supporting the main geodata functionality of a map. An example would be a list of place names with population, as described early in this section. I'm not going to go into all the details—it's a bit beyond the purview of this book—but an outline of such a process is as follows; it's built entirely from pieces that I *have* covered.

On the Server

The general steps you would take on the server are these, broadly following the structure of most PHP scripts in this chapter:

1. Clean the URL parameters, as necessary.

2. Retrieve the data from database.

3. Use a while loop to format each row as JSON. This would best be accomplished with a JSON array (see the preceding sidebar).

4. Return the data to the client, much as in Listing 10-11.

On the Client

The client side is both more flexible and harder to program than a basic GGeoXml solution, highlighting the contrast between JSON and geoXML generally. The general steps required are these:

1. Use json_parse to bring the data into a JavaScript variable, as in Listing 8-6.

2. Iterate through the array with a for loop, similar to Listing 9-11, creating map markers, sidebar content, or whatever the specific project requires.

Summary

After reading this chapter you should be able to produce your own geoXML, in both KML and GeoRSS formats as needed. For small, static geodata sets, Google's My Maps is an excellent graphical tool for creating KML. For larger or more dynamic situations, a database will be called for; you should now be familiar with the basics of configuring a MySQL table for storing geospatial data. And to produce geoXML from the database, simple server-side programming in PHP is within your grasp as well.

We've also covered a more advanced case, using KML network links and parameterized SQL to produce dynamic geodata that depends on the client map viewport. You should now be familiar with optimizing that geoXML for search engine listings and with producing geo sitemaps to guide the search engines to your content. Finally, JSON provides you with a powerful alternative for situations when geoXML just isn't up to the task.

This chapter has closed the geodata loop; you've now covered all aspects of participation in the geoweb. By both producing and consuming geospatial content in the standard KML and GeoRSS formats, you can easily map your own data in conjunction with that produced by others. Just as importantly, other map developers can mash up *your* geo content in new and interesting ways, producing synergies that will feed back and benefit your own site. Congratulations: it's a big world out there, and you're ready to map it!

In this book's final chapter, we'll be putting *all* these concepts to use, examining how a real-world web site makes use of both the Google Maps and Mapplets APIs—with geoXML tying everything together.

◼◼◼

CHAPTER 11

Case Study: Satellite-Friendly Campground Directory

In this final chapter, we're going to take a deep dive into a real-world web site that's utilizing all the key techniques from throughout the book, participating in the geoweb with vibrant, dynamic Google maps. My purpose here is twofold: first, to bring together all the underlying concepts from the entire book, showing how they cooperate; and second, to demonstrate those concepts in practical use by a real web application.

Major topics that you'll see include these:

- API maps tightly integrated with the pages on which they reside

- Managing the display of thousands of mapped locations

- Generation of geoXML from server-side PHP and MySQL

- Leveraging of prepackaged API features, like driving directions and local search

- A dynamic geo sitemap

- A simple geodata mapplet, driven from the same KML as the main web site

Along the way, I'll also introduce a few new techniques and features, expanding your own map programming capabilities even further.

Within a single chapter (albeit a long one), we won't be able to examine every line of code from the entire site. Instead, I'll be showing you the most important and relevant functions, in manageable pieces that should inspire and inform your own map integrations.

Introducing the Satellite-Friendly Directory

For this case study, I've chosen a web site of my own: www.satellitefriendly.com, a specialized directory of campgrounds in North America. The specialization (and the rationale for the name) is that these campgrounds have an unobstructed view of the southern sky, enabling a clear view of the satellites used for television and Internet access by suitably equipped travelers, usually in recreational vehicles (RVs). It's ideal for our purposes: a medium-sized store of geodata (11,000 locations as of this writing) that users want to search and browse, with maps as the natural platform for doing so.

Background

I started Satellite-Friendly in mid-2004, when I was traveling and working full-time in an RV with a satellite Internet connection. The satellite system was great, allowing near-broadband speeds from virtually anywhere—but at times, finding a campsite with a clear view of the sky was a hassle. So I created an online database, fed from software I'd already written to interface with the satellite hardware, and distributed it to the small community of fellow satellite-connected travelers. As we all moved around the continent, the database grew, and it soon became a handy resource for planning our stops.

When Google Maps were introduced, I immediately saw their potential for displaying the inherently geospatial contents of the database. Every entry already included latitude and longitude (the satellite hardware has a built-in GPS receiver), so the addition of mapping to the existing data was reasonably straightforward. As is always the case with legacy systems, however, a few oddities were unavoidable in the integration, as you'll see.

Overview of Map Architecture

Before we jump into the code, let's get our bearings with a high-level "satellite view" of the system's architecture. This should help provide some foundation for the common approach used throughout the various map implementations on the site.

On the server side, the Satellite-Friendly database is implemented in MySQL, with PHP providing the functionality layer. Using techniques based on those in Chapter 10, the geodata is extracted from MySQL (in response to client requests) and formatted into KML, GeoRSS, or JSON as appropriate.

The bulk of the functionality uses KML for geodata transfer and is processed on the client side using the third-party EGeoXml object introduced in Chapter 9. EGeoXml was chosen for this site primarily for its greater degree of control in handling the data returned; the dynamic geodata is viewport-based, as you saw with the UK Brewery map, so a similar display methodology is used here. In addition, EGeoXml's greater control over marker appearance is put to good use, as is its ability to generate content elsewhere on the page.

On other, more detail-oriented data pages, JSON is used instead, allowing more straightforward handling of data specific to this site than KML would permit. And finally, GeoRSS is made available for external consumption, as a standard geodata feed for interested users (and developers of other mashups, of course).

The Home Page

Satellite-Friendly is a map-centric web application, so it's no surprise that map integrations begin on the home page of the site. As you can see in Figure 11-1, there are two maps on the home page: a display of recent campsite entries on the left and a click-to-search map in at the top of the sidebar on the right.

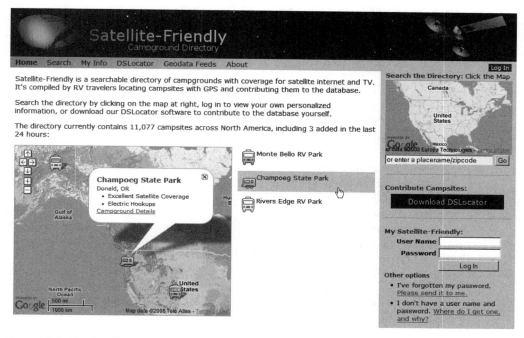

Figure 11-1. *The Satellite-Friendly home page*

The Recent Entries Map

The larger map on the home page is a display of campsites added to the directory within the last 24 hours; as well as the map itself, it includes a clickable list of the entries alongside it. This is a fairly basic geodata API map; the campsites are supplied via KML and added to both map and list with an EGeoXml object.

Server-Side: Generating KML for Recent Entries

The base PHP code on the web server that returns the recent-entries data can be found in Listing 11-1. It's fundamentally very similar to the geodata generators introduced in the previous chapter, with the few changes predominantly oriented around flexibility; the same script generates KML as well as GeoRSS, for both internal and external consumption.

Listing 11-1. *Server-Side Code for Recent Campground Data,* recent_campgrounds.php

```php
<?php
  // Process URL parameter
  $days = min(7, max(1, (integer) $_GET['days']));
  $filter = " and (dtmWhen > date_add(now(), interval -$days day))";
  $limit = 50;
```

```
// Connect to the database
include 'mod_sf_db_connect.php';

// Execute the database query
$query = "select sParkName,
                 Campground.nParkID,
                 Avg(fLatitude) fLatitude,
                 Avg(fLongitude) fLongitude,
                 Round(Avg(nCGRating)) nCGRating,
                 Max(nHookups) nHookups,
                 Max(dtmWhen) dtmWhen,
                 sTownName,
                 sState
          from Campsite
                 natural join Campground
          where (bSuspect <> 'Y')
            $filter
          group by Campground.nParkID
          order by dtmWhen desc
          limit $limit";
$result = mysql_query($query);
if (!$result)
  die("Unable to retrieve data");

// Build an array holding all the retrieved data to send to the formatting routine
$campgrounds = array();
while ($row = mysql_fetch_array($result))
  $campgrounds[] = array('lat'  => round($row['fLatitude'], 6),
                         'lon'  => round($row['fLongitude'], 6),
                         'id'   => $row['nParkID'],
                         'data' => $row);

if ($_GET['type'] == 'kml')
  // Return the results as KML
  include 'mod_produce_kml.php';
else
  // Return the results as GeoRSS (actually Atom)
  include 'mod_produce_atom.php';
?>
```

The first area of interest is a URL parameter, days; the script will display this many days'
entries. The first line of code cleans the parameter with an (integer) conversion and limits it
to between one and seven days; note that if the parameter is missing, this same line will default
$days to 1:

```
$days = min(7, max(1, (integer) $_GET['days']));
```

I then create a line of SQL, to be used in the database query, testing the dtmWhen column against a bit of date arithmetic using the MySQL date_add and now functions:

```
$filter = " and (dtmWhen > date_add(now(), interval -$days day))";
```

> ■**Note** As explained in Chapter 10, full coverage of SQL is beyond the scope of this book; accordingly, I'm not going to delve into every detail of the SQL syntax found in this chapter. For a complete introduction to SQL constructs, I recommend *Beginning SQL Queries: From Novice to Professional*, by Clare Churchill (Apress, 2008).

The next section of Listing 11-1 goes directly into the database retrieval. It's considerably more complicated than the SQL examples from Chapter 10, and much of it isn't especially relevant to the map integration, so I'll not say much more about it. Please note, however, that $query does include the $filter variable set earlier.

LEGACY DATABASE

I mentioned early in the chapter that Satellite-Friendly's maps were integrated into a web site with a pre-existing (or *legacy*) database structure. This is a common situation in the real world, and it can lead to some odd-looking code. A couple of examples you might notice from $query in Listing 11-1 are as follows.

- The query draws from two tables connected (or *joined*) together, rather than just one as in Chapter 10. Campsite contains information about specific site reports from users, including the satellite-coverage rating and site facilities, while Campground pulls out the data common to all the sites in a given park, such as the campground name. This means that, in order to determine coordinates for the campground, it's necessary to combine the coordinates for individual sites; I do this by averaging the latitude and longitude, using the avg function. Analogous grouping functions are used throughout the column list.

- The column names themselves use a naming convention not seen before in this book; they're all prefixed with one to three lowercase characters. This prefix indicates the *data type* of each column: s for string, dtm for date/time, and so on. Naming-convention clashes are fairly common when integrating with a legacy system. If you're interested, this specific convention is called *Hungarian notation*; you can read more about it at http://en.wikipedia.org/wiki/Hungarian_notation.

With the database result set in hand, you'd expect that I'm ready to generate the geoXML. You'd be correct, but in this case it doesn't actually happen in Listing 11-1; the geoXML production itself occurs in one of two external PHP files, depending on what type of geodata has been requested:

```
if ($_GET['type'] == 'kml')
  include 'mod_produce_kml.php';
else
  include 'mod_produce_atom.php';
```

The rationale for this bit of apparent misdirection goes back to my old friend, the OHIO principle: Only Handle It Once. Since there are a number of geodata feeds on Satellite-Friendly, all delivering either KML or GeoRSS (in this case, Atom), by centralizing the XML generation into external PHP modules I can simply include the appropriate file whenever I have the data ready for formatting. Not only does this mean that I only had to write the XML generators once, it also means that whenever I need to modify them, the modifications will automatically be consistent across all the site's feeds.

In order to make these external files work from disparate scripts, each calling script needs to put the geodata into a standard format, and that's what the other highlighted section of Listing 11-1 is about. Before calling the geoXML producer module, I move the data out of the $row variable and into a new array named $campgrounds:

```
$campgrounds = array();
while ($row = mysql_fetch_array($result))
  $campgrounds[] = array('lat'  => round($row['fLatitude'], 6),
                         'lon'  => round($row['fLongitude'], 6),
                         'id'   => $row['nParkID'],
                         'data' => $row);
```

Each element of $campgrounds is itself a small PHP array containing the coordinates, a campground ID, and the database $row itself. It may seem like extra work that wouldn't be needed if the geoXML was generated here (rather than in an external module), but it's worth it to centralize that functionality. The code in mod_return_kml.php and mod_return_atom.php closely follows the examples for producing geoXML presented in Chapter 10.

PHP MODULE SCRIPTS

Another naming convention: notice how the names of my geoXML producers, mod_return_kml.php and mod_return_atom.php, both begin with mod_? That's a convention I use to indicate that these are PHP *modules*, pieces of functionality ready to be "plugged in" to other routines, rather than full-fledged PHP scripts themselves.

There are two major reasons why I've found this convention worthwhile. First, as the number of PHP scripts for a complicated site like Satellite-Friendly grows, it's handy to be able to see at a glance which scripts are modules that I might want to reuse elsewhere. It's the purpose of a naming convention: to make the names work for you by conveying extra information.

The second advantage is more technical: it's possible to prevent these scripts from being served over the web on their own. This is important because such modules are only meant to run within other scripts, not independently, and doing so could potentially expose security vulnerabilities on your host. But if you're using Apache (the most popular web server software) and you're comfortable editing its configuration, the following lines in httpd.conf will prevent your PHP modules from being served on their own:

```
<Files ~ "^\mod_.+php">
  Order allow,deny
  Deny from all
</Files>
```

Client-Side: Displaying the Recent Entries

Having produced the required geoXML, we're ready to display the recent campground entries on the main home page map. As outlined earlier, the basic approach will be a standard Google Map, with geoXML data retrieved via EGeoXml and a customized display routine. Listing 11-2 gets things started with the map initialization; overall, the code is very like what we've been using throughout the book, but I have highlighted a few areas of interest for explanation.

Listing 11-2. *Initializing the Recent-Entries Map*

```
var options = {backgroundColor: '#D7D5E3', mapTypes: [G_PHYSICAL_MAP]};
recentMap = new GMap2(mapDiv, options);
recentMap.setCenter(new GLatLng(39.8, -98.5), 3, G_PHYSICAL_MAP);
recentMap.enableContinuousZoom();

// Limit the minimum zoom for the terrain map type
G_PHYSICAL_MAP.getMinimumResolution = function () {return 3};

// Add a couple of standard map controls
recentMap.addControl(new GSmallMapControl());
recentMap.addControl(new GScaleControl());

// Initialize the KML processor
var options = {createmarker: addDataPoint};
geoXml = new EGeoXml(recentMap, '/services/recent_campgrounds.php?type=kml',
                     options);
geoXml.parse();
```

- There's a new GMap2 option you haven't seen before, backgroundColor. This applies a standard CSS color specifier to the area visible before the map tiles load and off the polar extremes of the map. Here I'm using #D7D5E3, the same as the background of the site's right-hand sidebar.

- The new map function enableContinuousZoom turns on "smooth" zooming in response to double-click events, a nice refinement of the map user interface.

- Overriding the G_PHYSICAL_MAP type's getMinimumResolution property allows me to limit how far out the user can zoom the map (see the "Restricting Zoom Levels" sidebar). In this case, there's no need for a worldwide view, so I restrict it to zoom level 3.

- This map is fairly small on screen, so I don't include all the standard map controls, and I use GSmallMapControl.

- EGeoXml is loading the data from recent_campgrounds.php (Listing 11-1), with the KML option enabled.

Since most of the maps on Satellite-Friendly use a similar EGeoXml-based architecture, their initialization routines all generally resemble Listing 11-3.

RESTRICTING ZOOM LEVELS

In Listing 11-2, I'm using the `getMinimumResolution` property of the Terrain map type to restrict the minimum zoom level to 3. This is a standard technique in the Maps API, as is the equivalent `getMaximumResolution` at the other end of the scale, and their use is fairly straightforward.

The only cumbersome aspect is that you need to apply the limits to all map types that you're using. So for example, if your map had all the standard types and you wanted to restrict maximum zoom to level 10 (say to protect user privacy by disallowing zooming to street level), you'd need code like this:

```
G_NORMAL_MAP.getMaximumResolution    = function () {return 10};
G_SATELLITE_MAP.getMaximumResolution = function () {return 10};
G_HYBRID_MAP.getMaximumResolution    = function () {return 10};
G_PHYSICAL_MAP.getMaximumResolution  = function () {return 10};
```

A word to the wise: don't use `getMinimumResolution` if you have an overview map! You'll find that the same minimum zoom is applied to the overview as to the main map, and the usability of the overview will be severely impaired.

As in the later sections of Chapter 9, I'm using a custom data display option for EGeoXml: the addDataPoint function, which can be found in Listing 11-3. This is the heart of the recent entries map, creating both the map markers and the list alongside. Since this will again serve as a template for data-point handling throughout the site, it's worth going through addDataPoint section by section.

Listing 11-3. *The addDataPoint Function for recentMap*

```
function addDataPoint(coordinates, name, description, style)
{
  // Create and initialize the icon from the style in the KML
  var myIcon = new GIcon();
  myIcon.image       = geoXml.styles[style].image;
  myIcon.iconSize    = new GSize(32, 32);
  myIcon.shadow      = geoXml.styles[style].shadow;
  myIcon.shadowSize  = new GSize(59, 32);
  myIcon.iconAnchor  = new GPoint(16, 28);
  myIcon.infoWindowAnchor = getAnchor(myIcon.image);

  // Create a marker for this data point
  var options = {icon: myIcon, title: name};
  var thisMarker = new GMarker(coordinates, options);

  // Attach infowindow to the marker with content from the KML
  options = {maxWidth: 250};
  thisMarker.bindInfoWindowHtml('<div id="infowindow"><h3>' + name + '</h3>' +
    description + '</div>', options);
```

```
// Add the marker to the recent-entries map
recentMap.addOverlay(thisMarker);

// Also create a list entry (alongside the map) with the icon & name
var recentRow = document.createElement('li');
recentRow.innerHTML =
  '<img width="32" height="32" src="' + myIcon.image + '" />' + name;
document.getElementById('recent_list').appendChild(recentRow);

recentRow.onclick =
  function ()
  {
    // A click on the list entry triggers a click on its associated marker
    GEvent.trigger(thisMarker, 'click')
  };
};

function getAnchor(iconUrl)
{
  if (iconUrl.indexOf('bus') > -1)
    return new GPoint(16, 0);
  else if (iconUrl.indexOf('trailer') > -1)
    return new GPoint(19, 10);
  else
    return new GPoint(16, 6);
};
```

The first step here is to create a fully custom marker icon, and this generally follows the pattern laid out in Chapter 9, with one item to note: I get the image and shadow URLs from the styles property of geoXml. This property is actually an array of GIcons created by EGeoXml from the Style elements of the source KML, with the style parameter supplied to addDataPoint serving as an index to the array. So geoXml.styles[style] returns the appropriate GIcon object, and I can access its image and shadow properties as shown here.

If I'd wanted, I could have just gone ahead and used the icons that EGeoXml creates for me directly, but as the developer of those icon images I know more about their attributes than it does, so I can improve on its handling by manually setting such properties as iconAnchor and infoWindowAnchor. Note that, to keep addDataPoint cleaner, the latter is set in a little helper function, getAnchor.

Having created my icon, it's a simple matter to create a GMarker from it, which I then add to the map with the usual addOverlay function. Note that I create infowindow content from the campground's name and description parameters from the KML:

```
thisMarker.bindInfoWindowHtml('<div id="infowindow"><h3>' + name + '</h3>' +
  description + '</div>', options);
```

I also specify a title for the marker from name; this will be used by the API to generate a tooltip when the user hovers her mouse over a marker (see Figure 11-2):

```
var options = {icon: myIcon, title: name};
```

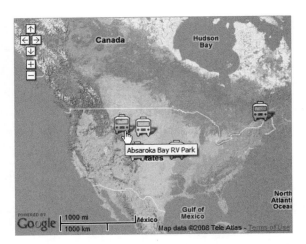

Figure 11-2. *The marker's* title *option creates a tooltip.*

We're now done with the map marker, so what remains is to generate the list entry for this campground. This is accomplished with a different DHTML (Dynamic HTML) technique than we've discussed before; here's how it works.

1. Create a new XHTML element of the type required; in this case, a list item:

```
var recentRow = document.createElement('li');
```

2. Set any needed properties of the element. Here, all that's required is innerHTML, the content of the list row:

```
recentRow.innerHTML =
    '<img width="32" height="32" src="' + myIcon.image + '" />' + name;
```

3. Add the new element to an existing element on the page; in this case, the recent-entries list:

```
document.getElementById('recent_list').appendChild(recentRow);
```

It's more work than just using innerHTML, as you saw in Chapter 9, but it's a more robust technique when *adding* content to an element rather than *replacing* it entirely.

With the new list item in place, I just need to attach an event handler to open the associated map marker's infowindow on a mouse click, like so:

```
recentRow.onclick =
  function ()
  {
    GEvent.trigger(thisMarker, 'click')
  };
```

Again, this is a slightly new construct, declaring a function on the fly for the event handler. It works much the same as any other function declaration you've seen, but it is particularly handy in a case like this. Because the handler for each list row is slightly different—each row links to a different map marker—I can't simply call the same event handler for each row. So I create a new function for each.

■**Note** This technique of declaring a function on the fly in JavaScript is called a *function literal*, and I discuss it more thoroughly (including tips and potential pitfalls) in Appendix B.

And we're done. You can see the recent entries map in action, including a click on a list row, back in Figure 11-1.

The Click-to-Search Map

The other map on the Satellite-Friendly home page is found in the upper-right corner, and it's a somewhat unusual case. The idea here is to provide a gateway to the site's search functionality by allowing the user to search the directory for any location clicked on the small map on the home page. The Maps API is indeed up to this task—it's not even very hard—but it does require slightly different handling than any map we've seen so far.

The key point to realize is that we want to *disable* much of the signature functionality of Google Maps. There's no need for the search map to pan or zoom, the user won't need to drag it or change map types; in essence, we just want a static map image, with the only functionality being a coordinates-from-click handler.

With this in mind, initializing the search map is quite simple:

```
searchMap = new GMap2(document.getElementById('search_map'));
searchMap.setCenter(new GLatLng(40, -96), 2);
searchMap.disableDragging();
```

It's very little more involved than the very first map you made, back in Chapter 3: create the GMap2 object, and call setCenter with just coordinates and a low level of zoom. My code obviously *doesn't* do all the other things you've come to expect when initializing a map, such as adding controls. The only other function required is disableDragging, which turns off the default Google Maps drag action. And that's it; I have an essentially static map on the page.

Adding the click-to-search functionality is then quite easy. It starts with an ordinary event listener, added after the initialization has finished:

```
GEvent.addListener(searchMap, 'click', searchMapClick);
```

This calls a handler function, which is itself only one line:

```
function searchMapClick(overlay, coordinates)
{
  document.location = 'search/#' + coordinates.toUrlValue() + ',8';
};
```

With the coordinates passed into the handler by the API, all that's required is to construct a specially formatted URL from them and set the document's location property to it. We haven't discussed this before, but setting document.location is how you change to a new browser page from within JavaScript. This particular URL sends the user to the main search page, with the clicked coordinates in tow—which is the subject of the next section.

STATIC MAPS

If I hadn't wanted the search map to be clickable, I wouldn't have used the full Google Maps API at all, but would instead have opted for its little brother, the *Static Maps API*. It's made for situations like this when all you need is an *image* of a map, not a full-functionality interactive map embedded in your page. It works entirely without JavaScript; instead, Static Maps are completely built into a single URL, for use in an `img` tag or a CSS `background-image`. Let's take a quick look at how they work.

To generate a static map image, the base URL is `http://maps.google.com/staticmap`; it's then controlled via standard URL parameters. Here are the basics:

- `center`: the coordinates of the map's center point, in *lat,lon* format.

- `zoom`: the zoom level, same as in the traditional Maps API.

- `size`: the pixel size of the map, in *widthxheight* format.

- `maptype`, either `roadmap` (what we know as `G_NORMAL_MAP`) or `mobile`, a high-contrast version.

- `key`, your usual Maps API key, registered for the domain where the image will be displayed.

So to replicate the appearance of the home page search map, the following URL would be used:

`http://maps.google.com/staticmap?center=40,-96&zoom=2&size=250x150&key=`*myapikey*

Note that I've omitted the `maptype` parameter, as I'm happy with the default of `roadmap`.

This URL would then go directly into an `img` element in my XHTML, like so:

`<img width="250" height="150" src="http://maps.google.com/staticmap?center=…" />`

And when the page was displayed by a browser, the map image would be served directly from Google, according to my specification. Here's the Static Maps API version of the search map:

It's also possible to add markers (though not custom icons) and even polylines to a static map; for the parameters involved, and more information generally on the Static Maps API, I refer you to the official documentation at `http://code.google.com/apis/maps/documentation/staticmaps`.

While clearly not a replacement for the full Maps API, static maps do load much faster thanks to the lack of JavaScript overhead. They can therefore be useful as placeholders on a page: show a summary static map when the page loads, then replace it with a full API map if the user clicks on it, thus only loading the JavaScript for the API if the user actively requests it. And as the `mobile` map type suggests, they are also useful on mobile devices, where low-capability browsers make the full API impractical.

Searching For Campgrounds

The home page search map leads the web site visitor into the Campground Search page, the heart of Satellite-Friendly, and at the heart of the search page sits a Google map. A typical Campground Search is shown in Figure 11-3; in this section of the chapter we'll go through this page in detail, discovering just what makes it tick.

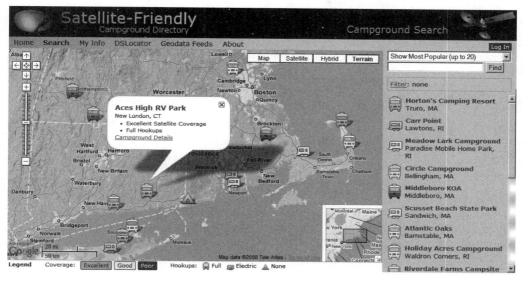

Figure 11-3. *The Campground Search page*

The core architecture of Campground Search is something of a hybrid between the UK Brewery map from Chapter 9 and the network-linked KML from Chapter 10. The underlying KML actually *is* a network-link server, returning only the data points within given geographic boundaries. And on the client side, I use EGeoXml to retrieve a new KML data set whenever the map is moved, and then display the new campgrounds in both the map and the sidebar list. It's yet another approach to handling a data set involving thousands of points, with support of network-linked KML similar to Google's own GGeoXml object, but with the greater display control that EGeoXml affords.

Campground Search also allows the user to select different data views based on her own preference (see Figure 11-4).

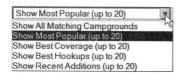

Figure 11-4. *Selecting different campground data views*

Behind the scenes, these views are selecting different KML data feeds. Here's the XHTML for the selector:

```
<select id="view" onchange="viewChange()" class="no_print">
  <option value="all">Show All Matching Campgrounds</option>
  <option value="popular">Show Most Popular (up to 20)</option>
  <option value="coverage">Show Best Coverage (up to 20)</option>
  <option value="hookups">Show Best Hookups (up to 20)</option>
  <option value="recent">Show Recent Additions (up to 20)</option>
</select>
```

And in the JavaScript, the viewChange event handler contains the following code:

```
var selected = view.options[view.selectedIndex].value;
if (selected == 'all')
  kmlUrl = '/services/all_campgrounds.php?';
else if (selected == 'recent')
  kmlUrl = '/services/recent_campgrounds.php?type=kml&';
else
  kmlUrl = '/services/top_campgrounds.php?sort=' + selected + '&';
```

As you can see, the value of the view selector drives a choice of data feed URLs: one for all campgrounds, one for recent entries (the same as was used in Listing 11-2), and a third for the top matching campgrounds. This last option takes an additional sort parameter, as the "top" selections can be most popular, best satellite coverage, or best hookups.

■**Note** In RV terminology, *hookups* refer to the utilities available at a campsite: *electric*, for a place to plug in your RV, or *full hookups*, electric plus a drinking-water outlet and a sewer inlet. On Satellite-Friendly, these facilities are indicated by different icons: a motor home for full hookups, a trailer for electric, and a tent for none.

So on the server, I have three PHP scripts backing up the Campground Search page, as highlighted in the JavaScript code. You've already seen recent_campgrounds.php, in Listing 11-1; top_campgrounds.php will be covered later in this section, in Listing 11-7; it is based on Listing 10-6.

That just leaves all_campgrounds.php, which is not closely based on code you've seen before, but instead implements a data-handling technique called *clustering*. This approach collects groups of data points into special "cluster" markers and plots these clusters on the map instead of the individual data points. In this way, the total markers to be plotted on the Google map will always be limited to a reasonable number; at lower zoom levels, the data points will just be grouped into larger clusters. This effect can be seen in Figures 11-5 and 11-6; the clusters are depicted as circular markers "hovering over" the area of the map where their corresponding campgrounds are.

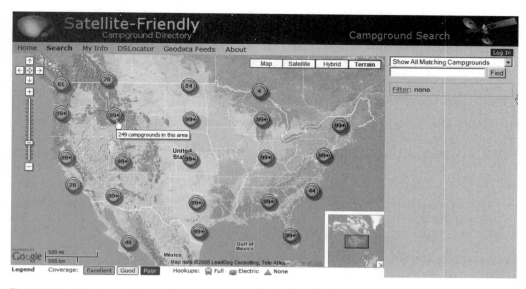

Figure 11-5. *Cluster markers at low zoom, containing hundreds of campgrounds each*

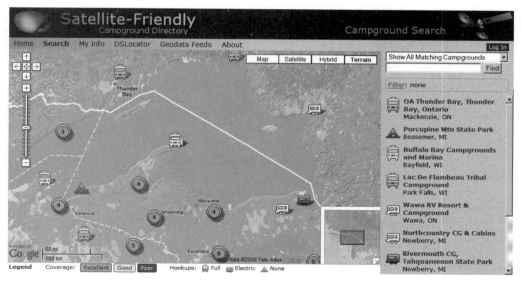

Figure 11-6. *An intermediate zoom level, mixing individual campgrounds with small clusters*

Unfortunately, the code behind this clustering is fairly advanced, beyond the scope of this book—so I'll not be delving into the internals of all_campgrounds.php. The server-side clustering code on Satellite-Friendly was originally based on that described in the Apress book *Beginning Google Maps Applications with PHP and Ajax.*

It's something to leave until your Google map programming skills are further along. For now, the thing to remember is that the client-side JavaScript code I will be showing you has very little that's cluster-specific; apart from just a few areas (that I'll point out), the bulk of the code is entirely applicable to the KML-generating PHP scripts covered in this book.

The Main Campground Search Data Display

As with Chapter 9's brewery map, the Campground Search will be dynamically loading and removing data points as it goes along, so as before, I use a JavaScript array to contain my markers. This array is declared and initialized at the beginning of the page's JavaScript like so:

```
var markers = new Array();
```

We'll be using markers throughout this segment of the code for handling the marker data.

I'll also need an EGeoXml object to retrieve the data and parse the KML; its initialization is much as it has been since Chapter 9 and will happen when the page loads:

```
options = {createmarker: addDataPoint, nozoom: true};
geoXml = new EGeoXml(map, null, options);
```

You've seen the createmarker and nozoom options before, so the only real difference is the null second parameter, where the geodata URL would usually go. Because I'll be changing this URL based on both the map viewport and the user's data selection, I leave it out for now and deal with it in the next section.

The mapMoveEnd Handler

As described earlier, the main data display is based on refreshing the display when the map viewport has moved, so (not surprisingly) it's triggered by a moveend event handler. This code can be found in Listing 11-4.

Listing 11-4. *The mapMoveEnd Event Handler*

```
function mapMoveEnd()
{
  // Get the map boundary coordinates
  var mapBounds = map.getBounds();

  // Parameterize the geodata URL based on those boundaries
  geoXml.urls = [kmlUrl + 'BBOX=' +
                 mapBounds.getSouthWest().lng().toFixed(6) + ',' +
                 mapBounds.getSouthWest().lat().toFixed(6) + ',' +
                 mapBounds.getNorthEast().lng().toFixed(6) + ',' +
                 mapBounds.getNorthEast().lat().toFixed(6)];

  // Load the KML - new markers will be added when it returns
  geoXml.parse();
```

```
// Remove markers from display that are no longer visible
for (var m = markers.length - 1; m >= 0; m--)
  if (!mapBounds.contains(markers[m].getPoint()))
    removeDataPoint(m);

// Also clear starting location out of the URL
location.hash = '#';
};
```

Most of the code here is essentially replicating the functionality of a KML network link: get the boundaries of the map viewport, with a map.getBounds call; add this to a BBOX parameter of the data URL, BBOX=*west,south,east,north* (as in Chapter 10); and process this URL with geoXml, my EGeoXml object, via its urls property and parse function.

Afterwards, while geoXml is off retrieving the new geodata (asynchronously, remember), I take the opportunity for a bit of housekeeping. First, because the map has moved, there are probably some data points that are no longer in the viewport mapBounds; for these, I call removeDataPoint, a function we'll delve into in a moment. And finally, there's a line to clear location.hash, but bear with me again until I discuss the related code in a few pages.

The addDataPoint Function

If you'll recall, when I initialized geoXml earlier I gave it a createmarker option, the callback function addDataPoint to use every time it extracts a single data point from the KML. So after parse returns from mapMoveEnd, geoXml will begin calling addDataPoint for campgrounds in the map viewport. This function can be found in Listing 11-5; it may look a bit daunting, but it's based closely on addDataPoint from Listing 11-3 on the home page. I've highlighted the few significant differences.

Listing 11-5. *The addDataPoint Function*

```
function addDataPoint(coordinates, name, description, style)
{
  // Check to see if this placemark is already displayed, and stop if it is
  for (var m = markers.length − 1; m >= 0; m--)
  {
    if (markers[m].getPoint().equals(coordinates))
      return;
  }

  // Create and initialize the icon from the style in the KML
  var myIcon = new GIcon();
  myIcon.image      = geoXml.styles[style].image;
  myIcon.iconSize   = new GSize(32, 32);
  if (myIcon.image.indexOf('circle') > −1)
  {
```

```
    // It's a cluster placemark
    myIcon.shadow     = '/images/icons/circle_shadow.png';
    myIcon.shadowSize = new GSize(40, 40);
    myIcon.iconAnchor = new GPoint(13, 13);
    myIcon.infoWindowAnchor = new GPoint(13, 0);
  }
  else
  {
    // Not a cluster => an individual campground
    myIcon.shadow     = geoXml.styles[style].shadow;
    myIcon.shadowSize = geoXml.styles[style].shadowSize;
    myIcon.iconAnchor = new GPoint(16, 28);
    myIcon.infoWindowAnchor = getAnchor(myIcon.image);
  }

  // Create a marker for this data point
  var options = {icon: myIcon, title: name};
  var thisMarker = new GMarker(coordinates, options);
  markers.push(thisMarker);

  // Some different handling for clusters and campgrounds
  if (myIcon.image.indexOf('circle') > -1)
  {
    // Cluster
    thisMarker.isCluster = true;

    GEvent.addListener(thisMarker, 'click',
      function ()
      {
        // Clicking on a cluster zooms the map on its location
        map.setCenter(coordinates, map.getZoom() + 2);
      });
  }
  else
  {
    // Individual campground
    thisMarker.isCluster = false;

    // Attach infowindow to the marker with content from the KML
    options = {maxWidth: 350};
    thisMarker.bindInfoWindowHtml('<div id="infowindow"><h3>' + name + '</h3>' +
      description + '</div>', options);
```

```
  // Also create a sidebar entry (alongside the map) with the icon, name, & descr
  var sidebarRow = document.createElement('div');
  sidebarRow.id = coordinates.toUrlValue();
  sidebarRow.className = 'sidebar_row';
  sidebarRow.innerHTML =
    '<img width="32" height="32" src="' + myIcon.image + '" /><h3>' + name +
    '</h3>' + description;
  sidebar.appendChild(sidebarRow);

  sidebarRow.onclick =
    function ()
    {
      // A click on the sidebar entry triggers a click on its associated marker
      GEvent.trigger(thisMarker, 'click')
    };
  }

  // Add the marker to the map
  map.addOverlay(thisMarker);
};
```

Overall, this function does just what it did on the home page: create a custom icon, use it when adding a marker to the map; and then create a DHTML entry in the list alongside the map (here called sidebar). The differences are primarily in two areas. First, I'm checking to see if the marker already exists on the map before I go ahead and add it again, thus avoiding duplicates. Second, I set a couple of additional attributes on the sidebar row element: id and className, which exactly correspond to the XHTML element attributes of id and class. As a result, each sidebar row will have DHTML something like this:

```
<div id="41.4045,-72.2234" class="sidebar_row">
```

■**Note** You will notice a couple of code blocks in Listing 11-5 relating to clusters. As I said, I'm not going into these, but I'm sure you can figure out what they're doing—and if you're implementing code like this without a clustering KML server, just leave them out.

The removeDataPoint Function

What gets added must get removed: enter removeDataPoint, shown in Listing 11-6. It's much simpler than addDataPoint because, as we know from the Second Law of Thermodynamics, it's easier to destroy than to create.

Listing 11-6. *The* removeDataPoint *Function*

```
function removeDataPoint(m)
{
  // Remove the marker from the map
  map.removeOverlay(markers[m]);

  // Find and remove the sidebar entry
  var id = markers[m].getPoint().toUrlValue();
  var sidebarRow = document.getElementById(id);
  if (sidebarRow)
    sidebar.removeChild(sidebarRow);

  // Remove the marker from our own array
  markers.splice(m, 1);
};
```

This function is quite straightforward: it takes an index m into my internal markers array as a parameter and removes that marker's data point from three places:

1. The map itself, using the standard removeOverlay API function

2. The sidebar list:

   a. The correct row is found using an id generated from the marker's coordinates, the same way I did in addDataPoint.

   b. That row is deleted using the removeChild function, counterpart to the DHTML addChild we've been using in this chapter.

3. My own markers array, using the splice function introduced in Chapter 9's *JavaScript 102*

■**Caution** Using the coordinates for an id (as I'm doing here) can lead to trouble if your geodata includes duplicate points. Duplicates can lead to other problems as well, such as indistinguishable map markers, so they're best avoided in your source data if at all possible.

With that, the data handling process is nearly complete; when the map moves, some old markers get removed, and other new markers get added. There's just one more piece of special handling required, when the map gets zoomed out.

The mapZoomEnd Handler

Handling geodata in this way—loading it dynamically and checking for duplicates in addDataPoint—makes for a smooth, responsive user experience, but does have a hole. With the code as it stands now, when the user zooms out all of the campgrounds in the old viewport are still visible, just concentrated into a small area. But the code will load an additional set of points spanning the new, wider viewport—leading to a concentration of points in the middle of the map. See Figures 11-7 and 11-8 for an illustration of this problem.

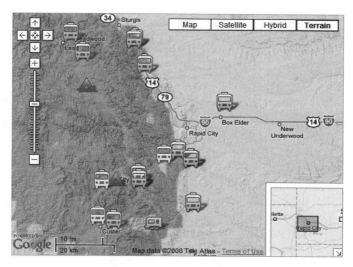

Figure 11-7. *What starts as a normal campground display…*

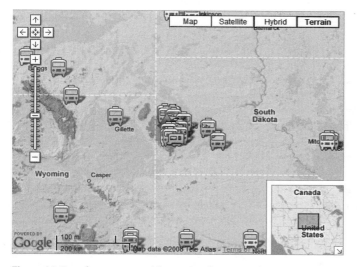

Figure 11-8. *…becomes problematic after zooming out.*

Fortunately, it's an easy hole to plug, as you can see here:

```
function mapZoomEnd(oldZoom, newZoom)
{
  for (var m = markers.length - 1; m >= 0; m--)
  {
    // The only markers we don't remove are individual campgrounds when zooming in
    if (markers[m].isCluster || (oldZoom > newZoom))
      removeDataPoint(m);
  }
};
```

The API gives us both the old and new zoom levels as parameters to the event handler. When the old is greater than the new, it means the map is zooming out, so I simply remove all markers. I also remove cluster markers when zooming in; they won't be applicable at the new, closer zoom level.

Filtering

The core data-display functionality for this page is now complete, so it's time to turn our attention to a couple of ancillary tasks. The first of these is *filtering*: allowing the user to restrict the locations shown by various attributes. It's a common requirement in mapping applications; with Satellite-Friendly, I support filtering by hookups, coverage rating, and satellite.

Unfortunately, filtering can be something of a hassle to implement, often involving heavily parameterized URLs and convoluted code to handle them. On this page, I take a different approach, based on browser cookies. Each of the three filter criteria has a different cookie assigned to it, and when the user selects a filter, I set the appropriate cookie in JavaScript and refresh the map. Then EGeoXml requests new data, and the browser *automatically* includes the filter cookies; it's a simple matter for the KML-producing scripts on the server to read those cookies and apply the filter to their database queries. With this approach, the browser handles all the mechanics of passing the filter between client and server.

MMMM, COOKIES

If you're not familiar with browser cookies, they're easy to explain. A *cookie* is a string of extra data that the browser includes with every request to a given web site, allowing the site to include information in addition to the URL of the request itself. This is what makes cookies useful here: they're included with *every* request, including the geodata requests that happen behind the scenes.

Importantly, once a cookie is set by a web site it remains in place until it either expires or is cleared by the site; expiration happens either after a certain amount of time, or when the user closes her browser session. Session cookies are often used to maintain a temporary presence on a web site, as when a user has logged in to her account. The site sets a cookie at login, and then as long as that cookie is attached to a request, the site knows that she's the same logged-in user. Conversely, cookies with longer expiration times are useful for keeping user information between visits; whenever you tell a web site to "Remember me," it's probably using cookies to do so.

I'm setting my filter cookies with an expiration time of one year, allowing them to do double duty for me. As well as passing the filter to the KML producers, they will also remain for the user's next visit to Satellite-Friendly, allowing the site to remember her preferred filter.

The user interface is also reasonably simple: the XHTML includes a div containing the filter controls, which is hidden when the page loads by a CSS rule of display: none. When the user clicks on the Filter link of the Campground Search page, I reveal the div with the following click event handler:

```
function showFilter()
{
  filter.style.display = 'block';
};
```

The div itself can be seen in Figure 11-9. When the user clicks Close, an equivalent handler hides it again by setting filter.style.display = 'none'.

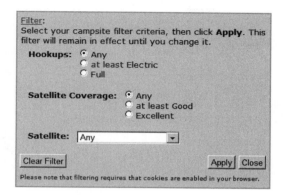

Figure 11-9. *The filter div*

The three filter controls have click event handlers that look like this:

```
onclick="setCookie('nHookups', value)"
```

The value here is the input element's value attribute. The setCookie function then uses the standard JavaScript document.cookie property to store this value in a cookie of the given name:

```
function setCookie(name, value)
{
  if (value == '')
    document.cookie = name + '=;expires=Sunday, 24-Apr-05 00:00:00 GMT;path=/'
  else
    document.cookie = name + '=' + value + ';expires=' + cookieExpire + ';path=/';
};
```

Note that, if value is blank, the cookie is cleared by setting an expiration time in the past.

And that's basically it on the client side. For the server side of this functionality, applying the filter to the MySQL query that retrieves the geodata, we need to return to PHP, as shown in Listing 11-7. I've highlighted the filter-handling code for you.

Listing 11-7. *Server-Side Code for Top-Ranked Campground Data,* top_campgrounds.php

```php
<?php
  // Bounding box from URL parameter

  $viewport = explode(',', $_GET['BBOX']);

  while ($viewport[0] > $viewport[2])
    $viewport[0] -= 360;
```

```php
$north = min(90,   (float) $viewport[3]);
$south = max(-90,  (float) $viewport[1]);
$east  = min(180,  (float) $viewport[2]);
$west  = max(-180, (float) $viewport[0]);

// Sort order, also from URL parameter
if ($_GET['sort'] == 'coverage')
  $order_by = 'nCGRating desc, dtmWhen desc';
else if ($_GET['sort'] == 'hookups')
  $order_by = 'nHookups desc, dtmWhen desc';
else
  $order_by = 'nCount desc, dtmWhen desc';

// Filter, from cookies
$filter = '';
if (is_numeric($_COOKIE['nCGRating']))
  $filter .= "and (nCGRating >= $_COOKIE[nCGRating])";
if (is_numeric($_COOKIE['nHookups']))
  $filter .= "and (nHookups >= $_COOKIE[nHookups])";
if (is_numeric($_COOKIE['nSatLon']))
  $filter .= "and (nSatLon = $_COOKIE[nSatLon])";

// Connect to the database
include 'mod_sf_db_connect.php';

// Execute the database query
$query = "select sParkName,
                 Campground.nParkID,
                 Avg(fLatitude) fLatitude,
                 Avg(fLongitude) fLongitude,
                 Round(Avg(nCGRating)) nCGRating,
                 Max(nHookups) nHookups,
                 Count(*) nCount,
                 sTownName,
                 sState,
                 date_format(dtExpire, '%Y-%m-%d') sExpire,
                 sResultsBlurb
            from Campsite
                 natural join Campground
                 left join Sponsor using (nParkID)
           where (fLatitude between $south and $north)
             and (fLongitude between $west and $east)
             and (bSuspect <> 'Y')
             $filter
        group by Campground.nParkID
           order by $order_by
           limit 20";
```

```
$result = mysql_query($query);
if (!$result)
  die("Unable to retrieve data");

// Build an array holding all the retrieved data to send to the formatting routine
$campgrounds = array();
while ($row = mysql_fetch_array($result))
  $campgrounds[] = array('lat'   => round($row['fLatitude'], 6),
                         'lon'   => round($row['fLongitude'], 6),
                         'id'    => $row['nParkID'],
                         'data'  => $row);

// Return the results as KML
  include 'mod_produce_kml.php';
?>
```

As you can see, the filter processing is quite simple. All of my filter fields are numbers, so the PHP is_numeric function both checks to see if they're set and cleans them for use in the query. Then for every filter cookie that's set, I add the appropriate SQL to a $filter string, which I then include in my $query. That's all there is to it.

■**Caution** Because cookies originate from the client, they do need to be cleaned before use, the same as URL parameters (as discussed in Chapter 10).

Before we move on, though, I would like to connect top_campgrounds.php back to recent_campgrounds.php, from Listing 11-1. First, note that this script uses the same mod_produce_kml.php module to generate the KML (from the $campgrounds array); and second, be aware that the filtering code from top_campgrounds will need to be replicated in recent_campgrounds. Because I hadn't discussed it until now, I left it out of Listing 11-1.

Location Search

There's one other user interface element on the Campground Search page that I'd like to touch on briefly, and that's the ability to search for locations by name, rather than just by interacting with the map. It's implemented using the Maps API geocoder, via the input element and Find button under the view selector, from the following XHTML:

```
<form method="get" action="#" onsubmit="geocode(); return false">
  <p>
    <input id="address" />
    <input type="submit" value="Find" />
  </p>
</form>
```

This should look very familiar to you from Chapter 5; the markup is extremely similar. The same goes for the JavaScript event handler:

```
function geocode()
{
  var address = document.getElementById('address').value;
  geocoder.getLocations(address, afterGeocode);
};
```

The only difference here is that I'm calling getLocations, rather than getLatLng as we did back in Listing 5-2. It's a somewhat more sophisticated version; where getLatLng just returned a single set of coordinates, getLocations returns an array of Placemark objects with additional information. This plays out in the callback, as you can see in Listing 11-8.

Listing 11-8. *The afterGeocode Callback Function*

```
function afterGeocode(response)
{
  if (response &&
      (response.Status.code == 200))
  {
    // Address was found - extract the map coordinates from the response
    var place = response.Placemark[0];
    var coordinates = new GLatLng(place.Point.coordinates[1],
                                  place.Point.coordinates[0]);

    // Move the map there, zooming further in for more accurate results
    map.setCenter(coordinates, place.AddressDetails.Accuracy + 5);
  }
  else
    alert('Address not found. Please try again.');
};
```

There's actually quite a lot that you can do with this list of Placemarks, such as asking the user "Did you mean..?" when there are multiple matches. I encourage you to peruse the Google documentation and examples (referenced in Appendix D) for more details.

In this case, though, I'm still only interested in the first match. I set my own place variable to the first Placemark (with index of 0) and extract its Point.coordinates to create a standard GLatLng object. I then have one more trick up my sleeve: I use those coordinates to recenter the map, *with the zoom determined by the Accuracy of the result*. The idea here is that the accuracy of the geocoding roughly reflects the specificity of the user's request. If the user has entered a full address, the specificity (and thus the accuracy) is generally high, and I zoom quite far in. On the other hand, if she's entered a more general location (like a ZIP code or, even more generally, just a state name), the resulting low zoom level will show a correspondingly wider area. It works pretty well on the whole.

Handling the Starting Location

The last item of interest on this page is to do with the map's starting location, the area it shows when the page loads. On all your previous maps, you've always either just shown the same initial area, or adjusted the map to fit the available data. And at times, that approach works fine on this page—the default is to show a zoom level 4 view of North America. But after seeing the click-to-search map on the home page, you know that I want to be able to override that default with a specific, requested location. How to make it happen?

If you recall, the click-to-search event handler on the home page contained the following line:

```
document.location = 'search/#' + coordinates.toUrlValue() + ',8';
```

And I said at the time that the document's `location` property sends the browser off to a new page—the Campground Search page. Specifically, a click on the Oregon coast (for example) will send the browser to the following URL:

```
http://www.satellitefriendly.com/search/#44.34,-124.11,8
```

So here the highlighted part of the URL—after the # character—indicates a latitude of 44.34, a longitude of –124.11, and a zoom level of 8.

This string following #, known as the *anchor* or *hash*, is then available from the `document.location.hash` property, and it's not especially hard to extract the map location from it. Listing 11-9 shows the way, with code to be dropped into the page initialization in place of our usual `map.setCenter` call.

Listing 11-9. *Loading the Start Position from the URL Hash*

```
// Check for a starting location in URL
var hash = location.hash.replace('#', '');
if (hash != '')
{
  // Found starting location - parse the coordinates & zoom from it
  var viewport = startLocation.split(',');
  var latitude  = parseFloat(viewport[0]);
  var longitude = parseFloat(viewport[1]);
  var zoom      = parseInt(viewport[2]);
}

// Initialize the core map object
var options = {backgroundColor: '#D7D5E3',
  mapTypes: [G_NORMAL_MAP, G_SATELLITE_MAP, G_HYBRID_MAP, G_PHYSICAL_MAP]};
map = new GMap2(mapDiv, options);

if (!isNaN(latitude + longitude + zoom))
  // Starting location supplied
  map.setCenter(new GLatLng(latitude, longitude), zoom, G_PHYSICAL_MAP);
else
  // Default starting location
  map.setCenter(new GLatLng(39.8, -98.5), 4, G_PHYSICAL_MAP);
```

There are three principal steps here:

1. The contents of the URL hash are extracted into a local variable (some browsers also include the # character, which must be removed).

2. If it's not blank, hash is separated on the commas into the three component fields: latitude, longitude, and zoom.

3. If all three are numbers, they're used in the initializing call to map.setCenter.

Fixing the Back Button

It's also possible to leverage this infrastructure into a fix for one of the biggest drawbacks to rich JavaScript-based web applications and make the browser's Back button function as the user expects it to.

Here's the issue. Most web directories simply show you a list of results, where clicking on one item takes you to the details for it—and clicking Back in the browser returns you to where you left the directory. But as it stands, my map-based directory won't do this. While browsing campgrounds in a specific area, if the user leaves this page and then comes Back to it, her last map view will be lost. She's likely to be quite annoyed by this behavior, and rightly so; it's not how she expects the Back button to work.

There's a good workaround to this problem, however, that makes use of a session cookie in conjunction with the code of Listing 11-9. Before the user leaves the page, I set a cookie containing the current map location. Then when the page loads, I check for that cookie in JavaScript and, if it exists, use it as the starting location.

The code to accomplish it is fairly straightforward. First, I need an unload handler for the page; this is most easily accomplished by adding it to the body tag:

```
<body onload="loadPage()" onunload="unloadPage()">
```

The unloadPage handler itself looks like this:

```
function unloadPage()
{
  var lastLocation = map.getCenter().toUrlValue() + ',' + map.getZoom();
  document.cookie = 'lastLocation=' + lastLocation + ';path=/';

  // Finalize the Maps API
  GUnload();
};
```

Essentially, I'm just interrogating the map about its current state—with getCenter and getZoom—and stringing them together into the lastLocation variable. This then gets dropped into a session cookie (Listing 11-10; note the lack of an explicit expiration date), and I'm ready to let the user leave the page.

Listing 11-10. *Loading the Start Position from Either the URL Hash or a Session Cookie*

```
var startLocation;

// Check for a starting location or search address in URL
var hash = location.hash.replace('#', '');
if (hash != '')
  startLocation = hash;

// No starting location in URL - check for a browser cookie
if (startLocation == null)
  startLocation = getCookie('lastLocation');

if (startLocation != null)
{
  // Found starting location - parse the coordinates & zoom from it
  var viewport = startLocation.split(',');
  var latitude  = parseFloat(viewport[0]);
  var longitude = parseFloat(viewport[1]);
  var zoom      = parseInt(viewport[2]);
}

// Initialize the core map object
var options = {backgroundColor: '#D7D5E3',
  mapTypes: [G_NORMAL_MAP, G_SATELLITE_MAP, G_HYBRID_MAP, G_PHYSICAL_MAP]};
map = new GMap2(mapDiv, options);

if (!isNaN(lat + lon + zoom))
  // Starting location supplied
  map.setCenter(new GLatLng(latitude, longitude), zoom, G_PHYSICAL_MAP);
else
  // Default starting location
  map.setCenter(new GLatLng(39.8, -98.5), 4, G_PHYSICAL_MAP);
```

When the user returns, just a small amount of additional code will be needed, as highlighted in Listing 11-10. If hash isn't set, I retrieve the starting location from the lastLocation cookie; doing things in this order allows the cookie to be overridden by the click-to-search map on the home page.

So I'm now ready to let the user go, confident that I can handle the Back button successfully. But where to?

Viewing Campground Details

As mentioned in the previous section, the obvious place to go from browsing a directory is to viewing details about a specific entry, and, Satellite-Friendly is no exception. If you look back at Figure 11-3, clicking a campground icon (or sidebar row) opens an infowindow with a summary for the campground—and a "Campground Details" link. So the Campground Details page, shown in Figure 11-10, is our next port of call.

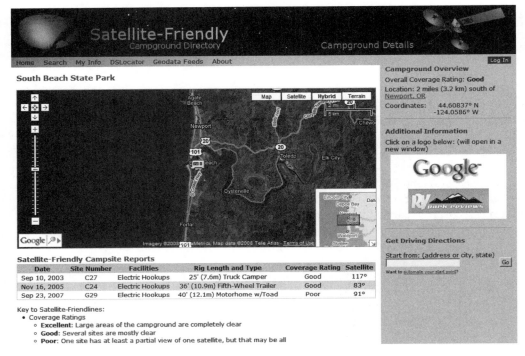

Figure 11-10. *The Campground Detail page*

The map here is far less complicated than on the Search page, because all it is doing is showing a single campground. There's no dynamic data to be loaded, so no behind-the-scenes round-trips to the server: all of the geodata is loaded when the page opens. What data there is, however, is more detailed: individual campsite reports, including date, facilities, and satellite coverage details.

Consequently, for this page I've chosen to leave the highway of geoXML and walk the path of JSON. It offers better support of the details that this page requires, and while it does mean that the campsite data won't be available on the larger geoweb, I'm not concerned about that. I'm already publishing my camp*ground* geodata; specific camp*sites* are less important.

There is another benefit as well. Virtually all the maps we've discussed up until now had a fundamental inefficiency: the page would load, the map would load, and then the map would go off to a server for its geodata—requiring one additional round-trip between client and server. On a fast Internet connection, this may not be especially important, but it is an inefficiency nonetheless, and on a high-latency connection—such as Internet over satellite, specifically—it may actually be noticeable.

JSON lets us sidestep this issue. Because we're not concerned about the data being independently available to the geoweb, it's possible to use PHP to place the data directly in the page itself, avoiding that extra server call. Listing 11-11 contains a PHP snippet to generate such embedded geodata; for the sake of brevity, I've omitted code not relevant to this discussion.

Listing 11-11. *Abbreviated View of campground_detail.php*

```
<!DOCTYPE html PUBLIC "-//W3C//DTD XHTML 1.0 Strict//EN"
                      "http://www.w3.org/TR/xhtml1/DTD/xhtml1-strict.dtd">
<html xmlns="http://www.w3.org/1999/xhtml">
  <head>
    <meta http-equiv="Content-Type" content="text/html; charset=UTF-8" />
    ...
    <?php
      include 'inc_sf_common.php';

      // Initialize variables
      $rows = 1;
      $sites = array();
      $totalRating    = 0;
      $totalLatitude  = 0.0;
      $totalLongitude = 0.0;

      // Clean the campground ID parameter
      $parkID = (integer) $_GET['nParkID'];

      // Connect to the database
      include 'mod_sf_db_connect.php';

      // Execute the database query
      $query = "select date_format(dtmWhen, '%b %e, %Y') sWhen,
                       Campsite.*,
                       sParkName
                  from Campsite
                       natural join Campground
                  where (Campsite.nParkID = $parkID)
                  order by dtmWhen asc";
      $result = mysql_query($query);
      if ($result)
      {
        // Query successful
        $rows = max(1, mysql_num_rows($result));

        while ($row = mysql_fetch_array($result))
        {
          // Accumulate data for the campground as a whole
          $totalRating    += $row['nCGRating'];
          $totalLatitude  += $row['fLatitude'];
          $totalLongitude += $row['fLongitude'];
          $maxHookups = max($maxHookups, $row['nHookups']);
          $parkName = htmlentities($row['sParkName']);
```

```php
        // Convert numeric hookup field into a text description
        switch ($row['nHookups'])
        {
          case -1: $hookups = 'Boondocking Area'; break;
          case  0: $hookups = 'Primitive Campsite'; break;
          case  1: $hookups = 'Electric Hookups'; break;
          case  2: $hookups = 'Full Hookups';
        }

        // Generate a JSON map data point for this site
        $icon = fsCGIcon($row['nCGRating'], $row['nHookups']);
        $sites[] = "
            {iconUrl: '$icon', number: '".$row['sSiteNum']."',
             hookups: '$hookups', date: '$row[sWhen]', satellite: $row[nSatLon],
             latitude: $row[fLatitude], longitude: $row[fLongitude],
             rating: '".$GLOBALS['asCGRating'][$row['nCGRating']]."'}";
      }
    }

    $parkRating = round($totalRating / $rows);
    switch ($parkRating)
    {
      case 0:
      case 1:  $color = '#FF0E0E'; break;
      case 2:  $color = '#FFFF0E'; break;
      case 3:  $color = '#0EFF0E'; break;
    }

    // Output the final JSON
    echo "
  <script type=\"text/javascript\">
    var campground = {name: '$parkName',
      iconUrl: '".fsCGIcon($parkRating, $maxHookups)."', color: '$color',
      latitude: {$totalLatitude}, longitude: {$totalLongitude}};

    var campsites = [".join($sites, ",")."];
  </script>";
    ?>
  </head>
  <body>
    ...
  </body>
</html>
```

In general, the PHP here follows the pattern for generating JSON laid out in Listing 10-11: retrieve data from the database, generate JSON code, and echo it back to the client. There are a couple of items of note, however:

- Because I'm returning multiple campsite rows, the $sites variable that holds their JSON is a PHP array, with one element for each site. This allows me to join them together with commas (near the end of the script) into a JSON array.

- The final JSON output is contained in <script> tags, making use of the fact that JSON *is* JavaScript.

And in Listing 11-12, we find the XHTML generated by this PHP (similarly abbreviated), containing the JSON for a typical campground with three campsite reports.

Listing 11-12. *Abbreviated XHTML Output of campground_detail.php*

```
<!DOCTYPE html PUBLIC "-//W3C//DTD XHTML 1.0 Strict//EN"
                    "http://www.w3.org/TR/xhtml1/DTD/xhtml1-strict.dtd">
<html xmlns="http://www.w3.org/1999/xhtml">
  <head>
    <meta http-equiv="Content-Type" content="text/html; charset=UTF-8" />
    ...
    <script type="text/javascript">
      var campground = {name: 'South Beach State Park',
        iconUrl: '/images/icons/trailer_yellow.png', color: '#FFFF0E',
        latitude: 133.82512, longitude: -372.1758};

      var campsites = [
            {iconUrl: '/images/icons/trailer_yellow.png', number: 'C27',
             hookups: 'Electric Hookups', date: 'Sep 10, 2003', satellite: 117,
             latitude: 44.6079, longitude: -124.059,
             rating: 'Good'},
            {iconUrl: '/images/icons/trailer_yellow.png', number: 'C24',
             hookups: 'Electric Hookups', date: 'Nov 16, 2005', satellite: 83,
             latitude: 44.60832, longitude: -124.0592,
             rating: 'Good'},
            {iconUrl: '/images/icons/trailer_red.png', number: 'G29',
             hookups: 'Electric Hookups', date: 'Sep 23, 2007', satellite: 91,
             latitude: 44.6089, longitude: -124.0576,
             rating: 'Poor'}];
    </script>
  </head>
  <body>
    ...
  </body>
</html>
```

Seeing the JSON *in situ* like this makes it obvious how convenient it is for JavaScript data loading. The data is *already in* the campground and campsites variables, just waiting for my map code to make use of it.

Displaying Both Campground and Campsite Details

Let's use it! With the JSON of Listing 11-12 in place, the following code is sufficient for my campground marker:

```
campground.coordinates = new GLatLng(campground.latitude, campground.longitude);
var options = {icon: createIcon(campground.iconUrl), title: campground.name};
campground.marker = new GMarker(campground.coordinates, options);
map.addOverlay(campground.marker);
```

It should be fairly clear what's going on here: I use the JSON-defined campground properties to create standard Maps API GLatLng and GMarker objects and then add the marker to the map.

Sharp-eyed readers will note the reference to createIcon in the previous listing; it's another "helper" function that's new to this page. Since both the campground and the campsites use the same icons, it's convenient to move the functionality out like this, where it can be used for both. OHIO is indeed my watchword. This is what createIcon looks like:

```
function createIcon(iconUrl)
{
  var result = new GIcon();
  result.image      = iconUrl;
  result.iconSize   = new GSize(32, 32);
  result.shadow     = iconUrl.replace('.png', '.shadow.png');
  result.shadowSize = new GSize(59, 32);
  result.iconAnchor = new GPoint(16, 28);
  result.infoWindowAnchor = getAnchor(iconUrl);
  return result;
};
```

Pretty standard custom-icon code, fairly familiar by now. The only item I'd like to call your attention to is the shadow; I've named my image files so that the shadow URLs are constructible in code as shown here. So trailer_yellow.png corresponds with trailer_yellow.shadow.png, and so on, making for nice, concise code.

Moving on to the campsite markers, however, we begin to encounter the fundamental split in the Satellite-Friendly data: this page is showing the details both for individual camp*sites* and for the camp*ground* as a whole. This is fine for the static data outside the map, but within the map it would be odd to display both simultaneously.

Instead, in Listing 11-13 I've chosen to implement this split along zoom-level lines: when the map is zoomed out beyond a certain threshold I show a single marker for the campground, and when closer than that threshold, I instead show markers for individual sites. This threshold will be calculated in code by effectively asking the API, "What's the highest zoom level at which all the campsites would be visible at once?"

Listing 11-13. *Creating the Campsite Markers*

```
// We'll also need the campground boundaries for use in zooming
campground.bounds = new GLatLngBounds();

// Create a map marker for each campsite to use when zoomed in
for (var c = 0; c < campsites.length; c++)
{
  // Extract the coordinates from JSON and add it to the campground boundaries
  campsites[c].coordinates = new GLatLng(campsites[c].latitude,
                                         campsites[c].longitude);
  campground.bounds.extend(campsites[c].coordinates);

  // Create campsite icon & marker
  campsites[c].title = 'Site number ' + campsites[c].number;
  options = {icon: createIcon(campsites[c].iconUrl), title: campsites[c].title};
  campsites[c].marker = new GMarker(campsites[c].coordinates, options);
  map.addOverlay(campsites[c].marker);

  // Immediately hide the marker (our initial zoom is too far out to show it)
  campsites[c].marker.hide();

  // Attach infowindow to the marker with content from JSON
  campsites[c].marker.bindInfoWindowHtml(
    '<div id="infowindow">' +
      '<h4>' + campsites[c].title + '</h4>' +
        '<li>' + campsites[c].rating + ' view of satellite at ' +
          campsites[c].satellite + '&deg;</li>' +
        '<li>' + campsites[c].hookups + '</li>' +
      '</ul>' +
      '<p>Reported on ' + campsites[c].date + '</p>' +
    '</div>');
}

// Calculate optimal campground-wide zoom level
optimalZoom = Math.min(15, map.getBoundsZoomLevel(campground.bounds) - 1);
```

With this approach in mind, let's look at Listing 11-13, showing the campsite marker initialization with the optimal-zoom code highlighted. It starts by creating a bounds property for the campground, of type GLatLngBounds, an API object used for establishing areas on the map. I then iterate through the campsites array that was created back in Listings 11-11 and 11-12; for each campsite, I create the custom icon, add the map marker (with infowindow), and extend campground.bounds to include that site.

After the for loop has processed all the campsites, I'm ready to establish the optimal campground zoom level. The API has a handy function for this, map.getBoundsZoomLevel, which takes the GLatLngBounds we want to fit and returns the maximum zoom level at which it will all be visible in the viewport. In order for the campsites' *markers* to fit comfortably as well, I reduce this maximum by one level, and I also limit it to 15 (as the highest zoom for which good satellite imagery is available in most places).

So then, what do we do with this optimal zoom level? I use it in two places. First and foremost is a handler for the map's moveend event (which also fires after the zoom level changes, remember). The logic is quite simple: if the current zoom level is well below the optimal, show the campground marker and hide the campsites; if not, hide the campground and show the individual sites instead. The code to do so can be found in Listing 11-14.

Listing 11-14. *The mapMoveEnd Handler to Switch Between Showing Campground and Campsites*

```
function mapMoveEnd()
{
  if (map.getZoom() < optimalZoom - 1)
  {
    // Zoomed far enough out to only show single marker for the campground

    // Hide all the individual campsite markers
    map.closeInfoWindow();
    for (var c = 0; c < campsites.length; c++)
      campsites[c].marker.hide()

    // Show (and track) the campground marker
    campground.marker.show();
    tracker.enable();
  }
  else
  {
    // Zoomed far enough in to see individual campsites

    // Hide the campground marker
    campground.marker.hide();

    // Show all the individual campsite markers
    siteVisible = false;
    var bounds = map.getBounds();
    for (var c = 0; c < campsites.length; c++)
    {
      campsites[c].marker.show()
      if (bounds.contains(campsites[c].coordinates))
        siteVisible = true;
    }

    // Only show the marker tracker if no campsite is visible
    if (siteVisible)
      tracker.disable();
    else
      tracker.enable();
  }
};
```

■**Note** There is some additional code in Listing 11-14, related to `tracker`, that I'll discuss in the next section.

The second use of the optimal zoom comes in a mouse-click event listener for the campground marker:

```
GEvent.addListener(campground.marker, 'click',
  function ()
  {
    map.setCenter(campground.bounds.getCenter(), optimalZoom);
  });
```

Basically, when the campground marker is clicked, the map zooms in to show all campsites by using the optimal zoom level. This lets the user move from a wide-angle view of the campground's location to a detailed view of its layout with a single click. In most areas, Google Maps' satellite imagery is sufficient to see individual campsites clearly, as shown in Figure 11-11.

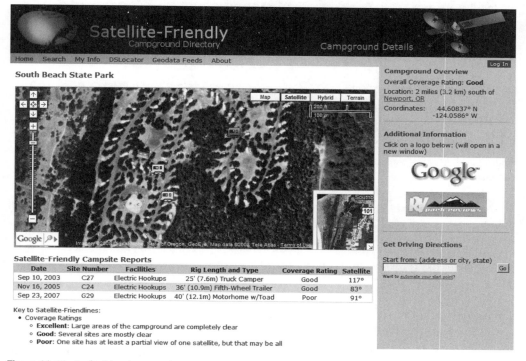

Figure 11-11. *Individual campsites*

Adding Bells and Whistles

We've now completed the core functionality of Campground Detail, so it's time to round out the page with some high-value add-ons, from both the API and elsewhere.

Tracking Off-Screen Markers

Our first addition to Campground Detail addresses a common issue with maps whose markers are highly localized. If the map is panned away from the campground, perhaps to look at a nearby point of interest, it's fairly easy to lose track of just where the campground was—leading, perhaps, to a frantic search around and user frustration.

To alleviate this problem, Maps API developer Dan Rummel created an add-on called the Marker Tracker, which Google has since adopted into their API utility library (like the LabeledMarker and MapIconMaker of Chapter 9). When activated, the MarkerTracker object waits quietly for its associated GMarker to disappear outside the map viewport—at which time it springs into action, displaying an arrow pointing toward the missing marker and a small copy of the marker itself. As you can see in Figure 11-12, it's a good, intuitive aid that shows the user the direction to the campground.

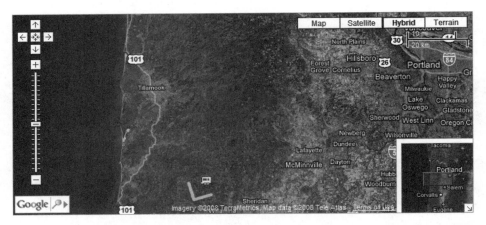

Figure 11-12. *MarkerTracker in action, indicating the campground's location off the bottom of the map*

MarkerTracker is also quite easy to add to a map. It's an external module, so you first need to link its JavaScript into your XHTML, like this:

```
<script type="text/javascript" src="http://gmaps-utility-library.googlecode.com ➥
/svn/trunk/markertracker/release/src/markertracker.js"></script>
```

Putting it to use requires just a couple of lines of JavaScript:

```
var options = {color: campground.color, weight: 5, length: 20};
tracker = new MarkerTracker(campground.marker, map, options);
```

The first option is a color for the arrow, which I set in JSON to match my campground icon (see Listing 11-12 again); it's a standard CSS-style color specifier string, like '#FFFF0E'. And the weight and length are pixel measurements for the "arms" of the arrow. The MarkerTracker object is then created, with the marker I want it to track and these options, and assigned to a tracker variable that I declared earlier. It's that easy.

Or rather, it would be if not for my campground/campsite split of the previous section. In order to avoid the MarkerTracker colliding with my campsite markers, I disable it (effectively hiding it from view) whenever a campsite marker is visible. This is the extra `tracker`-related code in Listing 11-14.

`MarkerTracker` has a number of other possible options as well; you can control the icon you want it to display, for instance. I encourage you to visit its official documentation at `http://tinyurl.com/5ga5oa` for more information.

Getting Directions to the Campground

A fairly obvious addition to the Campground Detail page is driving directions; once the user has found a campground that she wants to visit, it's a simple matter to give her full, turn-by-turn instructions from the Maps API.

I begin much as when we last used driving directions, in Chapter 5, with the following code in my page load handler:

```
var panel = document.getElementById('directions_response');
directions = new GDirections(map, panel);
GEvent.addListener(directions, 'addoverlay', directionsDone);
GEvent.addListener(directions, 'error',      directionsError);
```

The only change is the addition of the event listeners, which I'll cover in a moment. And as with `tracker` in the previous section, the `directions` variable was declared earlier.

The real directions handling occurs in three small functions, found in Listing 11-15. They're all event handlers: the first is attached to the click event of the "Go" button in XHTML, the same as in Listing 5-6, while the second and third are for the directions event listeners I just created. Let's look at each in turn.

Listing 11-15. *Driving Directions to the Campground*

```
function getDirections()
{
  // getDirections: retrieve driving directions to the campground

  var startAddress = document.getElementById('saddr');

  if (startAddress.value == '')
  {
    alert('Please enter a starting point for your driving directions.');
    startAddress.focus();
  }
  else
  {
    // Starting point looks good - load driving directions
    var endpoints = 'from: ' + startAddress.value + ' to:' +
                    campground.coordinates.toUrlValue();
    directions.load(endpoints);
  }
};
```

```
function directionsDone()
{
  // directionsDone: show the header above the driving directions area
  var status = directions.getStatus().code;
  if (status == 200)
  {
    document.getElementById('directions_header').style.display = 'block';
    tracker.disable();
  }
};

function directionsError()
{
  // directionsError: a problem occurred getting driving directions
  var status = directions.getStatus().code;
  if (status == 500)
    alert('Unable to load driving directions, sorry.');
  else
    alert('Unable to locate start point for driving directions.');
};
```

getDirections: Very similar to the last time you saw driving directions, in Listing 5-7, this function simply validates that a start point has been entered and then invokes the GDirections object. The only substantive difference is that here I'm using the load function, rather than loadFromWaypoints as in Chapter 5. The reason is that this page doesn't have starting *coordinates*, just an *address*, and load includes a call to GDirections' built-in geocoder.

directionsDone: This is effectively a callback for when the driving-directions call completes. I check to make sure it was successful (by checking its status for a code of 200, meaning success), show an XHTML header for the directions panel, and hide the MarkerTracker (it's not really needed with directions on the map).

directionsError: If Google was unable to find directions, this handler will be called, allowing me to tell the user about the problem. There are typically only two reasons why direction-finding will fail (see the last few lines of Listing 11-15), and I again use the status code to determine which is the case.

■**Tip** In other circumstances, you might find it useful to check for other status codes. Google maintains the complete list in the Maps API documentation at http://tinyurl.com/2bfbm2.

Finding Local Services

To finish off the Campground Detail map, I've included a couple of other standard API features to help the user find information on services local to the campground. These are both items that you've seen before, so I'm not going to spend much ink on them here. If you'd like a reminder, you can find complete coverage of each in earlier chapters.

The first is map advertising; as you'll recall from Chapter 5, the following two lines of code are sufficient to activate it:

```
var ads = new GAdsManager(map, 'pub-01234567890123456', {maxAdsOnMap: 10});
ads.enable();
```

The second feature is the GoogleBar, the small location-aware search control introduced in Chapter 4. It's even easier to add to the map:

```
map.enableGoogleBar();
```

Disseminating Geodata

We've now completed our tour of the core Maps API integrations for Satellite-Friendly. The whole of the directory is in place: a user can start a search by clicking a map on the home page, browse the directory on the Campground Search page, and view full information for any entry on Campground Detail.

And the bulk of this functionality is driven by standardized geoXML data. As a recap, Satellite-Friendly has the following geodata feeds:

- Recent campsite entries, as used on the home page (`recent_campgrounds.php` / Listing 11-1)

- Top campgrounds by several criteria, as used on the Campground Search page (`top_campgrounds.php` / Listing 11-7)

- All campgrounds, dynamically clustered as needed, also used on the Campground Search page (`all_campgrounds.php`)

In order to help users and other mashup-makers find my data, I've created a catalog page on the site listing the available feeds, as shown in Figure 11-13. All the various options are described here, with links directly to the data URLs for maximum ease of use.

The catalog also includes mention of a Satellite-Friendly mapplet. I'll be discussing the content of that mapplet in a moment; the link on this page (to add it to Google Maps) looks like this:

```
http://maps.google.com/maps/mpl?moduleurl=http%3A%2F%2Fwww.satellitefriendly.com ➥
%2Fservices%2Fcg_mapplet.xml
```

As described in Chapter 7, this is a special link Google provides to preview (and optionally install) a mapplet with one click. Note that my mapplet's location has been URL-encoded, with = changed to %3A and / to %2F.

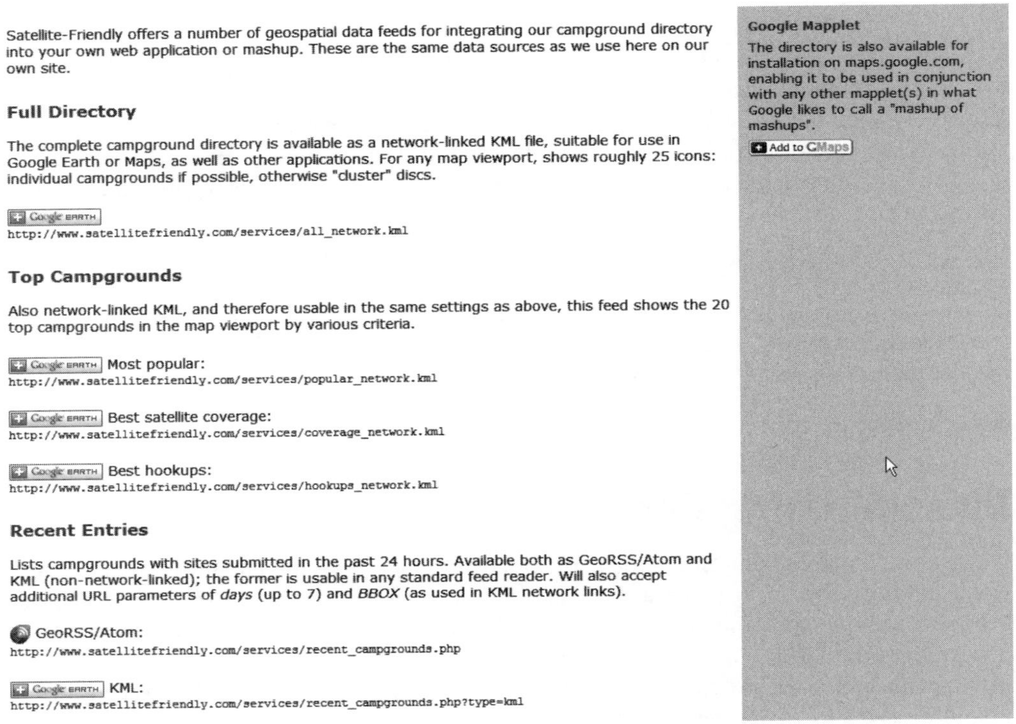

Satellite-Friendly offers a number of geospatial data feeds for integrating our campground directory into your own web application or mashup. These are the same data sources as we use here on our own site.

Full Directory

The complete campground directory is available as a network-linked KML file, suitable for use in Google Earth or Maps, as well as other applications. For any map viewport, shows roughly 25 icons: individual campgrounds if possible, otherwise "cluster" discs.

[Google EARTH]
http://www.satellitefriendly.com/services/all_network.kml

Top Campgrounds

Also network-linked KML, and therefore usable in the same settings as above, this feed shows the 20 top campgrounds in the map viewport by various criteria.

[Google EARTH] Most popular:
http://www.satellitefriendly.com/services/popular_network.kml

[Google EARTH] Best satellite coverage:
http://www.satellitefriendly.com/services/coverage_network.kml

[Google EARTH] Best hookups:
http://www.satellitefriendly.com/services/hookups_network.kml

Recent Entries

Lists campgrounds with sites submitted in the past 24 hours. Available both as GeoRSS/Atom and KML (non-network-linked); the former is usable in any standard feed reader. Will also accept additional URL parameters of *days* (up to 7) and *BBOX* (as used in KML network links).

⊙ GeoRSS/Atom:
http://www.satellitefriendly.com/services/recent_campgrounds.php

[Google EARTH] KML:
http://www.satellitefriendly.com/services/recent_campgrounds.php?type=kml

Google Mapplet

The directory is also available for installation on maps.google.com, enabling it to be used in conjunction with any other mapplet(s) in what Google likes to call a "mashup of mashups".

[➕ Add to GMaps]

Figure 11-13. *Satellite-Friendly's geodata feed catalog*

Geo Sitemap

Of course, for maximum geoweb participation I'd be remiss not to include a geo sitemap on Satellite-Friendly. With my large dataset and dynamically generated KML, however, a grid-based sitemap from PHP was the only practical choice. The source code can be found in Listing 11-16. Literally the only differences between this and the example from Chapter 10 are my database particulars, the size of my grid squares (one degree on a side), and the <loc> URL.

Listing 11-16. *Generating a Geo Sitemap for Satellite-Friendly*

```php
<?php
  include 'mod_sf_db_connect.php';

  $query = "select min(fLatitude) south,
                   max(fLatitude) north,
                   min(fLongitude) west,
                   max(fLongitude) east
              from Campsite";
  $result = mysql_query($query);
  $row = mysql_fetch_assoc($result);
```

```php
  // Boundaries for sitemap grid
  $north = ceil($row['north']);
  $south = floor($row['south']);
  $east  = floor($row['east']);
  $west  = ceil($row['west']);

  // Grid size, in degrees, with separate sizes for latitude and longitude
  $lat_grid = 1;
  $lon_grid = 1;

  // Prepare the sitemap XML header
  $header = '<?xml version="1.0" encoding="UTF-8"?>
<urlset xmlns="http://www.sitemaps.org/schemas/sitemap/0.9"
        xmlns:geo="http://www.google.com/geo/schemas/sitemap/1.0">';

  // Create a sitemap url element for each grid cell
  for ($lat = $south; $lat < $north; $lat += $lat_grid)
    for ($lon = $west; $lon < $east; $lon += $lon_grid)
    {
      $query = "select 1
                   from Campsite
                   where (fLatitude between $lat and ".($lat + $lat_grid).")
                      and (fLongitude between $lon and ".($lon + $lon_grid).")";
      $result = mysql_query($query);
      if (!mysql_num_rows($result))
        continue;

      $urls = $urls.'
  <url>
    <loc>
     http://www.satellitefriendly.com/services/top_campgrounds.php?BBOX='.
          $lon.','.$lat.','.($lon + $lon_grid).','.($lat + $lat_grid).'
    </loc>
    <geo:geo>
      <geo:format>kml</geo:format>
    </geo:geo>
  </url>';
    }

  // Prepare the sitemap XML footer
  $footer = '
</urlset>';

  // Output the final sitemap XML
  header('Content-type: application/xml');
  echo $header;
  echo $urls;
  echo $footer;
?>
```

A Satellite-Friendly Mapplet

The standardization of my geodata also makes it an easy matter to create a mapplet, distributing my content directly to maps.google.com. To finish off this chapter, let's take a look at the code to do so, in Listing 11-17.

Listing 11-17. *The Satellite-Friendly Mapplet*

```xml
<?xml version="1.0" encoding="UTF-8"?>
<Module>
  <ModulePrefs title="Satellite-Friendly Campgrounds"
          description="Campgrounds in North America with coverage for satellite ➥
TV and Internet. Results contributed by users on-site with GPS."
          author="Sterling Udell"
          author_email="sterling.udell+mapplet@googlemail.com"
          screenshot="http://satellitefriendly.com/images/cg_mapplet_scr.png"
          thumbnail="http://satellitefriendly.com/images/cg_mapplet_thm.png"
    <Require feature="sharedmap" />
    <Require feature="dynamic-height"/>
    <Require feature="setprefs" />
  </ModulePrefs>
<UserPref datatype="hidden" name="view" default_value="all" />
<Content type="html"><![CDATA[
    <style type="text/css">
      p, table {
        font-size: 90%;
        width: 100%;
        text-align: left;
      }
      h3 {
        margin: 0;
        font-size: 12pt;
      }
      img {
        vertical-align: middle;
      }
      .coverage {
        text-align: center;
      }
    </style>

    <p>
      Campgrounds in North America with coverage for satellite TV and Internet.
      Locations from
      <a href="http://www.satellitefriendly.com/">SatelliteFriendly.com</a>,
      contributed by users on-site with GPS.
    </p>
```

```
<p>
  View:
  <select id="view" onchange="viewChange()">
    <option value="all">All Campgrounds</option>
    <option value="popular">Most Popular</option>
    <option value="recent">Most Recent Entries</option>
  </select>
</p>

<h3>Legend</h3>
<table>
  <tr>
    <td colspan="2">
      <img src="http://satellitefriendly.com/images/icons/info_circle.png"
           width="32" height="32" /> Multiple campgrounds in area
    </td>
  </tr>
  <tr>
    <th>Campsite Hookups</th>
    <th class="coverage">Satellite Coverage</th>
  </tr>
  <tr>
    <td>
      <img src="http://satellitefriendly.com/images/icons/bus_gray.png"
           width="32" height="32" /> Full
    </td>
    <td class="coverage">
      <img width="64" height="18"
           src="http://satellitefriendly.com/images/excellent.png"
        title="Large areas of the campground are completely clear" />
    </td>
  </tr>
  <tr>
    <td>
      <img src="http://satellitefriendly.com/images/icons/trailer_gray.png"
           width="32" height="32" /> Electric
    </td>
    <td class="coverage">
      <img width="44" height="18"
           src="http://satellitefriendly.com/images/good.png"
        title="Several sites are mostly clear" />
    </td>
  </tr>
  <tr>
    <td>
      <img src="http://satellitefriendly.com/images/icons/tent_gray.png"
           width="32" height="32" /> None
    </td>
```

```
      <td class="coverage">
        <img width="39" height="18"
             src="http://satellitefriendly.com/images/poor.png"
          title="One site has at least a partial view of one satellite" />
      </td>
    </tr>
  </table>
<script type="text/javascript">
  function viewChange()
  {
    // viewChange: refresh the geodata display to match the new selection

    // Get the selection from the XHTML
    var selected = view.options[view.selectedIndex].value;

    // Save the new selection to hidden user preference
    prefs.set('view', selected);

    // Remove any previous data overlay
    if (geoXml != null)
      map.removeOverlay(geoXml);

    // Set the new geodata URL to use
    if (selected == 'all')
      geoXml = new GGeoXml(urlAll);
    else if (selected == 'recent')
      geoXml = new GGeoXml(urlRecent);
    else
      geoXml = new GGeoXml(urlTop);

    // Add data from the new URL to the map
    map.addOverlay(geoXml);
  };

  // END FUNCTION DECLARATIONS - BEGIN MAIN MAPPLET CODE

  // Initialize the map
  var map = new GMap2();
  var geoXml;
  var view = document.getElementById('view');
  var prefs = new _IG_Prefs();

  // Declare and initialize data source URLs
  var urlAll = 'http://satellitefriendly.com/services/all_network.kml';
  var urlTop = 'http://satellitefriendly.com/services/popular_network.kml';
  var urlRecent = 'http://satellitefriendly.com/services/recent_network.kml';
```

```
    // Adjust the height of the sidebar display
    _IG_AdjustIFrameHeight();

    // Initialize the data-view selector to the saved value
    for (var s = 0; s < view.options.length; s++)
      if (view.options[s].value == prefs.getString('view'))
      {
        view.selectedIndex = s;
        break;
      }

    // Initialize the data display
    viewChange();
  </script>
]]></Content>
</Module>
```

The JavaScript here is something of a simplified version of the Campground Search page: an XHTML select with an onchange event handler that swaps geodata-feed URLs appropriately. Since the logic is fundamentally the same, I'm not going to go into it in much more detail than that. The biggest difference is that I'm using Google's GGeoXml object rather than the modified EGeoXml. This is because GGeoXml handles networked-linked KML natively, and while it would certainly have been possible to implement my own EGeoXml-based version in a mapplet, the custom marker handling and sidebar entries aren't required here. So GGeoXml works, with minimal coding effort. See for yourself in Figure 11-14.

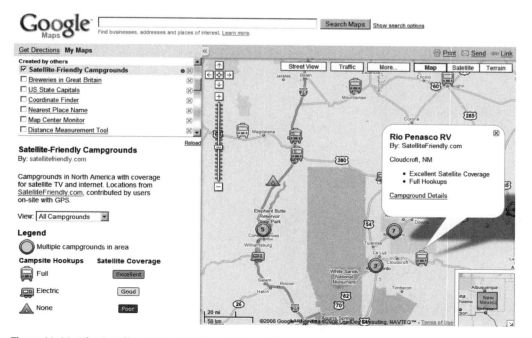

Figure 11-14. *The Satellite-Friendly Mapplet in action*

Overall, it's a fairly standard geodata mapplet, perfectly adequate for disseminating Satellite-Friendly's KML to the Google Maps channel. I've placed some ancillary content in the sidebar (promotional text and a marker icon legend), styled it with embedded CSS, and saved the user's preferred data view (recent, top, or all) in a hidden user preference—all techniques you saw in Chapter 8.

Summary

I hope you've enjoyed your tour of the Satellite-Friendly campground directory. Along the way, you've seen a full range of Maps API implementations, from the all-but-static click-to-search map on the home page to the highly dynamic main Campground Search map. All the major concepts of the book are represented here, on a working web site that RV travelers use every day: KML, GeoRSS, and JSON data, produced from MySQL and PHP, consumed by the Maps and Mapplets APIs, creating a rich and responsive cartographic application.

Of course, Satellite-Friendly goes beyond what I've been able to discuss here; I've mentioned a few such areas (such as clustering), though not all. For the complete picture, I invite you to examine the XHTML and JavaScript code yourself, at www.satellitefriendly.com. You'll find that viewing page source and inspecting the JavaScript in Firebug (see Appendix C) is a great learning tool, enabling you to dig into any page and see how it works.

This concludes the main section of the book; the remaining pages contain a few appendices with additional information and resources to help you on your way. But generally, you're now ready to go it alone. Your mapping skill set will always be growing, but you now have the techniques within your grasp to get underway. So get out there and make some maps!

Appendixes

Mapping Fundamentals

Not long ago, the specialized skills required to make accurate maps meant that the endeavor was restricted to trained cartographers. With the Google Maps API, you now have that ability yourself, with no more specialized knowledge than keeping your latitude and longitude coordinates straight (and some basic web design, of course). Nonetheless, some additional background on cartographic principles will make you a better map programmer, and that's what you'll find in this appendix.

Most of the information here is indeed to do with latitude and longitude: different formats you might encounter, how precise you need to be, and the relation of the two numbers to each other. You'll also learn about how to calculate distance between two locations using only their coordinates, and finally, I'll present some useful insights into map projections in general and the Mercator projection used by Google Maps in particular.

Latitude and Longitude

We've been using latitude and longitude throughout the book—there's very little that can be done in the Maps API without them—but until now, we haven't really talked much *about* them. And that's been fine; we haven't really needed to. But there are a couple of pitfalls lurking in this simple pair of numbers that could cause trouble for you, and my first task here is to guard you against them.

Degrees, Minutes, and Seconds

As you know by now, the numbers of latitude and longitude are generally expressed in *degrees*. This is because they are fundamentally measuring *angles* on the (roughly) spherical surface of the Earth. For latitude, it's the angle north of the equator; hence south latitudes are negative, and the North Pole has a latitude of 90°, "straight up" from the equator's "horizontal." Similarly, as the east-west circumference of the Earth measures 360°, longitude represents angles within that range. From an arbitrary zero line called the prime meridian, the angles run west to –180° and east to 180°, where they meet (in the mid-Pacific).

Following Google Maps' lead, we've been expressing these latitude and longitude angles in a format called *decimal degrees*: each number simply includes a few decimal places to specify partial degrees. However, there is an alternative method of expressing fractional degrees: each degree can be broken up into sixty *minutes*, with each minute further divided into sixty *seconds*. It's as if a degree was an hour of time. This approach is generally just called DMS, for Degrees/Minutes/Seconds.

Long before Google Maps hit the mainstream, DMS was the common format for expressing coordinates, and you still find it in use today. It's the default display setting on many GPS receivers, some paper maps show coordinates in this fashion, and certain organizations use it as their standard. Google never uses minutes or seconds, but as an API developer you may need to be aware that they exist, because you'll sometimes find coordinates in this format—from an external source, or a legacy database perhaps—and they cannot be plotted directly onto an API map.

Recognizing Minutes and Seconds

The first hurdle is recognizing when coordinates *need* conversion, and it's sometimes harder than you'd think. The easiest case is when the units are explicitly given, perhaps in separate database columns or labeled in text:

```
North 43 degrees, 28 minutes 3 seconds
West 103 degrees, 51 minutes, 27 seconds
```

It's also common to see quotation marks used as symbols, with single quotes (') for minutes and double quotes (") for seconds:

```
43° 28' 3" N
103° 51' 27" W
```

So quotes are a dead giveaway for DMS. But occasionally, you will just see bare numbers separated by spaces:

```
43 28  3 N
103 51 27 W
```

When greater precision is required, you will see decimal numbers on the seconds:

```
43 28  3.2
-103 51 26.9
```

Remember that negative longitudes are (almost) always west.

And finally, you will occasionally come across degrees plus decimal *minutes*:

```
43 28.053
-103 51.450
```

What do all of these possibilities have in common? In all cases, there are a couple of important clues that you're dealing with DMS, rather than decimal degrees.

- Each ordinate has a *several distinct numbers*, not just a single decimal number.

- Minutes and seconds, the second and third distinct numbers, are *never greater than 60*.

And finally, if you're plotting coordinates on a Google map and they're always coming out just a bit off, be suspicious: minutes and seconds may be your problem.

Converting to and from Decimal Degrees

Once you have established that coordinates are in DMS format, you need to convert them to decimal degrees before using them with the Maps and Mapplets APIs. It's actually quite easy, and in Listing A-1, you'll find a couple of JavaScript functions to do it.

Listing A-1. *DMS Conversion Functions*

```
function dms2decimal(deg, min, sec)
{
  // dms2dd: converts degree/minutes/seconds to decimal degrees
  if (sec == null)
    sec = 0;
  return deg + (min / 60) + (sec / 3600);
};

function decimal2dms(degrees)
{
  // dd2dms: converts decimal degrees to degree/minutes/seconds
  var minutes = (Math.abs(degrees) - Math.floor(Math.abs(degrees))) * 60;
  var seconds = new Number(((minutes - Math.floor(minutes)) * 60).toFixed(2));
  var minutes = Math.floor(minutes);
  var degrees = Math.floor(degrees);
  return {deg: degrees, min: minutes, sec: seconds};
};
```

The first function, `dms2decimal`, is the one you'll use more often. It converts DMS to decimal degrees, ready for use in any Google mapping API:

```
var latitude  = dms2decimal(43, 28, 3.2);
var longitude = dms2decimal(-103, 51, 26.9);
var coordinates = new GLatLng(latitude, longitude);
```

Note that the `min` and `sec` parameters can be decimal numbers themselves; if you have decimal minutes and not seconds, you can safely leave `sec` out.

The second function, `decimal2dms`, is for use if you need to convert API-standard decimal degrees to DMS. It returns a bit of JSON with the three components, used as shown here:

```
var dms = decimal2dms(coordinates.lat());
alert('Latitude is ' + dms.deg + ' degrees, ' + dms.min + ' minutes, ' +
    dms.sec + ' seconds');
```

So you simply use the `deg`, `min`, and `sec` properties of the returned value for the three DMS components.

■**Tip** A quick and easy way to convert a single DMS coordinate is by using Google Maps itself. Simply paste virtually any DMS format (such as 43 28 3, -103 51 27) into the Search Maps box at maps.google.com, and a map marker will be shown at the correct location, with the decimal degrees in an infowindow.

Other Coordinate Systems

Throughout the world and over the centuries, many different coordinate systems have been used to express location. You might encounter one of these when working with data predating the GPS era; others are still in use in particular areas of the world, such as Britain's National

Grid. It's beyond the scope of this book to cover them all in detail, especially since most are far more involved than the simple decimal-DMS conversions you've just seen. If you come across a different format or grid system, you will need to track down conversion routines yourself. Either a Google search or a query on the Maps API discussion group (see Appendix D) is a good place to start.

For reference, Google Maps latitude and longitude use a standard (called a *map datum*) known as WGS84, also the most commonly used by consumer GPS receivers.

Coordinate Precision

The other major numeric trap awaiting the unwary map programmer involves coordinate *precision*—essentially, how many decimal places to use with your latitudes and longitudes. Precision in coordinates directly translates to precision in mapping; more decimal places on your latitude and longitude means more exact placement on the map, and by extension, on the surface of the Earth.

Table A-1 illustrates this relationship, showing the accuracy of increasing decimal places at 40° latitude. These numbers are interesting from two directions, at both extremes.

Table A-1. *Coordinate Accuracy at 40° Latitude*

Decimal Places	Example	East/West Accuracy	North/South Accuracy
0	40°	44 miles	69 miles
1	40.1°	4.4 miles	6.9 miles
2	40.12°	0.44 miles	0.69 miles
3	40.123°	235 feet	364 feet
4	40.1234°	23 feet	36 feet
5	40.12345°	2.3 feet	3.6 feet
6	40.123456°	2.8 inches	4.4 inches
7	40.1234567°	0.3 inches	0.4 inches

Note East/west accuracy varies based on the exact latitude in question; this will be covered in more detail in a few pages, when I discuss map projections. The 40° values in Table A-1 are reasonable for middle latitudes, like those found in the continental USA.

First, it's important to have *sufficient* precision for the mapping task at hand. If you are giving the location of a specific address on a street, for example, a precision of one or two decimal places isn't really sufficient, but four probably is.

Second, it's all too easy to use *excessive* precision, which is useless at best and misleading at worst. Google maps clearly don't have sub-inch resolution, so anything more than six decimal places would be wasted. Even six is a bit much for most applications; consumer GPS receivers rarely have an accuracy better than ten or twenty feet, so for any coordinates relating to GPS, decimal places beyond five are meaningless.

And at worst, they are misleading. I once had a map-programming job where the client supplied coordinates for his customers and suppliers; my tasks included showing the existing customers on a map, and a system for geocoding the addresses of new customers. One day the client got it in his head to geocode one of his older customers—and immediately began complaining to me that the geocoder was broken, because it gave "entirely different coordinates" for the existing customers. The problem? The underlying software he was using showed the coordinates to eight decimal places, and after new geocoding, the last half of those decimal places were indeed "entirely different". So to the client, the latitude and longitude were "obviously" wrong, even though the marker hadn't visibly moved on the map.

As a rule, five (or maybe six) decimal places is a good target, neither insufficient nor excessive for most applications.

Avoiding Precision Problems

With one notable exception (covered in the next section), modern programming languages like JavaScript always have sufficient precision for good mapping. So as a developer, your major concern here should be avoiding excessive precision. For our purposes, there are two primary tools to use.

The first is native to JavaScript; all numbers have a built-in function, toFixed, that converts them to strings with the given precision. Here's an example of toFixed in use:

```
var latitude  = coordinates.lat();
alert('Latitude is ' + latitude.toFixed(5));
```

It's as easy as that; always using toFixed for your latitudes and longitudes should ensure that your users see just the right amount of precision. For an example of this technique in action, see Listing 8-9.

The second tool is built into Google's mapping APIs: toUrlValue, a function of the GLatLng object. This function accepts an optional precision parameter (which defaults to 6 if left out), and simply creates a string containing the coordinates, separated by commas and formatted with the given precision. So for example, the following code:

```
var coordinates = marker.getpoint();
alert(coordinates.toUrlValue(3));
```

would produce a message like this:

```
43.468,-103.858
```

As its name implies, toUrlValue was originally intended for adding coordinates as parameters to a URL, but it's handy whenever you need both latitude and longitude together. An example of such a usage can be found in Listing 5-7.

SQL Data Types

As mentioned, JavaScript and PHP always give you plenty of precision for good coordinate calculations, but with SQL, precision is an option. SQL allows several storage possibilities for decimal numbers, each with strengths and weaknesses for coordinate values. If you need to create geospatial databases, read on for full coverage; if not, feel free to skip to the next section.

The basic issue is precision versus storage space. It's certainly possible to always get plenty of precision from SQL, but for a large geodata table with millions of rows, conserving storage may be an issue. Table A-2 details the principal options for MySQL; other database systems are similar.

Table A-2. *MySQL numeric types*

Type	Coordinate Precision	Bytes per Field
FLOAT	3 decimal places	4
DOUBLE	12 decimal places	8
DECIMAL(9,6)	6 decimal places	11

As you can see, the DECIMAL type—good for fixed-precision values, like currency—isn't the most efficient choice for coordinates. You get more precision in fewer bytes with DOUBLE, and if the last digit isn't necessarily exact (the bugbear of floating-point storage), the four-millionths of an inch involved doesn't exactly matter.

The only real advantage of DECIMAL is that, with the precision specified in the database structure, you may be able to avoid formatting the results in JavaScript (as described in the previous section).

Finally, if your coordinates only need accuracy within a few hundred feet (see Table A-1) and space is at a premium, FLOAT is probably an even better option for you. But don't do this unless it's genuinely necessary; if the database truncates valid digits from your coordinates, that precision is gone forever.

Calculating Distance

Now that your latitudes and longitudes are in good shape, a common requirement is to calculate the distance between the coordinates of two points. On the curved surface of the Earth, such a calculation isn't trivial, but it's not insurmountable either.

If you have the two points in JavaScript, your easiest option is to let Google's API do the heavy lifting for you. The GLatLng object has a built-in function, distanceFrom, to calculate its distance (in meters) from another GLatLng. Here's how it's used:

```
var coordinates1 = new GLatLng(43.489532, -80.489487);
var coordinates2 = new GLatLng(43.487788, -80.498650);
var distance = coordinates1.distanceFrom(coordinates2);
alert('Distance is ' + distance.toFixed(0) + ' meters');
```

In this example, the result (displayed by the alert) will be "Distance is 765 meters." Note that again, I'm avoiding excessive precision by applying toFixed, rounding the displayed result to the nearest meter.

If you're not in JavaScript, you have to do the calculation yourself, and the best technique to use is generally one called the *spherical law of cosines*. I'm not going into the mathematical derivation of this formula, of course, but I will show you how to use it.[1] In fact, if you're working in SQL, I already have; this is the formula that was introduced in Listing 10-10.

The other programming language used in this book is PHP, and in Listing A-2 you can find an implementation of this distance formula. It shows a calculation using URL parameters, but of course the same technique will work wherever the numbers have come from.

Listing A-2. *Distance Calculation in PHP*

```php
<?php
  $lat1 = $_GET['lat1'];
  $lon1 = $_GET['lon1'];
  $lat2 = $_GET['lat2'];
  $lon2 = $_GET['lon2'];

  $distance = (6371008 * acos(cos(deg2rad($lat1)) * cos(deg2rad($lat2)) *
                    cos(deg2rad($lon2) - deg2rad($lon1)) +
                    sin(deg2rad($lat1)) * sin(deg2rad($lat2))));

  echo 'Distance is '.round($distance).' meters, '.
       round($distance / 1609, 3).' miles.';
?>
```

Note that both of the code samples in this section give the distance in meters, and Listing 10-10 in kilometers. For other units of measurement, simply apply the correct conversion factor. For example, for distance in miles, divide meters by 1609 (as shown in Listing A-2); for feet, multiply meters by 3.281; and for kilometers, divide by 1000.

Map Projections

We frequently talk about latitude and longitude as if they were a grid overlaid on the Earth's surface, and when discussing the coordinate system, that's quite convenient. But the reality is that they're not a grid: neither latitude nor longitude lines are parallel (as we generally understand the term[2]), and in fact all lines of longitude meet at both the North and South Poles. So, any talk of a latitude/longitude *grid* is fundamentally flawed—yet when working with maps, we continue to use the term.

The basic issue is that the Earth is round, and the conceptual lines of latitude and longitude represent angles (on that round surface) from agreed-upon starting points. Figure A-1 shows the general idea, with latitude and longitude lines drawn every twenty degrees on the

---

1. For background on the spherical law of cosines for distance calculations, I recommend http://www.movable-type.co.uk/scripts/latlong.html, where you'll also find formulae for other map-related computations.
2. Lines of latitude do describe parallel *planes* in three-dimensional space, and in fact are sometimes even called *parallels* (as in "the 49th Parallel"). On the Earth's surface, however, latitudes are actually large circles, not parallel grid lines.

globe. Note how the north-south longitude lines converge at the poles, while the east-west latitude lines remain separate from one another.

▪**Note** This convergence of longitude lines is why longitude precision improves as you approach the poles, as mentioned earlier in the appendix.

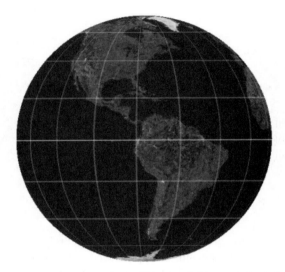

Figure A-1. *Latitude and longitude lines on the spherical Earth*

Of course, maps are flat, so a basic challenge of mapping is making the transition from the spherical Earth. It's done by a technique called *projection*, which is basically a consistent set of rules determining where every point on Earth will be represented on the flat map.

One of the simplest map projections, called *equirectangular*, has a rule that goes like this: Assume that latitude and longitude really *do* form a regular grid, and draw the Earth on that basis. The resulting map is shown in Figure A-2; it's twice as wide as it is tall, reflecting 360° of longitude by 180° of latitude, with the lines again drawn every 20°.

But like all map projections, the equirectangular Figure A-2 involves distortion. Here it's most obvious at the poles: the North Pole, for example, is a single point on the Earth's surface, but in Figure A-2 it occupies the entire top edge of the map. The same distortion exists at all high latitudes; notice how all the islands in northern Canada are horizontally elongated? They're not like that in reality. If you were to zoom in to the far northern or southern regions of an equirectangular projection, you'd find this distortion makes the map all but useless in those areas.

Over the years, cartographers have devised literally hundreds of different map projections, but they all distort sizes, shapes, distances, or directions in some area of the globe. As a newly-minted map programmer, it's important that you have some understanding of this issue: flat maps never represent the Earth perfectly. Google Maps are no exception, so to finish off this appendix, I'm going to acquaint you with the strengths and weaknesses of the map projection that Google uses.

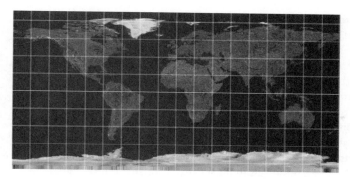

Figure A-2. *Equirectangular map projection, with the latitude/longitude lines forming a grid*

The Mercator Projection

Google Maps may be only a few years old, but the map projection it uses goes back centuries. It was created in 1569 by a Flemish cartographer named Gerardus Mercator, and it became a standard for maritime use because compass angles can be measured directly from straight lines on the map. This is very handy for navigation, and Mercator's is one of the few global map projections with which it is possible to do so. Figure A-3 shows a typical Mercator projection.

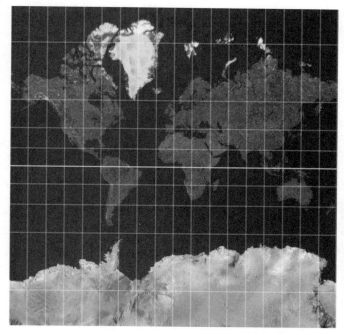

Figure A-3. *Mercator projection, also with latitude/longitude lines every 20°*

In recent decades, however, the Mercator projection had largely fallen out of favor because of a major drawback: the further you get from the equator (the thicker horizontal line in the middle of Figure A-3), the more regions become magnified. This is apparent if you examine the grid; the longitude lines (which converge at the poles in reality) remain parallel, while the latitude lines get progressively further apart (they're really equidistant, remember). For a real-world effect of this magnification consider that, in reality, Africa is roughly 14 times the size of Greenland, while on a Mercator map they appear roughly equal.

However, the high-latitude distortion isn't generally as extreme as with the equirectangular projection of Figure A-2, and is only visible over large latitude ranges. What this means in practice is that, as you zoom in to a Mercator-projected Google map, the distortions largely disappear, and the map view accurately reflects the surroundings that users experience around them. It also means that higher-zoom views can be overlaid seamlessly with undistorted aerial photographs anywhere in the world, from equatorial Sri Lanka to arctic Svalbard.

One other problem with all Mercator maps is that, because the latitude lines get progressively further apart, it's mathematically impossible to map all the way to the North and South Poles. And in reality, several degrees of the high arctic (and antarctic) regions are impractical to show on a Mercator map. But again, Google is not overly concerned with this problem, as there's essentially no population in these very high latitudes.

And for a web architecture, the Mercator map has a couple of advantages for Google. First, it's a rectangular projection, and this lends itself well to being constructed from rectangular XHTML `img` elements (see sidebar). And second, the math involved in the Mercator projection is reasonably simple. This is important because virtually all conversions between screen pixels and map coordinates are done using JavaScript in the browser, which isn't a very powerful computing platform.

GOOGLE MAP TILES

Google's take on the Mercator projection is a square map, cut into an array of 256-pixel square tiles, each of which is displayed on-screen in its own `img` element. Each successively-higher zoom level contains four times as many tiles as the level before it; each tile at a given zoom level is made up of four tiles at the next. For example, here's what the first two zoom levels look like. At zoom level 0, we have 1 tile:

At zoom level 1, we have four tiles:

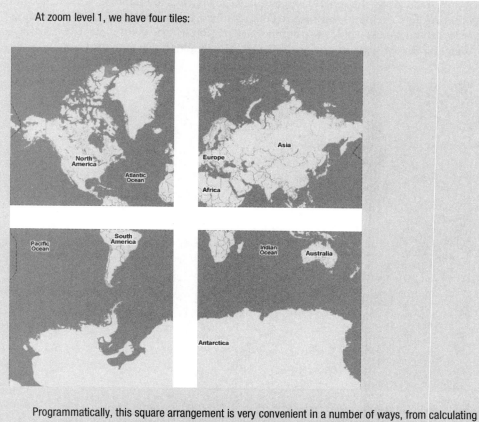

Programmatically, this square arrangement is very convenient in a number of ways, from calculating pixel coordinates within the tile array to the naming convention of the tile images themselves.

All of this comes together to make the Mercator projection quite convenient to work with. As a Google map programmer, however, you should be aware of the drawbacks. They're all to do with the high-latitude magnification effect; the following list sums up the major practical implications:

- Google maps are completely unusable for the North and South Poles, as they do not show any latitudes above about 85°.

- The scale of a Google map is not fixed for a given zoom level, but is larger at higher latitudes (further from the equator). GScaleControl accounts for this, and as you move a map north and south, you can actually watch it change size.

- As a result, distances on a Google map are not constant when moving the map north or south.

- At low zoom levels, the size discrepancy between high and low latitudes is extreme. Think of the Africa-Greenland contrast! So comparative areas on the map will be misleading below about zoom level 4. As an additional illustration, Figure A-4 shows two 1000-mile-diameter circles, with one centered on the equator and the other at 75° north.

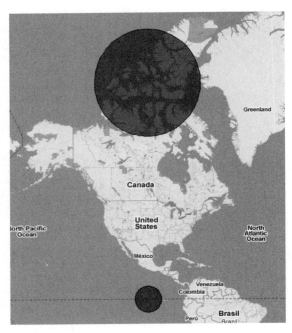

Figure A-4. *Thousand-mile circles at both low and high latitudes, showing the magnification effect of Mercator projection*

Summary

Although Google's mapping APIs insulate you from most cartographic technicalities, it is still beneficial to understand a few basic mapping principles. Being able to recognize and convert DMS-formatted coordinates will save you from puzzling inaccuracies in plotting. Avoiding excessive precision in coordinate displays should prevent some confusion for both you and your users. And being able to calculate distances between any two coordinates will definitely come in handy.

Finally, you now have a basic understanding of map projections, and especially the Mercator system used by Google Maps. As a result, you should know when to watch out for distortions of size and distance on all your maps.

Armed with all this knowledge, you can avoid several basic traps that commonly befall fledgling map programmers.

APPENDIX B

■ ■ ■

A JavaScript Primer

The native language of the Google mapping APIs discussed in this book is JavaScript, so some basic knowledge of JavaScript is necessary to program the maps effectively. In this appendix, you'll find an introduction to JavaScript, both as an elementary reference for readers who are new to programming and as a guide for those whose experience is with other languages. Like many of its counterparts (including C++, Java, and PHP), JavaScript bases its syntax on the programming language C; if you have experience with another C-based language, JavaScript will look very familiar to you.

The official name of JavaScript is ECMAScript, named for the European Computer Manufacturers Association (Ecma), under whose auspices it was standardized. However, this name is very rarely used; you'll far more often see it called JavaScript, the name under which Netscape created the language in the mid-1990s. So JavaScript is the generic name for the language that I use throughout this book.

The Mozilla Foundation, as successor to Netscape, still maintains the definitive reference to JavaScript at `http://developer.mozilla.org/en/JavaScript`. I recommend bookmarking it for detailed information on language particulars. At that URL you'll find several versions of JavaScript; as of this writing, I recommend adhering to the v1.5 standard, which is supported by all major modern browsers (Firefox 1+, IE 7+, Opera 7+, and Safari).

After Netscape first released JavaScript, but before it was standardized by Ecma, Microsoft (the other major browser developer at the time) created its own variant, called JScript. That is still the dialect of ECMAScript supported by Internet Explorer, and although it's largely interchangeable with JavaScript, there are occasional differences—mostly in the interactions with XHTML elements. For this reason, it's also worth noting Microsoft's official JScript reference, at `http://msdn.microsoft.com/yek4tbz0`; you'll want to check here when you find a piece of code that gives you trouble in IE.

While this appendix covers the aspects of JavaScript most commonly useful for map API development, it's not an exhaustive description of every language feature. The sites mentioned earlier, as well as in the next appendix, fulfill that role.

Statements

Predominantly, JavaScript is what is known as an *imperative language*;[1] this means that code consists of individual instructions that execute sequentially, one after another. Each instruction,

---

1. For those of you with a computer science background, JavaScript also has elements of functional programming.

called a *statement*, commands the computer to perform a task. You typically see JavaScript written with one statement per line, like this:

```
a = b;
c = d + e;
```

A *script* comprises a sequence of statements like this, generally contained within `<script>` tags in XHTML, or in an external file with a name ending in `.js`.

Semicolons

It's customary to end every JavaScript statement with a semicolon (;) as shown in the example above. The semicolon is not required as long as the next statement begins on the next line, so the previous example could be written without semicolons:

```
a = b
c = d + e
```

However, it is good practice to use semicolons at the end of each line, and a good habit to get into. First, many other languages (like PHP) *do* require semicolons, so acquiring such a habit will probably serve you well at some point. But also, when statements have semicolons, it is valid JavaScript to place multiple statements on a single line, like so:

```
a = b; c = d + e;
```

Although it's *not* recommended that you compose JavaScript like this yourself, there are a number of common tools that do, *compressing* JavaScript files by removing the line breaks (among other things). Ensuring that all of your statements end with semicolons will mean that your code is ready for such compression if necessary.

Block Statements

JavaScript statements can be grouped together into blocks by enclosing them in curly brackets, { and }, as follows:

```
{
  a = b;
  c = d + e;
}
```

Statements grouped into a block like this will execute together; they are effectively a single statement as far as JavaScript is concerned. We'll see block statements in action later in this appendix.

It's good practice to adopt formatting standards for block statements, as they make code easier for people to read and thus less prone to error. The standards I use are:

- Statements within each block are indented by two spaces at the beginning of each line. This groups them together visually as well as logically.

- The opening and closing curly brackets are on lines of their own, making it easier to see exactly which pair goes together.

Different people and organizations use different standards, and that's fine as long as it's consistent. Following your formatting standard consistently does make a real, positive difference for code readability.

Comments

Comments, embedded text the computer ignores, can be added to make the code more readable to people. JavaScript supports two types of comment syntax.

First, anything following two forward slashes // (on the same line of code) will be treated as a comment:

```
// This is a JavaScript comment
```

Second, comments can be surrounded by /* and */ (the same syntax as used for comments in CSS):

```
/* This is also a
   JavaScript comment */
```

A liberal use of comments is encouraged, again to make your code more readable. My own preference is to place a comment at the beginning of each function, explaining what it does, and then before every logical grouping of code lines.

Types and Objects

Information is handled within program code by placing it in *variables*. These variables can store any kind of program data, but before use each variable needs to be *declared*, a sort of "introduction" to tell the computer that what follows will be used as a variable. In JavaScript, variables are declared with the var keyword followed by the name you want to use, like so:

```
var variableName;
```

In this example, variableName is the name of the freshly declared variable and will be used whenever you need to refer to it later.

■**Caution** In some browsers (such as Firefox), the var keyword is optional—but leaving it out will cause errors in IE, so don't do it!

Variable names are case-sensitive, so that variablename, variableName, and VariableName would all refer to *different variables* as far as JavaScript is concerned. For this reason, it's a good idea to adopt a standard for the use of uppercase and lowercase in naming variables. I use the convention of capitalizing words within the variable name (but not the first word), like variableName in the example.

null, the non-Value

When a variable has first been declared, it's initialized to a special non-value, null. This essentially signifies an empty variable; it's the lack of a data value rather than a value in itself.

However, it is possible to test for null in code, as follows:

```
if (a == null)
{
  // a has not been initialized
  ...
}
```

This is often convenient for determining whether some action has yet occurred on the variable in question, and it's a technique that I use throughout the book.

Objects

All JavaScript data values are *objects*; in programming terms, this means that they encapsulate both data and functionality. In other words, in addition to containing information, objects also contain instructions for doing things with that information. For example, a string variable contains character data, such as 'banana', but as a String object it also has built-in functions that do things with that data, such as convert it to all uppercase ('BANANA') or count the number of characters within it (6). Such functions, built into objects, are called *methods*.

If you've worked with other programming languages, you'll know that even "object-oriented" languages rarely carry the object paradigm this far, to primitive types. JavaScript (in its current form) has other gaps in its object-orientation—it has no classes or true inheritance, for example—but this full objectification of all data is unusual. It even extends to most literals; it's valid JavaScript, for example, to write statements like this:

```
'banana'.toUpperCase();
```

In the following sections, I'll briefly describe the more important object types. A list of their methods is beyond the scope of this appendix; for a current reference, please see the links referenced earlier.

The String Type

As mentioned in the previous section, a String contains character data. Strings can be contained in either single or double quotes (' or "); they're equivalent. As a rule, I tend to use single quotes in this book, but if a string will *contain* an apostrophe, it's often more convenient to use double quotes:

```
var message = "Sorry, your browser doesn't support Google Maps.";
```

The alternative way to embed a quote mark within a string is to precede it with a backslash, like this:

```
var message = 'Sorry, your browser doesn\'t support Google Maps.';
```

It's also necessary to use this backslash technique to embed other special characters in strings. Table B-1 lists these character codes and their results; note that the last three are so-called "nonprintable" characters that are used to control formatting.

Table B-1. *Special Characters in Strings*

Code	Result
\'	Single-quote: '
\"	Double-quote: "
\\	Backslash: \
\/	Forward-slash: /
\n	New line
\r	Carriage return
\t	Tab

The Number Type

A Number is any simple quantity, such as 27 or 3.1415926535 (it may include a decimal point). It is used for anything involving counting or calculations in your code; the latitude and longitude values used throughout the book are perfect examples. You distinguish a number from a string by not enclosing it in quotes; 45 is a number, while '45' is a two-character string.

The Date Type

Date variables specify a particular date *and time*: for example, 2:26 PM on August 21, 2008. Using this type, you can format dates and time values for display, or perform date arithmetic such as determining how much time has elapsed since a specific event).

There are three principal ways to initialize a Date value, and they all involve the new keyword. The first, and simplest, just creates a Date with the current time and date when the code runs:

```
var d = new Date();
```

Be aware that this uses the time setting from the computer on which the script runs; for JavaScript on a web page, this means the client browser of the page visitor. So this relies on the accuracy of the user's own computer clock, a notoriously unreliable source. It's fine if you only need it for relative times—for code that needs to know when five seconds have passed, for example—but for the correct date and time in a larger context, you should either avoid this approach or warn the user of its shortcomings.

The second way to set a Date is from a string, as follows:

```
var d = new Date('21 Aug 2008 14:26:00 GMT+0100');
```

Note the specific format that the source string must take! Varying from this format may well result in an incorrect date/time value, and it may also display an error message.

So the third technique, and the most reliable, is to use separate numbers for the date and time components. They're supplied in order from largest to smallest units; our example date/time value would be created thus:

```
var d = new Date(2008, 7, 21, 14, 26, 0, 0);
```

There are, however, several important items to note about this format:

- The arguments are all assumed to be for local time on the client computer.

- The *months* value is zero-based, meaning 0 for January and 11 for December! This means that the month number used here is one less than usually expected.

- The *hours* are on a 24-hour clock, again zero-based, so that's 0 (for 12 AM) through 23 (for 11 PM). This is how 24-hour time is usually expressed, though.

- There's an extra 0 parameter, after the *seconds*: that's for *milliseconds* (1/1000 second), and is used for specifying fractions of a second.

- You can leave trailing parameters off from this format, which will then default to zero. So the same date/time value can be created more simply this way:

  ```
  var d = new Date(2008, 7, 21, 14, 26);
  ```

Note The new keyword used for Date can actually be used for any object, so in place of var = 5, it's equivalent to write var a = new Number(5). It is simpler and clearer, however, not to use new when a literal format is available for the variable type being created.

The Boolean Type

Boolean variables have only two possible values, true and false. They're used for logical operations, such as the code deciding whether or not to take a particular action. I'll discuss Boolean values (and their use) more thoroughly later in this appendix.

Booleans are initialized by simply setting a variable to one of the two possible values:

```
var b = true;
```

A Boolean variable can also be set as the result of a logical expression:

```
var b = (a > 0);
```

See how that works? If a is a number greater than zero, the expression is true, and b is set to true; otherwise, it's set to false. Again, you'll see more of these sorts of expressions in a little while.

The Array Type

Unlike the other types introduced so far, an Array contains a list of values, rather than a single value. As such, it's called a *compound type*. An array is initialized with a list of values in square brackets, [and]:

```
var a = ['apple', 'banana', 'cantaloupe'];
```

Here, a contains three strings (in this context, array *elements*) describing fruit. An array can contain values of any type; they will typically all be the same type, because arrays are usually used for lists of similar items, but this is not required. The number of elements in an array can be found from its length property.

The individual values are accessed using a number, called an *index*, also in square brackets. So a[0] is 'apple', and a[2] is 'cantaloupe'. Note that the index is *zero-based*, meaning that the first element has index 0, and the last has index a.length - 1.

Array indices can also be used to place values into the array. The following line changes the second element of the array:

```
a[1] = 'berry';
```

You can also add new elements to the array this way, and the array will automatically grow as needed to accommodate them. For example, if you ran the following line of code on our array:

```
a[23] = 'watermelon';
```

the array a would then have 22 elements: three strings, followed by 18 nulls, followed by another string. Arrays always fill themselves out like this; they never have gaps.

To create an empty array for later use, simply leave the square brackets empty:

```
var a = [];
```

The Object Type

The last basic type I'll cover is Object. While all the predefined JavaScript types you've seen are indeed objects, it's also possible (and useful) to create new object types, as a sort of "blank slate" for storing your own structured data—and functionality with it.

A basic Object is created with curly brackets, like this:

```
var x = {};
```

Like Array, Object is a compound type, but rather than specifying values by number we give each a name. Here's an example of defining an object containing three values:

```
var x = {'color': 'blue', 'size': 32, 'active': true};
```

So the object x contains three values: a String, a Number, and a Boolean. For objects, these internal values are called *properties*. Note that each property's name is a string (though in this special case, it's possible to leave off the quotes around property names).

■Note The curly brackets are the same symbol as used for block statements, but this is a different usage; the contents of the curly brackets in object definitions are *not* statements.

The properties of an object can be any JavaScript data type: strings, numbers, arrays, etc.—even other objects. Defining an object with named and initialized properties like this is the essence of JSON, JavaScript Object Notation, a technique for transmitting data in a format that's ready for use by client scripts (see Chapter 10).

Once you've created an object, you can access its properties by using array-like square brackets, this time containing the property's name, such as x['color']. Or, you can use *dot notation* to access properties, as in this example:

```
x.color = 'green';
var width = x.size;
```

Note that the property name is not in quotation marks with dot notation. There's generally no intrinsic advantage to square brackets versus dot notation; the two are functionally equivalent.

You can also add properties later using either notation. For example, if I wanted to add a date/time stamp to an object I'd already created, I could do it with code like this:

```
x['lastUpdate'] = new Date();
```

or

```
x.lastUpdate = new Date();
```

It doesn't matter that x didn't have a lastUpdate property before. It does now, set to the current time and date. You can do this with any object, even ones you didn't create yourself.

Finally, what makes an object an object is the ability to attach functionality, not just data. We do this by defining properties that are functions, as discussed later in the appendix.

■**Note** The Google mapping APIs make heavy use of custom objects like this; examples include GMap and GLatLng.

Expressions

To form JavaScript statements, variables are joined together into *expressions*. An expression usually performs some action (using the participating variables) and produces a *result* (the outcome of that action).

At its simplest, an expression is only one value, such as the number 8 or the variable a; there's no action here, and the result is simply the value. Variables and explicit values (called *literals*, like 8 in this case) are the building blocks of expressions.

Numeric and String Operators

More usefully, expressions are joined together using *operators*, symbols or keywords denoting the action to be taken. When this happens, a larger expression is formed from the component parts: some action is performed and a result returned.

The simplest JavaScript operators denote basic arithmetic; these are listed in Table B-2. For example, with the operator -, the action performed is subtraction, and the result is the difference of the two numbers.

Table B-2. *Basic Numeric and String Operators*

Operator	Description	Example	Result
+	Addition, of either numbers or strings	6 + 2	8
		'6' + '2'	'62'
–	Subtraction	6 – 2	4
*	Multiplication	6 * 2	12
/	Division	6 / 2	3
%	Modulus (remainder)	6 % 2	0
		7 % 2	1

Mixing Numbers and Strings

Note that the + operator in Table B-2 can take either numbers or strings as its *operands*, to different effect. With numbers, the result is their sum; with strings, it's a joining of the two (as in '6' + '2' gives '62'). Such joining of strings is called *concatenation*.

If a number is "added" to a string using +, the number is first converted to a string, and then the two strings are concatenated. So 5 + '1' is the string '51', not the number 6. In other words, adding a number and a string gives a string.

Increment and Decrement

There are two more basic numeric operators in JavaScript, ++ and --. Their basic usage is simply to add 1 to (or subtract 1 from) the variable they act upon. In other words, if a is 3, a++ changes the value of a to 4. Similarly, if a is 7, a-- will drop a down to 6.

As statements, they simply stand alone. So the following is a complete JavaScript statement:

```
a++;
```

These operators, called *increment* and *decrement* respectively, have one especially important use, within the loop structures you'll learn about later in the appendix. Those structures are so common in JavaScript programming, however, that these operators are worth mentioning now.

Assignment and Comparison

As you probably know by now, values are placed in (*assigned* to) variables using a single equal sign, =. So to set a variable a to a value of 11, we simply code it this way:

```
a = 11;
```

In English, that's "set a equal to 11." What you might not have realized is that = is the *assignment* operator, and it functions like any other operator: operands are supplied, action is taken, and a result is returned.

In everyday, natural language, we have another use for the equal sign, however: *comparison*, to check the equality between two values. So rather than "equal" as an imperative, as earlier, this is "equal" as a question: "Does a equal 11?" As humans, we work out which usage is meant by context and punctuation, but in programming we require a different operator (essentially, another form of punctuation). For JavaScript, the equals comparison operator is simply two equal signs together, `==`. Its usage in an expression looks like this:

```
a == 1
```

Table B-3 lists the various comparison operators available in JavaScript. The result of any numeric comparison is fairly obvious; what's less apparent is what happens when the operands are strings. In short, JavaScript does a character-by-character comparison, and stops as soon as it can give an answer. However, *all uppercase letters are "less than" all lowercase letters.* So `'apple'` is less than `'banana'`, but greater than `'Apple'` or `'Zebra'`.[2] This means that you can't use these operators to check alphabetic order unless all your operands are of the same case (upper or lower).

Table B-3. *Comparison Operators*

Operator	Description	Example	Result
==	Equal	3 == 3	true
!=	Not equal	3 != 3	false
>	Greater than	3 > 2	true
>=	Greater than or equal to	3 >= 2	true
<	Less than	3 < 3	false
<=	Less than or equal to	3 <= 3	true

Boolean Operators

All the comparison operators from Table B-3 give a Boolean `true` or `false` value as a result. That's fine if there's only a single comparison to make, but for more complicated questions, we need a few more operators. For example, you can use the `<` operator to determine if a variable a is below a certain threshold, like a `< 10`. But if you wanted to check that a was within a range—between 5 and 10, for example—you would need a `true` result from both a `< 10` *and* a `> 5`. This is where JavaScript's Boolean operators come in, as listed in Table B-4; they let us write this "and" expression as

```
(a < 10) && (a > 5)
```

Table B-4. *Boolean Operators (x is True, y is False)*

Operator	Description	Example	Result
&&	And	x && y	false
||	Or	x || y	true
!	Not	!x	false

---

2. String comparison is done based on each character's ASCII code, which can be found at http://asciitable.com.

Precedence

The (a < 10) && (a > 5) example uses one more set of symbols, parentheses (and). These aren't operators themselves, but they control the order in which operators take effect in an expression—basically, operations within parentheses go first. And this can be important; for example, (1 + 2) * 3 gives a result of 9, while 1 + (2 * 3) yields 7.

There are rules within JavaScript expressions to govern which operations happen first, or take *precedence*, in the absence of parentheses. However, they're fairly complicated (see http://tinyurl.com/6ouxdd for a complete list), so I strongly encourage you to use parentheses liberally if you're in any doubt.

Control Structures

So we now have a full set of variable types to store our data in, and operators to act upon them, combining to form expressions and statements. For anything interesting to happen, however, we also need to control the flow of our code as it moves from one statement to the next. Otherwise, we'd only have a static list of instructions, and the script would always consist of exactly the same sequence of events.

Enter *control structures*, specific keywords that divert the flow of the script, away from one statement (or statement block, remember) and toward another, based on conditions that we specify. In this section, I'll describe the most useful of JavaScript's control structures; there are others, but they mostly either duplicate what's found here or are used in more advanced settings.

The if/else Block

The most elemental control structure simply asks a yes/no question—is some condition true?— and performs one or more statements if it is. This is an if block, and at its most basic, it looks like this:

```
if (condition)
  statement;
```

As we know, a yes/no answer is a Boolean value, so condition is going to be a Boolean expression—possibly involving comparisons and Boolean operators.

In cases like these, we frequently want two options, corresponding to the two Boolean possibilities (true and false). In English, we would say, "If the condition is true; do this, otherwise, do that." In JavaScript, our word for otherwise is else, and bipartite if/else blocks are constructed as shown in Listing B-1. Of course, any Boolean expression could appear in place of a == b. There's only one caveat: the expression must be contained in parentheses. It's not valid to just write if a == b, it *must* be if (a == b).

Listing B-1. *An if/else Decision Block*

```
if (a == b)
{
  // Statements here execute if a is equal to b
  ...
}
```

```
else
{
  // Statements here execute if a is not equal to b
  ...
}
```

Since any statement can come after the else, and if is itself a statement, it's possible (and often useful) to string together if/else blocks as shown in Listing B-2. Here we have only two conditions, testing a against both b and c, but it's perfectly valid to continue chaining if after else as many times as you need to.

Listing B-2. *A Decision Block with else if*

```
if (a == b)
{
  // Statements here execute if a is equal to b
  ...
}
else if (a == c)
{
  // Statements here execute if a is equal to c
  ...
}
else
{
  // Statements here execute if a is not equal to b or c
  ...
}
```

The for Loop

The next step in script control, beyond a simple yes/no branching of the path, is to repeat a given block of code a certain number of times. This sort of repetition, called a *loop*, is most simply accomplished in JavaScript with a statement named for. A sample of its use is shown Listing B-3; it will perform the attached statement block five times.

Listing B-3. *A for Loop*

```
for (a = 0; a < 5; a++)
{
  // Statements here will execute five times
  ...
}
```

The for construct itself looks a bit intimidating the first time you see it, so let's go over it in more detail. Within the parentheses are three parts, separated by semicolons, in the following order:

a = 0   A statement initializing a, the *loop control variable*. By setting it to 0, we establish its starting value when the first loop begins.

a < 5   A Boolean expression, testing a against the limit for the loop (5 in this case). The code will continue looping as long as this expression evaluates to true; JavaScript will test this expression before each repetition of the loop.

a++   A statement incrementing a, adding one to its value every time the loop comes around.

The result is that a starts off at 0 and gets increased by one every time the loop repeats; the loop exits when a reaches 5. So the code loops five times. Many of the for loops you write will follow exactly this pattern: initialize a loop control variable to 0 in the first part, test it against the number of times you want the loop to repeat in the second part, and increment it (with the ++ operator) in the third part.

Note For simplicity in Listing B-3, a is assumed to have been declared earlier in the script (using var). If it hadn't been, you could declare it inside the for statement by writing for (var a = 0; a < 5; a++), as also shown in Listing B-4.

Why would you want to loop your code? Well, one of the most common uses of a for loop is to perform some action for every element in an array. If your array has five elements—or five hundred—and you need to do something for each (like place a marker on a map), a for loop is the natural tool for the job.

Listing B-4 shows a for loop constructed for exactly this purpose. The loop control variable (here also being declared with var) starts at 0 and finishes at array.length. Within the loop, anything can be done with the elements of the array by simply using a as the index, as in array[a].

Listing B-4. *Iterating Over an Array*

```
for (var a = 0; a < array.length; a++)
{
  // Actions can be performed here on array[a]
  ...
}
```

Well, *almost* anything. If your actions involve *removing* elements from the array, you need to do things a bit differently. To see why, imagine what happens the first time through the loop in Listing B-4: a is 0, and within the loop I delete array[0]. Fine, but as mentioned earlier, arrays never have gaps—which means that with the old array[0] gone, the old array[1] is now the new array[0] (and the old array[2] is now array[1], and so on). The next time through the loop, the control variable a will increment from 0 to 1, and I'll delete array[1]. But this is the original array[2] I've just deleted—I've skipped over the original array[1], now sitting at index 0. The array never has gaps, but my code does.

The simple solution to this problem is to walk *down* through the array rather than up. You start the loop control variable with the last element in the array (at zero-based index array.length - 1, remember), decrement it with each pass through the loop, and stop when it gets below 0 (the bottom end of the array). This code is shown in Listing B-5; the `array.splice` method does the actual deleting of elements.

Listing B-5. *Counting Down Over an Array When Deleting*

```
for (var a = array.length - 1; a >= 0; a—)
{
  // Actions can be performed here on array[a], before deletion
  ...

  array.splice(a, 1);
}
```

The while Loop

The majority of the time, `for` will satisfy your looping needs. But occasionally, you need to loop a less definite number of times; in effect, you don't know in advance how many passes through the loop you'll need. When this happens, call upon the `while` loop.

Listing B-6 shows the basic structure. It's actually simpler to write than a `for` loop; there's no explicit loop control variable involved, just a Boolean expression in the parentheses after the `while` keyword. JavaScript will evaluate that expression before every pass through the loop, and it will continue until the result is `false`—in other words, while it's `true`.

Listing B-6. *A while Loop*

```
while (a == b)
{
  // Statements here will execute until a is no longer equal to b
  ...
}
```

The biggest danger with `while` is that, if the condition (`a == b` in this case) never becomes `false`, the loop will never finish. To avoid such an *infinite loop*, it's absolutely crucial to ensure that your code will make the condition `false` at some point.

Note that `while` loops are trickier than `for` loops in this way: an infinite loop can't occur with a well-formed `for`, because the number of iterations is specified ahead of time. With `for`, it's only a danger if you modify the loop control variable within the loop itself.

The break Statement

There's also a way to break out of a loop before the main `for` or `while` end-condition is satisfied, and intuitively enough, it's the `break` statement.

This capability is often handy in a `for` loop when you might want to stop looping before the predetermined number of passes. For example, you might be looking for a specific element in an array, and you can stop looking once you find it. Listing B-7 shows an example of this situation.

Listing B-7. *Using break for Searching a String Array*

```
var found = -1;
for (var a = 0; a < array.length; a++)
{
  if (array[a] == 'banana')
  {
    found = a;
    break;
  }
}

if (found > -1)
  alert('banana found at element ' + found);
```

With while loops, break should usually not be used; reasons for stopping the loop should generally be incorporated into the main loop-control condition. This makes for more readable code; the structure is more obvious if the loop decision factors are all in the same place. However, JavaScript only tests the while condition at the beginning of each pass; if you need to end the loop midway through a pass, break may occasionally be necessary.

The switch Block

The last basic control structure we'll look at is switch, something of a specialized variant of the if/else construct. If you're testing a single variable against a (potentially lengthy) list of possible values, switch offers a concise and readable structure for doing so.

It's easiest to understand switch by example, so take a look at Listing B-8. It's logically equivalent to Listing B-2, simply rewriting the else if code using switch.

Listing B-8. *A Decision Block with switch*

```
switch (a)
{
  case b:
    // Statements here execute if a is equal to b
    ...
    break

  case c:
    // Statements here execute if a is equal to c
    ...
    break;

  default:
    // Statements here execute if a is not equal to b or c
    ...
}
```

The guidelines you need to be aware of for constructing a switch block are as follows:

- The expression to be tested (a in this case) goes inside parentheses after the switch keyword.

- The remainder of the block is surrounded by curly brackets; these are the only grouping required with switch.

- Each expression you're testing against (in Listing B-8, b and c) is preceded by the keyword case.

- After every conditional code block, you need break to exit the switch block. *This is important*; without it, the script would simply continue into the next case.

- At the end of the switch block is a special case, default. This code executes if no other listed case is true; it's equivalent to the final else in a chain of if/else blocks. The default case is optional.

As shown in Listings B-8 and B-2, any switch block could be constructed using a series of if and else blocks, but in certain situations switch is much clearer. One common use is when coding a *lookup table*, where one set of values equates to another. A real-world example of a lookup table can be found in Listing B-9, showing switch put to good use.

Listing B-9. *A Currency Code Lookup Table Using switch*

```
switch (currencyCode)
{
  case 'AUD':
  case 'CAD':
  case 'USD':
    var symbol = '$';
    break;

  case 'GBP':
    var symbol = '£';
    break;

  case 'JPY':
    var symbol = '¥';
    break;

  default:
    var symbol = currencyCode;
}
```

Note that multiple cases can be handled by the same code block: in Listing B-9, several different dollar currencies result in the same symbol, $. This is actually made possible because there's no break between these cases, illustrating why break is required elsewhere in the switch.

Functions

I'll finish this tour of control structures with something a bit different, function. Unlike the other structures described earlier, function doesn't perform any action at the point in the JavaScript code where it occurs. Instead, function is used to define a block of code for later use—and potentially for reuse, as many times as you'd like.

It works by attaching a statement block to a name, the same as a variable name; this is called *defining* the function. Then, at any point when you want to execute that block of code, you can do so simply by calling its name. Listing B-10 shows a simple example of a function.

Listing B-10. *A function Definition and Call*

```
function doSomething(a)
{
  var b;
  // Actions can be performed here on the parameter, a
  ...

  return b;
};


...
// Later in the code, we can invoke those actions:
var c = doSomething(d);
```

Note that I include a semicolon after the function's closing curly bracket. Functions are a bit different from other statement blocks in that they can occasionally be used as expressions, inside other statements. To avoid any confusion, it's good practice to include this ending semicolon, just as you would after any other statement (and for the same reasons).

Parameters and Return Values

Much of function's power comes from two other features shown in Listing B-10. First, a function can accept one or more *parameters*, variables that are *passed* into the function by including them in parentheses after the function name. So in Listing B-10, doSomething takes a single parameter, a. Within the function definition, a is an ordinary variable and can participate in any valid JavaScript statements. What makes this powerful is that the function can be called with different values at different times; here, d is being passed into the doSomething function, and whatever it does will be done with the value of d.

The second important feature is the counterpart to parameters, the ability for a function to *return* a value. This allows data to be passed back out of the function, generally as a result of the actions that occurred within it. So in Listing B-10, the variable b (inside the function) is passed back out, using the return keyword, and externally is stored in c.

The concepts of parameters and return values are easier to see in a concrete example, as in Listing B-11. The function square takes any number and returns its mathematical square (the number multiplied by itself). It's declared with one parameter, x; multiplies x by itself; and then returns that result. The listing also shows square being called with two different parameters, 3 and 6, with their respective results being stored in the eponymous variables.

Listing B-11. *A Simple Function,* `square`

```
function square (x)
{
  var sqr = x * x;
  return sqr;
};


var nine = square(3);
var thirtySix = square(6);
```

Functions as Variables

I've mentioned that function names work in the same way as variable names, but JavaScript takes this one step further. Function names actually *are* variable names; when a function is defined, that definition is stored in a variable with the function's name.

This relationship becomes clearer if we examine an alternative (but equally valid) way of declaring the function from Listing B-10:

```
var doSomething = function (a)
{
  var b;
  ...
  return b;
};
```

Using this property of functions, we can handle them the same as any other variable. Throughout this book, there is considerable use of callbacks, in which one function is passed as a parameter to another; this is a perfect example of using the first function's name as a variable, passing it as a value.

Taking this one more step, recall that I've said all JavaScript values are actually objects. This holds true even for functions: they are instances of the `Function` object, and have properties and methods like any other object. I exploit this fact in Listing 9-13, with an expression like this:

```
new Function('showDetail(' + m + ')')
```

This uses the `new` keyword to create a function whose body is composed of the string `'showDetail(' + m + ')'`, and since `m` is a variable, the body of the function varies as well. This allows me to create a function on the fly, using the loop control variable of a `for` loop, that will then do something different for each iteration.

Object Methods

Finally, the fact that functions are just variables at heart allows us to use them to add functionality to objects. In JavaScript, this is done simply by defining an object property that is a function; if you'll recall, these are called *methods* of the object.

Listing B-12 shows the way. The first line defines an object, `x`. Then, using the "function as a variable" syntax from the previous section, we simply add a function property to `x`.

Listing B-12. *Defining an Object Method*

```
var x = {length: 6, width: 4, color: 'gray'};
x.area = function ()
{
  return this.length * this.width;
};
```

Notice the use of the this keyword inside the area method: it's a special syntax that enables you to access other properties of an object from within that object's methods. Since the primary purpose of a method is to perform actions on an object's encapsulated data, it's important to be able to access that data, and this is what provides that access.

It's also worth noting that area isn't computed until the method is called, so if length or width changes, area will always return the current, correct result.

Additional JavaScript Topics

The preceding sections have covered the basics of JavaScript, giving you some grounding in all the core elements of the language. To round off this appendix, there are just a few additional areas that you'll find it helpful to understand as you get out and work with scripts.

The Math Object

JavaScript creates a few predefined object variables as "containers" for related groups of functionality, and one of the most useful is Math. As you might expect, it contains functions (and a few properties) related to mathematical operations. You use these functions simply by prefacing them with the name Math; for example, to use the min function to find the smaller of two variables, you'd write:

```
var c = Math.min(a, b);
```

As usual, I refer you to the documentation for a full list of the Math methods, at http://tinyurl.com/5rhw5o.

This is primarily of interest for JavaScript developers coming from other languages; most programming languages have the same functions as contained in Math, but without the containing object: just min(), for example, not Math.min().

The DOM

Up to this point, I've been discussing JavaScript in isolation, small blocks of self-contained code that had no connection to the wider world. For scripts to be useful, however, they need to interact with the outside world. For JavaScript,[3] running within the context of a web browser, these interactions occur primarily via the web documents that the browser displays. This being JavaScript, those XHTML documents are naturally encapsulated as objects, and the structure in which they reside is called the *Document Object Model*, or *DOM*.

---

3. JavaScript can run in other places besides a web browser, but these uses are far less common, and it's quite likely that you may never come across one.

The primary way that JavaScript interacts with the DOM is by accessing the properties of these document objects. In this way, scripts can take different action for different page content, or they can actually modify the content displayed to the user. This latter technique, modifying XHTML in code, is known as *DHTML*, for *Dynamic (x)HTML*.

One important aspect of this object interaction takes the form of *events*. Briefly, an event is a specific action that occurs outside the code, usually in response to a user activity, such as a mouse click on a link. The browser lets us attach JavaScript code to virtually any event; this code, called an *event handler*, will then run when the event occurs. This allows our script to perform tasks in response to the user's actions.

In this section, I'll briefly discuss a few of the more important DOM objects, and what you need to know about them. More complete information is hosted by Mozilla (http://developer.mozilla.org/en/Gecko_DOM_Reference), and by Microsoft (http://msdn.microsoft.com/ms533050) for the JScript dialect.

The window Object

The root DOM object is window, and it essentially represents the browser window itself, separate from the web page it displays. This is where JavaScript gains access to browser-window properties like innerHeight and innerWidth (the dimensions of the page canvas), and methods like alert (which displays a dialog box, as in Figure 5-2).

For our purposes, JavaScript is *always* running within a browser window, and for this reason window is actually implied. In other words, you don't need to preface its properties and methods with window; rather than writing window.alert, you can simply call alert.

The window object also has a number of events that you'll find useful, particularly in map API programming. The onload event fires when the browser page finishes rendering, and onunload, just before the user leaves for another page. The simplest way to attach a handler to these events is within the body tag of the page, like so:

```
<body onload="loadPage()" onunload="GUnload()">
```

Then separately, in your JavaScript, you'll define the loadPage function:

```
function loadPage()
{
  // Map initialization code goes here
  ...
};
```

Note that GUnload is a function, predefined by Google in the Maps API, that "cleans up" after the map when the page unloads and should generally be included in the onunload handler of any page with an API map.

The document Property

Arguably the most useful property of window is document; as its name implies, this object is the root of the XHTML document rendered within the browser. As such, most of the interactions you'll have with the page itself will come through document. It has some important properties and methods of its own—like location, the URL displayed in the browser's address bar—but document also provides access to all the other XHTML elements on the page.

The chief function for gaining this access is getElementById; this method of document returns the object representing any XHTML element on the page, simply by providing its id attribute. So for example, an XHTML div defined thus:

```
<div id="container_div"></div>
```

would be accessed from JavaScript by the following DOM method:

```
var containerDiv = document.getElementById('container_div');
```

This would set the containerDiv variable to an object representing the div on the page. From here, any of that div's own properties can be retrieved or modified.

The element Object

Which brings us to element, the base object for all XHTML elements within the page proper. These DOM objects constitute the main point of contact between JavaScript and the page the user sees on screen. As described in the previous section, elements are most often retrieved via the document.getElementById method.

Once retrieved, most element objects have properties corresponding to the attributes of their XHTML counterparts. For example, the element for an img tag has height and width properties, allowing the size of the image to be adjusted in code. Virtually all elements have a className property, a string containing their class from the XHTML source; modifying className can change what CSS is applied to that element. Or, elements have a whole slew of style properties by which their appearance can be modified directly. For a complete list of element properties, see the reference links I provided earlier.

One property I do want to mention specifically is element.innerHTML. With this, our code can directly set the content displayed within any element on the page. For example, consider the following code:

```
var containerDiv = document.getElementById('container_div');
containerDiv.innerHTML = ' <p> Hello! </p> ';
```

The effect of this code is *exactly the same* as if the following had been in the page's original XHTML source:

```
<div id="container_div"> <p> Hello! </p> </div>
```

Setting the innerHTML of various elements is one of the most powerful techniques for JavaScript user interaction.

Most DOM elements also have events; one of the most obvious is a click event, which occurs when the user clicks the element on the page with his mouse. Attaching a JavaScript event handler to a DOM object in XHTML is accomplished much as it was for the body tag earlier; here's an example of a click listener on a link:

```
<a href="#" onclick="linkClick()">Click Here</a>
```

Not surprisingly, this will run a JavaScript function named linkClick when the link is clicked. In Appendix C I'll introduce another technique for attaching handlers to DOM events from within JavaScript itself.

Scope of Variables

One area that often trips up beginning programmers is the issue of where different variables can be used—their *scope*. In a nutshell, where a variable can be used depends on where it was declared, meaning where it first appeared with the var keyword. And the rule is this: *a variable can't be used outside the function where it was declared.*

Let's look at an example. Listing B-13 shows a very simple script, with one function and a couple of variables.

Listing B-13. *Variable Scope*

```
var a;

function doSomething()
{
  var b;
  var c = a + b;
  ...
};
...
var d = a + b;   // This statement will produce an error!
```

As pointed out in the comment, the last statement in Listing B-13 is erroneous, because b can only be used within the function where it was declared, doSomething. More accurately, b only *exists* within doSomething, so attempting to use it outside of the function is not valid JavaScript. This concept is called the *scope* of a variable; the scope of b is *local* to doSomething.

What about a, which isn't declared inside any function? It has a scope described as *global*,[4] and as the name implies, global variables can be used anywhere. So the expression inside the function, c = a + b, is perfectly valid.

So why not declare all variables as global? Technically, that would be valid JavaScript, but it's not good practice. The whole idea of functions is to encapsulate the code to perform a specific task, and if a variable is only needed for that task, it should be encapsulated in that function too.

In general, you should make sure that only variables used exclusively inside a single function are declared there.

Function Literals and Closures

To finish this appendix, I'm going to dip into a slightly more advanced feature of JavaScript, but one that's useful enough to bear introducing here: *function literals*.

As mentioned earlier, a JavaScript function is an object like any other value, and its declaration is a normal JavaScript expression. This makes it possible to declare functions on the fly, at the point where they are needed. Listing B-14 shows an example of this, in one of its most common use cases: a callback.

---

4. Technically, JavaScript in a browser doesn't have true global variables; all variables in the "global" scope are actually properties of the window object the script is running within. So in Listing 5-12, it would also be valid to refer to window.a. But effectively, these variables can be thought of as global.

Listing B-14. *A Function Literal as a Callback*

```
GEvent.addListener(map, 'zoomend',
  function (oldZoom, newZoom)
  {
    // Perform actions here, after the map zooms, using the old and new zoom levels
    ...
  });
```

For programmers with experience in other languages, this construct is often unprecedented. Essentially, it's defining a function without a name, an *anonymous function* or *function literal* (a literal, recall, is a value that's not in a variable, like 27 or 'foo'). In the example here, I know that the zoomend event handler callback will need two parameters, oldZoom and newZoom, so I define a function on the fly to use those zoom levels as required. JavaScript creates the function, sends it to the addListener API method, and all is well. Like any function definition, this callback does not execute at the time it's defined; the code inside the block only runs when the zoomend event is triggered.

▮**Caution** Notice that the closing curly bracket of the function literal *doesn't* have a semicolon, as I recommend other functions should. That's because the function here isn't a complete statement. The only semicolon comes outside the parentheses, ending the GEvent.addListener statement.

It's a neat trick; when a callback requires only a couple of lines of code, it's much cleaner to include it at the point of assignment (as here) than to declare another function, elsewhere in the script, and pass it by name. As a practice, though, it's best to not use function literals if they'll be much longer than this, as they will significantly disrupt the visual flow of the surrounding code.

Building on function literals, JavaScript has one more trick up its sleeve, to do with variables within these functions. Take a look at Listing B-15, a snippet taken directly from Listing 11-5 with only the relevant lines shown. It's a classic function literal, this time being used for a DOM event handler rather than a callback.

Listing B-15. *A Function Closure*

```
function addDataPoint(coordinates, name, description, style)
{
  var thisMarker = new GMarker(coordinates, options);
  ...
  var sidebarRow = document.createElement('div');
  ...
  sidebarRow.onclick =
    function ()
    {
      // A click on the sidebar entry triggers a click on its associated marker
      GEvent.trigger(thisMarker, 'click')
    };
};
```

Note the variable `thisMarker`, declared outside the function literal but used inside it. As you know, the code in the literal won't execute at the time it's defined, but later on when the `sidebarRow.onclick` event occurs. But by that time the `addDataPoint` function will long since have finished—and you know from the previous section on variable scope that `thisMarker` will no longer exist. So how will this code work?

The key is a JavaScript feature called a *closure*, which essentially keeps a copy of `thisMarker` around *purely for use by the function literal*. This opens the door to one of the handiest aspects of function literals, the ability to write variable functions. In Listing B-15, for example, every time `addDataPoint` is called to create a marker (`thisMarker`) and add it to the map, a corresponding div (`sidebarRow`) is also created elsewhere on the page. The use of a closure allows us to connect the `click` event on `sidebarRow` with the correct, corresponding map marker. Without the function literal and the closure, linking these two newly created objects would have required quite a lot more code.

■**Note** Older versions of Internet Explorer had a bug that frequently caused them to lose (or "leak") memory when closures were used. However, this bug was fixed in IE7 and retroactively in an update to IE6; see `http://tinyurl.com/2mmusb`.

One warning: the closure, the copy of the local variable, is created with the last value that the variable has—not necessarily the value it had when the function literal occurred. So for example, if you have a function literal within a `for` loop, you can't create a closure on the loop control variable, because it will have changed by the time the function literal gets called. I described a workaround to this a few pages back, in the "Functions as Variables" section.

Summary

If you're new to JavaScript, this appendix should have helped you get up to speed on the essential concepts. You should now be comfortable with variables of different types, constructing expressions from them, and assembling expressions into statements. You should also have a working knowledge of the basic control structures, including decision blocks, looping, and function definitions. Finally, you've learned the key DOM concepts linking pure JavaScript to XHTML documents, and you know how to make the scope of variables work for you rather than against you.

For a more complete guide to learning JavaScript, I recommend the online tutorial at the W3C (`http://www.w3schools.com/js`), or the Mozilla Foundation's Core JavaScript Guide (go to `http://developer.mozilla.org/en/JavaScript` and click the "Guide" link).

Douglas Crockford, one of the giants of JavaScript, has called it "the world's most misunderstood programming language." I hope it's now a bit better understood by you.

■ ■ ■

JavaScript Techniques
for Map Developers

In this appendix you'll find a few slightly more advanced JavaScript techniques to improve your map pages and make the task of developing them easier. First up are two debugging tools, crucial weapons in the daily struggle against recalcitrant code. They're followed by a little-used API feature to improve your page structure; a code snippet to handle Google Maps API keys for multiple domains; and finally, a feature borrowed from the Gadgets API to make your mapplets more scalable.

Like all the appendixes, this one is primarily meant as a reference to dip into as needed while working through the rest of the book. Different topics here will be useful to you at different times.

Debugging Map Scripts

It's inevitable that program code will contain bugs, so it shouldn't come as too much of a surprise that programmers have developed tools to help in tracking down and eliminating those bugs. In this section I'll first outline what debugging tools need to accomplish and then introduce you to two of the most useful for developing API maps, the `GLog` object in the Maps API and the Firebug add-on to Firefox.

You can find more information on both of these tools, as well as a few others, at `http://code.google.com/apis/maps/articles/debuggingmaps.html`.

Debugging Basics

If you don't have much experience in software development, a few words about the basic principles of debugging are probably in order. At its core, *debugging* is about getting inside your code and seeing what's going on internally, rather than just observing the external symptoms.

For example, say you had JavaScript that was meant to place a map marker at a certain location, but when you loaded the map the marker didn't appear. Without debugging tools, that's about all that you would be able to tell: that it doesn't work. But if you can get inside the code and take a look at what's going on in more detail, you can often see the exact cause of the problem.

The first main aspect of debugging is to *examine* aspects of the code as it's running, usually the contents of variables. If your marker isn't appearing, perhaps the coordinates you're trying to place it at are wrong; being able to look at the contents of a `coordinates` variable directly will give you this insight.

Second, a good debugger will let you *step* through your code line by line, rather than executing functions all at once, as ordinarily occurs. This is incredibly helpful, as you can often see exactly where an error is occurring, letting you know which line of code needs fixing. And in combination with examining variables, you can actually watch what's happening inside your script. If you can see that `coordinates` gets initialized correctly, but is wrong by the time the marker gets created, by keeping an eye on it you can see just where it goes astray—and from there, find out why.

The GLog Object

The first debugging tool is actually built into the Maps API, as an object called `GLog`. It fulfills the first debugging role, allowing you to examine variables or expressions by *logging* their values to a special window that appears on top of the map.

The basic `GLog` function is `write`, and it's used in this form:

```
GLog.write(expression);
```

Note that `GLog` requires no initialization; you just include a line like the preceding at any point in your code where 'it would be helpful to see what the value of *expression* is.

Listing C-1 shows a simple Maps API script with `GLog.write` in action, logging the new center coordinates whenever the map is moved. Typical output of this script (after a couple of map moves) is shown in Figure C-1.

Listing C-1. *Using GLog.write to Log the Map Center Coordinates*

```
var map;

function loadMap()
{
  var mapDiv = document.getElementById('map');

  if (!GBrowserIsCompatible())
    mapDiv.innerHTML = 'Sorry, your browser isn\'t compatible with Google Maps.';
  else
  {
    map = new GMap2(mapDiv);
    map.setCenter(new GLatLng(39.8, -98.5), 4);

    GEvent.addListener(map, 'moveend', mapMoveEnd);
  }
};

function mapMoveEnd()
{
  GLog.write(map.getCenter().toUrlValue());
  ...
};
```

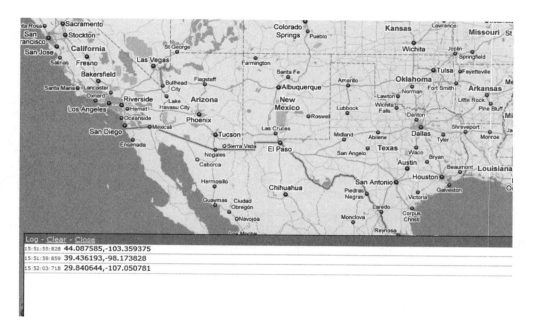

Figure C-1. *Typical output of* `GLog.write`

The `write` function also takes an optional second parameter for the color of the message, as follows:

```
GLog.write(expression, color);
```

The *color* value is a string containing an ordinary CSS-style color specifier, such as `'red'` or `'#FF0000'`. If you are logging a number of different values from different places in your code, `color` is useful in keeping track of which is which.

While `GLog` isn't a full-fledged debugger, the fact that it's built into the API means that it's always available, and it's quite handy to be able to simply add `GLog.write` to your code when you need to see what a given variable is up to. Just don't forget to remove the statements again before release; I've occasionally been using live Maps API web sites and seen the `GLog` window appear!

Firebug

When your bugs are too big or numerous for `GLog`, it's time to move up to a real debugger, and my recommendation is one called Firebug. It's an add-on to the Firefox browser, and you can download and install it from its homepage at `http://getfirebug.com`. Of course, you'll need to have Firefox installed first.

Once Firebug is installed, you'll need to enable it for the web site containing the script you want to debug (for performance reasons, Firebug is disabled for all web sites by default). So browse to the site in Firebox and click the Firebug icon in the lower-right corner of the Firefox screen (see Figure C-2). When Firebug opens, check all three boxes and click Enable (Figure C-3). The page will reload with Firebug enabled.

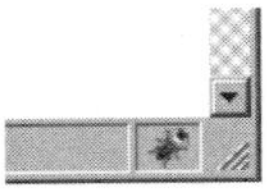

Figure C-2. *The Firebug icon in Firefox*

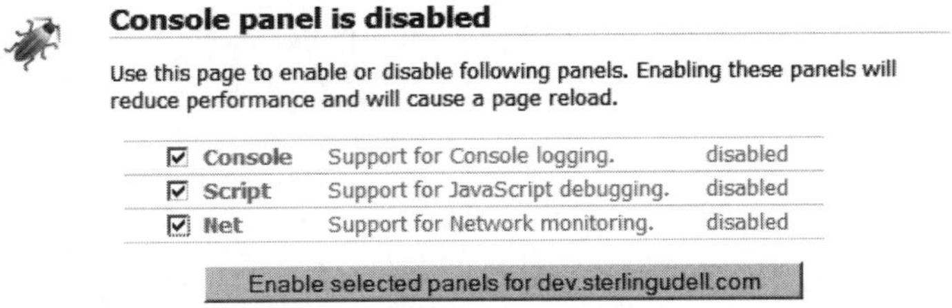

Console panel is disabled

Use this page to enable or disable following panels. Enabling these panels will reduce performance and will cause a page reload.

☑	**Console**	Support for Console logging.	disabled
☑	**Script**	Support for JavaScript debugging.	disabled
☑	**Net**	Support for Network monitoring.	disabled

Enable selected panels for dev.sterlingudell.com

Figure C-3. *Enabling Firebug for a domain*

Firebug is quite a powerful debugger; although I'm only going to discuss two aspects specifically useful for Maps API JavaScript debugging, I encourage you to explore its many features. The following web sites contain documentation and tutorials on its use:

- `http://getfirebug.com/docs.html`, at the Firebug home page

- `http://code.google.com/support/bin/answer.py?answer=94630`, a Google Code article

JAVASCRIPT DEBUGGING IN INTERNET EXPLORER

Although I recommend Firefox for Maps API development, if you need (or prefer) to use Internet Explorer, you will also need to take a different route for JavaScript debugging. `GLog` will still work fine—it's browser-independent—but for a true debugger, you have a few options.

- Microsoft Script Debugger is a free add-on for IE that offers most of the basic debugging features, such as stepping through code, examining variables, and a console. Install it from `http://tinyurl.com/6gc69`.

- Internet Explorer 8 includes an integrated JScript debugger; more information can be found at `http://msdn.microsoft.com/cc848892`.

- If you have Office XP or 2003 installed, it includes Microsoft's Script Editor, a reasonable debugging tool. A good getting-started guide can be found at `http://tinyurl.com/py2zz`.

- Microsoft's Visual Studio development environment can be linked to IE for integrated debugging of JavaScript code. Instructions for doing so can be found in Visual Studio's help files, or online at `http://msdn.microsoft.com/7seh8d72`.

The Console Tab

The Firebug window is organized into tabs, and by default, the Console tab is open initially. The Console can be thought of as a real-time view into browser activity, displaying messages as various events occur in the browser window, as well as in response to your own requests.

In the following sections, I'll cover a couple of the Console features of greatest use to Google Maps developers. In addition, Firebug's Console can also be used for sophisticated logging, similar to GLog but with more features. For more information on this, see http://getfirebug.com/console.html.

Page Errors

The first step in fixing code errors is finding them, and to this end, the most obvious usage of Firebug is as a JavaScript error console. Whenever any JavaScript error occurs on a web page, Firebug will display a message in the lower-right corner of the Firefox window (see Figure C-4). Clicking this message will open Firebug's Console, where you'll see a detailed error message (displayed in red), along with the script name and line where it occurred, as shown in Figure C-5. These latter are clickable, and doing so will take you directly to the offending statement on the Script tab.

Figure C-4. *Firebug tells you when an error occurs...*

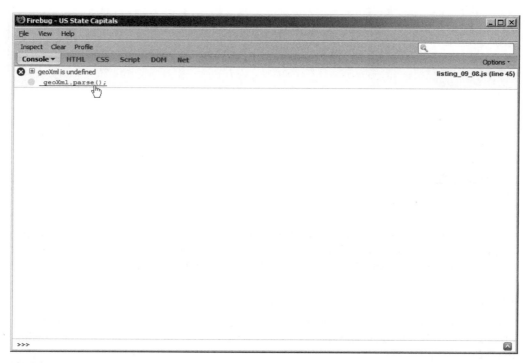

Figure C-5. *...and then shows you details about what went wrong.*

Interactive JavaScript

The other Console feature of greatest use to JavaScript developers is the ability to evaluate expressions interactively. At any time, you can type a JavaScript expression into the entry area at the bottom of the Console tab, and Firebug will evaluate it and display the results.

For an example, see Figure C-6. The entry area is adjacent to >>> at the bottom of the window; here, I've entered map.getZoom(), so when I press Enter, Firebug will show me the current map zoom level. Also in Figure C-6, I've already entered map.getCenter(), and you can see the results further up the Console: the latitude and longitude of the map center.

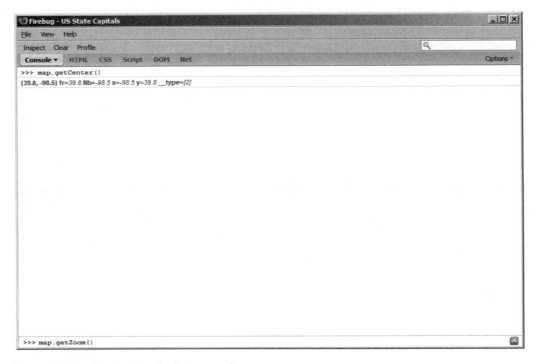

Figure C-6. *Evaluating JavaScript expressions*

Any JavaScript expression can be evaluated in this way: variables, expressions, functions, or object methods. It's a very useful tool when tracking down a bug, enabling you to get inside the page and determine whether the values within are what they should be.

The Script Tab

Not surprisingly, Firebug's most advanced JavaScript tools are found on the Script tab. The other Firebug tabs get you inside your web page, but here, you can get inside your scripts while they're running.

A typical Script tab view can be found in Figure C-7, and before I discuss what you can do here, a bit of orientation will be helpful.

- In the left half of the window is a pane showing the script itself, the same as you would see in a text editor while you're writing or modifying the source code. This is where you set and modify breakpoints (discussed in the next section).

  - Above the script pane is the name of the script (`listing_c_01.js` in this case). If your page has multiple scripts, clicking here will open a menu listing them, allowing you to select one to work with.

  - Next to the script name is the *call stack* (here, `loadMap < onLoad`). This tells you where in the code you are: within the `loadMap` function, which has been called by the `onLoad` event. For a complicated script, this reference can be invaluable.

- The right side of the window serves multiple functions:

  - By default (and in Figure C-7), it shows the Watch pane. Here you can see the values for all local variables at once, as discussed later in the appendix.

  - Clicking the Stack tab will show a more detailed view of the call stack.

  - The Breakpoints tab lets you see and manipulate all your code breakpoints in one place (see the next section).

As with Firebug generally, the Script tab has a lot more features than I can effectively cover in this appendix. Once you're comfortable with the basic techniques described in the following sections, I encourage you to take Firebug further, starting with the reference at http://getfirebug.com/js.html.

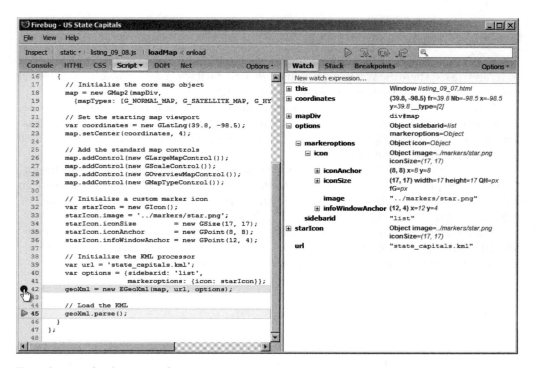

Figure C-7. *Firebug's Script tab*

Breakpoints

The key to the Script tab's usefulness is the ability to stop the execution of your JavaScript on any line; this enables you to have a good look around and see what's going on, analogous to pausing a video. The primary method for making this happen is to set a *breakpoint* in your code; effectively, a breakpoint is like a stop sign that tells Firebug to put everything on hold and await further instructions from you.

You set a breakpoint in the Script tab by clicking to the left of the line number where you want the code to pause; this will create a red dot next to that line (visible next to line 42 in Figure C-7). You need to do this *before* Firefox executes that line of code, either before its containing function is called, or before reloading the page. Firefox will execute your code normally until it reaches the line containing the breakpoint, it will then pause all page activity and bring the Firebug window to the fore.

■**Tip** Breakpoints can only be set on *executable* code; not blank lines, comments, nor curly-brackets ({ and }).

When code is paused, Firebug displays a small yellow triangle alongside the *next* line of code that will be executed. In Figure C-7, this can be seen at line 45. This is your indicator of where in the script the action is currently stopped and is called the *current line* of the script; I'll discuss moving from one line to another in a moment.

To clear a breakpoint, click on the dot again, and it will vanish. Your code will then execute uninterrupted.

Watching Variables

When your code has stopped at a breakpoint, it's a good opportunity to examine the program state, and this is where the Watch pane comes into its own. By default, it shows (or *watches*) all variables local[1] to the function where the code is paused.

For example, in Figure C-7, options was set (on line 40) to an object literal, so when the code is paused on line 42, options shows as an object in the Watch pane. Note that its watch value has been expanded to show its markeroptions and sidebarid properties, and that markeroptions is itself an object (also shown expanded).

As well as displaying the local variables, you can create your own watches by clicking on "New watch expression…" at the top of the pane. For example, if you wanted to keep an eye on a global variable, you could create a watch for it here. And watches don't have to be simple variables; they can be any JavaScript expression, such as functions.

Finally, the Watch pane also lets you modify variables by double-clicking on their values. So if you think a given bug is being caused by an incorrect value, you can actually set it right here and then confirm that the script runs correctly as a result.

---

1. See the discussion on variable scope in Appendix B.

Stepping Through Code

You've paused your script and examined all the relevant variables, and you're ready to move on. To do so, the Script tab gives you fine-grained control of how and where to watch your code run after a breakpoint, using the four icons visible above "Breakpoints" in Figure C-7.

The first icon, a simple right-pointing triangle, is Continue. Clicking it will resume normal execution of your script, with no further Firebug interaction unless another breakpoint is reached.

The remaining three icons all *step through* the code, meaning that Firebug will execute the current line of the script and pause again, moving the yellow arrow (from line 45 of Figure C-7) to indicate the new current line. But they all work in slightly different ways. From left to right, here's what they do:

- The second icon is Step Into, and it will pass execution into the first function on the current line; in Figure C-7, this would mean geoXml.parse. This will change which lines are displayed in the script pane, and the new current function will be added to the call stack (above the script pane). So the new current line will be the first executable line of code within that function.

- The third icon is Step Over; it simply executes the current line of code and makes the next executable line current. If the current line of code contains functions, they are executed without pause (rather than being stepped into).

- The fourth and final icon is Step Out, and it's somewhat the opposite of Step Into. It will execute (without pause) every line of code between the current one and the end of the current function, pausing again when the script returns to whatever function called it. Step Out is essentially saying to Firebug, "Get me out of the current function."

If you've not used a debugger before, the preceding descriptions may sound somewhat confusing, but the use of these controls will become natural with a bit of practice. Initially, I recommend that you predominantly use Step Over (the third icon), until you become comfortable with stepping into and out of functions.

And in general, the only way to become comfortable with a debugger (and recognize its full value) is to use it. When the inevitable bugs occur in scripts, Firebug is priceless, and I encourage you to take the time to get to know it.

The Art of Debugging

Finding bugs in program code is as much an art as it is a skill, and its full coverage is well beyond the scope of this appendix. If you're pulling your hair out trying to quash an ornery insect, I recommend the article on the essentials of debugging at http://tinyurl.com/61859d.

Better Event Listeners

Throughout the book, we've been attaching handlers to events for web page elements by including them directly in the XHTML. Examples of this include:

```
<body onload="loadmap()" onunload="GUnload()">
```

and

```
<a href="#" id="link" onclick="clickLink()">Click Here</a>
```

This technique works, and it's quite straightforward as an introductory technique for beginners. However, when using the Maps API, there is a better, more standards-compliant way to accomplish the same end.

To understand what's wrong with coding the handlers directly in the XHTML, it might be easiest to draw an analogy with CSS. As I'm sure you're aware, it's not recommended that CSS rules be included directly in XHTML elements using style attributes, as in

```
<p style="text-align: center">
```

Good web design practice is to separate content from presentation by placing CSS in style sheets, usually external to the XHTML. Similarly, JavaScript is generally not included in the XHTML. By placing it in external .js files, we're separating content from functionality; the argument is exactly analogous to that for external CSS. But look again at the onload, onunload, and onclick event handlers discussed earlier: they're little snippets of JavaScript embedded in the XHTML, no different than the style attribute of the p tag.

So how do we avoid this, and create a clean break between content and functionality? Recall that, for API objects, we use GEvent.addListener to attach event handlers. Well, GEvent has another method used for attaching handlers to XHTML objects, called addDomListener. Its syntax is almost exactly the same as addListener's; it should look very familiar to you. Listing C-2 shows it in use.

Listing C-2. *Attaching Page Events with addDomListener*

```
var map;

GEvent.addDomListener(window, 'load',   loadMap);
GEvent.addDomListener(window, 'unload', GUnload);

function loadMap()
{
  var mapDiv = document.getElementById('map');

  if (!GBrowserIsCompatible())
    mapDiv.innerHTML = 'Sorry, your browser isn\'t compatible with Google Maps.';
  else
  {
    map = new GMap2(mapDiv);
    map.setCenter(new GLatLng(39.8, -98.5), 4);
  }
};
```

You can probably see how it works already. At the beginning of the script (outside of any function definitions) I've called addDomListener twice, for the standard body events that virtually every map script in this book uses. That's all it takes; the event handlers are now attached, and my XHTML body tag is clean, as seen in Listing C-3.

Listing C-3. *XHTML without Event Listeners*

```
<!DOCTYPE html PUBLIC "-//W3C//DTD XHTML 1.0 Strict//EN"
                      "http://www.w3.org/TR/xhtml1/DTD/xhtml1-strict.dtd">
<html xmlns="http://www.w3.org/1999/xhtml" style="height: 100%">
  <head>
    <meta http-equiv="Content-Type" content="text/html; charset=UTF-8" />
    <title>Better Event Listeners</title>
    <link type="text/css" rel="stylesheet" href="figure_c_01.css" />
    <script type="text/javascript"
            src="http://maps.google.com/maps?file=api&amp;v=2.124&amp;key="></script>
    <script type="text/javascript" src="listing_c_02.js"></script>
  </head>
  <body>
    <div id="map"></div>
  </body>
</html>
```

The same technique can be used for events attached to any element on the page. For example, to replicate the link-click handler example from the beginning of this section, we would need the following JavaScript:

```
GEvent.addDomListener(document.GetElementById('link'), 'click', clickLink);
```

This will attach a function named `clickLink` to the `click` event for the a element, exactly the same as `onclick="clickLink()"` but without breaching the content/functionality divide.

GEvent.addDomListener VERSUS EVENT PROPERTIES

If you've done much JavaScript programming before, you may be aware that XHTML elements in JavaScript have event properties that can be used to attach handlers directly. So for example, the `loadMap` function from Listing C-2 could be attached with the following JavaScript:

```
document.body.onload = loadMap;
```

Again, this works, but it's not the best solution. The main reason is that it's exclusive: you can only attach one handler to each event this way. If other code elsewhere on the same page needed to be attached to the `onload` event, it would be unable to, because the listener is already occupied by `loadMap`. Worse yet, if other code on the page were *already* attached to `onload`, this line of JavaScript *would destroy that attachment*.

The `GEvent.addDomListener` method doesn't work this way; you can attach as many listeners as you like to each event, with no interference. You can even remove them independently (using a separate `GEvent.removeListener` function). You, the programmer, have complete control.

Using Multiple API Keys

The Google Maps API key system introduced in Chapter 2 generally works quite seamlessly; once you have your key, you can usually just paste it into the appropriate `script` tag and forget about it. But because the key system is based on domains, it can be problematic if the same map page needs to be served from completely different domains. Here are a few examples of such situations:

- Parallel live and development systems, where a given page is written and tested on a development server and then deployed to the live system.

- "White-label" systems, where different branding (including the serving domain) is applied dynamically to a single page.

- Country-specific domains, where the same page may be served to multiple top-level domains (such as `.com`, `.ca`, and `.co.uk`).

In cases such as these, the API key system doesn't natively offer a solution, and it's up to us to develop one ourselves. In this section I'll give you code you can use to overcome the problem.

The first step is that you need to generate API keys from Google for all the domains that you'll need, at `http://code.google.com/apis/maps/signup.html`. Simply repeat the signup process for each domain, copying each key to a safe place; you'll need them in a moment.

With API keys in hand, we're ready to start coding. The key (if you will) is to include the API indirectly, via an intermediary JavaScript that dynamically inserts the correct key for the requesting domain. So your XHTML will look something like Listing C-4; note that in the first script element, the `src` is `listing_c_05.js`, rather than the usual `http://maps.google.com/maps?file=api&v=2.124&key=`. And the heart of the solution can be found in Listing C-5, the intermediary that holds all the keys.

Listing C-4. *The XHTML for Dynamic API Keys*

```
<!DOCTYPE html PUBLIC "-//W3C//DTD XHTML 1.0 Strict//EN"
                      "http://www.w3.org/TR/xhtml1/DTD/xhtml1-strict.dtd">
<html xmlns="http://www.w3.org/1999/xhtml" style="height: 100%">
  <head>
    <meta http-equiv="Content-Type" content="text/html; charset=UTF-8" />
    <title>Multiple API Keys</title>
    <link type="text/css" rel="stylesheet" href="figure_c_01.css" />
    <script type="text/javascript" src="listing_c_05.js"></script>
    <script type="text/javascript" src="listing_c_02.js"></script>
  </head>
  <body>
    <div id="map"></div>
  </body>
</html>
```

Listing C-5. *The Basic JavaScript for Dynamic API Keys*

```
var scriptUrl = 'http://maps.google.com/maps?file=api&v=2.124&key=';

if (location.host == 'www.somedomain.com')
  // Live server
  scriptUrl = scriptUrl + 'ABQIAAAA5wG_Upp3E2E2FvbwfSzPchQEMNwiYNXG5Xk21FzWxftqhFg';
else
  // Development server
  scriptUrl = scriptUrl + 'ABQIAAAAN_IKAOv-fz9s2G9ZOihkhRQRiYyMmFOXXgCIe1BMmHtWUkP';

document.write('<script type="text/javascript" src="' + scriptUrl + '"></script>');
```

In this example, I have a system to support two domains (for live and development servers) but the principle is the same for any such situation.

1. Test `location.host` against one of your domains.

2. If it matches, add the key for that domain to `scriptUrl`.

3. Repeat for as many domains as you need to support (using `if`/`else` or `switch` blocks, as covered in Appendix B).

4. Use `scriptUrl` to generate the `script` element dynamically, linking in the Maps API.

Note step 4, using `document.write`; it's another example of DHTML, introduced in Chapters 9 and 11, here creating a `script` element on the fly. We'll use it again in the next section, for a similar purpose.

MULTIPLE API KEYS AND SUBDOMAINS

As you know from Chapter 2, a page served from multiple subdomains (such as `sub1.mydomain.com` and `sub2.mydomain.com`) doesn't require multiple API keys; a single key registered for `mydomain.com` is sufficient. But if your page is served from both multiple domains *and* subdomains, a little bit more work is required.

The first option is to extend Listing C-5 to include each subdomain, like so:

```
if ((location.host == 'mydomain.com') ||
    (location.host == 'sub1.mydomain.com') ||
    (location.host == 'sub2.mydomain.com'))
  // Use key for mydomain.com
  scriptUrl = scriptUrl + 'ABQIAAAAN_IKAOv-fz9s2G9ZOihkhRQqF5vs-amCUIieOBLhZ3';
else
  // Use key for mydomain.co.uk
  scriptUrl = scriptUrl + 'ABQIAAAAN_IKAOvfz9s2G9ZOihkhRQRiYyMmFOXXgCIe1BMmHt';
```

> However, if you have many subdomains, such a solution may be impractical - and in any event, there's a more elegant approach. The idea here is that, rather than testing `location.host` against each individual subdomain, we can match a *pattern* instead. Here's an example in action:
>
> ```
> if (location.host.search(/mydomain.com$/) > -1)
>     // Use key for mydomain.com
>     scriptUrl = scriptUrl + 'ABQIAAAAN_IKAOv-fz9s2G9ZOihkhRQqF5vs-amCUIieOBLhZ3';
> else
>     // Use key for mydomain.co.uk
>     scriptUrl = scriptUrl + 'ABQIAAAAN_IKAOvfz9s2G9ZOihkhRQRiYyMmFOXXgCIe1BMmHt';
> ```
>
> The idea is the same as in Listing C-5, but rather than a simple string comparison, an advanced technique called a *regular expression* is used. You can utilize it in the same way, however; simply substitute in your own API keys and top-level domain (ensuring that you leave the special characters, / and $/, intact).

Using the Gadgets API Cache in Mapplets

To close out this appendix, I'm going to introduce a technique that's specifically useful in Mapplets, but which is not available in the traditional Maps API. It's a feature of the Google Gadgets API, which (as you'll recall from Chapters 6 through 8) is the foundation of Mapplets.

More specifically, it's an additional utilization of Google's caching servers, and its goal is to make your mapplets more scalable. This is potentially an issue because maps.google.com (where mapplets run) has many millions of users, and if even a small fraction were to install your mapplet, the load on your own server could become overwhelming. Google mitigates this problem somewhat by caching your main mapplet specification. However, if your mapplet uses external JavaScript, images, or other files, they are *not* automatically cached by Google. The purpose of this section is to demonstrate how they can be.

As mentioned, the key is a function from the Gadgets API, named _IG_GetCachedUrl. When supplied with the URL for any resource on the web, it returns a new URL for that same resource, but *cached through the Google Gadget servers*. So your code can then use the new, cached URL in place of the original, confident that Google will bear the load and only check back with your original once every hour or two.

With that background, let's see it in action. For this example, I'm going to revisit the US State Capitals mapplet from Chapter 9; it uses both external JavaScript and image files, the latter in the form of a custom map icon. For review, please see Figure 9-10 for the mapplet's appearance, and Listing 9-9 for the XML on which this section is based. Listing C-6 shows the new mapplet specification with the changes for caching highlighted.

Listing C-6. *The US Capitals Mapplet, Modified to Use the Google Cache*

```
<?xml version="1.0" encoding="UTF-8"?>
<Module>
  <ModulePrefs title="US State Capitals"
               description="The capitals (and capitols) of the 50 US states."
               author="Sterling Udell"
               author_email="sterling.udell+mapplet@googlemail.com"
```

```
            screenshot="http://sterlingudell.com/bgmm/chapter_09/state_scr.png"
            thumbnail="http://sterlingudell.com/bgmm/chapter_09/state_thm.png">
  <Require feature="sharedmap" />
  <Require feature="dynamic-height" />
</ModulePrefs>
<Content type="html"><![CDATA[
  <style type="text/css">
    p {
      font-size: 90%;
    }
  </style>

  <p id="list"></p>

  <script type="text/javascript">
    var scriptUrl = _IG_GetCachedUrl('http://sterlingudell.com/bgmm/egeoxml.js');
    document.write(
      '<script type="text/javascript" src="' + scriptUrl + '"><\/script>');

    function xmlParsed()
    {
      // xmlParsed: After KML processing, adjust the height of the sidebar display
      _IG_AdjustIFrameHeight();
    };

    function loadMap()
    {
      // Initialize the map
      var map = new GMap2();

      // Initialize a custom marker icon
      var starIcon = new GIcon();
      starIcon.image = 'http://gmodules.com' +
        _IG_GetCachedUrl('http://sterlingudell.com/bgmm/markers/star.png');
      starIcon.iconSize        = new GSize(17, 17);
      starIcon.iconAnchor      = new GPoint(8, 8);
      starIcon.infoWindowAnchor = new GPoint(12, 4);

      // Initialize the KML processor
      var url = 'http://sterlingudell.com/bgmm/chapter_09/state_capitals.kml';
      var options = {sidebarid: 'list',
                     markeroptions: {icon: starIcon},
                     nozoom: true};
      var geoXml = new EGeoXml(map, url, options);
```

```
      // Attach an event handler for after the KML is processed
      GEvent.addListener(geoXml, 'parsed', xmlParsed);

      // Load the KML
      geoXml.parse();
    };
    _IG_RegisterOnloadHandler(loadMap);
  </script>
]]></Content>
</Module>
```

The first occurrence is for the external JavaScript file, and you'll notice that it requires two lines. The first is to get the cached URL, as outlined earlier:

```
var scriptUrl = _IG_GetCachedUrl('http://sterlingudell.com/bgmm/egeoxml.js');
```

Simple enough; scriptUrl is set to the Google-cached URL for egeoxml.js.

To link it into the mapplet, I use the document.write technique described earlier in this appendix:

```
document.write('<script type="text/javascript" src="' + scriptUrl + '"><\/script>');
```

There's just one slight oddity here: notice how I have an extra backslash in the closing script tag? That's required because, if I simply had </script>, the browser would interpret it as the end of *the mapplet's main script element*, not the one within my document.write function. I avoid the problem by "breaking up" the closing tag with a backslash plus forward-slash, which JavaScript prints as a simple forward-slash (see the section on Special Characters in Appendix B).

The second occurrence of _IG_GetCachedUrl (for the icon image) doesn't involve script but has its own minor quirk:

```
starIcon.image = 'http://gmodules.com' +
                 _IG_GetCachedUrl('http://sterlingudell.com/bgmm/markers/star.png');
```

Note the highlighted string prepended to the cached URL, 'http://gmodules.com'. It's needed because the URL returned from _IG_GetCachedUrl is *relative*; this works fine in the main body of the mapplet, which is contained in an iframe served from gmodules.com. But for images that will appear on the map itself, like markers, we need to make the URL absolute, as shown here.

And that's all there is to it. The same technique can be used for all external files used by your mapplets, such as stylesheets or any sort of image; you just need to follow the guidelines here. A mapplet using Google's cache in this way should be free of any scaling problems.

■■■

Mapping Resources Online

While I hope that you've found this book to be a useful introduction to Google's mapping APIs, no single book could cover the topic exhaustively. For a complete reference, as well as the most up-to-the-minute information, online resources are your best option. In this appendix, you'll find links to the most helpful of those resources, covering all areas of Maps and Mapplets API development.

For your convenience, this list of links can also be found at `http://sterlingudell.com/bgmm/appendix_d`.

API-Related Documentation

Let's get the boring-but-indispensable items out of the way first. In this section you'll find the actual reference materials, providing the foundation for all information about the mapping APIs.

Official Google

Your first port of call for any API-related questions should usually be Google's own documentation. It's not always the most helpful—Google documentation tends toward brevity, sometimes too strongly–but it is always the most complete, and certainly the most authoritative.

Maps API

`http://code.google.com/apis/maps/documentation`

The original Google Maps API is documented here, including a Developer Guide, code samples, and much more. I especially recommend the API Reference; it contains an explanation of every object, property, and function in the Maps API.

Mapplets API

`http://code.google.com/apis/maps/documentation/mapplets`

Same as previous, but for the Mapplets API. Note that this is not usually as up-to-date as the documentation for the traditional Maps API, so while the information here is correct, it's just not as complete, especially for newer features. Use the Maps API reference as a guide, and you'll find that many features also exist for Mapplets, even if they're not mentioned here.

Gadgets API

http://code.google.com/apis/gadgets/docs/legacy/reference.html

This is the reference for Gadgets API features that are available in mapplets but are not part of the Mapplets API itself, such as the Dynamic Height and User Preferences libraries. Note that the Mapplet-compatible version referenced here is not the default iGoogle Gadgets API, but instead what Google refers to as the "legacy" API.

Maps Utility Library

http://code.google.com/p/gmaps-utility-library-dev/wiki/Libraries

Here's where you'll find Google's documentation for their API add-ons, like LabeledMarker and MapIconMaker. It's a bit more fragmented than the core API's documentation, but it's still quite complete.

KML

http://code.google.com/apis/kml

Although KML is now an open standard, Google still maintains the definitive documentation for it. As with the other API sites, this link will lead you to a Developer's Guide, a complete Reference, and many other useful resources.

Third-Party

The resources here supplement Google's own information about the Maps API, as well as documenting useful third-party add-on modules described in this book.

Mike Williams

http://econym.googlepages.com/index.htm

Mike is a giant of the Maps API world, and his tutorial has helped many a map developer out of tight spot, or guided them towards a little-known feature of the API. It's no exaggeration to say that he knows the Maps API like no-one else outside of Google.

Mike is also the author of the original EGeoXml KML processor, and for information on its use, his site is the best place to go. Its home page can be found at http://econym.googlepages.com/egeoxml.htm.

■**Caution** I've extended EGeoXml myself for some of the examples in this book, so in order to use it as I describe, you'll need to download it from http://sterlingudell.com/bgmm/egeoxml.js, not Mike Williams' site.

Michael Geary

`http://mg.to/2007/06/22`

Another Mike; this one's the author of `GAsync`, a module that lets you run the same code in both the Maps and Mapplets APIs. This handy add-on, described in Chapter 9, is documented on his web site at the URL shown here, from where it can also be downloaded.

Mapki

`http://mapki.com`

The Google Maps API wiki. There's plenty of good information here, if a bit disorganized. As with any wiki, you can add or modify it yourself as needed. One of the most useful items in the Mapki is an API version tracker, showing which versions are current and what has changed in every version Google has released.

Discussion Groups

Although the reference sites in the previous section are usually the best place to start, they don't have all the answers. Sometimes there's no substitute for experience, and when you're stuck, asking more experienced developers is an excellent way to get moving again. In this section you'll find the main discussion groups related to topics covered in this book.

All of these groups are frequented by developers and users at the tops of their specialties, and they're happy to answer your questions. However, answering questions takes their time, and you'll have much better success if you observe a few simple posting guidelines (especially on the developer groups):

- **Search past discussions before you post.** Many questions have been asked before, and you will often find your solutions here without covering the same ground again.

- **Ask specific questions, not general ones.** An expert isn't likely to talk you through an entire project, but if you can point to a specific problem you're having, he might well advise you on it.

- **Be polite.** The other group members are helping you out of their own generosity, which will be much more forthcoming if you're civil.

- **Post links, not code.** There are many reasons for this; high among them is that it enables others to go try your code in action rather than simply looking at it. Also, your problem may not be where you think it is, so the code snippet you post might not even contain your bug.

One additional benefit to the Google groups listed here is that Google employees participate in them as developer liaisons. They will respond to questions on the groups when appropriate, and this is often the most practical way to contact Google directly regarding their APIs.

Google Maps API Group

`http://groups.google.com/group/Google-Maps-API`

This is the place to ask any question relating to the Maps or Mapplets APIs. It's an incredibly active group, so you're likely to have a response within hours.

iGoogle Developer Forum

`http://groups.google.com/group/Google-Gadgets-API`

Although the Maps API group does cover mapplets, it is far more focused on the traditional Maps API. Conversely, this group is specific to iGoogle gadgets, which share much of the same infrastructure as mapplets. If you have a question specifically related to gadget functionality, or you're not getting anywhere with the Maps API group, try asking here.

KML Developer Support

`http://groups.google.com/group/kml-support`

If your question is more related to KML than the mapping APIs, this is the place to ask it.

Google Earth Community

`http://bbs.keyhole.com`

This is a forum of Google Earth users rather than map developers, but since KML was originally developed for Earth, there's a lot of KML expertise here. In addition, searching this group is a good way to find KML files online.

Map-Oriented Weblogs

Keep up-to-date with the latest happenings in the Google mapping world by subscribing to these blogs.

Google LatLon

`http://google-latlong.blogspot.com`

This blog contains general news from Google about their participation in the geoweb, from product announcements to spotlights on interesting uses of their APIs. It's a good place to keep your finger on the pulse of all Google's geospatial initiatives.

Google Geo Developers Blog

`http://googlegeodevelopers.blogspot.com`

More technical than LatLon, this blog is pitched at map developers of all levels. Here you'll find announcements of new aspects, features within the mapping APIs, Google initiatives to assist the developer community, and occasional guides on the use of specific API modules.

Google Maps Mania

`http://googlemapsmania.blogspot.com`

This blog isn't run by Google; rather, it's an outsider's take on the most interesting map mashups of the moment. Not only is it fun to see what other developers are doing, this blog is a great source of inspiration, and a good way to promote your own mashup when it's ready for the world to see.

Related Resources

Moving beyond the mapping APIs themselves, the following resources provide other information useful to map developers.

GeoRSS Information

Google maintains good information about KML (see the previous sections), but for GeoRSS—the other side of geoXML—you need to turn elsewhere.

GeoRSS.org

`http://georss.org`

The definitive site for the emerging GeoRSS standard. There's not a huge amount here, but it is the place to go for the official standards.

RSS 2.0 Specification

`http://cyber.law.harvard.edu/rss/rss.html`

GeoRSS is of course an add-on to Real Simple Syndication, and this site hosts the core RSS documentation. It's the definitive source for answers when your GeoRSS issues aren't confined to the "Geo" aspect.

AtomEnabled

`http://atomenabled.org`

Atom is the other feed standard into which GeoRSS fits, and AtomEnabled is its official site. You'll probably be most interested in their Developers section, where you can find the XML specification, a tutorial, and other resources.

XML Validators

When you have your geoXML written, it's important to test it, and the following sites will help you to do that. Ill-formed XML can cause many problems, so checking its validity is always a good idea.

World Wide Web Consortium

http://validator.w3.org

Although the W3C's validator is intended for use with X/HTML, it will check the structure of any XML document (with one warning, "No DOCTYPE found"). So it will work with KML, GeoRSS, Geo Sitemaps, or mapplet specifications.

Feed Validator

http://feedvalidator.org

Specifically for Atom, RSS, and KML, Feed Validator will therefore also check GeoRSS. It produces more specific and informative error messages for these standards than does the W3C's.

JavaScript References

As the native language of Google's mapping APIs, JavaScript is where you'll spend most of your time, so good JavaScript references are indispensable.

World Wide Web Consortium

http://w3schools.com/js

The W3C maintains a wealth of good information for web developers, and their JavaScript reference is no exception, especially for beginners.

Mozilla

http://developer.mozilla.org/en/JavaScript

This is another excellent JavaScript site, containing a reference section, guide, change log, and more. It also highlights aspects specific to the Mozilla family of browsers (Firefox, Netscape, and so on). The reference here is slightly more technical than on the W3C site, but in my opinion it's easier to navigate.

Microsoft

http://msdn.microsoft.com/hbxc2t98

Internet Explorer uses JScript, a slightly different dialect, so occasionally you'll need to come here to find ways in which the language diverges from standard JavaScript.

JSON

http://json.org

JavaScript Object Notation is usually quite straightforward (see Chapter 10 and Appendix B), but if you'd like more information on its whys and wherefores, Douglas Crockford's site is the go-to guide.

DOM References

As you're working with JavaScript on web pages, you'll often find yourself interacting with the Document Object Model and needing a guide to its mysteries. Although the DOM is fairly well standardized across browsers, there are some slight differences, so again you'll need to visit the web sites of the different vendors at different times.

Mozilla

`http://developer.mozilla.org/en/Gecko_DOM_Reference`

Mozilla's DOM implementation is quite standards-compliant, so their reference is a good place to start. For a change, however, I find it a bit hard to navigate.

Microsoft

`http://msdn.microsoft.com/ms533050`

The MSDN (Microsoft Developer Network) DOM reference, internally called the "DHTML Object Model," is arguably easier to get around than Mozilla's. However, it contains quite a few IE-only extensions to the standard; whether that's a good or bad thing depends on what you're looking for.

Server-Side Programming Guides

Although the Google mapping APIs are fundamentally client-based, a complete map application may also involve programming on the server, as discussed in Chapter 10. The following references document the technologies used in that chapter.

PHP

`http://php.net/manual/en`

PHP is an incredibly rich programming language, and its online manual is correspondingly huge. It's relatively easy to find your way around, however, and includes an excellent search function. A nice bonus is the user comment section you'll find on virtually every page, containing useful code snippets and time-saving tips.

MySQL

`http://dev.mysql.com/doc`

In addition to covering the MySQL database manager itself, this documentation also includes a general SQL tutorial for beginners. From the URL shown, I recommend going to the basic HTML manual for the version of MySQL your system is running.

Sitemaps

`http://sitemaps.org`

A brief introduction to the fundamentals of sitemap XML files, from which geo sitemaps are based.

Geospatial Calculations

`http://www.movable-type.co.uk/scripts/latlong.html`

This excellent page, hosted at Moveable Type Scripts, has a variety of formulas in various programming languages (including JavaScript) for calculating geographic distances, bearings, and so on, along with a good discussion of each.

Index

Numbers and symbols

(hash character), 289

$ (dollar sign) for variables in PHP, 233

/* and */ in JavaScript, 327

// (forward slashes) for JavaScript comments, 52, 327

; (semicolons) in JavaScript, 326

{ } (curly brackets) in JavaScript, 331

3-dimensional icons, 181, 326

A

addControl function (GMap2), 22

addDataPoint function, 270–271, 279, 281

addDomListener, attaching page events with, 358

addOverlay function, 32

addresses

    geocoding, 80–86, 185–186

    retrieving directions from, 91

    verification of, 186–187

AdSense program, Google, 100

advertising, map, 100–101

afterGeocode callback function, 85, 288

alert function, 84

anchor points (icons), 179

anonymous functions, 347

API (Application Programming Interface)

    API keys, using multiple, 14–16, 360–362

    cross-API development, 213–219

    Gadgets, 362–364

    linking into mapplets, 114

    mapping documentation, 365–367

    mapplets API services, 168

    maps. *See* Maps API

arrays

    Array type, 330–331

    iterating over, 337

    JavaScript, 200, 204–205

    JSON, 260

assignment operators (expressions), 333–334

asynchronous mapplet functions, 116, 159

asynchronous quality of GGeoXml, 35

Atom feed format, 7

Atom specification/documentation, 242

AtomEnabled site, 369

attribution, 249

author attribute (ModulePrefs tag), 129

author_location attribute (ModulePrefs tag), 130

B

Back button function, 290–291

backgroundColor GMap2 option, 269

Beginning Google Maps Applications with PHP and Ajax (Apress), 277

Beginning SQL Queries: From Novice to Professional (Apress), 267

Berners-Lee, Tim, 5

between operator, 246, 258

bindInfoWindow

    bindInfoWindowTabs (National Park example), 64–65

    mapplet application, 123

block statements (JavaScript), 326–327

blocks, switch (JavaScript), 339–340

blowup infowindows (National Park example), 57–60

bool datatype, 141

Boole, George, 141

Boolean operators (expressions), 334

Boolean type (JavaScript), 330

break statements (JavaScript), 338–339

breakpoints (Firebug), 356

Breweries in UK (example), 199

button element, 90

■C

cache, Gadgets API, 362–364

caching, GGeoXml, 33

calculations
    of distance between coordinates, 318–319
    geospatial, 372

call stacks, 355

callback functions
    geocoding and, 82
    JavaScript, 35
    Street View, 96–98

camel case naming, 31

campground application. *See*
    satellite-friendly campground
    directory (case study)

center coordinates, confirming changes in,
    161–162

Chadwick, Bill, 252

character data (CDATA), XML, 122

Churchill, Clare, 267

circular icons, 175

class label option, 177

clicks
    capturing map clicks, 143–145
    click-to-search map (campground
        application), 273
    single-click timeout workaround
        (geonaming), 144–145

client-side programming, 231

closures, function (JavaScript), 346–348

cluster markers, 276–278

code
    breaking down, 161
    defensive coding, 83–85
    gadget-related (mapplets), 120–122
    parameterizing, 239
    stepping through (Firebug), 357

collaboration on My Maps, 225

comments, JavaScript, 51–52, 327

comparison operators (expressions),
    333–334

compound types, 330

concatenation, 333

Console tab (Firebug), 352

consuming geodata, 29

Content element, XML, 121

content tags, GeoRSS, 40

control structures
    break statements, 338–339
    defined, 335
    functions. *See* functions (JavaScript)
    if/else blocks, 335–336
    for loops, 336–338
    switch blocks, 339–340
    while loops, 338

controls, Google Maps
    GLargeMapControl (pan and zoom), 22
    GMapTypeControl, 23
    GOverviewMapControl, 23
    GScaleControl (scale for distance), 23
    GSmallMapControl (pan and zoom), 24

cookies, 284, 287

Coordinate Finder mapplet, defined, 10

coordinates
    calculating distance between, 318–319
    callback function to receive center
        coordinates, 159–161
    different systems for, 315
    formatting for display, 162–163
    map, 10

precision of, 316–317

saving, 187–188

SQL data types for precision of, 318

cosines, spherical law of, 319

Craigslist, 4

Crockford, Douglas, 256, 348, 370

cross-API development, 213–219

CSS (Cascading Style Sheets)

display limitations and, 40

for location entry page, 185

mapplets and, 122–123

for sidebar (National Park example), 50–51

for tabbed infowindow content (National Park example), 62–64

Transit Links example, 44–45

for UK Brewery map page, 202

current lines, script (Firebug), 356

custom marker icons

changing icons, 174

designing, 178–182

Google pre-made icons, 174–175

labeled markers, 175–177

Map Icon Maker, 177

National Park example, 53

overview, 173–174

use in mapplets, 169

■ **D**

data

data handling, dynamic, 219–220

filtering, 246–248

formatting as JSON, 258–260

PHP and dynamic, 238–239

data sets, large

displaying 20 data points, 204–207

executive summary, 199

infowindow fix, 208–212

loading data, 200–203

overview, 199

data transfers on client-side/server-side (JSON), 261

data types

datatype attribute (UserPref element), 139

JavaScript, 327–332

Placeopedia content mapplet, 142

data values as objects (JavaScript), 328

data views, selecting different (campground application), 276

databases

connecting PHP to, 237

database_connect.php, 237

storing geodata in MySQL, 228

date function (PHP), 231, 241

Date type (JavaScript), 329–330

datum, map, 316

debugging map scripts

basics, 349–350

Firebug debugger. *See* Firebug debugger

GLog object, 350–351

in Internet Explorer, 352

debugging mapplets, 117–118

decimal degrees

converting coordinates to, 314–315

defined, 313

DECIMAL numeric type (MySQL), 318

decimal2dms function, 315

declaring variables, defined, 17

decrement/increment numeric operators, 333

default_value attribute (UserPref element), 139

defensive coding, 83–85

degrees/minutes/seconds (DMS). *See* DMS (degrees/minutes/seconds)

deploying mapplets, 124–129

description attribute (ModulePrefs tag), 129

description tags, KML, 40

designing icons, 178–179

destination, selecting (Route Finder application), 86–88

Developer Mapplet, 128

DHTML (Dynamic HTML), 344

directions, driving. *See* driving directions

directory, Google mapplet, 130

directory_title attribute (ModulePrefs tag), 130

discussion groups (Google), 367–368

displaying maps, 16–19

display_name attribute (UserPref element), 139

distance between coordinates, calculating, 318–319

distanceFrom function (GLatLng object), 318

DMS (degrees/minutes/seconds), 313–316

dms2decimal function, 315

documents
    defined (XML), 120
    document property (window object), 344–345
    document.createElement function, 97
    document.getElementById method, 345
    document.location.hash property, 289
    element, defined, 121

DOM (Document Object Model)
    document property (window object), 344–345
    element object, 345
    overview, 343–344
    references, 371
    window object, 344

domains, enabling Firebug for, 352

double (double-precision) datatype, 229

DOUBLE numeric type (MySQL), 318

driving directions
    campground application, 301–302
    event handler for (Route Finder application), 90–91
    retrieving from addresses, 91
    XHTML for (Route Finder application), 89–90

Dyas, Lance, 41

dynamic API keys, 360–361

dynamic data handling, 219–220

dynamic data, PHP and, 238–239

dynamic geo sitemaps, 251–254

dynamic GeoRSS, 239–241

dynamic-height Gadget library, 132–134

dynamic KML, 236

dynamic XHTML, JavaScript and, 206

■E

echo statement, 231

ECMAScript. *See* JavaScript

Editor, Google Gadget, 125–126

EGeoXml object, 191–195
    as alternative to GGeoXml, 41
    drawbacks of, 195
    geoXML data retrieved via, 269
    in campground application, 264
    initialization of, 194
    KML processor, 366
    modifying, 198
    to retrieve new KML data sets, 275

elements
    array, 331
    element object (DOM), 345
    element.innerHTML property, 345
    XML, 6

enableContinuousZoom function, 269

enum values (UserPref element), 140, 141

equirectangular map projections, 320

errors, page (Firebug), 353

eval function, JavaScript, 88

event handlers
    attaching (Map Center Monitor mapplet), 157–158
    defined, 344
    destinationChange (Route Finder application), 86–87
    for driving directions (Route Finder application), 90–91

implementing (Map Center Monitor mapplet), 158–159

JavaScript, 16

marker drag, 187

triggering, 45

event listeners, JavaScript, 60, 357–360

events

defined, 344

properties, 359

triggering (JavaScript), 45

expressions

assignment operators, 333–334

Boolean operators, 334

comparison operators, 333–334

defined, 332

evaluating JavaScript, 354

numeric operators, 332–333

precedence among operators, 335

string operators, 332–333

external map content (National Park example), 68–70

■**F**

feeds

defined, 30

Feed Validator, 370

filtering

campground application example, 284–287

data, 246–248

by geographic area, 242

Firebug debugger

breakpoints, 356

Console tab, 352

interactive JavaScript, 354

overview, 351–352

page errors, 353

Script tab, 354–355

stepping through code, 357

watching variables, 356

flags

flag variables, 159

setting moving, 163

Flash panorama viewer object, 98

FLOAT numeric type (MySQL), 318

for loops (JavaScript), 336–338

form validation, 191

formatting

coordinates for display, 162–163

data as JSON, 258–260

place names (Geonaming mapplet), 147–149

functions (JavaScript)

closures, 346–348

defining, 341

function, defined, 17

literals, 273, 346–348

object methods, 342–343

parameters, 18, 341

return values, 341

as variables, 342

■**G**

gadgets

Gadget API cache in mapplets, 362–364

Gadget API reference, 366

Gadget Editor, Google, 125–126

gadget-related code (mapplets), 120–122

mapplets as, 109

GAdsManager, 100–101

GAsync

function, 213–219

module, 367

G_DEFAULT_ICON, 173

GDirections object, 91

Geary, Michael, 367

Geo Developers blog, Google, 368

geo sitemaps

basic example, 250

campground application, 304

dynamic, 251–254

overview, 248

SEO for GeoXML, 248–249

submitting to Google, 254–255

geocoding

addresses, 185–186

caveats regarding, 85–86

defensive coding in geocoder callback
function, 83–85

defined, 10, 80

interface added to route finder
application, 80–83

saving latitude and longitude, 86

verified. *See* verified geocoding

geodata

consuming, 29

controlling display of, 41

feeds and catalog (campground
application), 303

potential uses of, 3–4

preparing for indexing, 238

producing, 221

producing KML manually. *See* KML

producing with PHP and MySQL, 227–228

storing in MySQL database, 228–230

as XML, 5

geographic area, filtering by, 242

geoname table, MySQL, 229–230

Geonaming mapplet

calling geoname service, 147

capturing map clicks, 143–145

formatting place names, 147–149

full specification of, 150–153

functionality required, 143

order of functions, 153–154

placing markers, 145–146

GeoRSS

in campground application, 265

feed, using GGeoXml with, 33

generating via PHP, 239–242

GeoRSS.org, 369

vs. KML, 8–9

My Maps and, 222

standard, 7–8

geospatial calculations, 372

geospatial extensions, 258

Geospatial Web (Geoweb)

basics, 3–4

geodata as XML, 5

GeoXML. *See* GeoXML

mapplets and, 117

mashups overview, 4

Semantic Web, 4–5

GeoXML

alternatives to, 42–43

defined, 29

examining source, 40

GeoRSS standard, 7–8

how to find, 45

JSON vs., 255–256

KML standard, 6

KML vs. GeoRSS, 8–9

latitude and longitude, defined, 9

mapplets, quick and dirty, 135

XML overview, 5–6

getArray data type, 142

getBool function, 142

getElementById function, JavaScript, 63, 345

getInt (integer) data type, 142

getMinimumResolution property, 269, 270

getPoint function, 116

getString data type, 141, 142

getView function, 96

GEvent.addDomListener method, 359

GEvent.addListener function, 60

GGeoXML object

alternatives to, 41–42

caching, 33

closed functionality of, 41

defined, 29

drawbacks of, 191

hide and show function, 36

illustrating use of, 30

incomplete support of KML, 42

inflexible data display with, 40–41

map viewpoint, automatically moving, 34–36

Transit Links JavaScript example, 43–45

using with GeoRSS feed, 33

using with KML feed, 30–33

GIcon object, 174

GLargeMapControl (pan and zoom), 22

GLatLng object, 21, 318

GLog object (Maps API), 350–351

GMap2 map object, 20

GMapTypeControl, 23

GMarker object, 21–22

Google

AdSense program, 100

directory, submitting mapplets to, 130

Geo Developers blog, 368

GoogleBar, local search with, 72–73, 303

Icon Maker Wizard, 177

LatLon blog, 368

map tiles, 322

My Maps, 221–225

pre-made icons, 174–175

submitting geo sitemaps to, 254–255

Webmaster Tools, 254

Google Earth

browser plug-in, 73–74

Community, 47, 368

creating/editing KML in, 226

defined, 10

Google Gadget

Editor, 125–126

servers, 362

Google Maps

adding functionality to, 143

API. *See* Maps API

Mania blog, 369

GOverviewMapControl, 23

GPoint API object, 180

GPS receivers, defined, 10

Greenwich, England, 9

grids

grid-based geo sitemap, 252

latitude and longitude, 319

ground overlays, 39

GScaleControl, 23, 323

GScreenOverlay API object, 156–157

GScreenPoint object, 156

GScreenSize object, 156

GSmallMapControl, 24, 269

GUnload function (Maps API), 16, 344

■H

height of maps in IE, 13

Hello World mapplet application, 119–122

hidden data type, 141

hide and show function, GGeoXml, 36

home page (campground application), 264

hosting mapplets, 124–126

HousingMaps, 4

href attributes, 68

Hungarian notation, 267

■I

icons

creating custom, 169

custom marker. *See* custom marker icons

defined (JavaScript), 54

if/else blocks (JavaScript), 335–336

if/else blocks (PHP), 231

IG_GetCachedUrl function, 362

_IG_SetTitle function, 163

imperative languages, 325

include statements, 237

increment/decrement numeric operators, 333

indexes
defined, 230
preparing geodata for indexing, 238
zero-based, 331

infowindows
content, sanitized, 115
fix, 208–212
making from geoname results, 147–148
showing from outside map (National Park example), 66–68
tabbed (National Park example), 60–62

innerHTML property, 345

installing
mapplets, 111
mapplets by URL, 126–127

interactive JavaScript, 354

Internet Explorer, debugging map scripts in, 352

is_numeric function (PHP), 287

■ J

JavaScript
arrays. *See* arrays, JavaScript
to assign 3-dimensional icon properties, 181
basics, 13
block statements, 326–327
callback functions, 35
case-sensitivity of, 31
comments, 51–52, 327
complete geocode verification, 188–191
control structures. *See* control structures
debugging in Internet Explorer, 352
debugging map scripts. *See* debugging map scripts
DOM and. *See* DOM (Document Object Model)

dynamic XHTML and, 206
eval function, 88
event handlers, 16
event listeners, 60, 357
expressions. *See* expressions
function closures, 346–348
function literals, 346–348
function parameters, 18
Gadgets API cache in mapplets, 362–364
getElementById function, 63
GEvent.addDomListener method, 359
Hello World mapplet code, 123–124
interactive, 354
loadMap function, 17–19
main code (Map Center Monitor mapplet), 155–157
Math object, 343
naming conventions, 31
null keyword, 84
objects, 20
objects in mapplets, 113
online help, 348
optional parameters, 25
overview, 325
Placeopedia application, 134–135
references, 370
Route Finder page (complete), 102–106
scope of variables, 346
semicolons (;) in, 326
for State Capitals page, 192–194
statements, defined, 325
strings, 55
triggering events, 45
using multiple API keys, 360–361
variables and functions, 17
variables, basics, 327
variables, reusing, 66

jEdit XML editor, 226

JScript (Microsoft), 325, 352, 370

JSON (JavaScript Object Notation), 42
  arrays, 260
  basic format of, 256–257
  in campground application, 292–296
  formatting data as and returning to client,
    258–260
  vs. GeoXML, 255–256
  large data transfers, 261
  references, 370
  results from geoname service, 148
  retrieving Nearest Place Name, 257–258

■K

keys, API, 14–16, 360–362
kludge, 241
KML
  creating/editing in Google Earth, 226
  creating in PHP, 233–235
  developer support, 368
  document to be generated in PHP,
    232–233
  documentation, 366
  dynamic, 236
  feed, using GGeoXml with, 30–33
  generating for recent entries
    (campground application), 265–268
  vs. GeoRSS, 8–9
  GGeoXml incomplete support of, 42
  Google My Maps to produce, 221–225
  KMZ files and, 38
  managing KML files, 225–226
  network links, 242–243
  producing manually, 221
  returning KML document to client,
    235–236
  standard, 6
  styling marker icons within, 238
  validating, 226
  viewport-parameterized KML
    generator, 243

■L

labeled marker icons, 175–177
latitude and longitude
  defined, 9
  DMS (degrees/minutes/seconds) format,
    313–316
  LatLon blog, Google, 368
legacy databases, 267
length function (arrays), 204
links
  linking API into mapplets, 114
  publishing to mapplets, 130
list data type, 141
literals
  defined, 332
  function (JavaScript), 346–348
loadMap function, JavaScript, 17–19
loc tags, 251
local search, 72–73, 303
location data type, 141
location search (campground application),
  287–288
longitude and latitude, defined, 9
loops (JavaScript)
  for loops, 336–338
  while loops, 338

■M

machine-readable data, 3
Map Center Monitor mapplet
  asynchronous mapplet functions, 159
  confirming changes in center coordinates,
    161–162
  event handlers, attaching, 157–158
  event handlers, implementing, 158–159
  formatting coordinates for display,
    162–163
  full specification of, 164–167
  main JavaScript code for, 155–157
  overview, 154–155

setting moving flag, 163

updating map center display, 159–161

updating mapplet title, 163

Map Icon Maker, 177

map markers. *See* markers

mapMoveEnd event handler, 278–279

Mapki (Google Maps API wiki), 367

mapplets

additional functionality for, 167

advantages of, 116–117

API services, 168

asynchronous functions of, 116

combining, 111–112

convert existing Maps API to, 195–199

creating (campground application), 306–310

CSS and, 122–123

Developer Mapplet, 128

drawbacks of, 117

functionality mapplets. *See* Geonaming mapplet; Map Center Monitor mapplet

as gadgets, 109

Gadgets API cache in, 362–364

geodata mapplets. *See* Placeopedia content mapplet

geonaming. *See* Geonaming mapplet

Hello World mapplet, 119–122

hosting, 124–126

installing, 111

installing by URL, 126–127

JavaScript code and, 123–124

JavaScript (Placeopedia application), 134–135

limited adoption of, 118

linking API into, 114

Map Center Monitor mapplet. *See* Map Center Monitor mapplet

map-centered designs and, 113

map marker tips, 169

map object creation and, 114

Mapplet Scratch Pad, 129

Mapplets API documentation, 365

and Maps APIs compared, 113–116

ModulePrefs (Placeopedia application), 132

ModulePrefs tag metadata, 129–130

on My Maps page (maps.google.com), 110

overview, 109

Placeopedia mapplet specification, 131–132

Placeopedia thumbnail, 132–133

publishing links to, 130

quick and dirty GEOXML mapplets, 135

sanitized infowindow content, 115

shared maps and, 113

sidebar content (Placeopedia application), 133

submitting to Google directory, 130

uploading, 124–126

using, 110–111

XHTML, XML and, 113–114, 122–123

maps

advertising, 100–101

blowup infowindows (National Park example), 57–60

center display, updating, 159–161

clicks, capturing (Geonaming mapplet), 143–145

containers (XHTML), 12

coordinates. *See* coordinates

creating with My Maps, 222

Google map tiles, 322

map datum standard, 316

map page basic XHTML, 11–12

map page, complete JavaScript, 25

map page stylesheet (CSS), 12–13

mapping APIs documentation, 365–367

objects, simplified creation of, 114

projections, 319–320

shared, 113

sharedmap feature, 121

small, 24

Static Maps (API), 274

utility library, 366

viewpoint, automatically moving, 34–36

Maps API

adding map to Web page, 26–27

adding to map page, 13

API keys, 14–16, 360

complete map page JavaScript, 25

consuming geoXML in. *See* GGeoXml object

controls. *See* controls, Google Maps

converting to mapplets, 195–199

documentation, 365

displaying maps, 16–19

GLatLng map object, 21

GMap2 map object, 20

GMarker map object, 21–22

JavaScript and, 13

latest version of, 196

and mapplets API compared, 113–116

versions of, 14, 27–28

Maps Mania blog, Google, 369

mapTypes, 24

mapZoomEnd handler, 282–284, 298–299

marker icons

custom. *See* custom marker icons

custom (National Park example), 53

defined, 54

styling within KML, 238

markers

custom, 169

defined, 54

labeled icon, 175–177

Marker Tracker, 300–301

placing map (Geonaming mapplet), 145–146

saving private, 146

tips, mapplets, 169

Markup Validation Service (W3C), 12

mashups

danger of, 33

definition and background, 4

mashup of mashups, 112

Math object (JavaScript), 343

Math.abs function, 162

Mercator map projection, 321–324

metadata, 121

methods

defined, 328

of objects, 342

Microsoft

and JScript, 325

DOM reference, 371

JScript reference, 325, 370

minutes and seconds, recognizing, 314

mktime function (PHP), 240

Module element, XML, 121

ModulePrefs element, 121, 132

ModulePrefs tag metadata, 129–130

Moveable Type Scripts, 372

Mozilla reference to JavaScript, 325, 370, 371

MSDN (Microsoft Developer Network). *See* Microsoft

multiple API keys, 361–362

My Maps (Google), 110, 221–225

myIcon.image property, 174

MySQL

database, storing geodata in, 228–230

documentation, 371

mysql_fetch_array, 234

numeric types, 318

producing geodata with, 227–228

■**N**

name attribute (UserPref element), 139

naming conventions, JavaScript, 31, 327

National Grid (Britain), 315

National Park example
    basic XHTML for map page, 49–50
    bindInfoWindowTabs, 64–65
    CSS for tabbed infowindow content, 62–64
    custom marker icons, 53
    full XHTML for National Park page, 74–78
    Google Earth browser plug-in, 73–74
    infowindow, showing from outside map,
        66–68
    JavaScript for basic map, 51–52
    JavaScript with custom map markers,
        54–55
    JavaScript with optional geodata, 70
    local search with GoogleBar, 72–73
    map blowup infowindows, 57–60
    optional external content, adding, 68–70
    sidebar basic CSS, 50–51
    sidebar content, adding, 56
    sidebar links, 67
    sidebar stylesheet, 56
    tabbed infowindows, 60–62
Nearest Place Name mapplet. See
        Geonaming mapplet
Nearest Place Name, retrieving, 257–258
Nearest Place Name Server, 258–259
network links (KML), 242–243
new keyword (JavaScript), 330, 342
null (JavaScript), 84, 328
numbers
    MySQL, 318
    Number type (JavaScript), 329
    strings and, 333
numeric operators (expressions), 332–333

■O
objects
    JavaScript, 20
    mapplets and JavaScript, 113
    object methods, 342–343

objects, JavaScript
    Array type, 330–331
    Boolean type, 330
    data values as, 328
    Date type, 329–330
    Number type, 329
    Object type, 331–332
    String type, 328–329
off-screen markers, tracking, 300–301
offset label option, 176
OHIO (Only Handle It Once), 86
onclick events, 16
onload event handlers, 17
onload events, 16
openInfoWindow function, 98
operands, 333
operators (expressions)
    assignment, 333–334
    Boolean, 334
    comparison, 333–334
    increment/decrement numeric, 333
    numeric, 332–333
    precedence among, 335
    string, 332–333
optional parameters (JavaScript), 25
overlay, defined, 32
overview, map, 23

■P
page errors (Firebug), 353
panoramic photos, 94
parameterizing code, 239
parameters
    cleaning, 246
    function (JavaScript), 18, 341
    optional (JavaScript), 25
    receiving viewpoint, 245–246
parseFloat function (JavaScript), 149
passing, defined, 18, 341

PHP (PHP Hypertext Preprocessor)
  basics, 230–232
  connecting PHP to database, 237
  creating KML in, 233–235
  database retrieval with SQL statement
      in, 233
  distance calculation in, 319
  dynamic data and, 238–239
  filtering by geographic area, 242
  filtering data, 246–248
  generating GeoRSS via, 239–242
  KML document to be generated in,
      232–233
  module scripts, 268
  modules, centralizing XML into, 268
  network links (KML), 242–243
  PHP to produce dynamic KML, 236
  preparing geodata for indexing, 238
  producing geodata with, 227–228
  programming language reference, 371
  receiving viewpoint parameters, 245–246
  returning KML document to client, 235–236
  styling marker icons within KML, 238
place names, formatting (Geonaming
      mapplet), 147–149
placeMarker function, 145
Placemarks, 233–235, 238
Placeopedia application
  JavaScript, 134–135
  mapplet specification, 131–132
  sidebar content, 133
  thumbnail, 132–133
Placeopedia content mapplet
  alternative data types, 142
  extending, 137
  user interface, 140
  user preferences, 139–140
  UserPref data types, 141
  using preferences in JavaScript, 141–142
polygons and polylines, 37–38

POV (point of view), 98
precedence among operators
      (expressions), 335
precision, coordinate, 316–317
preferences
  module, 121
  UserPref options in JavaScript, 141–142
prime meridian, 9
private markers, saving, 146
projections
  defined, 320
  equirectangular, 320
  map, 319–320
  Mercator, 321–324
properties
  defined, 20
  event (JavaScript), 359
publishing
  links to mapplets, 130
  mapplets, 129

Q

quick and dirty geoXML mapplets, 135

R

Rademacher, Paul, 4
recent entries (campground application)
  client-side display of, 269–270
  map, 265–273
regular expressions, 362
removeDataPoint function, 281–282
Require feature elements, 132
required attribute (UserPref element), 139
resources online
  API-related documentation, 365–367
  discussion groups (Google), 367–368
  DOM references, 371
  GeoRSS information, 369
  geospatial calculations, 372
  JavaScript references, 370
  map-oriented weblogs, 368–369

server-side programming guides, 371

XML validators, 369–370

restaurant chain (example), 221

return keyword, 341

return values (JavaScript functions), 341

reverse geocoding, 143

root domain keys, 15

Route Finder web page application

basic starting XHTML, 79–80

destinationChange Event Handler, 86–87

driving directions event handler, 90–91

driving directions XHTML, 89–90

geocoding. *See* geocoding

getView function, 96

map advertising, 100–101

Route Finder page JavaScript (complete),
102–106

selecting destination, 86–88

Street View button XHTML, 94–96

Street View callback function, 96–98

style for Street View panorama, 99–100

traffic overlay, JavaScript to control, 93–94

traffic overlay XHTML, 92–93

RSS (Real Simple Syndication)

2.0 Specification, 369

standard, 7

Rummel, Dan, 300

■**S**

sad camel case naming, 31

sanitized infowindow content, 115

Satellite-Friendly Campground Directory
(case study)

addDataPoint function, 270–271, 279–281

afterGeocode callback function, 288

Back button function, 290–291

background, 264

click-to-search map, 273

client-side display of recent entries,
269–270

cluster markers, 276–278

data views, selecting, 276

details, viewing, 291–296

displaying campground/campsite details,
296–299

driving directions, 301–302

filtering, 284–287

geo sitemap, 304

geodata feeds and catalog, 303

home page, 264

legacy database and, 267

local services, finding, 303

location search, 287–288

map architecture overview, 264

mapMoveEnd event handler, 278–279

mapplet, creating, 306–310

mapZoomEnd handler, 282–284, 298–299

off-screen markers, tracking, 300–301

PHP module scripts, 268

recent entries map, 265–273

removeDataPoint function, 281–282

search data display, 278–284

search page, 275

server-side code for recent data, 265–268

server-side code for top-ranked data,
285–287

starting location handling, 289–290

Static Maps API, 274

zoom levels, restricting, 270

saving

latitude and longitude, 86

saveCoordinates function, 187

scope of variables (JavaScript), 346

Scratch Pad, Mapplet, 129

screenshot attribute (ModulePrefs tag), 130

scripts

defined (JavaScript), 326

element, JavaScript, 13

Script Debugger, Microsoft, 352

Script Editor, Microsoft, 352

Script tab (Firebug), 354–355

searching

    locally with GoogleBar, 72–73

    search engine optimization (SEO). *See* SEO (search engine optimization) for GeoXML

select element, 86

Semantic Web, 4–5

semicolons (;)

    in JavaScript, 326

    in PHP, 231

SEO (search engine optimization) for GeoXML, 248–249

server-side

    code for top-ranked data (campground application), 285–287

    programming, 227–228, 231

    programming guides, 371

setTimeout function, 145

settitle Require element, 167

shadow generator, automated, 181

sharedmap feature, 121

showMapBlowup function (National Park example), 57

sidebars

    added content in, 167

    adding content to (National Park example), 56

    defined, 41

    sidebar content (Placeopedia application), 133

    sidebar links (National Park example), 67

    stylesheet (National Park example), 56

single-click timeout workaround (geonaming), 144–145

sitemaps

    defined, 248

    fundamentals reference, 371

    geo. *See* geo sitemaps

small map type control, 24

special characters in strings, 329

specifications, mapplet, 120

spherical law of cosines, 319

splice function (arrays), 205

SQL (Structured Query Language)

    data types, for precision of coordinates, 318

    Injection attacks, 246

starting location handling (campground application), 289–290

State Capitals Page example, 191, 195–196, 199

statements (JavaScript)

    break, 338–339

    defined, 325

Static Maps API, 274

stepping through code (Firebug), 357

Street View feature, Google (Route Finder application)

    callback function, 96–98

    fundamentals, 94–96

    panorama, style for, 99–100

strings

    data type, 141

    JavaScript, 55

    numbers and, 333

    operators (expressions), 332–333

    PHP, 233

    special characters in, 329

    String type (JavaScript), 328–329

style attributes (CSS), 358

styling marker icons within KML, 238

subdomains

    API keys for, 15

    multiple, 361–362

switch blocks (JavaScript), 339–340

T

tabbed infowindows (National Park example), 60–64

tags, XML, 6

Terrain map type, 23–24

text label option, 176

this keyword, 343

thumbnail attribute (ModulePrefs tag), 129

tiles, Google map, 322

timeouts, JavaScript, 144

titles, updating mapplet, 163

toFixed function (JavaScript), 149, 317

toUrlValue function (Google mapping APIs), 317

tracking off-screen markers, 306–310

traffic overlay (Route Finder application)

    JavaScript to control, 93–94

    XHTML for, 92–93

Transit Links (JavaScript example), 43–45

triggering events (JavaScript), 45

■U

Udell, Sterling (author), 87

UK Brewery (example), 199

Universally Unique Identifiers (UUIs), 241

updating

    map center display, 159–161

    mapplet title, 163

uploading mapplets, 124–126

US capital mapplet, 362–364

user interface (Placeopedia content mapplet), 140

user preferences (Placeopedia content mapplet), 139–140

UserPref

    data types, 141

    module, 139–140

    options in JavaScript, 141–142

UTF-8 encodings, 120

■V

validating KML, 226

values, XML data, 6

var keyword, 346

variables (JavaScript)

    basics, 327

    declaring, 17

    and functions, 17

    functions as, 342

    reusing, 66

    scope of, 346

    watching (Firebug), 356

verified geocoding

    address geocoding, 185–186

    address verification, 186–187

    form validation, 191

    JavaScript for complete geocode verification, 188–191

    location entry page, 183–185

    location selection by map click, 191

    overview, 182–183

    saving coordinates, 187–188

viewport parameters

    receiving, 245–246

    viewport-parameterized KML generator, 243

■W

W3C Geo format, 33

watching variables (Firebug), 356

web-logs, map-oriented, 368–369

web sites, for downloading

    automated shadow generator, 181

    Coordinate Finder mapplet, 10

    Developer gadget, 126

    egeoxml.js, 192

    Firebug debugger, 351

    geonames.org free web service, 143

    Google Earth browser plug-in, 74

    Google Gadget Editor, 125

    icon image files, 53

    Icon Maker Wizard, 177

jEdit guide, 226

My Maps page, 221

Udell, Sterling (author), 87

Webmaster Tools, 254

XML Notepad (Microsoft), 226

web sites, for further information

API documentation, 128

API keys, 15, 360

Atom specification/documentation, 242

AtomEnabled.org, 369

closure bug fix, 348

content tags and attributes allowed, 115

DOM objects, 344

EGeoXml, 41

EGeoXml KML processor, 366

essentials of debugging article, 357

Feed Validator, 370

Firebug debugger, 349, 352

Gadgets API reference, 366

GAsync module, 367

GeoRSS content, 47

GeoRSS.org, 369

geospatial calculations, 372

GLog object, 349

Google AdSense program, 100

Google Earth Community, 47, 368

Google Earth icons, 238

Google Geo Developers blog, 368

Google LabeledMarker, 177

Google LatLon blog, 368

Google Maps, 47

Google Maps API documentation, 365

Google Maps API group, 368

Google Maps API wiki, 14

Google Maps Mania blog, 369

Hungarian notation, 267

iGoogle developer forum, 368

JavaScript online help, 348

JScript debugger (IE 8), 352

JSON guide, 254

JSON reference, 370

KML developer support, 368

KML documentation, 366

Lance Dyas designs, 41

links for online resources, 365

Mapki (Google Maps API wiki), 367

Mapplets API documentation, 365

Maps API documentation, 302

maps utility library, 366

Markup Validation Service (W3C), 12

Microsoft JScript reference, 325

Microsoft Script Debugger, 352

Microsoft Script Editor, 352

Microsoft Visual Studio, 352

Mike Williams tutorial, 366

Moveable Type Scripts, 372

Mozilla reference to JavaScript, 325, 370

MSDN (Microsoft Developer Network) DOM reference, 371

MySQL documentation, 371

PHP reference, 371

RSS 2.0 Specification, 369

satellite-friendly.com, 263

sitemaps, 248, 371

SQL Injection attacks, 246

Stanford University Census data, 47

Static Maps API documentation, 274

Universally Unique Identifiers, 241

validating geoXML, 227

World Wide Web Consortium (W3C), 370

while loops (JavaScript), 234, 261, 338

Williams, Mike, 41, 198, 366

window object (DOM), 344

World Wide Web Consortium (W3C), 370

write function, GLog, 350–351

■X

XHTML (eXtensible HTML)

basic XHTML for Route Finder application, 79–80

for driving directions (Route Finder application), 89–90

dynamic, 206

elements, defined, 6

framework, 11–13

for map page (National Park example), 49–50

mapplets and, 113–114, 122–123

for National Park page, 74–78

for State Capitals page, 192

for Street View button (Route Finder application), 94–96

for traffic overlay (Route Finder application), 92–93

for UK Brewery map page, 200

viewing source in Firefox, 40

XML (eXtensible Markup Language)

character data (CDATA), 122

Content element, 121

geodata as, 5

mapplets and, 113–114

Module element, 121

Notepad (Microsoft), 226

overview, 5–6

validators, 369–370

■Z

zero-based indexes, 331

zoom levels, 19, 270

You Need the Companion eBook

Your purchase of this book entitles you to buy the companion PDF-version eBook for only $10. Take the weightless companion with you anywhere.

We believe this Apress title will prove so indispensable that you'll want to carry it with you everywhere, which is why we are offering the companion eBook (in PDF format) for $10 to customers who purchase this book now. Convenient and fully searchable, the PDF version of any content-rich, page-heavy Apress book makes a valuable addition to your programming library. You can easily find and copy code—or perform examples by quickly toggling between instructions and the application. Even simultaneously tackling a donut, diet soda, and complex code becomes simplified with hands-free eBooks!

Once you purchase your book, getting the $10 companion eBook is simple:

1. Visit **www.apress.com/promo/tendollars/**.

2. Complete a basic registration form to receive a randomly generated question about this title.

3. Answer the question correctly in 60 seconds, and you will receive a promotional code to redeem for the $10.00 eBook.

THE EXPERT'S VOICE™

2855 TELEGRAPH AVENUE | SUITE 600 | BERKELEY, CA 94705

Offer valid through 6/09.